THE
IRISH BOATS

VOLUME I
LIVERPOOL TO DUBLIN

THE
IRISH BOATS

VOLUME I
LIVERPOOL TO DUBLIN

Malcolm McRonald

TEMPUS

First published 2005

Tempus Publishing Limited
The Mill, Brimscombe Port,
Stroud, Gloucestershire, GL5 2QG
www.tempus-publishing.com

British Library Cataloguing in Publication Data.
A catalogue record for this book is available from the British Library.

ISBN 0 7524 3541 8

Typesetting and origination by Tempus Publishing Limited
Printed in Great Britain

CONTENTS

ACKNOWLEDGEMENTS

This book and its companion volumes have been in preparation for more than seven years. I owe a great deal to my wife, Gill, and to our three daughters, Fiona, Ailsa and Elspeth, for their understanding and tolerance of my absences from home to carry out some of the research. My brother, Derek, and his wife, Margaret, have willingly provided bed and breakfast for my visits to Kew and Greenwich.

Many of the black-and-white photographs have been supplied by my longstanding friend Keith P. Lewis. I am very grateful for his permission to use these largely unpublished photographs from his extensive collection. Another major source of photographs has been the collection built up over many years by the late Raymond Brandreth. I acknowledge his help in supplying these photographs and in encouraging me in my research before his untimely death. Thanks are also due to the other people who have supplied photographs: the late Ray Pugh, Colin Campbell, Stuart Turpin, Bryan Kennedy and Gordon Ditchfield.

I have been greatly assisted in my research by the staff of museums, record offices and libraries all over the country and in Ireland, and by Customs and Excise in Ireland. First and foremost have been the staff of the National Galleries and Museums Merseyside (the Merseyside Maritime Museum), whose excellent reading room provided the necessary facilities for much of my research. I have also made substantial use of the facilities offered by the Public Record Office, Kew; the National Maritime Museum, Greenwich; the Public Record Office of Northern Ireland, Belfast; the Mitchell Library, Glasgow; and the Irish National Archives, Dublin. Irish Customs and Excise were particularly helpful in allowing me unrestricted access to the Dublin and Cork Shipping Registers, and the Port of Cork gave similar access to the Cork arrival and departure books.

I must also thank Tempus Publishing and, in particular, Campbell McCutcheon for their encouragement in the later stages of this project, and for the discipline of a deadline without which I might have continued searching indefinitely for additional information.

Many other individuals and organisations have been helpful. I hope that the list below is a complete list of all those who have assisted in any way, together with the sources consulted at their respective locations. In order to keep the list to a reasonable size, I have not included those organisations and people whose help relates purely to the later volumes of the series. I apologise if I have missed anyone from this list, but their help has been equally appreciated.

Merseyside Maritime Museum, Liverpool: Shipping register for Liverpool; Lloyds List, Lloyds Register, Mercantile Navy List, Mersey Docks & Harbour Board Dock Registers; Shipping library.

Public Record Office, Kew: Series BT 107, BT 108, BT 109, BT 110, BT 340, CUST 130.

National Maritime Museum, Greenwich: Coast Lines archives; Mercantile Navy List.

PRONI, Belfast: Shipping registers for Belfast, Londonderry and Newry; Belfast Berthing Records.

Irish National Archives, Dublin: Shipping registers for Waterford and Limerick; Waterford berthing records.

Irish Customs & Excise: Shipping registers for Dublin and Cork.

Port of Cork: Berthing records.

University Of Glasgow Archives & Business Records Centre (G. Gardner): Clyde Shipping Co. archives; Launch dates.

Local Record Offices/Archives:

Aberdeen: Shipping register for Aberdeen

Berwick-upon-Tweed: Shipping register for Berwick

Cumbria: Shipping registers for Whitehaven, Workington and Barrow; Barrow arrival and departure books

East Riding: Shipping register for Goole

Flintshire: Shipping register for Chester

Glamorgan: Shipping register for Cardiff

Glasgow: Shipping register for Glasgow; Glasgow berthing records

Gloucester: Shipping register for Gloucester

Gwynedd: Shipping register for Beaumaris

Hull: Shipping register for Hull

Tyne & Wear: Shipping register for North Shields

HM Customs & Excise, Greenock: Shipping register for Greenock

Isle of Man Marine Administration: Queries on the current shipping register for Douglas.

Manx National Heritage

Dublin Port Co. (G. Daly)

Shannon Estuary Ports, Limerick. Royal Naval Museum, Portsmouth: Naval Movements Book

Admiralty Librarian, London

Maritime Institute of Ireland, Dun Laoghaire

National Railway Museum, York

Libraries:

Aberdeen City Library
Birkenhead Central Library (microfilm copies of the Liverpool Mercury)
Birmingham Central Library
Carlisle Library.
Cork City Library
Gilbert Library, Dublin
Mitchell Library, Glasgow.
Goole Library (Jennifer Briody)
Greenock Central Library
Guildhall Library, London (Ruth Barraskill)
Hartlepool Central Library
Hull Central Library.
Limerick City Library
Limerick County Library
Liverpool City Library (Lloyds Register and Mercantile Navy List)
Newcastle upon Tyne City Library

World Ship Society: Central Register and Yard Lists

Gary Andrews; David Asprey; Andrew Bowcock; Dr Ian Buxton; Colin Campbel; Gordon Ditchfield; Patrick Flood; Rowan Hackman (late); Bryan Kennedy; Bernard Lawley; Andreas von Mach; John Shepherd; Robert Sinclair; Stuart J. Turpin; Mike Walker; John Winser.

Irish Ferries
Norse Merchant Ferries
P&O Ferries
Stena Line

Finally, it remains only for me to apologise for those mistakes that have slipped 'through the net'. They are my sole responsibility.

INTRODUCTION

This volume is the first in a series covering the passenger shipping services between Liverpool and Ireland. The title of the series is taken from the practice, common around Liverpool, of referring to cross-Channel passenger ships as 'boats'. This is perhaps best illustrated by a typical instruction to a taxi driver: 'Please take me to the Dublin (or B&I) boat'.

My first introduction to the 'Irish boats' was in 1946 when, as a six year old, I was taken to visit Irish relatives in Dublin. We were a family of four, sailing on *Longford* or *Louth* in a third-class cabin. I can still remember the excitement of making such a daring journey and waking up to look through the porthole and see one bank of the Liffey slipping past.

In later years, I often saw the Irish passenger vessels in Princes Dock in Liverpool. The Dublin vessels were identical, although the differences between the two Belfast vessels were very clear. During the autumn and winter months, the relief vessel, *Irish Coast*, appeared on both services. Photography, except in the confined conditions of the dock, was difficult, because departures were always in the dark; even around the longest day, the Dublin vessel docked too early for good photographic lighting conditions.

Through the good services of Captain R.G. Morrison, the Marine Superintendent of Coast Lines, the principal company of the group operating the passenger services from Liverpool to Dublin, Cork and Belfast, I was able several times to arrange for members of the Coastal Cruising Association to visit the ships in dock at Liverpool. I also used the ships for crossings to Ireland, although I never again ventured a passage in third class. From 1963 onwards, I held a season ticket with the Isle of Man Steam Packet Co. and I began to discover the sailing possibilities that occasionally occurred through a combined use of the 'Irish boats' and the 'Isle of Man boats'. I discovered that Burns & Laird Lines, the Scottish company in the Coast Lines group, operated some interesting daytime sailings at peak periods on services that were normally overnight runs. In 1966, I sailed on a Thursday night from Liverpool to Belfast on board *Ulster Monarch*, made a magnificent Saturday daytime sailing on board *Lairds Loch* from Londonderry to Greenock and then returned from Ardrossan to Liverpool via the Isle of Man. In 1967, I sailed on a Saturday from Liverpool to Ardrossan via the Isle of Man, made a Sunday daylight sailing from Glasgow to Belfast on board *Royal Ulsterman* and then returned to Liverpool that night on board the new car ferry, *Ulster Prince*. One Saturday morning in 1968, *Manxman's* Purser was surprised to find a small group of North Western enthusiasts waiting to board his vessel in Belfast; we had travelled overnight from Liverpool on board *Ulster Prince* for the rare opportunity of daylight sailings by the Isle of Man steamers from Belfast to Liverpool, changing ships at Douglas.

From 1967, the pattern of Irish Sea services changed very rapidly. The Dublin and Belfast vessels were replaced by car ferries, and the luxury of having a special relief vessel for winter overhaul periods could no longer be justified. I was privileged to be on board the final sailings of *Ulster Prince* (1937) from Liverpool to Belfast and *Munster* (1948) from Dublin to Liverpool. I was also able to enjoy two daylight sailings on board *Leinster* (1948) in her final year of service and made some sailings on the new car ferries.

From the start of the car ferry era, the area around Princes Dock became less interesting, since only the Belfast service continued to use that dock. The closure of P&O's Belfast service in 1981 left Princes Dock deserted and today all the buildings surrounding the dock have been demolished, leaving a finger of water in the middle of a property development site, now rapidly being covered with offices and a hotel. The Waterloo entrance lock has been filled in.

B&I's Dublin service fared little better than P&O's Belfast service, and was withdrawn in favour of Holyhead in 1988. Attempts by new operators to take over the routes at first proved no more successful. The major selling point of the services was the opportunity for passengers to enjoy an undisturbed night's sleep on a long crossing. The growth of air travel took away many of the business travellers who used the services and the more recent growth of low-cost airlines further eroded the market. The present trend towards cars using short sea crossings has also reduced demand for a long overnight crossing between city centres. However, growth in freight traffic, brought about partly by restrictions on drivers' hours, has brought a new generation of ro-ro ships with some capacity for passengers and cars, and fast craft have made it possible to carry larger numbers of passengers and cars at speed, at least on the Dublin route.

For nearly forty years of the period covered by this book, the Irish Sea passenger services of the Coast Lines group were provided by a remarkable series of thirteen motorships, which were well ahead of their times when first designed. The earliest was *Ulster Monarch* (1929), whose design could be traced in all the ships that followed her up to the final vessel in the series, *Scottish Coast* (1957). Four of the pre-war vessels in the series were war losses or did not return to passenger service after the war, and were replaced by four new vessels built between 1948 and 1952. After the completion of *Scottish Coast*, the surviving nine vessels were then in service together for a little less than ten years. In view of the fact that I was able to sail on seven of the nine ships operating after the war, I have a particular affection for them and I do not apologise for the fact that some emphasis in these volumes is placed on this remarkable series of ships.

These volumes cover all the passenger routes from Liverpool to Ireland, including all the services of companies in the Coast Lines group and its predecessors, its successors P&O Ferries, and Pandoro and the other companies that have operated passenger services more recently. This includes Sealink's Liverpool–Dun Laoghaire service. A later volume also includes the Liverpool–Waterford service, operated by the Clyde Shipping Co., which was never part of the Coast Lines group. The main emphasis is on the ships operating from 1918 onwards, although a history of the earlier years is also given for each route.

It was interesting, when researching this book, to discover that the name of P&O occurs in the early days of Irish Sea services, as a result of the involvement of Irish shipowners in its formation. It is a tribute to the foresight of those early pioneers that some of today's Irish Sea services should be carried on by that same group of companies.

I hope that this book will be a happy reminder of the 'Irish boats' to the many people who have used them over the years and to those who observed them in the daytime at their dockside berths in Liverpool, or at their quayside berths in Belfast or Dublin.

Malcolm McRonald

ONE

AN ACCOUNT OF SAILINGS FROM LIVERPOOL TO DUBLIN AND RETURN

This account describes sailings from Liverpool to Dublin and return made by the author for a short holiday in Ireland in late March 1963.

I felt that my journey really started when, one Tuesday night, I boarded a Birkenhead ferry at Woodside for the short crossing to Liverpool. The overnight Liverpool–Dublin service was operated by the sisters *Munster* and *Leinster*, but at that stage I did not know which ship would be sailing from Liverpool that night. After leaving the ferry at Liverpool, a walk along George's landing stage past the Seacombe ferry as far as the Isle of Man steamer *Manxman*, berthed overnight, and then up the floating roadway, brought me to the entrance gate of the Dublin service at South East Princes Dock. The gate had the name Dublin in large letters above it, suspended between its two pillars. Large pictorial advertising hoardings either side of the gateway proclaimed the merits of the Dublin and Belfast services. The entrance to the Belfast terminal was round to the left, closer to the river. A further walk under a covered walkway, alongside the former passage to George's Dock, now being used as a cargo berth, led to the terminal building. Here tickets were inspected, or purchased if the passage had not been pre-booked, and customs formalities were carried out. After a further walk through a warehouse, which seemed dirty and a poor introduction to the ship, I arrived at the warehouse doors, which had been rolled open to give access to the ship, revealing her green hull and pale yellow superstructure and her identity as *Leinster*. At this stage, signs directed passengers to two gangways, one towards the after end of the main superstructure for first-class passengers and one leading to the stern accommodation for second-class passengers. Passengers' tickets were re-checked at the gangway to ensure that they were entering the correct accommodation and I then went up the gangway into the first-class entrance.

The reception area made a favourable contrast to the warehouse approach. It was on B Deck and contained the purser's office, where I joined a short queue of passengers wishing to claim their pre-booked cabins or buy cabin tickets. Once these formalities were completed, a courteous and friendly Irish steward was on hand to carry my luggage to my designated cabin. The cabins were located forward of the reception area and on the deck above and were approached along a port or starboard corridor. My cabin was small, but quite adequate for an overnight crossing. There was a single bunk, with a washbasin, a mirror, and a writing desk and chair, with notepaper and envelopes showing the name of the ship and her owners. Toilet facilities were not provided in the cabin, but were only a short distance away outside, between the two corridors. I was pleased to see that my cabin had a porthole.

There was now time to explore the ship. I returned to the reception area and admired its wooden panelling. There was a dining saloon at its after end and some passengers were enjoying a late dinner. A staircase led up to A Deck, where there was a drawing room above the dining saloon. A further staircase led up from there to the Boat Deck, where there was a bar and lounge, and doors leading to the open deck. Passengers could walk right round this deck, mainly in the open, although the forward end was enclosed by a glass screen and offered some protection from the elements. From the after end of this deck, passengers could look over the Well Deck to the cramped second-class accommodation in the stern. An outside staircase led up to another open deck, aft of the green, white and black funnel. From the open decks, I could see that the ship was berthed starboard side to the quay, with her bows pointing away from the Pier Head and towards the lock leading to the river.

Opposite *Leinster*, on the other side of the dock, was the Belfast vessel, the single-funnelled *Ulster Prince*. Before the war, she had been named *Leinster* and had herself operated on the Liverpool–Dublin service. The other Belfast vessel was the two-funnelled *Ulster Monarch*, dating from 1929. *Ulster Prince* was due to sail at 21.30, half an hour before *Leinster*, to allow sufficient time for her to clear the lock into the river. As *Ulster Prince*'s departure time approached, a number of *Leinster*'s passengers came out on deck to watch. She sailed promptly, moving out into the middle of the dock and then away from *Leinster* and into the darkness of the night. We settled down for another half hour's wait, during which further passengers boarded.

I returned inside, as the night was cold, and went to sit in the drawing room. This was an opportunity to examine my fellow passengers. There were businessmen in suits, who appreciated the opportunity of having an unbroken night's sleep. There were priests and nuns returning home to Ireland. It was less easy to identify other passengers, but some of them appeared to be families visiting relatives in Ireland, or returning from visiting relatives in Britain. It was too early in the year for there to be many tourists like myself.

As *Leinster*'s departure time approached, I returned out on deck, along with other interested passengers. At midsummer, there would still be some daylight for the departure but, at this time of the year, it was dark. As soon as the Liver Building's clock had finished striking ten, the gangways were lowered to the dock, the ship's passenger doors were closed and the warehouse doors were rolled shut. A small boat took a heaving line to the other side of the dock, so that *Leinster* could pull her bow out from the dockside. The lines were cast off, the propellers turned and *Leinster* began to move out from the quay into the middle of the dock and then along the dock. The entrance to Princes Dock was crossed by a bridge carrying the railway line to the Riverside Station, used by Liverpool's liner passengers. The bridge had been swung open for *Leinster*, but the passage was very narrow and careful handling was needed to pass through without touching either side. *Leinster* then crossed Princes Half Tide Dock at an angle, before turning to go through another narrow passage into West Waterloo Dock. She stopped at the far end of that dock, a head rope was attached to the quay and her stern was swung to port, to align her with the entrance lock. When that manoeuvre had been completed successfully, the head rope was cast off and *Leinster* moved astern into the lock. Once in the lock, she stopped again and tied up. The inner lock gates were closed and the water in the lock was then lowered to bring *Leinster* down to river level. This took about fifteen minutes and the outer lock gates were then opened. *Leinster* cast off again and moved astern into the river, where she was suddenly subjected to the Mersey's tidal forces. Sometimes a tug was needed to help the ship away from the river wall, but tonight there was no such problem. Once she was clear of the lock, *Leinster*'s telegraphs signalled full ahead and she moved further out into the Mersey, bound for the open sea. This complicated manoeuvre, requiring skilful vessel handling, had again been accomplished successfully.

It was now time to move to the forward end of the Boat Deck, behind the glass screen, for shelter from the cold wind. The Mersey slipped by quickly and soon we passed New Brighton and entered the Crosby Channel. Half an hour after leaving the dock system, we passed the Crosby lightship and I decided that it was time to retire for the night. There would be little else to be seen during the night, except for passing *Munster*, off Anglesey, around 01.45. Most other passengers did the same, although some stayed in the bar for a nightcap, and those who had not booked a cabin settled down for the night in a chair in the lounge or drawing room.

I soon fell asleep, to the background noise of the ship's engines and enjoyed a reasonable night's sleep. Next morning, I was woken by my steward, who brought me tea and biscuits. Through my porthole, I could see that we were still moving. I dressed and went out on deck, where I found that we were sailing up the river Liffey. Some passengers were already in the dining saloon, enjoying a hearty Irish breakfast. Shortly afterwards, *Leinster* turned, so that she could complete her passage up the Liffey, stern first, with her bow pointing towards the sea, ready for that evening's return sailing to Liverpool. She berthed on time at 07.30 at B&I's North Wall terminal, near the city centre, with her port side to the quay. The ship's side doors were opened, the specially designed gangway was extended from the terminal building and all passengers were asked to proceed ashore. I soon completed Customs formalities and was ready to start my brief holiday in Ireland.

On the Saturday evening, I returned to the terminal for my return sailing to Liverpool, knowing that I would be sailing on *Munster*. I was pleased that I would have sailed on both sister ships, although I could detect no difference between them. The embarkation procedures were similar, although the passenger entrance, which was one floor above the cargo warehouse, gave a much better impression than the approach at Liverpool. The departure from Dublin was earlier, at 20.00, and the ship sailed direct from the quay. Unfortunately it was dark, so I saw little of the river as we sailed out to sea. Unlike the outward crossing, this passage was very rough and I was glad to retire to my cabin. I woke occasionally during the night and each time I was aware of an unusual degree of motion. I slept through our arrival in the Mersey, but we probably called at Woodside to disembark cattle. I also slept through the complicated manoeuvres needed to take *Munster* through the river lock and astern up to her berth. I was woken by my steward with tea and biscuits. By this time, *Munster* was tied up quietly in Princes Dock. I walked down the corridor to the toilet and realised that I was swaying from side to side, striking the sides of the corridor as I did so. The ship was not moving, but I was still being affected by the motion experienced earlier, while out at sea. It must have been quite a crossing!

After dressing, I disembarked through the dingy warehouse and went through Customs. I then walked down to the landing stage and crossed by ferry back to Birkenhead. My Irish holiday was over.

TWO

EARLY DUBLIN SERVICES

City of Dublin Steam Packet Co.

The first steamship sailings between Liverpool and Dublin were made in 1819 by *Waterloo* and *Belfast*, both owned by George Langtry, who had already established sailings between Belfast and Liverpool. From 1822 he also used *Mountaineer*, which had previously operated on London–Leith and later served on the Shannon. In 1821, the former Holyhead mail packets *Talbot* and *Ivanhoe* made a brief appearance on the route. The newly established Saint George Steam Packet Co. placed *St Patrick* on the route in 1822, as part of a longer weekly service from Liverpool to Dublin, Tenby and Bristol. The history of the Saint George Steam Packet Co., and its brief involvement with Liverpool–Dublin, is given in the Cork volume.

The City of Dublin Steam Packet Co.'s Liverpool–Dublin service dated from 1824. The Dublin firm Charles Wye Williams & Co. had been established in 1823 and ordered two paddle steamers from a Liverpool shipbuilder, Thomas ('Frigate') Wilson, for a new Liverpool–Dublin service. As Wilson's new shipyard was not ready, the first ship was built under Wilson's supervision by another Liverpool shipbuilder. Named *City of Dublin*, her first sailing was on 20 March 1824. The second was built by Wilson and named *Town of Liverpool*. She was originally advertised to commence service in June 1824, but was not completed until September, making her first sailing on 5 October. These ships were the first on the route to carry cargo, in addition to passengers and livestock, and operated to Dublin's Custom House Quay. Around the end of 1824, the new competition persuaded George Langtry to withdraw from Dublin and concentrate his efforts on his home port of Belfast.

The City of Dublin Steam Packet Co. was established by a trust deed dated 10 May 1825 and took over the business operated by Charles Wye Williams & Co. In addition to Charles Wye Williams, the company's directors included Francis Carleton and Richard Bourne, all of whom were later to be involved in establishing P&O. In 1833, the City of Dublin Steam Packet Co. was incorporated by an Act of Parliament.

A further two newly built ships, *Hibernia* and *Britannia*, joined the fleet in 1825 and were the first to be registered in the new company's name. The initial advertisements referring to these ships stated that they were to be named *Free Trader* and *Union*, but the names were changed before the first ship had been completed. In 1826, the company acquired the Dublin & Liverpool Steam Navigation Co., which had started a competing service towards the end of 1824. It owned three ships, *Liffey*, *Mersey* and *Commerce*. Its fleet also included a chartered ship, *Mona*, which was advertised as carrying passengers only. In due course, *Mona* also passed into the City of Dublin company's ownership. The new company's rate of expansion was remarkably rapid. In 1826 it acquired the Liverpool and Belfast Steam Packet Co., together with its ship, *Shamrock*, and took delivery of another four new ships, *Manchester*, *Leeds*, *Birmingham* and *Sheffield*. *Shamrock* had been completed towards the end of 1824 and began her first sailing, to Belfast, on 8 December 1824. Her acquisition gained the company a new Liverpool–Belfast service, which it operated continuously until 1851, in co-operation with Langtrys. The ship most frequently associated with the early years of Liverpool–Belfast, which normally operated weekly, was *Hibernia*. A further ship, *Nottingham*, was built in 1827, bringing the fleet to fourteen ships. With so many ships, mostly operating Liverpool–Dublin, a frequent service was possible and sometimes there would be several sailings in each direction in the course of a single day.

In 1827, because of price competition for cargo, a sailing vessel, *Tyne*, was chartered for a number of sailings between Dublin and Liverpool, carrying rough goods at lower rates equivalent to those charged by sailing ships. The company stated that half to three-quarters of *Tyne*'s space was used to carry coal to Dublin to re-fuel its steamships. She was towed into and out of port so the punctuality of her sailings could be guaranteed. At that time, the company owned one tug, *Mars*, and possibly a second, *Venus*. In later years, *Mars* was used as a cattle tender.

The company suffered its first loss when *Town of Liverpool* was wrecked on 18 March 1828, while operating a Liverpool–Waterford sailing. *Sheffield* was wrecked at Ballywalter in a gale on 30 December 1828, while sailing Liverpool–Belfast. *Manchester* went aground near Dublin lighthouse in late November 1829, but was refloated with little damage and towed to Dublin for repairs, but within a few days, on 3 December, she had sunk off the Skerries. It has been stated that *Britannia* was lost in 1829. An older *Britannia*, built in 1815, but not owned by the City of Dublin company, did indeed sink at Donaghadee on 21 November 1829, but the City of Dublin company's *Britannia* continued in service until 1859, when she was broken up.

The company's final new ship of the decade was *Ballinasloe*, which was fitted with a 'blast cylinder' to ventilate her cattle accommodation.

As the fleet expanded, additional routes were opened up, including Liverpool–Londonderry (1830–1833), using first *Commerce* and later *Nottingham*, Dublin–London, Dublin–Belfast, Dublin–Bordeaux, Belfast/Dublin–Le Havre, Liverpool–North Wales and a Liverpool–Kingstown (now Dun Laoghaire) mail service.

An associated company, the Dublin & London Steam Packet Co., which was owned by Richard Bourne, started the Dublin–London service in 1826. The first vessels on that service were *Thames* (1826) and *Shannon* (1826). *Thames* had the same name as a very early steamship that had made a single sailing from Dublin to London, departing on 28 May 1815. In 1830, they were joined by *City of Londonderry* (1827), giving a regular weekly service. She had previously operated a Liverpool–Londonderry service, which was continued by the City of Dublin company. Later vessels to operate on the route were *Royal Tar* (1832) and *William Fawcett* (1828), which, together with *City of Londonderry*, were to become the first ships in the fleet of the Peninsular Steam Navigation Co., P&O's predecessor. By the mid 1830s, the same ships also operated Belfast–London, with some sailings being routed via Dublin. The Dublin–London sailing took eighty hours, including a call at Plymouth. The London agents for the service were Brodie M'Ghie Willcox and Arthur Anderson, who later established the Peninsular Steam Navigation Co. and became founder directors of P&O. In 1835, some of the ships sailed to Spain and Portugal between their Dublin–London sailings. In 1836, the newly formed British & Irish Steam Packet Co. took over the interests of the Dublin and London company, leaving that company's directors and most of its ships free to concentrate on the Peninsular Steam Navigation Co. The two oldest Dublin & London ships were sold, *Thames* to the City of Dublin Steam Packet Co. and *Shannon* to B&I, and continued to operate Dublin–London. *Thames* remained regularly on the service until she was wrecked off the Isles of Scilly in January 1841, with the loss of more than sixty lives; there were only four survivors. *Shannon*, despite being damaged by a fire in 1846, was not broken up until 1855. The City of Dublin company began operating ships on the London–Dublin/Belfast routes from 1837, in conjunction with B&I, with the first City of Dublin sailings being made by *Leeds*. Most early City of Dublin ships operated on the route. Some former Dublin and London ships, notably *William Fawcett*, continued to sail on London–Dublin/Belfast, in addition to their Peninsular sailings. The interchanges also operated in the reverse direction; in 1841, *Leeds* made several sailings to Spain, Portugal and Gibraltar, from both Liverpool and Southampton.

The ship particularly associated with the Dublin–Bordeaux service was *Leeds*, which departed from Belfast on 17 June 1827 and from Dublin on 20 June. The service operated approximately monthly, but only during the summer season, giving round-trip passengers four or five days in Bordeaux. Later Bordeaux sailings in 1827 started from Liverpool, calling at Dublin, but from 1828 the service started at Dublin, with Belfast, Liverpool and Cork passengers being offered free passage to/from Dublin. A call at Plymouth was included from 1832. *Leeds* was replaced on the service in 1836 by the company's newly built ship *City of Limerick*, because of the latter's more powerful engines, which made her 'one of the fastest steamships in the kingdom'. However, after the end of the 1836 season *City of Limerick* was chartered and later sold to B&I. The 1837 season saw the return of *Leeds* as the Bordeaux vessel. This was the last year when a regular service was operated, although *Royal William* made a single sailing on the route in May 1840.

Once Liverpool–Dublin had been firmly established, Charles Wye Williams' company set out to consolidate its position by providing connections to other parts of Ireland by inland waterways. The Grand Canal system connected Dublin with the river Shannon at Shannon Harbour. From there it was possible to sail north to Athlone and Carrick-on-Shannon, or south through Lough Derg to Limerick. In 1828, Charles Wye Williams set up the Irish Inland Steam Navigation Co. and acquired an existing vessel, *Marquis Wellsley*, which had been built at Tipton, in Staffordshire, in 1822. The new company ordered a steam lighter, *Wye*, from the Birkenhead Ironworks and it was duly assembled on the Shannon by workmen from John Laird's new yard. The successful completion of *Wye* was followed by other vessels. The most famous of the river Shannon vessels, *Lady Lansdowne*, was the first ship built by John Laird and was assembled on the Shannon in 1833. In all, the Irish Inland Steam Navigation Co. owned eight river vessels.

The river Shannon sailings connected with services from Limerick, which made the four-hour journey down the Shannon estuary to Kilrush, with intermediate calls at Tarbert, Glin and Foynes. From Kilrush, it was a short land journey to the popular seaside resort of Kilkee. The service was started in May 1829, when *Mona* was transferred from the Irish Sea. She was unsatisfactory, as her draught prevented her from reaching the quay at Limerick except at high tide, so she was replaced by a smaller vessel, *Kingstown*, in January 1830. *Kingstown* had been built in 1827 for the Saint George Steam Packet Co. and may have been chartered, as there is no record of her sale. The City of Dublin company abandoned the Shannon estuary service later in 1830, but resumed it in 1832, using the chartered Clyde steamer *Clarence*, which also operated in 1833 and 1834. *Kingstown* appears to have returned to the Shannon in mid-1834, having spent the period away from the Shannon on a Dublin–Waterford–Cork service.

In December 1834, *Garryowen*, also built by John Laird, arrived at Limerick to take up the service. *Garryowen* was an outstandingly successful ship, named after a district of Limerick. When launched, she was the largest iron ship in the world. Her iron construction meant that her draught was considerably less than that of a similar-sized wooden ship, facilitating berthing at Limerick. She was the first vessel built with watertight bulkheads. The strength of her construction was designed to deal with the conditions which sometimes prevailed in the more westerly parts of the Shannon estuary, especially in winter. She broke away from her moorings at Kilrush during a gale in January 1839, when her survival was attributed to her bulkheads. In addition to her regular sailings, she was used by the Admiralty in October 1835 to investigate the behaviour of magnetic compasses in iron ships.

In 1835, *Kingstown* was chartered for a service between Goole, Hull and Newcastle, calling off Bridlington, Scarborough, Whitby, Hartlepool and Sunderland; the charter lasted for several months, but she then appears to have returned again to the Shannon, where she assisted *Garryowen*. *Clarence* was back on the Clyde in 1835, but returned to Limerick by 1837, to operate a separate service from Limerick to Clarecastle and Ennis. The services catered for goods and livestock, as well as passengers; on their outward sailings from Limerick, the ships carried supplies for the local communities, while the return sailings carried agricultural produce and livestock. *Clarence* was sold to the Carlisle Canal Co. in 1838, but there is conflicting evidence over her date of departure from the Shannon. She was advertised on the Clare service as late as April 1840, although the local Carlisle newspaper had expected her in service there in June 1838. At Carlisle she was used as a passenger ferry on the Solway Firth, carrying passengers between Port Carlisle and Annan Waterfoot, with connecting sailings to and from Carlisle by canal passage boats. She also acted as a tender to the Liverpool and Belfast steamers at low water and carried out some towage duties. She was sold again in 1847 and finished her life as a Mersey ferry, sailing between Liverpool and Eastham.

In April 1841, there were radical changes. The local vessel *Dover Castle*, which had been based at Limerick since her arrival there on 7 November 1838, was acquired. The origins of her highly inappropriate name lay in the fact that she had been built for a Dover–London service. She was joined in the same month by a new paddle steamer, *Erin go Bragh*. It was probably after *Erin go Bragh*'s arrival that *Kingstown* finally departed from the Shannon. The three-ship service, using *Garryowen*, *Dover Castle* and *Erin go Bragh*, lasted only until 1843, when *Erin go Bragh* was transferred to Liverpool to start the City of Dublin company's new Liverpool–North Wales service. She did not return to the Shannon until 1847.

All Shannon services, both inland and estuary, were withdrawn in 1861. The inland vessels were left in the waterway system. *Lady Lansdowne* was scuttled in Lough Derg, where her remains can still be seen. *Lady Burgoyne* was sold in 1867 to other owners at Killaloe. *Dover Castle* was broken up by 1863. There was a long interval between the closure of the services and the disposal of *Garryowen* and *Erin go Bragh*. *Garryowen* was sold in 1866 to Liverpool owners, who removed her engines and converted her to a sailing ship. She made a single voyage out to West Africa, and was then converted to a storage hulk. Clearly this had been a successful venture, as the same treatment was in store for *Erin go Bragh* the following year.

Two of the company's ships, *Birmingham* and *Leeds*, were chartered in 1833 by Willcox and Anderson as transports for the Royalist side in the Portuguese Civil War. *Birmingham* brought the news to England that the opposing side, headed by Dom Miguel, had been defeated. A similar charter, of *Royal Tar*, owned by the Bourne family, was arranged in 1835, during the Spanish Civil War. It was from these connections that the Peninsular Steam Navigation Co. developed its Iberian service. A later connection came through the sale, in 1847, of *Royal Tar* to the Portuguese Government, for naval service. After a brief period in service as *Royal Tar*, she was captured by enemy forces on 30 May. She was recaptured on 3 June, and renamed *Infante D Luis*. She remained in Government service, including carrying troops, until 1863, when she was decommissioned.

The only addition to the fleet in the first half of the 1830s was *William Huskisson*, which was acquired in 1832. She had been built for a Liverpool–Glasgow service and had spent a short time on Liverpool–Waterford for the Saint George Steam Packet Co., before joining the City of Dublin fleet. Her career with the company was destined to be relatively brief. She sprang a leak in rough weather during the evening of 11 January 1840, when she was about 15 miles off Holyhead, on passage between Dublin and Liverpool with cattle and about 120 passengers. With her fires extinguished, she drifted northwards during the night and, by 7.30 next morning, was some 18 miles from the Calf of Man. Fortunately she was then spotted by the sailing ship *Huddersfield*, which sailed alongside her four times to allow her passengers and crew to be transferred.

Several passengers fell into the sea during this procedure and six people were left on board, as it had become too rough to attempt another approach. In all, *Huddersfield* rescued ninety-four people. *William Huskisson's* remains were found in 1919 during dredging operations at the Burbo Bank in the Mersey. Much of her machinery had disappeared, but her engine bedplate and funnel had survived, along with pottery relics and other items. There were other less serious casualties in this period; *Nottingham* ran aground at Larne in September 1833, while on Liverpool–Londonderry; and *Leeds* sank at Holyhead after striking a rock on 6 November 1834, but was raised and returned to service.

A new building programme started in 1836, with *Athlone* and *City of Limerick*. Most of *Athlone's* career was spent on Liverpool–Belfast. Two other vessels were ordered by the company, which intended to name them *Roscommon* and *Roscrea*. *Roscommon* was launched on 14 September 1836 and both ships featured in press reports before and after the launch, but they were never delivered to the company.

The Liverpool–Kingstown mail service commenced operations in the same year, so five new vessels were built for the mail service: *Royal William* and *Queen Victoria* in 1837, *Duchess of Kent* in 1838, and *Prince* and *Princess* in 1839. *Princess* was the final wooden steamer built for the company. *Royal Adelaide* was also built in 1838, but was not advertised to sail on the mail service, operating instead on Dublin–London, on which she was often partnered by *Royal William*. The mail service at first competed with the Admiralty packets on the same route, but an agreement was reached in 1839 under which the Admiralty packets took the morning sailings and the City of Dublin vessels the evening sailings from Liverpool. The City of Dublin company operated the 18.30 mail sailing from Kingstown. These services carried saloon passengers in addition to the mail, but no cargo or deck passengers. The mail service used the most modern, and fastest, ships. In 1850, sailings from Ireland were advertised to leave Kingstown at 18.00 and to arrive at Liverpool in time to catch the morning mail train, which was due in London at 13.00. In that year, the ships on the service were advertised as *Eblana*, *Iron Duke* and *Trafalgar*. Despite the acquisition of the Holyhead mail contract, Liverpool–Kingstown was continued, albeit less frequently. In 1855, *Iron Duke*, *Trafalgar* and *Windsor* were advertised to leave Princes pierhead for Kingstown, at 19.00 on Mondays, Wednesdays and Fridays.

The building programme of 1838–39 required more capital than was available to the company and it was prevented by law from raising extra capital. As a result, a new company, the Dublin and Liverpool Steam-Ship Building Co., was established, with capital provided mainly by City of Dublin shareholders. The first ship to be funded by the new company was *Princess*. Various ships were funded in this way, including some inland vessels on the Shannon. The company was also involved in funding *United States* for transatlantic service and as a result became a shareholder in P&O for a period. All ships were hired to the City of Dublin company. At first the ships were registered in the company's name, but in 1851 they were registered in the individual names of the owner's trustees.

A new area of operations for the City of Dublin company opened up on 5 July 1838, when *Royal William* sailed from Liverpool to New York. This sailing was advertised by the City of Dublin Steam Packet Co. itself, and was the first westbound sailing under power between the two ports. *Royal William* reached New York after a passage of eighteen days twenty-three hours and remained there for ten days, allowing sufficient time for sightseeing by round-trip passengers, before starting her return sailing to Liverpool on 4 August. She reached Liverpool on 19 August. She returned briefly to Liverpool–Dublin, but then made two further Atlantic crossings, this time under charter to the Transatlantic Steamship Co. *Royal William* then returned to Liverpool–Kingstown, and was replaced by a new larger vessel, *Liverpool*, which had been built for transatlantic service. The Transatlantic Steamship Co. merged with the Peninsular Steam Navigation Co. in 1840 to form the Peninsular and Oriental Steam Navigation Co., and *Liverpool* was renamed *Great Liverpool* by P&O. A second vessel ordered by the Transatlantic Steamship Co., which was intended to be named *United States*, was completed for P&O as *Oriental*.

The period around the late 1830s was an active one. In addition to its six new ships, the company acquired two newly built steamers, *Devonshire* and *Duke of Cambridge*, from the Goole Steam Navigation Co., which had put them up for sale without them ever having entered service, because of financial problems. They had been built for a new Goole–Hamburg service and were named *Vanguard* and *Jason*, respectively, when they were launched, but were registered with names chosen by the City of Dublin company. *Devonshire* was used on Dublin–London, and was sold to B&I within two years of her acquisition, but *Duke of Cambridge* remained in the City of Dublin fleet.

After the ending of the summer-only Bordeaux service, the company started a new year-round Belfast–Le Havre service, calling at Kingstown and Plymouth, in 1838. The first sailing was made by *Thames*, which sailed from Belfast on 23 July 1838. A free passage to Belfast or Kingstown was offered for goods and passengers from Liverpool. At first, a variety of ships operated on the route, but in 1839 most sailings were by *Duke of Cambridge*. It appears that this service was unsuccessful, with the final sailing, by *Duke of Cambridge*, leaving Belfast on 17 January 1840. The service was revived in March 1840, using P&O's *William Fawcett*, but starting from Liverpool before Belfast. From the advertising, it appears that this was a P&O service for which the City of Dublin company acted as agents in Liverpool. The new service was no more successful than the old, and was withdrawn before the end of the year.

In December 1840, an order was placed with Thomas Wilson for a further two ships to operate the Liverpool–Kingstown mail service, but as no new ships were delivered to the company until *Iron Duke* in 1844 and *Albert* in 1845, it is not clear whether these ships were ever built.

Nottingham was severely damaged in a collision with the sailing ship *Governor Fenner* off Holyhead on 20 February 1841; she was struck amidships with the complete destruction of her starboard paddle wheel and shaft, considerable damage to her starboard engine and the loss overboard of her funnel. *Governor Fenner* was carrying emigrants and sank within one minute; only her Captain and Mate had time to scramble on board *Nottingham* and the remaining 122 people on board died. After two days adrift, *Nottingham* fell in with another steamer, which towed her to Liverpool.

A special sailing by *City of Dublin* from Liverpool to Havana, calling at Lisbon, Madeira and Barbados, departed from Liverpool on 20 September 1841. It was advertised to appeal especially to passengers wishing to visit Madeira. The advertisement stated that the ship had recently undergone 'a most extensive and complete overhaul'. The reason for the sailing was not to start a new route for the company, but was due to the sale of the vessel to the Mexican Government. After her arrival at Havana on 28 November, she sailed for Mexico, arriving at Vera Cruz on 22 December. She was renamed *Regenerador*, but had a short career, being lost in 1845. By the time this sailing took place, there were regular transatlantic steamship sailings, notably by the Cunard Line, which had started its service in 1840. This single crossing therefore attracted little attention and is not referred to in literature about early transatlantic steamships. However, *City of Dublin*, dated from 1823, was a generation older than *Sirius* and *Royal William* and one of the smallest steamships ever to make an Atlantic crossing. Hers was a remarkable achievement.

October 1842 saw an outbreak of the competition that periodically characterised the Irish Sea routes. The starting point was the decision of the Saint George Steam Packet Co. to re-enter Liverpool–Dublin, which it had abandoned to the City of Dublin Steam Packet Co. many years before. The City of Dublin company retaliated almost immediately, placing *Royal Adelaide* and *Leeds* on a London–Cork service, with almost identical sailing days to those of the Saint George company's established weekly service. Although the Saint George company withdrew from Liverpool–Dublin in December, the City of Dublin company continued to operate the same ships on London–Cork until February 1843. An accommodation then appears to have been reached with the Saint George company, as a result of which the service became joint, with each company providing a single ship. The contribution from the City of Dublin company was *Duke of Cambridge*. This situation continued until May when the City of Dublin company withdrew from the route, apparently after the intervention of Malcomson Brothers of Waterford, who placed their *Mermaid* on London–Cork.

The City of Dublin company's design policy was very progressive at the time and it was one of the early companies to standardise on iron ships. Apart from the experiment of *Garryowen*, its first iron ship was *Erin go Bragh* (1840), followed by *Iron Duke* (1844). There was then a flurry of shipbuilding, with the completion of *Albert* in 1845, *Roscommon*, *Prince of Wales* and *Windsor* in 1846, and *Trafalgar* in 1848. In addition, the company took delivery of three auxiliary screw vessels, *Pearl*, *Emerald* and *Diamond*, the company's first screw vessels. They were intended to carry only cargo and livestock but, as a result of a decision by another operator, the newly formed Dublin and Liverpool Steam Ship Co., to carry emigrants to Liverpool in auxiliary steamers, the three City of Dublin vessels were used for the same purpose. Passengers travelled on deck, with no shelter. Conditions were so bad that a Government enquiry was established.

The company had been loyal to Liverpool shipbuilders while building wooden ships and its first iron ships were also built there. However, *Pearl* was built at Blackwall in 1845. Several other ships were built in Liverpool for the company in 1845 and 1846, but *Diamond* (1846) was the final vessel built there for the company.

In 1843, the company acquired the year-round Liverpool–North Wales passenger and cargo service from the Saint George Steam Packet Co. It operated to the Menai Straits (Beaumaris, Bangor and Menai Bridge); some sailings were extended to Caernarfon and some called off Llandudno, although, in the early years, those calls were not advertised in Liverpool. The Saint George company had also enjoyed a period of rapid expansion and its fleet in 1842 numbered around twenty ships. However, its financial position was weak, so it was reorganised in 1843 and many of its routes and ships were sold. The City of Dublin company did not acquire any ships from the Saint George company, but provided a ship for its new service by transferring *Erin go Bragh* from Limerick. She made her first sailing on 15 April 1843. In summer, the service operated outwards from Liverpool on Tuesdays, Thursdays and Saturdays, returning from North Wales on Mondays, Wednesdays and Fridays. There were also a few weekend excursions and occasional summer sailings from Liverpool to Kingstown via Menai Bridge, using other vessels of the fleet. *Erin go Bragh* made a sailing from Douglas to Menai Bridge on 15 July 1843. A similar service covering the 'missing' City of Dublin days was provided by a local competitor, Price and Case, using *Ayrshire Lassie* in 1843 and 1844. Their new ship *Cambria* took over in 1845. For a short period in 1844, the two services were advertised jointly, but they reverted to separate advertising before the end of the summer season. *Erin go Bragh* also operated in winter, but on a twice-weekly frequency. The City of Dublin company built *Prince of Wales* for Liverpool–North Wales and she entered service on 18 April 1846. *Erin go Bragh* was then laid up in Liverpool for most of that summer. *Prince of Wales* operated a summer service similar to that given by *Erin go Bragh*, but in winter she only made one weekly sailing. Between October and December 1846, *Erin go Bragh* operated a twice-weekly Liverpool–Caernarfon service, until she was replaced by *Mersey* in December. She left Liverpool on 7 January 1847, bound for Limerick. *Prince of Wales* was joined in 1849 by *Fairy*, a smaller vessel, which was used in the Menai Straits. The fourth of the early mail packets, *Prince Arthur*, was transferred to Liverpool–North Wales in 1863. There seems to have been relatively little interchange of vessels between the North Wales and Dublin services. The Liverpool–North Wales service was transferred to the Liverpool, Llandudno and Welsh Coast Steam Boat Co., a predecessor of the Liverpool & North Wales Steamship Co., in 1881, together with *Prince of Wales*, *Prince Arthur* and *Fairy*. The City of Dublin company had a significant shareholding in the new company.

Athlone went aground on Mew Island, at the entrance to Belfast Lough, on 4 July 1847 during a morning fog. At the time, she was nearing the end of a sailing from Dublin. Langtrys' *Sea King* also went aground close by for the same reason. *Athlone* was fortunate in being refloated on the next high tide without any serious damage, unlike *Sea King*, which was wrecked.

The Admiralty transferred the British terminal of its mail service to Holyhead in 1848 when the railway line from Chester was completed. It took over the whole service in 1849, using four packet vessels. The Government soon realised that the Admiralty service was too costly, so tenders to take over the service were invited from private operators. Two tenders were submitted: one from the Chester and Holyhead Railway, which had been taken over by the London & North Western Railway in 1848, and one from the City of Dublin Steam Packet Co. Despite much manoeuvring by the Railway, the contract was awarded to the City of Dublin Steam Packet Co., which was to retain it for the next seventy years. The contract commenced on 1 June 1850. During the contract negotiations, the City of Dublin company did agree to buy four ships, *Anglia*, *Cambria*, *Hibernia* and *Scotia*, which had been built recently for the Railway, but that arrangement was never implemented, apparently by mutual agreement, and the four ships were used by the Railway on its Holyhead–Dublin service. The City of Dublin company used two of the former Admiralty packets, *St Columba* and *Llewellyn*, with the latter renamed *St Patrick* in 1865, and provided two of its own vessels, *Eblana* and the newly built *Prince Arthur*. The two former Admiralty mail vessels were not registered in the name of the City of Dublin Steam Packet Co. until 1854 and 1865, respectively, suggesting that they had been on charter in the intervening period. The new mail service competed for passengers with the Railway's Holyhead–Dublin service.

Initially, the Holyhead mail service was viewed as supporting the company's main Liverpool–Dublin service, but by 1860 the position had been reversed and it became the City of Dublin company's most important service. The company continued a Liverpool–Dublin passenger service using its older ships, but nearly twenty years were to pass before the Liverpool route was to see another newly built vessel.

Serious competition between the various Irish companies operating cross-Channel services in the Irish Sea erupted in 1850. Its cause was the City of Dublin company's decision to enter Liverpool–Waterford with *Devonshire*, chartered from B&I, in opposition to the Waterford Steamship Co., which was closely connected to the Cork Steamship Co. The City of Dublin company then extended the competition to Liverpool–Cork, using *Duke of Cambridge* and *Albert*, and to Cork–London, with *Royal William* and *Royal Adelaide*. *Royal Adelaide* was on one of these sailings when she was wrecked off Margate in March 1850, with the loss of everyone on board. The Waterford and Cork operators responded by starting London–Dublin, Liverpool–Belfast and Liverpool–Dublin services, and threatening to start a Holyhead–Dublin service. Some of the City of Dublin and B&I ships on Dublin–London added a call at Waterford to their schedules, to carry the war right into the Malcomsons' heartland. After twelve months of competition, a meeting between the parties reached an amicable agreement on the redistribution of services. The City of Dublin company gave up Liverpool–Belfast in favour of the Cork Steamship Co., transferred its Dublin–London rights to B&I, which was to operate the service jointly with Malcomson Brothers, and ended its connection with B&I. In return the City of Dublin company obtained exclusive rights to Holyhead–Dublin/Kingstown and the other companies withdrew from Liverpool–Dublin. The Railways were not included in these discussions, so they were not precluded from developing their own Holyhead services.

The first four vessels on the mail service served the route for ten years, until the completion in 1860 of four new 17½-knot paddle steamers, *Ulster*, *Munster*, *Leinster* and *Connaught*. *Leinster* was built on the Thames, but the other three were built by Laird's. The appearance of two of these ships was unusual; *Leinster* and *Connaught* had four

Connaught (1860), as built, departing from Kingstown. (R. Brandreth collection)

bell-topped funnels, arranged in pairs fore and aft of the paddle boxes, while the other two ships had two funnels. This difference was due to the fact that two different engine builders had been used. After a short period in service, they were all given a turtle-back forward to assist them in coping with heavy seas.

A new mail contract was agreed in 1882 and the four paddle steamers were re-engined by Laird's to give them the increased speed required under the new contract. *Leinster* and *Connaught* re-entered service as two-funnelled vessels, like their sisters. On trials after re-engining, the ships reached 19½ knots. The first sailing under the new contract was made by *Leinster* in February 1885. As a backup for the mail service, a fifth two-funnelled paddle steamer, *Ireland*, was built by Laird's in 1885 and made her maiden voyage in August.

A further mail contract was signed in 1895. This contract required the sea passage to be completed in two hours forty-five minutes. The old steamers were incapable of this, so the company ordered four new ships from Laird's, each named after one of the four original paddle steamers, and took delivery of them in 1896 and 1897. They were two-funnelled screw vessels, again featuring a turtle-back forward, with a normal service speed of 23½ knots and a maximum in excess of 24 knots.

The new contract came into force in 1897, and was due to last until 1917, but was extended because of the First World War. During that war, *Connaught* and *Leinster* were torpedoed, the former on 3 March 1917 while on Government service between Le Havre and Southampton, and the latter on 10 October 1918 while sailing Kingstown–Holyhead. After the end of the war, the mail service was continued with the assistance of chartered vessels, but the company was in a weak position when tenders for a new

Connaught (1860), after re-engining. (R. Brandreth collection)

mail contract were called for. The London & North Western Railway put in the lower tender, and was awarded the new contract. The final mail sailings by the City of Dublin Steam Packet Co. took place on 27 November 1920. The two remaining mail steamers were laid up at Holyhead, and sold for breaking up in 1924.

After the award of the first Holyhead mail contract, the City of Dublin Steam Packet Co. continued to operate Liverpool–Dublin with a fleet of secondary steamers. In 1850, a daily service, Sundays excepted, was advertised, with steamers leaving Dublin two hours before high water. Following the building of new mail vessels in 1860, three of the former mail packets were transferred to Liverpool–Dublin, *Eblana* in 1861, *St Columba* in 1863 and *St Patrick* (ex-*Llewellyn*) in 1865. The fourth packet, *Prince Arthur*, was transferred to Liverpool–North Wales. Throughout this period, the frequency of sailings was maintained, with one or more sailings each day except Sunday. A surprising feature was that no new ships were built for the route until 1867; the most modern vessel used dated from 1849. By the 1860s, the ships on the service were completely outdated and very slow; the absence of new ships demonstrated the neglect by the City of Dublin company of its Liverpool service.

Two vessels employed on Liverpool–Dublin were lost in the early 1850s. *Leeds* suffered heavy-weather damage off Point Lynas on 24 January 1852, and was abandoned before she sank. All on board were saved by an American vessel, *Empire State*. On 15 February 1853, *Queen Victoria*, which was sailing from Liverpool to Dublin, ran aground on the Baily Light Rock, off Howth Head. She had been engulfed by a snowstorm, which had completely obscured the coastal lights. Her engines were put astern to pull her off the

Ireland (1885), entering Kingstown. She only served for fourteen years. (R. Brandreth collection)

The old and the new – *Connaught* (1860) and *Ulster* (1896) at Kingstown. (R. Brandreth collection)

rocks, but she sank about twenty yards from the shore as soon as she reached deep water. She had been carrying 120 passengers, of whom only forty survived. Some survivors were rescued by *Roscommon*, which had come to the aid of the stricken steamer. This was not the first incident involving *Queen Victoria*; she had run aground on the North Bank, off Rhyl, on 9 December 1842, but had quickly been refloated.

A greater emphasis on the Liverpool–Dublin route in the second half of the 1860s resulted in orders for a series of iron paddle steamers with passenger accommodation. The decision to build paddle steamers seems surprising; in earlier years, the company had been very innovative, especially in the introduction of iron steamers, but by this date it seemed unwilling to keep up with the latest developments. The final paddle steamer for Liverpool–Dublin, *Galway*, was built as late as 1891. The policy of using Irish counties as names for the company's secondary vessels was introduced in 1867 by the first vessel, *Kildare*, although an Irish county name, *Athlone*, had been used as early as 1836, followed by *Roscommon* in 1846. The names of the four Irish provinces were always reserved for the company's mail ships.

Kildare had accommodation for sixty first-class passengers and for some deck passengers. She started her maiden voyage from Liverpool to Dublin on 15 August 1857. She was followed by *Mullingar* (1868), which was the only vessel not to receive a county name, *Longford* (1870), *Leitrim* (1874), *Cavan* (1876) and *Mayo* (1880). All these paddle steamers were built at Birkenhead, by Fawcett, Preston, except for *Mullingar*, which was built at Dublin with engines supplied by Laird's. *Mayo* had no passenger accommodation. They normally took between seven and eight hours to complete a crossing, compared with eleven or twelve hours previously.

Leitrim was to enjoy an unusual and extended career. After some years as a passenger and cargo ship, she was downgraded to a cattle carrier, still operating between Liverpool and Dublin. On 20 December 1896, she sank with the loss of seventy-five cattle after being struck by another vessel, *Nicosian*, while she was berthing at Liverpool in dense fog. She was then laid up until June 1899, when she was sold for breaking up at Preston, and much of her was indeed dismantled. However, her remains were rebuilt as a twin-screw self-propelled grain elevator. She was based at Sharpness until 1959. The elevator was then sold for further service at Hull and left Sharpness on 30 September, towed by a Grimsby tug, *Lady Cecilia*, arriving at Hull on 3 October. After a short period of service there, she was sold for breaking up at Dunston-on-Tyne and left Hull under tow on 18 June 1963. She was the company's last surviving vessel.

Another of this group to enjoy an extended life was *Cavan*. She was sold for breaking up in 1897 and her registry was closed. Her engines were removed, but she was then converted to a sailing ship and re-registered under the same name in 1899. After four years' ownership by a Swansea shipowner, she was sold to Italians, who re-named her *Ero*. In the following year, she returned to British ownership and reverted to *Cavan*. One year later, she was registered in Australia, where she survived until 1932, aged fifty-six years.

The City of Dublin company acquired the Dublin and Liverpool Screw Steam Packet Co. in the early 1880s, together with its fleet of three screw vessels, *Standard* (1854), *Star* (1860) and *Express* (1874). A fourth vessel had been ordered by the acquired company, but was delivered to the City of Dublin company in 1884 as *Belfast*. However, the company remained loyal to the paddle wheel after the acquisition, building two further paddle steamers, *Meath*, again from Laird's, in 1884 and *Galway* in 1891. *Galway* was the City of Dublin company's first new steel vessel, and the first in a series to be built for the company at Port Glasgow by Blackwood & Gordon.

The next generation was built between 1894 and 1903, with six passenger/cargo steamers replacing the five oldest paddle steamers, together with *Standard* and *Star*. Their names – *Louth* (1894), *Wicklow* (1895), *Carlow* (1896), *Kerry* (1897), *Cork* (1899) and *Kilkenny* (1903) – followed the Irish county pattern. All six ships were built by Blackwood & Gordon, except for *Kilkenny*, which was built by the Clyde Shipbuilding & Engineering Co., Blackwood & Gordon's acquisitor in 1900. It is possible to trace the development of passenger accommodation in successive vessels. *Louth* and *Wicklow* each accommodated seventy first-class passengers in a saloon on the poop deck aft. Above this was a deckhouse with a smoking room and a lounge. In the forward part of the ship, there was a room for cattle dealers, and sheltered accommodation and seating for deck passengers. In *Carlow* and *Kerry*, the poop deckhouse was used to provide cabins for thirty first-class passengers, in addition to the seventy accommodated in the saloon, so the smoking room was positioned amidships on the Bridge Deck. *Cork* had accommodation for 150 first-class passengers, which was achieved by including cabins on the Bridge Deck, in addition to those on the poop deck, and she retained the smoking room in the midships accommodation. For the first time in the series, separate apartments were provided for male and female steerage passengers. The final vessel in the series, *Kilkenny*, had first-class accommodation for 154 passengers, but otherwise was similar to *Cork*. All six vessels had space for 500 head of cattle and general cargo.

The Liverpool berth was in Clarence Dock, but it was moved to Nelson Dock in July 1903. From the time when Princes landing stage was opened, the company's ships also called there to embark or disembark passengers. *Iron Duke* was the first ship to tie up at the first Princes stage when it opened. By the 1880s, the service comprised a single sailing every day, Sundays excepted, in both directions. In July 1902, with five modern vessels in operation, the frequency of the service was increased to twice daily, Sundays excepted, in both directions, throughout the year, with both an overnight and a daytime sailing. The twice-daily service lasted until the end of 1908, but it then reverted to once daily, although there were occasional twice-daily sailings on busy days in 1909 and 1910. There was also a single-ship Manchester–Dublin service, usually by *Wicklow*.

The final vessel to enter the company's fleet, in 1910, was *Mystic* (1893), previously owned by the Belfast Steamship Co. She was renamed *Carrickfergus* and employed on Dublin–Belfast.

On 11 July 1913, there was a Royal visit to Liverpool to open the new Gladstone Dock, which at that time comprised a single graving dock, of a size sufficient to accommodate the largest Cunard liners of the era, *Mauretania*, *Lusitania* and *Aquitania*. There was a parade of 109 ships and smaller vessels in the river, in which *Kilkenny* represented the City of Dublin Steam Packet Co. She was anchored close to the Isle of Man steamer *Ben-my-Chree*, the Belfast Steamship Co.'s *Patriotic*, Powell, Bacon & Hough's *Powerful* and the Cork Steamship Co.'s *Bittern*.

Louth (1894) –the first screw vessel ordered by the City of Dublin Co. (R. Brandreth collection)

Wicklow (1895). Obviously a coal burner! (R. Brandreth collection)

Carlow (1896). (R. Brandreth collection)

Kerry (1897) in the Mersey. (Author's collection)

Cork (1899). (Author's collection)

Galway (1894) in 1938. She was originally the City of Dublin Co.'s *Louth*. (K.P. Lewis)

Wicklow (1895) in 1938, the former final City of Dublin Co. vessel within Coast Lines. (K.P. Lewis)

At the outbreak of war in 1914, the company's six Liverpool-based ships were requisitioned and spent the period between 8 and 24 August carrying troops from Ireland to England. They then returned to their normal service. In their absence, *Belfast* and *Carrickfergus* maintained the service. During the war, the ships continued to operate intermittent services when there was sufficient traffic. The nadir of the service was reached in the early months of 1916, when the sole vessel in service was *Wicklow*, making only one round sailing each week, while *Kerry* and *Cork* were laid up in Liverpool. Between 25 April and 5 May 1916, *Louth*, *Wicklow*, *Carlow* and *Kerry* were requisitioned to carry troops to Ireland following the rising there.

Some of the company's ships were requisitioned for general trooping or other services. *Carrickfergus* carried stores across the English Channel between September 1915 and April 1917. *Cork* carried mail from Dover or Newhaven to Dunkerque between April 1916 and July 1917. *Louth* carried troops from Ireland to England during January 1917.

During August/September 1917, *Louth* was employed salving cargo from the wrecked vessel *Camito*. Immediately afterwards, she was chartered by the Admiralty and ran between Aberdeen and Norway. Her passengers included Secret Service agents, diplomatic representatives and British refugees from Russia. On 17 October 1917, while crossing the North Sea, *Louth* arrived at the scene of the sinking of two destroyers, HMS *Mary Rose* and HMS *Strongbow*. She was able to rescue two officers and twelve ratings, the sole survivors.

The City of Dublin company's only war loss from its Liverpool fleet was *Cork*, which was torpedoed by a German submarine, *U-103*, 9 miles off Point Lynas on 26 January

1918 on a Dublin–Liverpool sailing, with a loss of twelve lives among the passengers and crew on board.

Kilkenny was requisitioned and left Liverpool under sealed orders on 22 December 1915. She spent some time carrying refugees from Holland to London, and ended her requisition in June 1916. While carrying out a Liverpool–Cork sailing, she ran aground on 15 May 1917 at Knockadoon Bay, at Youghal, north-east of the entrance to Cork harbour. She was then sold to the Great Eastern Railway. She was requisitioned again in November 1918 and chartered to the City of Cork Steam Packet Co., which used her on Liverpool–Cork and Fishguard–Cork. In July, she was handed back to the GER, renamed *Frinton* and re-built before entering railway service on Harwich–Antwerp, normally as a cargo vessel. In 1920, she was transferred to Harwich–Rotterdam. She passed to the London & North Eastern Railway in 1923, when the Railway companies were amalgamated. She was sold to Greek owners in 1926, but retained the name *Frinton* and remained in their service until 22 April 1941, when she became a war loss.

Towards the end of the war, most of the company's Liverpool fleet came under Government requisition, but continued in Irish Sea service. Several of them were managed by B&I during this period.

Following its loss of the mail contract, the City of Dublin Steam Packet Co. decided to cease operations. Its trade from Dublin to Liverpool/Manchester was sold to B&I in 1919, together with five ships, *Louth, Wicklow, Carlow, Kerry* and *Belfast*. The five ships were sold first to the London Maritime Investment Co., a Royal Mail subsidiary set up in 1897 to acquire new companies, and then on to B&I. The City of Dublin business was merged with that of Tedcastle, McCormick, under the B&I name, on 17 October 1919.

The City of Dublin Steam Packet Co. was wound up in 1924 by an Act of Parliament, one hundred years after it had started its first service, although the legal procedures continued until at least 1931. The winding up itself presented constitutional difficulties, since it first had to be established that Westminster, which had passed the Act establishing the company, still had jurisdiction following the passage of the Irish Free State Act.

Tedcastle, McCormick & Co.

Tedcastle, McCormick & Co.'s origins lie in the coal trade. As Ireland lacked indigenous supplies of coal, numerous colliers were employed over the years to carry coal between British and Irish ports. Robert Tedcastle started in the coal trade in Liverpool around 1840 and built up a fleet of sailing vessels carrying coal to Kingstown. He bought his first steamer, *Dublin*, in 1869 and extended his operations to include general cargo and passengers in 1872, trading as the Tedcastle Line. However, the space on the ships actually allocated to passengers appears to have been fairly limited. He acquired the trade of the Whitehaven Steam Navigation Co. from Liverpool to Maryport/Whitehaven in 1885 and used this as the basis of a triangular Dublin–Liverpool–Maryport–Whitehaven service, returning direct to Dublin.

One ship in Robert Tedcastle's fleet, between 1876 and 1882, was a small wooden paddle tug, *Toiler*. Her principal claim to fame lies in her subsequent history, in becoming Aberdeen's first trawler. She was sold in 1882 to Aberdeen owners and sailed there through the Caledonian Canal. Her owners were headed by Mr Robert Brown, later the Manager of the Bon-Accord Ice Co. At the time, trawling was just being developed, but there were no trawlers at Aberdeen. *Toiler* was fitted out as an experimental trawler, with a net weighted with a heavy oak beam. She made her first trip on 23 March 1882, but managed to catch little more than enough fish for those on board to enjoy a 'fry'. Subsequent trips were more successful and she made a profit of £769 in her first six months. Unfortunately, she soon proved a financial burden, needing repairs costing £1,000. She sank on 31 March 1887 while on a fishing trip in the Moray Firth. This was not quite the end of the story. Her successor, the trawler *North Star*, trawled up some of her remains two years later. Her oak beam was taken to the residence of Mr William Pyper, one of her later part owners, and erected there with due ceremony.

J. McCormick & Co. was established in Dublin in 1848, when John McCormick acquired another coal merchant's business. He became a shipowner in the early 1870s and built up a fleet of sailing ships. He later acquired some steamers and, in 1891, established the Dublin & Mersey Steam Shipping Co., which carried goods, passengers and livestock between Liverpool and Dublin. The service was extended to include Manchester when the Ship Canal opened.

The two businesses amalgamated in 1897 as Tedcastle, McCormick & Co. The Tedcastle business contributed four ships, *Adela* (1878), *Marlay* (1890), *Eblana* (1892) and *Cumbria* (1896), while the McCormick business contributed two, *Blackwater* (1883) and *Blackrock* (1892). Further vessels built after the merger were *Dublin* (1904), *Blackwater* (1907) and *Killiney* (1918). *Dublin* was a replacement for *Marlay*, which sank during a gale in 1902. The second *Blackwater* replaced her namesake, which sank in a collision in 1905. The Maryport/Whitehaven service, operated by the appropriately named *Cumbria*, was sold in 1916. The company's ships were less involved than the City of Dublin company's ships in wartime requisitions, but *Eblana* was a Fleet Messenger Ship in 1917–18, *Dublin* became a naval collier in 1918–19 and *Blackwater* carried stores across the English Channel between 1915 and 1919. *Adela* was torpedoed on 27 December 1917, while on her regular service. She was the company's only war loss.

B&I acquired the company in September 1919, along with its six ships, *Eblana*, *Cumbria*, *Blackrock*, *Dublin*, *Blackwater* and *Killiney*. *Blackwater* was transferred direct to Coast Lines without ever entering B&I's fleet. The ships carried a few passengers, but four were typical engines-aft coasters. Only the most modern, *Killiney*, could justify being described as a passenger vessel. She had both first-class and steerage passenger accommodation, and was a great advance over previous ships because, for the first time, steerage passengers were housed aft rather than being crowded together forward, and there were separate rooms for men and women. After she had entered the B&I fleet, she was renamed *Lady Killiney*. The other five ships retained their Tedcastle, McCormick names.

THREE

BRITISH & IRISH STEAM PACKET CO.

The British & Irish Steam Packet Co. (B&I) operated the Liverpool–Dublin service between 1919 and 1988. It had a long history from its establishment in 1836 but, until 1919, its main service had been Dublin–London via the south coast of England. B&I was acquired by Coast Lines in 1917 and became the means of developing a major route in Coast Lines' network of passenger, cargo and livestock services across the Irish Sea. In 1919, B&I acquired five ships from the City of Dublin Steam Packet Co., together with its Dublin–Liverpool/Manchester trade. Just before that acquisition, B&I had bought Tedcastle McCormick & Co., which operated six ships on the same two routes. In the space of one month, B&I had become the sole operator between the Mersey and the Liffey, laying the foundations of a new service that was to become far more significant than B&I's original Dublin–London service, which it continued to operate until 1939. Apart from the period 1940–1946, B&I operated the passenger service until 1988, when it withdrew from Liverpool in favour of Holyhead. It continued to operate a freight ro-ro service until 1994.

In 1836, B&I took over the Dublin–Plymouth–London service previously operated by the Dublin & London Steam Packet Co. The service was initially operated by chartered ships, *City of Limerick*, from the City of Dublin Steam Packet Co. and *Mermaid*, from the Waterford Steam Navigation Co., with the latter soon replaced by *Royal William*. Later, the company purchased three ships – *Shannon* from the Dublin & London Steam Packet Co., and *City of Limerick* and *Devonshire* from the City of Dublin Steam Packet Co. The sailings were supplemented by *Nottingham*, chartered from the City of Dublin Steam Packet Co. The service was operated jointly with the City of Dublin Steam Packet Co. itself, which supplied other ships.

There were a number of close links between B&I and the City of Dublin company, in addition to the joint Dublin–London service and the sale of City of Dublin ships to B&I. The City of Dublin company's Liverpool–Dublin service was advertised as a convenient method of travel from Liverpool to London, connecting at Dublin with the London sailings. The City of Dublin company occasionally used B&I's ships on its

Liverpool service and both companies shared the same agents at Dublin. The close ties with the City of Dublin Steam Packet Co. were further emphasised by the presence of Francis Carleton among the first directors of B&I. He was a director of the City of Dublin Steam Packet Co. and later became a director of the Transatlantic Steamship Co., and then of P&O.

An ingenious theft connected with *City of Limerick* took place in April 1839. The ship had called at Falmouth to pick up two boxes of gold dust, which had been brought there from Brazil by a naval vessel. When she arrived at London, the boxes were handed in at the agent's offices, where a man presented apparently correct documents and claimed the boxes. Two hours later, the mining company's real representative arrived to collect the gold. It turned out that the planning of the theft had involved a company employee. Two men were later tried and sentenced to transportation to Australia for fourteen years. The agent, James Hartley, had been so diligent in discovering the perpetrators of the crime that he was made a director of B&I. He had earlier become a founder director of P&O, as a representative of the City of Dublin company's interests.

B&I's first new ship, *Duke of Cornwall*, was built in 1842. A vessel named *Prince Albert* was launched for the company on 16 September 1841, but no ship of that name was ever delivered, so it seems likely that she became *Duke of Cornwall*. She was a wooden paddle steamer, the only such vessel ever built for the company. All B&I's future vessels would be built of iron or steel and with propellers. B&I's policy contrasted markedly with that of the City of Dublin company, which continued to build paddle steamers until 1891. Two ships with auxiliary screw propulsion, *Rose* and *Shamrock*, were built in 1845. The company's first proper screw steamship, *Foyle*, was bought in 1850.

From 1850 onwards, there was fierce competition between B&I, the City of Dublin company, the Waterford Steamship Co., the Cork Steamship Co. and Langtrys. Following an initial move by the City of Dublin Steam Packet Co., the Waterford Steamship Co. opened a Dublin–London service. In response, B&I opened new Waterford–London, Waterford–Liverpool and London–St Petersburg services, all being routes already operated by the Waterford company. Under the terms of an agreement reached in 1851, B&I and the Waterford company shared the Dublin–London traffic and B&I withdrew its other services. The City of Dublin Steam Packet Co. withdrew from Dublin–London and severed its connections with B&I.

Following the agreement, B&I's service was extended to Liverpool. The service also introduced calls at more ports on the south coast of England, normally Falmouth, Torquay, Southampton and Portsmouth, in addition to Plymouth. The company also introduced a Limerick–London service, using *Rose*, but that service was transferred to Limerick operators when *Rose* was sold to them in 1853.

In 1853, B&I augmented its fleet with two further screw steamers intended for Liverpool–London: a chartered steamer, *Nile*, which had been built in 1852, and *Lady Eglinton*, which was newly built for the company. *Lady Eglinton* was the first B&I ship to carry a 'Lady' name. This style was used with most subsequent B&I vessels until 1937, when it was changed to that of the former City of Dublin company, using Irish provinces for the major passenger ships and counties for secondary vessels.

Nile was wrecked on the north Cornish coast, between St Ives and Portreath, on 30 November 1854, with the loss of all on board. The British Government chartered *Lady Eglinton* and *Foyle* in 1855 as Crimean War transports. The shortage of ships resulting from this loss and the Government charters necessitated the withdrawal of the Liverpool extension, which was never reinstated.

Lady Eglinton is widely credited with two transatlantic voyages from Galway to Quebec and Montreal in 1858. It is less well known that she made three earlier Atlantic crossings in 1853, just after her delivery. The first two voyages were under charter to the Canadian Steam Navigation Co., which had been established by the Liverpool firm of McKean, McLarty & Lamont under a mail contract with the Canadian Government. The company at first relied on chartered vessels, including *Lady Eglinton*, which sailed from Liverpool for Quebec and Montreal on 16 June and again on 18 August. The third crossing was under charter to the South American & General Steam Navigation Co., which was also awaiting the delivery of new ships. She sailed from Liverpool on 24 October, with calls at Lisbon, St Vincent, Pernambuco, Bahia, Rio de Janeiro and Montevideo, and arrived back at Liverpool on 13 January 1854. The 1858 crossings were operated by B&I as the British & Irish Transatlantic Steam Packet Co. and departed from Galway on 4 August and 23 September. Galway had some advantages as a transatlantic passenger port, since it provided the shortest sea journey to America. The service attracted good passenger numbers but the port had few advantages for cargo, little of which was offered, so the venture was not repeated. *Lady Eglinton* was chartered again in 1862; after Malcomson Brothers had lost *Malvina*, *Lady Eglinton* was her short-term replacement on their Belfast–Waterford–London service.

In 1858, B&I acquired the paddle steamer *Mars* (1853), for a Dublin–Wexford service. She had been built for service between London and Gravesend. In addition to Dublin–Wexford, she also operated local excursions from Dublin to Lambay Island. This short-lived service ended in 1863, when *Mars* was sold as a blockade-runner in the American Civil War. She operated successfully and avoided capture; after the end of the war, she was broken up at Nassau.

Two years later, in 1865, *Lady Wodehouse* was delivered to B&I. At the same time, *Lady Eglinton* was lengthened by the Dublin builders of *Lady Wodehouse*. After the work, her length was similar to that of the new ship. A third ship, *Countess of Dublin*, was completed by the same builders in 1869. B&I became the sole operator on Dublin–London in 1870, when it bought out the Waterford interests in the route, together with two ships, *Avoca* and *Cymba*.

The year 1879 was notable in B&I's history because of its registration as a limited company. The change in status was celebrated by the delivery of another new steamer, *Lady Olive*. She brought the number of first-rate vessels in the B&I fleet to four.

B&I's next new vessel, *Lady Martin*, was not built until 1888, at Belfast. She was notable as the first B&I vessel with a steel hull and triple expansion engines. She replaced *Lady Eglinton*, which was broken up. B&I's next new vessel was *Lady Hudson-Kinahan*. She was built at Troon in 1891 and brought the number of first-rate vessels in the fleet up to five. Two further new vessels followed at three-yearly intervals. *Lady Wolseley* was built at Barrow in 1894 and replaced *Countess of Dublin*, which had been involved in a collision in March that year, and was then broken up. B&I returned to Troon for *Lady Roberts*, which was completed in 1897. She took the place of *Lady Wodehouse*, which was also broken up. Since *Lady Wodehouse* was older than *Countess of Dublin*, it seems probable that *Lady Wolseley* had been intended as a replacement for *Lady Wodehouse*, which gained a three-year reprieve as a result of the accident to *Countess of Dublin*.

On completion of *Lady Roberts*, the four most modern vessels maintained the regular service, with *Lady Olive* being held in reserve. The ships all had berths for around 120 saloon and fifty second-cabin passengers, and also carried unberthed steerage passengers. There was a full complement of stewards and stewardesses. The service was fashionable and a piano was put on board each ship during the summer. The ships' normal speed was 13 knots. They also operated cruises from Dublin, usually to Falmouth and Plymouth, and offered through fares to Brittany, via Southampton and St Malo.

The company took delivery of two small vessels, the cargo steamer *Calshot* in 1905, and the barge *Camber* in 1907, but it was not until September 1911 that another major vessel was delivered. This ship was *Lady Gwendolen*, which was built at Port Glasgow. She was a replacement for *Lady Olive*, which had been sold to Greek owners in 1910.

There were further important changes in 1914. After Powell, Bacon & Hough Lines (later renamed Coast Lines) had acquired a minority shareholding in B&I that year, a fleet disposal programme was started, with the sale of three of the five major ships. The first vessels to be sold were *Lady Martin* and *Lady Roberts*, both in July. *Lady Martin* was sold to Turkish buyers and renamed *Bimbashi Riza Bey*. She was still at Glasgow at the outbreak of war, so was seized by the British authorities and re-sold to B&I in March 1915, when she resumed her previous name. *Lady Roberts* was sold to Italian buyers and renamed *Sassari*. The year's final sale took place in October, when *Lady Hudson-Kinahan* was sold to Greek owners and renamed *Elsie*. A further sale took place in December 1915, of *Lady Wolseley* to the Limerick Steamship Co., who renamed her *Kinvarra*. Allowing for the return of *Lady Martin*, there had been three disposals, which were replaced with one new vessel, *Lady Wimborne* (1915), and a purchased vessel, *Tees Trader* (1913), which was renamed *Lady Olive*. Gaps in the schedule resulting from the disposals were filled with chartered vessels.

Some sources refer to a vessel named '*Lady Roberts*', which was completed for B&I in 1915 and traded for about two years before becoming a war loss. Those sources give no details of tonnage, dimensions or builder of the vessel. It is impossible to find any record of a vessel with that name either being launched or completed in 1915, or becoming a war loss or casualty. Dublin Customs records contain no reports of any '*Lady Roberts*' calling at Dublin in 1915/16, although arrivals and departures of the known members of B&I's fleet were reported regularly. It therefore seems certain that this '*Lady Roberts*' never existed. The most likely explanation for the error is that there was some confusion in Lloyd's Register with *Lady Wimborne*, which was completed in 1915 with an initial gross tonnage of 1,532, not long after the sale of the 1897 *Lady Roberts*. B&I's fleet list in Lloyd's Register for 1915 shows a '*Lady Roberts*' of 1,532 gross tons built in 1915, but no *Lady Wimborne*; the alphabetical list of ships in the main Register shows the reverse.

The fleet list showed both ships in 1916, but only *Lady Wimborne* in 1917; 'Lady Roberts' never appeared in the main Register.

There were two further additions to B&I's fleet in 1916, *Lady Cloé* and *Lady Patricia*. They were balanced, by the sales, in 1916 of *Lady Olive* back to her original owners for use as a naval 'Q'-ship (*Q 18*), and early in 1917 of *Lady Martin* (for the second time), which went to Cunningham, Shaw & Co. as *Purfleet Belle*. *Lady Patricia*, which had been commissioned into the Royal Navy as a Special Service Ship (*Q 25*), was sunk north-west of Ireland by *U-46* on 20 May 1917. One further vessel disposed of during the war was *Lady Gwendolen*, which had previously been lent to the Russian Government between May 1916 and April 1918 and used by the Governor of Archangel. Only seven years old, she was sold to the Dundee, Perth & London Shipping Co. in July 1918. She was used on that company's Dundee–London passenger/cargo service without change of name, but was not really suitable. As soon as other ships became available after the war, she was withdrawn and sold in 1919 to sail, as *Rosalind*, between New York and Canada. She was bought by a subsidiary of Furness, Withy in 1929 and had a number of further ownership changes, not being broken up until 1952.

Coast Lines completed its purchase of B&I's shares by July 1917. After the war, B&I's fleet had been reduced by war losses and sales to two ships, *Lady Wimborne* and *Lady Cloé*, with accommodation for seventy passengers each. Two war-standard ships were bought from the British Government in 1919 after their launch. *War Spey* was completed as *Lady Patricia* and *War Garry* became *Lady Emerald*. Unlike their predecessors, these two ships had no passenger accommodation. These four ships covered Dublin–London calling at Cork, Falmouth, Torquay and Southampton. There were twice-weekly sailings in each direction, one by a passenger ship and one by a cargo ship. The passenger service was reduced in the early 1930s, when most passenger accommodation was removed, leaving only a few cabins for men. All passenger carrying ceased in 1937, but the cargo service continued until 1939.

Having completed the acquisition of the fleet of the City of Dublin Steam Packet Co. and Tedcastle McCormick & Co. in 1919, B&I turned its attention to building up its Irish Sea services. With the acquisitions, it had obtained five passenger/cargo vessels, four of which, *Wicklow*, *Carlow*, *Kerry* and *Killiney*, operated an interim Liverpool–Dublin service until new vessels could be built. Each of the four had 'Lady' prefixed to her name. The fifth, *Louth*, was renamed *Lady Louth*, but was transferred in 1920 to the City of Cork Steam Packet Co. to help make good its war losses, and renamed *Bandon*. B&I then brightened the image of its ships by changing its all-black funnel colour to green with a black top.

Lady Louth, Lady Longford and *Lady Limerick*

Although both the City of Dublin Steam Packet Co. and Tedcastle McCormick & Co. had operated Liverpool–Dublin passenger services, their services were fairly well run down by the end of 1918. B&I's passenger service combined the best of both fleets, using *Lady*

Lady Louth (1923) – B&I's first ship built for the Liverpool–Dublin service. (R. Brandreth collection)

Wicklow, Lady Carlow, Lady Kerry and *Lady Killiney*, and briefly in 1920/21 the Belfast Steamship Co.'s *Classic*, but sailing times varied with the tides. B&I needed modern ships operating at fixed times for a proper daily passenger service, so placed an order with the Ardrossan Dockyard Co. for two steamers to operate the service. Departures were to be from Liverpool at 22.00, arriving in Dublin at 08.00, and from Dublin at 20.15, arriving in Liverpool at 07.00. On Saturday nights, departure was at 23.00. The timings would enable passengers to use the same trains as the Liverpool–Belfast passengers.

There seem to have been some doubts about the new vessels' intended use. Both orders were transferred from B&I to Burns & Laird Lines on 10 December 1922. There are shipyard references to the first vessel under the name *Ermine*, which had previously been used by G.&J. Burns. She was launched on 7 March 1923 without a name. Press reports merely stated that she was building for Irish Sea service with a Coast Lines' associate. Both orders were transferred back to B&I in May 1923.

The first vessel was delivered in June 1923 as *Lady Louth*. However, her crewing arrangements caused a strike, which closed down all B&I's Liverpool sailings from 23 June. After arriving at Liverpool from Ardrossan on 27 June, *Lady Louth* lay idle until she took over Coast Lines' cruise programme from *Tiger*. She operated five cruises between 19 July and 26 September, and was then laid up again in Liverpool because the strike had not been settled. It was not until 5 November that she was able to make her first Liverpool–Dublin sailing.

Initially, *Lady Louth* operated the service with *Lady Killiney*, but they were joined on 5 December by *Ardmore*, built in 1921 for the City of Cork Steam Packet Co.'s Liverpool–Cork service. At the beginning of 1924, *Ardmore* was renamed *Lady Longford*

Lady Limerick (1924) sailing from Princes Stage. (K.P. Lewis)

and *Lady Killiney* was renamed *Ardmore*. The three ships continued to operate the service, but for the summer of that year, *Classic* re-joined the service, replacing *Ardmore*. On 29 July, while in Dublin, *Classic* was renamed *Killarney*. In October 1924, the second vessel ordered from the Ardrossan Dockyard was delivered as *Lady Limerick*, making her maiden voyage from Liverpool to Dublin on 17 October. Her advent enabled *Ardmore* to be released to Liverpool–Cork. On 8 December, *Lady Limerick* operated a trip around Dublin Bay for 200 of Dublin's leading citizens.

Lady Louth and *Lady Limerick* were sister ships. They were three-island type vessels, with two masts placed well forward and aft and one tall thin funnel, with a cowl top. There was little rake to the funnels and masts. Each well deck had two large cranes. Their overall appearance was rather severe. There were two features by which the ships could be differentiated. *Lady Louth* had cowl ventilators at the after end of her Boat Deck and a galley chimney that was carried into the funnel at an angle. *Lady Limerick* had cylindrical ventilators and lacked the galley chimney extension.

Both ships had cabin accommodation for eighty first-class passengers, including sixty single cabins, and housed ninety steerage passengers aft. They carried general cargo and 800–1,000 head of cattle. There were four passenger decks amidships for saloon passengers. The Upper Deck had a forward lounge extending across the full width of the ship. Immediately aft, there was a bar. The rest of the accommodation on that deck was set back from the sides of the ship to provide some promenade space. The ship's main entrance was immediately behind the lounge and had a purser's room and stairs to the next deck down, the Saloon Deck. The rest of the Upper Deck was used for thirty-three single-berth cabins, two cabins de-luxe and one special cabin, which was also used as a writing room. On the Saloon Deck, there was a dining room forward, underneath the lounge; the remainder of the accommodation comprised cabins. The other cabins were on the Main Deck. There was some open space on the Boat Deck, above the Upper Deck. Their passenger facilities were very advanced for the time, with hot and cold seawater spray-baths and a 'hairdressing establishment'. This appears to have served the same purpose as the barber's shops installed in the Belfast vessels around the same time, to allow male passengers to be shaved despite the absence of hot water in the cabins. Their machinery could not make any similar claim to be advanced. They were the last Irish Sea passenger vessels built with reciprocating engines and coal-fired boilers, giving a leisurely speed of 15 knots.

Lady Longford's design was similar. She had been built in 1921 as *Ardmore* for Liverpool–Cork, with only a limited amount of passenger accommodation. Additional passenger accommodation was fitted later, involving little change in her external appearance, except for four extra lifeboats, making eight in total. A flying bridge was fitted above her wheelhouse; three cabs were added to her flying bridge later. Her appearance lacked the severity of her two companions. Although she was two years older than her coal-fired running mates she was oil-fired, but her reciprocating engines were less powerful and managed only 14 knots.

Both *Lady Louth* and *Lady Longford* spent over two months at Ardrossan early in 1925. It was probably at this stage that *Lady Longford's* passenger accommodation was increased, bringing her into line with the other two ships. Their absence from the service was covered by *Killarney* from Fishguard–Cork and by *Ardmore* from Liverpool–Cork.

Lady Longford (1921). She was formerly *Ardmore*. (R. Brandreth collection)

Lady Longford (1921), after alterations in 1925. (R. Brandreth collection)

The vessels were based in Nelson Dock, Liverpool. They often called at a Wirral cattle stage, and at Princes Landing Stage to disembark their passengers, on their arrival from Dublin.

By the late 1920s, the three ships had succeeded in re-establishing the Liverpool–Dublin passenger service and larger ships were needed. After the delivery of *Ulster Monarch* and her two sister ships to the Belfast Steamship Co., B&I acquired *Graphic*, *Heroic* and *Patriotic* from the Belfast company. They took over Liverpool–Dublin from the older ships, which in turn were transferred in 1930 to Coast Lines' Scottish subsidiary, Burns & Laird Lines. The Dublin service was transferred to a new Liverpool berth, at South East Princes Dock, from 22 March 1930.

Lady Longford was the first to be withdrawn from Liverpool–Dublin, making her final sailing from Dublin to Liverpool on 6 July 1929, but she was then used by the City of Cork Steam Packet Co. on Fishguard–Cork. She also made a round sailing on her original Cork–Liverpool route in December 1929.

Lady Limerick was the first ship transferred to her new owners. She left Glasgow on her first sailing to Belfast on 17 April 1930, and was renamed *Lairdscastle* at Glasgow on 15 May. She was followed on 14 June by *Lady Louth*, which was renamed *Lairdsburn* on 25 June. They were placed on the overnight Glasgow–Belfast service and offered greatly improved facilities over *Lairdswood* and *Lairdsloch*, which they replaced. Those two were transferred to Glasgow–Dublin. Some of *Lairdscastle*'s single cabins were converted to doubles, resulting in the number of berths being increased to 130.

The new *Innisfallen* took over Fishguard–Cork from *Lady Longford* on 16 June 1930. *Lady Longford* relieved *Kenmare* on Liverpool–Cork for the remainder of that month and then left Cork light for Ardrossan on 30 June, following the other two ships into

Lairdshill (1921) in the Mersey. She was formerly *Lady Longford*. (K.P. Lewis)

Burns & Laird's ownership on 2 July. Her first sailing on the overnight Glasgow–Dublin service began on 14 July and she was renamed *Lairdshill* on 23 July. Once in service, all three ships made periodic deviations from their normal routes, usually to Londonderry. One of Burns & Laird's routes was the summer-only Ardrossan–Belfast daylight service. It had been closed after the 1920 season, but was re-started in 1925, operated by a variety of Burns & Laird vessels. In 1932, *Lairdscastle* was used. From 1933 onwards, it was operated by *Lairds Isle*, formerly the Southern Railway vessel *Riviera*, which had been acquired specifically to operate this service.

Lairdscastle went aground on West Twin Island, at the entrance to Belfast Lough, in foggy conditions, on 22 January 1932. She was refloated without assistance. On 12 January 1936, a foggy night, *Lairdscastle* was forced to anchor in the Clyde, off Dalmuir, on a sailing to Belfast. While she was anchored, she was struck by two vessels, first *Baron Renfrew* and then *Dromara*.

After their acquisition by Burns & Laird, both *Lairdsburn* and *Lairdscastle* lost the cowls from their funnels. Around 1936, one or both ships received a white hull, but the change did not last long.

Further changes took place with the delivery of the new motor vessels, *Royal Ulsterman* and *Royal Scotsman*, for Glasgow–Belfast. *Lairdscastle* and *Lairdsburn* were transferred to Glasgow–Dublin in June 1936, while *Lairdshill* had already been returned to B&I on 31 December 1935. In anticipation of that transfer, *Lairdshill* carried out Christmas relief sailings on Fishguard–Cork between 13 December 1935 and 3 January 1936. Later in 1936, her name reverted to *Lady Longford* and her masts were cut down so that she could pass under the bridges across the Manchester Ship Canal. Despite this alteration, she spent much of January 1937 and the period between 22 February and 28 April 1937 back on Liverpool–Cork. Her career with B&I then ended abruptly. Another Burns & Laird vessel, *Lairdsmoor*, was sunk in a collision with the Shaw Savill cargo liner *Taranaki* on 7 April 1937. *Lady Longford* was handed back to Burns & Laird at Dublin on 1 May and made her first sailing from Dublin to Glasgow that evening. After two round Glasgow–Dublin sailings, she was laid up at Ardrossan to await the main summer season, and then resumed the name *Lairdshill*.

Lairdshill was again used mainly on Glasgow–Dublin, together now with *Lairdscastle* and *Lairdsburn*, although all three appeared on other routes, especially during overhauls and at peak holiday periods. There were four Glasgow–Dublin round sailings per week in winter, increasing to five from early March and to six in the main season. This frequency required a minimum of two ships, but a third was needed to cover overhauls and peak summer traffic. All three vessels were used on the service throughout the year; this resulted in under-utilisation of the ships for most of the year. *Lairdscastle* relieved *Innisfallen* on Fishguard–Cork between 1 and 22 April 1939.

The Glasgow–Dublin passenger service was suspended soon after the outbreak of war. *Lairdshill* made the final passenger sailing on 16 September 1939, but continued on the route in a cargo-only capacity. *Lairdscastle* was chartered to the Belfast Steamship Co. as a replacement for the requisitioned *Ulster Monarch*, and made her first sailing from Belfast to Liverpool on 8 September 1939. After a single round sailing, she returned briefly to her owners, but rejoined Liverpool–Belfast on 16 September. After *Ulster Monarch*'s return from requisition, *Lairdscastle* transferred to Liverpool–Dublin between 25 October and 6 December, when she was returned to her owners. *Lairdsburn* took over Liverpool–Belfast on 6 February 1940, replacing the requisitioned *Louth*. She was joined on 12 February for two weeks by *Lairdshill*, as a replacement for *Munster*, which had been sunk. *Lairdscastle* again resumed on Liverpool–Belfast on 23 February 1940, replacing *Lairdshill*, and operated with *Ulster Queen* and *Lairdsburn*. The two sisters spent some eight weeks together on Liverpool–Belfast, with *Lairdscastle* finishing at Liverpool on 24 April and *Lairdsburn* at Belfast on the following day. Their hasty withdrawal left Liverpool–Belfast reduced to a single vessel, but was necessary in order to replace the requisitioned *Royal Ulsterman* and *Royal Scotsman* on Glasgow–Belfast.

Lairdscastle was sunk in a collision with the Reardon Smith steamer *Vernon City* on 4 September 1940, while on passage from Glasgow to Belfast. Her seventy-two passengers and twenty-nine crew took to the lifeboats and were picked up later by a destroyer. Thereafter *Lairdshill* joined *Lairdsburn* on Glasgow–Belfast. *Lairdsburn*, on passage from Belfast to Glasgow, was in collision with the Clyde steamer *King Edward* early on 21 October 1941, off Gourock. *King Edward*, which had no passengers on board at the time, was badly damaged at the bow and returned to Gourock. *Lairdsburn* suffered little damage. A more serious accident took place on 4 September 1942, off Gourock Bay. *Lairdsburn* was on passage from Glasgow to Belfast, when she sank the Alexandra Towing Co.'s tug *Romsey*. Fifteen of the twenty people on board the tug died.

Lairdshill (ex-*Lady Longford*), showing her cut-down funnel after war. (C. Campbell collection)

Normal shipping services to and from Ireland were withdrawn in April 1944, to prevent information about the Allied plans for the D-Day invasion from reaching the German embassy in Dublin. *Lairdsburn* arrived at Glasgow from Belfast on 22 April, followed by *Lairdshill* on 23 April. Both ships were employed carrying cattle from Glasgow to Birkenhead. Normal services to and from Ireland were resumed on 10 July 1944, with *Lairdshill* sailing from Glasgow and *Lairdsburn* from Belfast.

After the war, *Royal Scotsman* returned to Glasgow–Belfast on 26 December 1945, displacing *Lairdshill*. *Royal Ulsterman* resumed on 27 September 1946. *Lairdsburn* and *Lairdshill* returned to the Glasgow–Dublin passenger service, which was reopened on 21 June 1946. As in the pre-war years, the service operated on at least four nights per week and two ships were therefore needed to maintain the timetable. Both ships also operated as reliefs on Burns & Laird's Glasgow–Belfast and Glasgow–Londonderry services. In the post-war years, *Lairdshill* had accommodation for 195 first-class and 271 third-class passengers. By 1948, part of *Lairdshill's* funnel had been cut off, leaving it with an angled top, which did nothing for her appearance. *Lairdshill* was in collision with a Brocklebank cargo vessel, *Malakand*, in the Clyde on 12 August 1952.

Irish Coast was delivered to Coast Lines in October 1952. She was intended as a relief vessel for all Coast Lines' major passenger services and to operate Glasgow–Dublin in the summer. As a result of her introduction, *Lairdsburn* was sold for breaking up at Port Glasgow, where she arrived in May 1953. *Irish Coast's* greater capacity allowed Glasgow–Dublin's frequency to be reduced to three round sailings per week in summer, so only one ship was needed to maintain the timetable. As a result, from 1953, *Lairdshill* operated

Lady Brussels (1902), notorious for the execution of Capt. Fryatt in 1916. (J. Clarkson)

Glasgow–Dublin only in the winter months, and was used as a general relief vessel on other routes during the summer. When she was not in use as a passenger vessel, she operated Irish Sea cargo/livestock sailings. In 1953, Burns & Laird Lines acquired *Rathlin* from the Clyde Shipping Co. and renamed her *Lairdscraig*. She was used as the relief vessel for Glasgow–Londonderry until her transfer to the City of Cork Steam Packet Co. in May 1956, so it is unlikely that *Lairdshill* operated to Londonderry after 1952.

In summer 1956, *Lairdshill* made several livestock sailings from Dublin to Continental ports. In June 1957, she was as usual replaced on Glasgow–Dublin by *Irish Coast*. In July, *Irish Coast* was in turn replaced by *Scottish Coast*, which had been built for year-round operation on that route. *Lairdshill* no longer had a role, and was put up for sale. On 9 July 1957 she arrived at the Hammond Lane Foundry in Dublin to be broken up. Her bell was sold to Clonliffe Harriers and is now in the Billy Morton Stadium, in Santry.

Captain Fryatt and *Brussels*

This book sets out to describe the passenger ships operating between Liverpool and Dublin, and has referred to cargo ships only incidentally. However, no work dealing with B&I would be complete without some reference to its most famous cargo vessel, *Lady Brussels*, which was better known as *Brussels*.

Brussels was built in 1902 as a passenger ship for the Great Eastern Railway's Harwich–Antwerp service, with occasional Harwich–Hook of Holland and Harwich–

Zeebrugge sailings. After the outbreak of war in 1914 and the German occupation of Belgium, she continued an intermittent Tilbury–Holland civilian passenger service. *Brussels* had avoided an attack on 3 March 1915 by the use of her speed. However, on 28 March 1915, when bound for Rotterdam under the command of Captain Charles Fryatt, *Brussels* was challenged by a German submarine (*U-33*) near the Maas lightship, off the Dutch coast. The Captain ignored the submarine's signal and changed course, but it was clear that the submarine was manoeuvring into a position where it could fire a torpedo at *Brussels*, so Captain Fryatt, following secret Admiralty instructions, steered at full speed directly for the submarine, forcing it to dive in order to avoid a collision. By the time the submarine was able to re-surface, *Brussels* was several miles away and out of danger. Captain Fryatt's entry in *Brussels'* log read as follows:

> *1.10 p.m. Sighted submarine two points on starboard bow. I altered my course to go under his stern. He then turned round and crossed my bow from starboard to port. When he saw me starboard my helm he started to submerge and I steered straight for him. At 1.30 his periscope came up under my bows, port side, about 6 feet from the side and passed astern. Although a good look out was kept, I saw nothing else of him. I was steering an E. by S. course at the time of sighting him and brought my ship to a north-easterly course when I was over the top of him. The lat. was 51 08 N., long. 3 41 E.*

Captain Fryatt was awarded an inscribed gold watch by the Admiralty to commemorate the escape.

The German Naval authorities took a different view and ordered that no efforts were to be spared to capture or destroy *Brussels* and her captain. During the next three months, *Brussels* thrice evaded submarines by use of her speed. A torpedo was fired at her on 20 July, but missed. Despite these attacks, she continued sailing to Holland and Captain Fryatt remained on her. Nearly one year later, on 22 June 1916, *Brussels* left Rotterdam for Tilbury. She called briefly at the Hook of Holland for mail and sailed from there at 23.00 but, as she sailed, a rocket was fired from the shore. When *Brussels* was about one hour out to sea, she passed a small unidentified vessel, which was seen to send a signal by lamp after passing *Brussels*. Captain Fryatt was alarmed by these events, so he ordered the passengers below and extinguished all the ship's lights, but continued on his normal course at full speed. Around 24.30, the ship's lights were switched on briefly to alert another unlit ship, which was sailing on the same course, to *Brussels'* presence. About fifteen minutes later, *Brussels* was stopped by a number of German Naval vessels. Captain Fryatt had time to throw confidential documents, including the secret Admiralty instructions, into the ship's furnace before the Germans boarded the ship. *Brussels'* engine room failed to respond to the Germans' telegraph instructions because the entire engine room crew had been transferred to a German vessel, but this resulted in threats against Captain Fryatt. German engineers were then put into the engine room and a German crew took the ship to Zeebrugge. Later that day, she was sailed up the canal to Bruges, with German troops lining both banks. Members of *Brussels'* crew were sent to a prison camp, where they remained for the duration of the war. Captain Fryatt was kept in a prison in Bruges and interrogated for three weeks. He was court-martialled on 27 July 1916, on a charge that, as a civilian, he attempted to cause injury to the forces of Germany. The evidence presented against him included the entries in the ship's log describing the events of 28 March 1915. He did not reveal the existence of the secret Admiralty instructions, which would have proved his innocence, so he was found guilty and executed by firing squad two hours after the sentence had been passed. This harsh treatment of a non-combatant caused great indignation in Britain. After the end of the war, a German commission of enquiry upheld the sentence but regretted the speed with which it had been carried out.

Brussels was renamed *Brugge*. She was used as a submarine depot ship at Bruges and later as an accommodation ship at Zeebrugge. She was attacked by British naval forces during the raid on Zeebrugge on 23 April 1918, in which two Wallasey ferries, *Iris* and *Daffodil* (later renamed *Royal Iris* and *Royal Daffodil*), participated. When the Germans retreated towards the end of the war, *Brugge* was mined and sunk on 5 October 1918 to act as a blockship at the entrance to Zeebrugge harbour.

After the war, Zeebrugge harbour contained many wrecks and a British Admiralty salvage expert was put in charge of clearing them all. *Brugge* was found to be upright, but had sunk into 18ft of mud, which had filled her. It took four lifting craft and sixteen steel wires underneath the ship to raise her on 4 August 1919. She was then beached, and moved progressively further towards the shore over the next two days. Once there, she was patched up and pumped out before being refloated. As she had been under water for ten months, she was covered with marine growth.

As *Brugge* was in Belgian waters, international law made her the Belgian Government's property. However, in view of the circumstances surrounding her capture, she was returned to the British Government on 26 April 1920, in a ceremony at Zeebrugge attended by HMS *Dragon*. She was renamed *Brussels* and towed back to Britain.

In August 1920, *Brussels*, which had been lying on the river Tyne, was sold at a public auction, with bids restricted to British buyers, to a broker acting on behalf of Preston owners, who planned to use her to carry cattle and sheep from Dublin to Preston. She was towed to Leith in March 1921, for conversion by Henry Robb. By the time her conversion had been completed, she was owned by a Dublin company, the Dublin & Lancashire Shipping Co., which had been set up on 17 February 1921. She was registered in Dublin, but her management was based in Preston. Her two funnels had been painted red, with a thin black top, separated by a thin green band. Preston was very proud of its new service and *Brussels* was given a great welcome on her first arrival in the port on 5 September 1921. She was visited by a civic party, which was particularly interested in a framed copy of the death sentence on Captain Fryatt, displayed near the captain's quarters. She left Preston on her first sailing to Dublin on 7 September. On 14 March 1922, the Guild Mayor of Preston unveiled a memorial plaque on the bridge of *Brussels*. The words on this plaque read:

Captain Charles Fryatt, when gallantly endeavouring to save this ship and the lives on board from capture during the Great War, was himself taken prisoner and subsequently shot. His name is honoured in the history of the British nation and his deeds have added lustre to the records of the British

Merchant Service. This memorial is placed here by the chairman and committee of the Charles Fryatt Memorial Fund, founded by the Imperial Merchant Service Guild, of which he was a member.

Since *Brussels* was in competition with B&I's established Dublin–Liverpool livestock service, the new competition was unwelcome. *Brussels* was one of the largest ships to use Dublin, but the Port Authority allocated her to a shallow berth, which she had difficulty in using at low tide. A subsequent enquiry by the Dail Eireann (Irish Parliament) found that a B&I cargo vessel, *Blackrock*, had been laid up in a deep water berth between July and October 1922 and that a deep water berth could have been found for *Brussels* without unduly inconveniencing other port users. The matter was resolved when the Dublin & Lancashire company was acquired by B&I on 16 August 1922. *Brussels* was transferred to B&I's ownership. Thereafter, *Brussels* continued to sail on Dublin–Preston, but also served on Dublin–Liverpool. In 1923, she was renamed *Lady Brussels*. She ran into the lock gates at Preston on 30 July 1926. One gate was badly damaged and had to be removed for repairs. She remained in service until 1929, arriving at Preston for the last time on the morning of 19 April. After discharging her livestock, she sailed on the evening tide for Port Glasgow, where she was broken up.

There was a sequel to Captain Fryatt's execution. On 4 December 1916, Anchor Line's *Caledonia* was torpedoed in the Mediterranean by a German submarine, *U-65*. *Caledonia*'s Captain had attempted to ram the submarine and nearly succeeded. He was taken prisoner and sent for trial in Germany. However, the German Government was told via the American Ambassador in Berlin that, if there were a 'similar occurrence', a German officer prisoner of equivalent rank would be shot by the British. As a result, Captain Blaikie spent the rest of the war in an officers' camp at Friedberg.

Reference to the Dublin and Lancashire company requires a mention of the vessel *Lydia*, which the company had contracted to buy shortly before it was acquired by B&I. *Lydia* had a history nearly as colourful as *Brussels*. She had been built in 1890 for the London & South Western Railway's Southampton–Channel Islands services. In 1915, she was taken over for military service and continued in that role until October 1919. She was then sold to Southampton buyers and laid up in Southampton Water until March 1921, when she was re-sold to Captain Montagu Yates. He placed her in service between Malta and Syracuse. In September 1921, Captain Yates was arrested at Syracuse by the Italian Police after a two-day siege of the ship. The 1921 vendors had not been paid in full for the ship, so they repossessed her under a mortgage and later contracted to sell her to the Dublin and Lancashire company. *Lydia* was towed back from the Mediterranean to Ardrossan and delivered in October 1922. By then the Dublin & Lancashire company had been acquired by Coast Lines, in whose ownership *Lydia* was registered. However, she was no longer needed and was laid up at Ardrossan. Her ownership was recorded in B&I's books, although that change was never officially registered. *Lydia* was sold to Greek owners in May 1923 and the loss of more than £8,000 arising on her sale was shown in B&I's accounts. Coast Lines stated at the time of the sale that she had never traded during the period of her ownership by Coast Lines. After her sale, she returned to the Mediterranean, under the Greek flag, and was renamed *Ierac*. She was broken up in 1937.

Lady Munster/Louth, Lady Connaught/Longford and *Lady Leinster/Lady Connaught*

B&I's regular overnight Liverpool–Dublin service had been re-established in 1923, using *Lady Louth*, *Lady Limerick* and *Lady Longford*. They had only a limited amount of passenger accommodation and the success of the service made it clear that vessels with more passenger capacity were needed. The Belfast Steamship Co. had ordered three new motor vessels for Liverpool–Belfast and its three old vessels were transferred to B&I.

The first vessel transferred was *Graphic*, on 10 June 1929; she was renamed *Lady Munster*. Before entering service from Liverpool on 12 July, she went to Harland & Wolff at Belfast, where her appearance was altered by shortening her funnel in 'motorship style', while a second dummy funnel was added. The bridge and boat decks were lengthened to the mainmast, bringing her into line with *Patriotic*, the railings on the forward half of her open fore deck were replaced with solid bulwarks, and the steerage accommodation in the poop was extended to the stern. Her hull was painted grey, although this proved unserviceable and was later repainted black. Her funnels assumed B&I's colours – green with a black top. Despite these external changes, no internal alterations were made. *Heroic* was transferred to B&I on 5 March 1930 and renamed *Lady Connaught*; *Patriotic* followed on 22 March 1930, and was renamed *Lady Leinster*. Both ships received similar alterations by Harland & Wolff before entering service from Liverpool, *Lady Connaught* on 16 April and *Lady Leinster* on 16 May. In Liverpool, the ships used the new B&I berth at South East Princes Dock, although *Lady Munster* used B&I's Nelson Dock berth until the transfer to Princes Dock on 22 March 1930.

Lady Munster (1906), formerly *Graphic*. (R. Brandreth collection)

Lady Leinster (1912) at the Dublin berth in Princes Dock, Liverpool. She was formerly *Patriotic*. (K.P. Lewis)

During the 1930s the three 'Ladies' were occasionally chartered by the Belfast Steamship Co. for additional Liverpool–Belfast sailings. One would also supplement Burns & Laird's Friday Glasgow–Belfast sailings during Fair weeks. *Lady Connaught* was involved in two small accidents. On 9 March 1932, she was in a collision with the Watts, Watts vessel *Star of Cairo* in the Crosby Channel. Both vessels suffered some damage above the waterline. On 21 March 1936, her foremast was struck by lightning when she was off the Skerries, between Dublin and Liverpool. The mast's truck was torn away and landed on the deck.

In 1938, B&I took delivery of two new motorships, *Leinster* and *Munster*, for Liverpool–Dublin. *Lady Connaught* and *Lady Munster* were withdrawn. *Lady Connaught* was renamed *Longford* in March 1938, made her final sailing from Dublin to Liverpool on 18 March and was then laid up in Wallasey Dock, Birkenhead. *Lady Munster* was renamed *Louth*, made her final sailing from Dublin one day after her sister and was also laid up in Wallasey Dock.

Louth's lay-up lasted only a short time. She was given yellow funnels and placed on Coast Lines' new Liverpool–Greenock cruise service taking visitors to the British Empire Exhibition at Bellahouston Park, Glasgow. The service had been planned to operate twice weekly throughout the summer, except for the three peak weeks in July, but it seems probable that bookings were far below expectations, as the service was cut back severely. The revised schedule showed only four sailings, all around Bank Holiday weekends:

Lady Munster (1906) in 1937. Later colours. (K.P. Lewis)

Louth (1906), sailing from Liverpool for the Clyde and the British Empire Exhibition on 4 June 1938. *Lady Connaught* (1912) is behind. (K.P. Lewis)

Saturdays 4 June and 30 July dep. Liverpool 19.00, Sunday cruising in the Firth of Clyde, Monday arr. Greenock 08.00, dep. Greenock 22.30, Tuesday arr. Liverpool 11.30.

These Saturday cruises cost between 90/- (£4.50) and 120/- (£6.00), with a maximum of 200 passengers.

Wednesdays 8 June and 27 July dep. Liverpool 19.00, Thursday arr. Greenock a.m., Friday dep. Greenock 23.00, Saturday arr. Liverpool 11.00.

The price of these Wednesday cruises ranged between 55/- (£2.75) and 100/- (£5.00), with a maximum of 250 passengers.

Even this programme was reduced; the cruise on Wednesday 27 July did not take place, as *Louth* operated a round trip to Dublin between 26 and 28 July, although the cruise on Saturday 30 July probably did take place, as it was over the Bank Holiday weekend and *Louth* made no Dublin sailings during that period.

After the first two Greenock cruises, *Louth* returned to Wallasey Dock between 11 June and 7 July, and was then chartered to Burns & Laird over the Glasgow Fair and Belfast holidays, operating mainly between Ardrossan and Belfast. Afterwards, from 21 July, she made some Liverpool–Dublin sailings, in addition to her final Greenock cruise, before re-joining *Longford* on 14 August.

Lady Leinster was renamed *Lady Connaught* on 4 April 1938 and remained on Liverpool–Dublin as the third ship on the nightly service. Her funnels were painted in B&I's new colours with a white band separating the green from the black top.

Lady Connaught (1912) in the Mersey. (K.P. Lewis)

Lady Connaught (1912), formerly *Lady Leinster* and *Patriotic*. This is a B&I postcard. (K.P. Lewis collection)

A proposal to spend £50,000 on converting *Lady Connaught* for cruising was authorised by Coast Lines' board in 1938, but within two months the decision had been deferred. In addition to her regular Liverpool–Dublin sailings, she continued to make occasional Liverpool–Belfast sailings and some Glasgow–Belfast overhaul reliefs.

Louth's port of registry was transferred from Dublin to Liverpool in April 1939. She re-entered service on 6 July 1939 with a light sailing to Belfast, and was then chartered to Burns & Laird, sailing from Belfast to Glasgow/Ardrossan over the Fair periods. After some Liverpool–Belfast/Dublin supplementary sailings, she returned to Birkenhead on 14 August.

Following the outbreak of war on 3 September 1939, *Ulster Prince* was requisitioned immediately. Her place on Liverpool–Belfast was taken by *Louth*, which made her first sailing from Liverpool on 9 September. *Louth* completed a sailing from Belfast to Liverpool on 27 January 1940, and was requisitioned to carry troops to France. She sailed for Southampton on 30 January and made her first troop sailing from there to Cherbourg on 2 February. *Longford* was brought out of lay-up on 3 January 1940, but needed attention after her long lay-up. It was not until 1 March that she made her first Liverpool–Belfast sailing, having had her port of registry transferred to Liverpool on the previous day.

Initially, *Lady Connaught* continued to operate Liverpool–Dublin with *Leinster* and *Munster* until both of the latter pair were laid up at Barrow early in October 1939. *Lady Connaught* continued the service with *Innisfallen*, transferred from Fishguard–Cork. *Lady Connaught* was also withdrawn after her arrival at Liverpool on 27 October and sailed to Barrow on 1 November. She was covered by *Lairdscastle*, which had been released from Liverpool–Belfast by the return of *Ulster Monarch* after her initial requisition.

Lady Connaught's stay at Barrow was short; she departed on 5 December and arrived at Liverpool next morning, sailing for Dublin that same night. *Lady Connaught* then remained on the service until her arrival at Liverpool from Dublin on 5 May 1940.

Lady Connaught was transferred to Liverpool–Belfast on 11 May, rejoining *Longford*, and her port of registry was changed to Liverpool four days later. *Louth* completed her final troop sailing on 4 May, with an arrival at Southampton from Le Havre. She arrived back from Southampton on 6 May and resumed Liverpool–Belfast on 18 May, shortly before the commencement of the Dunkirk evacuation. The Liverpool–Belfast service was now back in the hands of the three ships that had previously operated it between 1912 and 1929, excluding the First World War years, but they now all had B&I names and Liverpool as their port of registry. *Longford* had seen no service since 1938 and *Louth* had only operated for a few weeks in the summers of 1938 and 1939. It showed a remarkable degree of foresight that those two ships, whose services were to be invaluable over the next eight years, had been retained, when there must have been a strong financial temptation to sell at least one of them.

Lady Connaught was involved in a number of small incidents early in the war. Two days after re-starting on Liverpool–Dublin, on 8 December 1939, she collided in the Mersey with the coaster *Holme Force*, damaging her bow and superstructure. On 9 February 1940, while on passage from Liverpool to Dublin, she hit an unknown object but, as no damage was apparent, she continued her voyage. On 26 July 1940, she was damaged by an incendiary bomb falling on her at Liverpool and, on 30 October 1940, while on passage from Liverpool to Belfast, she collided with a cargo vessel, *Don*. These incidents were a foretaste of worse to come. On 20 December 1940, she was caught in an air raid on Liverpool. After sheltering in the river for some time, she made her way out to sea through a low anti-aircraft barrage. On her way up the Crosby Channel, she was attacked by two aircraft, one of which dropped a bomb that fell near her. Six days later, *Lady Connaught*, carrying 120 passengers, was mined near the Bar lightship while on passage from Liverpool to Belfast. Passengers and some crew abandoned ship and were picked up shortly afterwards by the cargo vessel *Greypoint*, which started to tow *Lady Connaught* back to Liverpool. The tow was later taken over by the tug *Crosby*; shortly afterwards *Lady Connaught* collided with a Naval trawler and lost two lifeboats. The Dock Board salvage vessel *Vigilant* put a pump board to help keep the water in check. After *Lady Connaught* had arrived at Liverpool, a second pump was put on board to help pump her out before she was dry-docked to make her watertight. She was then laid up in Princes Dock, where she suffered additional damage in later air raids. In due course, she was abandoned to the underwriters.

Following the loss of *Lady Connaught*, *Longford* and *Louth* continued on Liverpool–Belfast. Liverpool suffered further heavy air raids and, on the night of 3/4 May 1941, *Louth* was damaged by debris from a demolished warehouse at South Wellington Dock. In the same night, Brocklebank's vessel *Malakand*, which was carrying explosives, was set on fire in Huskisson Branch Dock No.2 and later blew up. Debris from the explosion damaged one of *Louth*'s funnels. *Louth* was moved to Princes Dock on 5 May and suffered more damage that night, caused by debris from a warehouse. She was attacked by a German plane in June 1941, while on passage from Belfast to Liverpool, and fired back, but the attacking plane escaped.

Despite *Lady Connaught* having received damage which, at other times, would have ensured her sale to ship-breakers, the wartime need for shipping was so great that it was decided to re-build her. Late in 1941, she was taken from Liverpool to Belfast for dry-docking. On 12 January 1942, her hulk was bought back from the underwriters. She was sent to the Liffey Dockyard in Dublin for conversion to a cattle-carrier. The damage was so extensive that more than a year was to pass before she re-entered service on 24 June 1943 between Liverpool and Belfast, carrying cattle and cargo only. The repairs did not involve major changes to her passenger areas; it seems likely that the possibility of re-converting her for passenger service at a future date was being kept in mind.

In January 1944, *Lady Connaught* had a further change of role, which would have a major effect on her post-war service. She started her final sailing from Liverpool to Belfast on 1 January, and was then sent to Barclay Curle's Clyde shipyard, where she arrived on 5 January for conversion into a hospital carrier. The conversion was extensive and included considerable refrigeration capacity. She lost her dummy funnel and her superstructure was extended aft over her well deck. Her rectangular saloon windows were replaced by portholes and the solid bulwarks in the forward half of her foredeck were extended aft to the superstructure. She was equipped with water ambulances, which were landing craft modified to carry casualties from the beaches, and became *Hospital Carrier No.55*, with accommodation for 341 patients. For the D-Day invasion, *Lady Connaught* was one of three hospital carriers assembled at Milford Haven; the other two were *Duke of Lancaster*, from Heysham–Belfast and *St Julien*, from GWR's Channel Islands service. *Lady Connaught*'s medical and nursing staff were all American. She sailed to the Solent and made her first crossing to Utah beach on 7 June. She was employed carrying the wounded from the Normandy campaign back to Southampton. On 18 November 1944, her bow was badly damaged in a collision with an American LST in Southampton Water; she was out of service until the middle of February 1945. Her war service ended on 18 June 1945, when she arrived back at Belfast.

Louth was withdrawn from Liverpool–Belfast after arriving at Liverpool on 31 December 1943. She was chartered to the LMS Railway and commenced running Heysham–Belfast on 5 January 1944 in conjunction with the Railway's own *Cambria* from Holyhead–Dun Laoghaire. The three 'Dukes', which were normally on the route, were all engaged in war work. *Louth*'s manoeuvring qualities are reported to have won the admiration of the Railway's marine authorities. *Louth* was requisitioned by the Government and left Heysham–Belfast on 21 April, arriving back in Liverpool on 24 April. Initially, she was used on Irish Sea troop carrying from Liverpool and the Clyde. She sailed from the Clyde on 16 June for the follow up to D-Day. She entered service on 21 June, sailing from Newhaven to Gold beach, and continued to ferry troops across the English Channel until November 1944. She then returned to Liverpool, arriving on 23 November. She re-entered Heysham–Belfast service on 18 December and remained on that route for the rest of the war. For a period in 1945 she operated the service alone because *Cambria* had returned to Holyhead for her sister, *Hibernia*, to have a leak repaired.

Longford continued on Liverpool–Belfast alone until 21 April 1944, when she was withdrawn from service because travel to Ireland had been prohibited in the period before D-Day. The Liverpool–Belfast passenger service was then suspended, for the first time in more than ninety years.

Following her withdrawal, *Longford* was requisitioned and employed initially on trooping duties in the Irish Sea, making her first sailing from Liverpool on 14 May. After D-Day, she sailed from the Clyde on 16 June and entered the cross-Channel troop service, from Newhaven to Juno beach. Until Christmas 1944, she was employed on cross-Channel trooping voyages from Southampton and Newhaven. She was then transferred to the Tilbury–Ostend troop service. After completing that service, she sailed from London back to Liverpool, arriving on 23 March 1945.

Longford reopened Liverpool–Belfast on 18 June 1945. She had not been fully refitted after her year away trooping and did not carry any cargo. With only war ballast aboard, some passages were extremely lively. Her funnels were painted in the Belfast Steamship Co.'s colours, which at that time were still crimson with a black top, separated by a saxe blue band, but her hull and upperworks remained in wartime grey. *Louth* arrived back from Heysham on 13 December and relieved *Longford* on 18 December. Her painting was similar to *Longford*'s. After overhauls, the two ships operated a passenger-only service. Both ships were still owned by B&I, on charter to the Belfast Steamship Co.

Ulster Prince (ex-*Leinster*) made her first sailing from Belfast to Liverpool on 28 February 1946. This allowed *Longford* to receive an overdue refit before re-starting Liverpool–Dublin on 22 May 1946. This was the first sailing on the route since the loss of *Innisfallen* in December 1940. *Louth* continued to operate Liverpool–Belfast with *Ulster Prince*, jointly making sailings four nights per week in each direction during winter and nightly during the summer. By this time, *Louth*'s hull was black but her upperworks were still grey. Following *Ulster Monarch*'s return to service on 9 August 1946, *Louth* was transferred to Liverpool–Dublin, making her first sailing on 15 August. Their hulls were painted in their pre-war B&I colours, and their funnels were green with a black top, separated by a white band. Despite the fact that they were running a B&I service and were owned by B&I, their port of registry remained at Liverpool and neither ship was ever again registered at Dublin. The two ships kept the service going until 1948.

Longford lost a sailing from Liverpool on 21 October 1946, when a rope fouled her propeller, forcing her to return to dock. In the following year, *Longford*, which was berthed at the landing stage on 21 October, was struck by a destroyer, HMS *Sluys*, which was returning from trials. *Longford* did not suffer any damage and remained in service.

B&I's two new motor ships, *Munster* and *Leinster*, entered service in early April 1948. As the Waterloo river entrance at Liverpool had not been completed, three ships were still needed to operate a full nightly passenger and cargo service. *Longford* therefore remained on Liverpool–Dublin, but *Louth* was able to return to Liverpool–Belfast on 31 May 1948. She was painted in the Belfast Steamship Company's colours. This transfer enabled both services to be operated nightly during the summer and provided each service with a spare ship for reliefs during winter overhauls. On 6 October 1948,

Louth (1906) in the Mersey, formerly *Lady Munster* and *Graphic*. (K.P. Lewis)

Longford (1906) in the Mersey in 1948. She was formerly *Lady Connaught* and *Heroic*. (K.P. Lewis)

Louth was transferred to the Belfast Steamship Co., renamed *Ulster Duke* and registered at Belfast. Both *Longford* and *Ulster Duke* now received a thorough refit during which the deckhouse on the after end of the boat deck was further enlarged. *Ulster Duke's* remaining history is covered in the Belfast volume.

After *Ulster Duke* had been withdrawn from service at the end of January 1950, *Longford* was retained as the relief ship for both services. In the summers of 1951 and 1952, she was chartered to Butlins and sailed between Liverpool and Dublin, carrying holidaymakers to Butlins' Irish holiday camp at Mosney. Her final sailing, on 31 October 1952, was on her original Belfast–Liverpool route, although she was wearing B&I's colours. She was replaced by Coast Lines' new motor vessel, *Irish Coast*, which was to act as a winter relief vessel on all Coast Lines' major services. *Longford* was laid up in Morpeth Dock, Birkenhead, and like her sister, *Ulster Duke*, was sold to Italian ship-breakers. However, the Ministry of Transport refused to give permission for the sale, so instead she was sold in January 1953 to the British Iron and Steel Corporation. She sailed for Barrow on 29 January 1953 to be broken up.

Lady Connaught had been laid up at Belfast in 1945, with her future prospects uncertain. Her engine bed had been damaged in 1940 but had not been fully repaired. This limited her speed and consequently her usefulness as a regular overnight vessel. Coast Lines' pre-war cruise vessel *Killarney* had been used for most of the war as a depot and accommodation ship at Rosyth. After the war, she was towed back to Liverpool. However, in view of her age and her inactivity for the previous five years, she was not felt to be worth re-converting. On the other hand, Coast Lines believed that there would be demand for cruises, since few ships were likely to offering cruises for several years to come. As a result, it was decided that *Lady Connaught* should be converted for operation as a permanent cruise ship, in succession to *Killarney*. She was to be renamed *Lady Killarney*, a combination of her own name and that of her predecessor. On 2 April 1947, her ownership was transferred from B&I to Coast Lines, but her Liverpool registration required no change. Her first duty after completing her refit, before taking up her new cruise service, was to relieve *Longford* and *Louth* on Liverpool–Dublin between 19 April and 8 June 1947. This was to be her final spell of duty as an Irish Sea ferry. The remainder of her history appears in the volume dealing with cruises.

Leinster (1937) and *Munster* (1938)

By 1936, Coast Lines had built new ships for all its most important overnight passenger services, except Liverpool–Dublin. This service was being operated by the three former Belfast vessels, *Lady Munster*, *Lady Connaught* and *Lady Leinster*. The service had enjoyed considerable success since its re-establishment in 1923 and it was time to replace the vessels operating the services, which were already up to thirty years old.

An order for two new ships was placed with Harland & Wolff at Belfast. It was significant that the order was for two ships, rather than the three needed in 1929 to give a nightly service between Liverpool and Belfast. Discussions were taking place with the

Mersey Docks & Harbour Board to provide a new river entrance at Waterloo Dock to allow ships to enter or leave the dock system at any state of the tide. This would permit a nightly service to be operated with just two ships and it was planned that one 'Ulster' vessel would act as a relief ship covering both Belfast and Dublin services from Liverpool. The new lock's construction was planned by 1936, but the war delayed its completion by thirteen years.

A complication at this stage was that Coast Lines was seeking its freedom from the remains of the Royal Mail group. One condition imposed by the bank handling the share flotation was that a controlling interest in B&I and the other Irish companies in the Coast Lines group should be offered to the Irish Government. In the arrangements for the possible sale of part of B&I, a new company, British & Irish Steam Packet Co. (1936) Ltd, was set up to take over the assets and business of B&I and the other Irish companies. It appears that the orders for the two ships were placed at a time when this sale was still under discussion. *Leinster*'s cost was £293,693, with a similar figure for *Munster*. Most of the finance for the ships was made available by the Midland Bank, with a guarantee from the Ministry of Finance in Northern Ireland. In view of the uncertainty over B&I's future, the Ministry insisted that the ships must not be registered in B&I's name until the loans had been repaid. Technically, the ships were chartered to B&I by Coast Lines, the registered owners of the ships, but these arrangements were not obvious to the passengers. As events turned out, B&I's sale to the Irish Government did not go ahead at that time and it was nearly thirty years before the sale did take place. In 1938, the 'new' B&I dropped the '(1936)' from its name.

The two ships adopted a style of naming revived by B&I, which went back to the days of the City of Dublin Steam Packet Co. They were named *Leinster* and *Munster*, after two of the four Irish provinces. *Leinster* was launched on 24 June 1937. She left for trials on 26 October 1937; during these she assisted the Greek steamer *Anastassios Pateras*, which was in difficulties in the Irish Sea. She was handed over to her owners on 2 November, one day before *Munster*'s launch. *Munster*'s trials took place during February 1938 and she was delivered on 22 February.

At the time of their launches, the ships carried Liverpool on their sterns as their intended port of registry. *Leinster* was registered at Liverpool before her delivery and transferred to the Dublin register in January 1938. *Munster* was registered at Liverpool on 23 February 1938, immediately after her delivery, but was transferred to the Dublin register about two weeks later, before she entered service.

The ships introduced a new colour scheme for B&I passenger steamers. The B&I funnel had been green with a black top, but a white band separating the other two colours was now added. It has been suggested that the white band incorporated part of the white funnel of the City of Cork Steam Packet Co. The new funnel colours were subsequently given to the company's other ships. *Leinster* and *Munster* received a yellow hull, with white upperworks. The choice of hull colour seems strange, since the grey in which the three 'Ulster' vessels, *Innisfallen* and some of the 'Ladies' had first appeared soon gave way to black for practical reasons. It is probably significant that the yellow was not repeated after the war.

Leinster (1937), anchored in the Mersey before embarking her passengers in 1939. (K.P. Lewis)

The appearance of the two ships showed a few changes from the previous two vessels, *Royal Ulsterman* and *Royal Scotsman*. They were the longest two ships in the series and so had a reasonable amount of space clear of the lifeboats at the after end of the Boat Deck. The poop extended further forward, with the result that the mainmast was mounted on the poop, rather than in the after well. The bridge front had two steps in it, rather than the single step in Burns & Laird's ships. B&I's ships also lacked the Burns & Laird ships' docking bridge at the after end of the superstructure and their stern anchor. The greater length of the new ships made them appear better proportioned than any of their predecessors. They were the largest cross-Channel motorships in the world at that time.

The ships' internal layout followed the general pattern of all the ships in the series. In the first-class accommodation, the public rooms were located aft and the cabins forward, to ensure a peaceful night for cabin passengers. There was a reception area and shop on B Deck, with a dining saloon seating eighty-six passengers at the after end of that deck. There was a lounge at the after end of A Deck and a large smoke room and bar on the Boat Deck. Open promenade space was provided on the Boat Deck, which was screened at its forward end, and on the Sun Deck over the smoke room. However, one major change was a reversion to the pattern last used in the three 'Ulster' vessels, in which the first-class cabins were spread over four decks, from A Deck down to D Deck. This gave the ships berths for 425 first-class passengers, at the expense of the cattle accommodation, which had traditionally been an important revenue earner on the route. With their enlarged poops, the ships carried 1,075 third-class passengers, of whom 120 had berths in two- and four-berth cabins, and a general room and a ladies' room. The third-class passengers also had a restaurant and a smoke room. General cargo, including passengers'

Munster (1938), anchored in the Mersey in 1938. (K.P. Lewis)

Munster (1938), viewed aft from the bridge. (K.P. Lewis)

Munster (1938), viewed ahead from bridge. (K.P. Lewis)

cars, was carried in the holds. As the passenger traffic using Liverpool–Dublin had a heavy seasonal bias towards the summer months and Christmas, it seems surprising that livestock space, which would have earned revenue throughout the year, was excluded to provide additional cabins that would earn revenue only for a short period each year. The design of the post-war ships showed that the mistake had been recognised.

Leinster had been delivered on 2 November 1937, but did not start her normal service immediately. A relief vessel was needed to replace *Ulster Monarch* on Liverpool–Belfast, while her builders made some improvements to her. There was also the problem that not all the necessary shore installations were in place. Finally, it seemed that more publicity would be obtained if both ships started service together. As a result, it was decided that *Leinster* should enter service on Liverpool–Belfast and so she made her maiden voyage on 4 November from Belfast to Liverpool. After the work on *Ulster Monarch* had been completed, *Leinster* remained on Liverpool–Belfast until 9 March 1938 to cover the two other vessels' overhauls. *Leinster* had the 'honour' of introducing the new Belfast Steamship Co. funnel colours of crimson with a black top, separated by a saxe blue band.

One reason for the delay in putting the new ships on the service was the plan to build a new passenger terminal at Dublin's North Wall. The new building had separate sections for the two classes on the ship. It included special gangways designed so that their steps were always horizontal, regardless of the state of the tide and the height of the ship. The Liverpool passenger terminal in Princes Dock was used to embark passengers whenever the tide permitted. For other departures and most arrivals, passengers used Princes Landing Stage. The departure time from Liverpool was 22.15, with arrival at Dublin at 06.00. In the reverse direction, departure was at 20.30, with arrival at Liverpool at 06.00, except on Saturdays/Sundays, when the times were 23.00 and 08.00, respectively.

Munster (1938). First-class smoke room. (K.P. Lewis)

With *Munster*'s delivery, B&I's two new ships were ready to enter service. *Leinster* first made a four-hour cruise from Dublin with invited guests on 19 March 1938. She then made her maiden voyage from Dublin to Liverpool on 21 March. There was a noisy send off from Dublin, with a firework display. *Munster* had sailed light from Belfast to Liverpool and made her maiden voyage from there on the same night. There was a repeat of the firework display on the following night for *Munster*'s first sailing from Dublin. With the service taking the form of overnight sailings, there was no need for high speed, except when it was needed to reach Liverpool in time to dock on the tide, so a service speed of around 17 knots, with a maximum of a little over 19 knots, was sufficient. An indication of the standards on board was given in the first-class dining saloon, which had an electric food trolley, for hot joints to be served at diners' tables, while after dinner there was dancing with music provided by a musical trio supplied by the Empire Theatre in Liverpool.

Lady Leinster, renamed *Lady Connaught*, was retained as the third ship on Liverpool–Dublin, pending the completion of the new river entrance.

Not long after the ships had entered service, woodworm was found in the wood panelling in some cabins. One man was employed for several months injecting chemicals into the wood to eliminate the problem.

While the ships were normally employed on their regular route, there were occasional diversions. On one occasion, *Munster* made a special sailing from Swansea to Dublin for a football match. *Munster* was in the news for a less welcome reason on 19 July 1938 when, in foggy conditions, she was in collision with a cargo ship, *West Cohas*, owned by the American company Lykes Brothers Steamship Co., at 02.30 while off the Skerries, bound from Liverpool to Dublin. She was struck and holed about 6 feet forward of the engine room's forward bulkhead. Had she been holed aft of this bulkhead, the damage could have affected the engine room and would have been very serious. Some eighteen cabins were damaged and one passenger was injured. *Ulster Queen*, on passage to Belfast, stood by until the inbound *Ulster Prince* replaced her and escorted *Munster* back to Liverpool. *Munster* was withdrawn from service for repairs at Belfast. In the following year, *Leinster* and *Ulster Monarch* collided in the Mersey on 6 May, but neither vessel suffered much damage.

B&I was very proud of its new ships. In summer 1939, the opportunity was taken to celebrate them, when one of the pair operated a special cruise in Dublin Bay for B&I employees and their families and friends.

Sadly, the splendid service operated by these fine ships was not to last long. Until the outbreak of war in September 1939, ships registered at Irish ports generally flew the red ensign and were described as British. After the outbreak of war, the Irish Government set up its own registry and all ships registered at Irish ports were required to fly the Irish flag. *Leinster* and *Munster* both substituted the Irish flag for the red ensign. However, as there was a manning dispute over danger money for Irish seamen both ships were withdrawn from service. *Leinster* arrived at Liverpool on 28 September and then moved to Barrow, where she arrived on 4 October. She was followed by *Munster*, which arrived at Liverpool on 3 October and at Barrow on 7 October. Despite substitutions, the service was reduced to two ships. After agreement had been reached with the crews, *Munster* departed from Barrow on 11 December. She left Liverpool on 12 December on Liverpool–Belfast, replacing the requisitioned *Ulster Monarch*. Her hull was painted black, with a large Irish tricolour on each side of her hull. Her partner on the service was *Ulster Queen*. Sadly, the Irish flag was no protection against mines and she activated a magnetic mine just before 06.00 on 7 February 1940, some 20 miles from the Bar lightship, inward bound for Liverpool with 200 passengers and fifty crew. The explosion wrecked the bridge, carried away the wireless transmitter and cut off the electricity. In the explosion, the ship's captain suffered a broken arm and dislocated shoulder, and four other crewmen were also slightly injured. The damage to the ship was so severe that an immediate evacuation was ordered; this prompt action ensured that all passengers and crew escaped safely. About one hour after the explosion, the collier *Ringwall* arrived on the scene, took everyone on board and carried them all to Liverpool, where they arrived at midday. *Munster* was last seen with a heavy list to port and her propellers in the air. Her wreck still lies where it came to rest.

Leinster stayed at Barrow until 3 May 1940, when she sailed for Liverpool. She re-entered Liverpool–Dublin on 9 May, making twelve round sailings on the route, with the final sailing ending at Liverpool on 19 June. On the following day, she again departed for Barrow, arriving on 21 June. *Innisfallen*, previously on Fishguard–Cork, had been operating Liverpool–Dublin since 29 September 1939. After *Leinster*'s final withdrawal, she remained alone on the service until 21 December 1940, when she was sunk. The passenger service was then withdrawn for the remainder of the war, and was not reinstated until 22 May 1946.

Keeping the Dublin and Belfast services from Liverpool operating after the outbreak of war involved considerable switching of ships. The complexity of the Dublin sailing arrangements from the outbreak of war until the withdrawal of the passenger service in December 1940 is shown by this table of deployments on the service over the period:

Date	Vessel 1	Vessel 2	Vessel 3	Comments
1939				
3 September	*Leinster*	*Munster*	*Lady Connaught*	
28 September	*Munster*	*Lady Connaught*		*Leinster* laid up
29 September	*Innisfallen*	*Munster*	*Lady Connaught*	*Innisfallen* from Cork
3 October	*Innisfallen*	*Lady Connaught*		*Munster* laid up
25 October	*Innisfallen*	*Lairdscastle*	*Lady Connaught*	*Lairdscastle* from Belfast
27 October	*Innisfallen*	*Lairdscastle*		*Lady Connaught* laid up
6 December	*Innisfallen*	*Lady Connaught*		*Lady Connaught* from lay-up. *Lairdscastle* charter ended
1940				
16 April	(*Innisfallen*)	*Lady Connaught*		*Innisfallen* to overhaul
17 April	(*Innisfallen*)	*Kenmare*	*Lady Connaught*	*Kenmare* from Cork
3 May	(*Innisfallen*)	*Lady Connaught*		*Kenmare* to Cork
5 May	(*Innisfallen*)			*Lady Connaught* to Belfast
6 May	*Innisfallen*			*Innisfallen* from overhaul
9 May	*Innisfallen*	*Leinster*		*Leinster* from lay-up
19 June	*Innisfallen*			*Leinster* laid up
21 December	Service withdrawn			*Innisfallen* sunk

Leinster was re-registered at Liverpool on 11 September 1940. After being requisitioned, she left Barrow and returned to Liverpool on 19 September, for conversion to a hospital ship. She departed from Liverpool on 23 November, and was based at Akureyri, in the north of Iceland, for six months. During part of this period, she was frozen in. After her return to Britain, she was fitted out for trooping. On her first voyage as a troopship, she sailed from the Clyde on 15 July 1941, in a convoy to deliver troops and supplies to Malta, but ran aground on 21 July soon after leaving Gibraltar, and so did not attempt the rest of the voyage. She was repaired at Gibraltar and returned to Liverpool, from where she made a further trooping voyage to Gibraltar. She then made a series of trooping voyages to Iceland, grounding again on 15 January 1942 and being refloated two days later. The North African landings brought about a change of route for *Leinster*, which departed from the Clyde on 26 October, carrying troops bound for the beachhead at Oran. During her return to Britain, she picked up survivors from the torpedoed Union-Castle liner *Warwick Castle* on 14 November 1942. Because of the heavy seas at the time, it was not possible to launch any of the ship's boats, so she had to be manoeuvred alongside men in the water without swamping them or running them down. *Leinster* then returned to Icelandic trooping for a further six months, during which she also made two calls at the Faroes. Her final departure from Iceland was on 14 May 1943.

Leinster was then re-converted to a hospital carrier and equipped with six water ambulances. She sailed on 25 June from the Clyde to Sicily, which was invaded by Allied forces on 10 July. She arrived off Sicily on 15 July. As there were no docking facilities, the water ambulances brought casualties to her. From Sicily, she sailed to Salerno, where she arrived three days after the landings on 9 September. She was immediately subjected to air attacks. On 13 September, she was in international waters 25 miles off Salerno with three other hospital ships, each fully illuminated in accordance with the Geneva Convention, when all four were attacked from the air. *Leinster* escaped with little damage, but the hospital ship *Newfoundland* was sunk and *Leinster* took part in the operation to rescue survivors.

Leinster spent the next four months on a variety of hospital sailings. Her next area of operation was further north in Italy, at Anzio; the landings there took place on 22 January 1944 and she arrived from Naples on 24 January. She experienced heavy raids and shellfire, and was hit by a radio-controlled bomb, which bounced on the siren lanyard, struck and destroyed some davits and set fire to a water ambulance. Fortunately the bomb landed in the water and did little further damage when it exploded. On that same night, *Leinster* was able to rescue survivors when a nearby hospital ship, *St David*, from the GWR's Fishguard–Rosslare service, was bombed, sinking in less than five minutes. *Leinster* left for Naples on the same day, carrying 100 survivors from *St David*. She made a total of thirty-nine trips to the Anzio beaches before her service there ended with the entry of American troops into Rome on 4 June 1944. She was then transferred to the Adriatic, where she remained until the end of the war, carrying casualties between Ancona and Bari. She was at Bari when an American ammunition ship, *Charles Henderson*, blew up on 9 April 1945. She escaped, albeit with extensive superficial and internal damage, and rescued many survivors. Her final departure from Ancona was on 1 May; she left Taranto on 4 May and arrived back at Liverpool on 14 May. After her service her master was sent a message from Field Marshall Alexander:

> *Please accept and convey to all under your command my grateful thanks for splendid work during the past two years. The wounded and sick from the battlefields of Italy owe much to the staffs of the ship which carried a large proportion of them to comfort and safety. The part you played in the Sicily landing, the Anzio beach head, at Ancona and Bari, has been most praiseworthy.*

For the rest of her career with the Coast Lines group, she carried an oak memorial plaque recording the decorations awarded to her crew.

After her arrival back in the Mersey, *Leinster* sailed to Harland & Wolff, Belfast, on 5 June for her refit. It was decided that she would not return to B&I's Liverpool–Dublin service, but would be transferred to the Belfast Steamship Co. to operate on Liverpool–Belfast. During the war, the Belfast company had lost *Ulster Prince*, while *Ulster Queen* had been so greatly altered for war service that there was no prospect of her returning to passenger service. The Belfast company therefore required a ship to run alongside its sole survivor, *Ulster Monarch*. A further factor was *Leinster*'s lack of livestock accommodation and her large number of first-class cabins, both of which were better suited to Liverpool–Belfast than to Liverpool–Dublin. After her refit, her name was changed to *Ulster Prince* and she was registered at Belfast. She made her first sailing from Belfast on 28 February 1946. It was a notable coincidence that she would spend the remainder of her years within the Coast Lines group on the route on which she had served for the first four months of her career. The remainder of her story belongs in the volume dealing with Liverpool–Belfast.

Munster (1948) and *Leinster* (1948)

After the war, Liverpool–Dublin was reopened by *Longford* on 22 May 1946. In August, her sister ship, *Louth*, joined her on the service. They were old ships, dating from 1906, but they had to maintain the service until B&I could take delivery of two new ships, *Munster* and *Leinster*. Both these ships were ordered in December 1945 from Harland & Wolff, Belfast, costing £565,000 each. They were similar to the two pre-war vessels of the same names, but a little smaller and with cattle accommodation.

Although the war was over, sanction from the British Ministry of Transport was needed for the two ships and the new *Innisfallen* to be registered at Dublin. As a contingency, *Munster* and possibly the other two ships were launched with the port of registry on their sterns showing as Liverpool. Approval for Irish registry was advised to Coast Lines in January 1948.

Munster (1948), fitting out at Belfast, with Liverpool as the intended port of registry. Moss Hutchison's *Kantara* is fitting out alongside. (R. Brandreth collection)

Munster was launched by Lady Glenavy on 25 March 1947, when she sustained some damage. This appears to have been underwater, as it was not reported until December, when the vessel was almost complete. Her fitting out was characterised by delays caused by shortages of materials and components. Hopes that she would be ready before the end of the summer season gave way to an expectation of her being in service for Christmas. In fact, she was not delivered until 17 January 1948, when her cost had risen to around £700,000. As her sister was still being built and there was no urgent seasonal need for her presence on Liverpool–Dublin, *Munster* was used on Fishguard–Cork, starting her maiden voyage from Fishguard on 20 January. *Leinster* was launched by Mrs R.W. Linott, the wife of B&I's General Manager, on 20 May 1947. She suffered delays in fitting out similar to those of her sister, and was delivered on 25 March 1948. She started her maiden voyage from Liverpool on 5 April. *Munster* arrived at Liverpool from Cork on 6 April, having carried twelve passengers, but no cargo, and began her first Liverpool–Dublin voyage on the following evening. *Munster*'s sailing from Cork was the last occasion on which one of Coast Lines' large passenger vessels carried passengers on a scheduled sailing on that route.

The pre-war use of light hull colours had proved unsuccessful and the two post-war passenger ships introduced a new and more serviceable scheme. They wore a dark green hull with a pale yellow line, orange boot-topping and a pale yellow superstructure. Their funnels continued the final pre-war arrangement of green with a white band and black top.

The sisters accommodated first- and third-class passengers. First class occupied the entire midships superstructure of the vessels, with public rooms comprising a smoke room with bar and a lounge on the Boat Deck, a drawing room on A Deck and a

Leinster (1948), as new at Princes Stage. (K.P. Lewis)

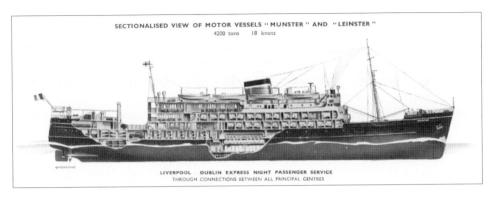

A sectionalised view of *Munster* and *Leinster* (1948). (Author's collection)

dining saloon, passenger reception area, shop and purser's office on B Deck. The dining room had permanent seats for seventy diners and a further twelve portable seats could be added. There were 193 single- and two-berth and two de-luxe cabins, sleeping 225 passengers. Later in their careers, some of their single cabins had a second berth added, increasing the number of berths to 266. Third class occupied the stern of the vessel from the well deck aft in accommodation that appeared to be crowded, although it did include berths for 107 passengers in twenty-four two-berth cabins and two dormitories. In the early years, the company's timetables advertised two- and four-berth cabins in third class but, by 1956, second-class (third class was renamed second class in 1956) cabins were advertised as two-berth only, although it seems likely that they were still used as four-berth cabins when necessary. The ships had passenger certificates for 700 first-class and 800 third-class passengers, so substantial numbers were carried unberthed, especially in third class. During their overhauls in winter 1959, both ships received some improvements to their second-class accommodation.

Both vessels were intended for night service only and, with a few exceptions after 1950, they provided a regular service six nights per week. There were no sailings on Sunday nights. Sailing times were 20.00 from Dublin and 22.00 from Liverpool. The departure from Liverpool was changed to 22.15 from 18 April 1966 to allow the Belfast vessel to connect with a later train from London. Scheduled arrivals were 07.00 at Liverpool and 07.30 at Dublin, although actual arrivals were often earlier.

In Liverpool, the ships berthed in South East Princes Dock, close to Pier Head and the Liver building. Until the completion of the Waterloo river entrance lock in 1950, access to and from the dock was at high tide only and it was often necessary for passengers to disembark at Princes Landing Stage while the ship awaited high tide before proceeding to her dock berth. Since the ships also carried cargo, the tidal delays prevented cargo being discharged and re-loaded in a single day, so the return sailing from Liverpool was roughly 1½ days after arrival. Departures followed a similar pattern, with high tide sailings direct from Princes Dock and all others from the landing stage. As a result, *Longford* was needed to maintain a nightly service. The full nightly service, overhaul periods excepted, started during 1949; in the previous winter, the two modern vessels had operated alone, giving

Irish Coast (1952) at a Dublin berth in Princes Dock. She was the relief vessel between 1952 and 1966. (R. Brandreth collection)

four sailings per week in each direction and *Longford* had acted as a reserve vessel. From March 1950, it was possible to enter Princes Dock at any state of the tide and turn the ship round in twelve hours, so the service then became nightly throughout the year. From that date, the landing stage was used only for arrivals delayed by bad weather and for a short period in 1966 when the Waterloo entrance was under repair. During that period, passengers were disembarked at the landing stage and the ships used the Langton river entrance. In Dublin, the ships used B&I's North Wall quay, which was directly alongside the river Liffey and could be used at any state of the tide.

In addition to their cargo holds, both vessels had accommodation on C and D Decks for up to 484 head of cattle, which were carried from Ireland. They were embarked during the day at North Wall and were disembarked in the early morning at the northern end of Woodside landing stage, which had direct access to the lairage at Woodside, before the vessel crossed the river to berth in Princes Dock. This activity explains the longer scheduled passage from Dublin.

During annual overhaul periods in January and February, a relief vessel was provided from elsewhere in the Coast Lines group; in the early years it was normally *Longford*, but from 1953 onwards the relief vessel was *Irish Coast*. In common with the other vessels of the class built at Belfast, annual overhauls were carried out by their builders at Belfast. The overhauls were extensive, normally taking about one month for each ship, and were intended to ensure a long life for the ships.

The two ships normally enjoyed uneventful lives, but it was inevitable that, over a period of more than twenty years, there would be a few incidents. On 24 March 1949, *Munster* was rounding up in the Mersey at 03.55 before berthing at Woodside landing

Munster (1948), shown with collision damage on 24 October 1961. (K.P. Lewis)

stage to discharge cattle when she came into contact with the Birkenhead ferry *Claughton*, moored at the landing stage. *Leinster* grounded in the Mersey between Wallasey and Seacombe landing stages for over two hours on 5 March 1950. On 1 December 1953, she struck the Birkenhead ferry *Thurstaston*, which was tied up at Woodside landing stage. In 1954 *Leinster* was damaged on 15 November when she struck the dock wall while locking out at Liverpool; she had to be withdrawn for repairs. *Innisfallen* was withdrawn from her normal service and sent from Fishguard to Dublin, where she arrived on 20 November and sailed the same evening on the Liverpool service. *Leinster* resumed her service from Liverpool on 26 November. *Irish Coast* was already relieving on Liverpool–Belfast, so was not available to relieve *Leinster*. In July 1959, *Leinster* suffered superficial damage in a similar incident. *Munster*, during her sailing from Liverpool on 23 October 1961, was in collision at 23.20, about 16 miles out from Liverpool, with the Norwegian tanker *Jakinda*. She suffered damage to her port side, with a gash extending over three decks, resulting in one unoccupied first-class cabin being flattened and four others badly damaged. Parts of the ship were flooded when the sprinkler system came into operation. The force of the impact swung her round and back onto *Jakinda*, damaging her bow. After she had returned to Liverpool, five passengers were taken to hospital for treatment for shock and minor injuries. The accident resulted in her immediate withdrawal from service. On 27 October, she was sent to Harland & Wolff at Belfast for repairs and an early overhaul. Her replacement was Burns & Laird's Dublin–Glasgow vessel *Scottish Coast*. *Munster* did not return to service until 16 December. On 15 January 1961, *Leinster* collided with the vessel *Cameo* off the Bar Lightship, in foggy conditions. On 1 January 1963, *Munster*, while berthed at Dublin, was struck by the Spanish steamer *Monte de la Esperanza*; the accident

Scottish Coast (1957) at the Dublin berth in Princes Dock on 5 November 1961, in Burns & Laird colours, relieving *Munster* after her collision. (Author)

happened in high winds. There was some damage above the waterline, but *Munster* was able to remain in service. The damage was repaired during her annual overhaul in February. On 10 November 1963, while swinging at the mouth of the Liffey in a gale, *Leinster* fouled both anchors in a dredger mooring. After buoying her anchors, she berthed at the nearby Ocean Pier. The anchors were recovered in time for a normal sailing to Liverpool that evening. On 30 January 1964, *Munster* damaged her belting in a collision with the dredger *W.D. Fairway* in the Mersey. On 12 December 1964, *Munster* received slight damage in a collision in the Mersey approaches with the Chilean cargo ship *Lebu*.

Both vessels carried passengers' cars, but under very restrictive conditions. Cars to be carried on the passenger vessels were required alongside no later than 16.00 (12.30 on Saturdays) at Dublin and 15.30 (10.30 on Saturdays) at Liverpool. On Sundays, cars for Dublin were only unloaded during the summer. With the steady growth in car traffic, it was decided in 1961 that a Coast Lines' cargo vessel should be employed as a summer car carrier, backing up the passenger vessels by giving three sailings per week in each direction. The vessel chosen was *Antrim Coast* (1937). She carried fifty cars, but had no passenger accommodation, so drivers and passengers travelled on the passenger ship. Some of her sailings to Liverpool called at Princes Landing Stage, to allow passengers on the passenger vessel to collect their cars there. In 1962, *Pacific Coast* (1947) replaced *Antrim Coast*. She had accommodation for twelve passengers and had previously been on Coast Lines' Liverpool–London service. Her passenger accommodation was advertised, with departures at 18.00 from both ports. In 1963, a nightly service was provided, using both ships. *Antrim Coast* was replaced in 1964 by *Adriatic Coast* (1949), which also did not carry passengers. In 1965 there was again a two-ship service given by *Pacific Coast*

Pacific Coast (1947) – a 12-passenger Coast Lines' ship used to carry cars for several summers in the 1960s. (R. Brandreth collection)

and *Mersey Coast* (1938). The 1966 service was operated by *Pacific Coast* alone, although she was unable to commence service until the end of the British seamen's strike in early July. In 1967 it was taken over by B&I's cargo vessel *Wicklow*. Following the introduction of a car ferry in 1968, this supplementary service ceased.

On 22 March 1965, Coast Lines sold its shareholding in B&I to the Irish Government for £3.6 million. Following its change to Irish ownership, B&I ordered two new car ferries for Dublin–Liverpool. The first vessel, *Munster*, was already on order; the second vessel, *Leinster*, was an improved version of the new *Munster*.

Under its new management, B&I adopted a different image. Its trading style became B+I Line and the traditional B&I colours were changed during overhauls in the winter of 1966/67. The new colours were those of the City of Cork Steam Packet Co. (black hull with a white line, red boot topping, white superstructure and a white funnel with a black top), but the funnel now displayed B&I's new logo, an orange device comprising an arrow within a broken circle. There had been a change in plan over the funnel colours, since both *Leinster* and *Innisfallen* had initially been given a blue funnel with the device in white, which was in line with the drawing used on the cover of the 1967 timetables; in March 1967, all three colour schemes could be seen simultaneously on different vessels of the fleet. In this period *Innisfallen* made some Liverpool–Dublin sailings while *Munster* and *Leinster* were being overhauled. *Innisfallen*'s Fishguard–Cork service had been closed for the winter as an economy measure, but the move also avoided the cost of hiring a relief vessel from Coast Lines.

Pending the arrival of the new car ferries, the old *Munster* and *Leinster* continued to operate the nightly service until October 1967. *Munster* made her final sailing from

Munster (1948) in new B&I colours before her final sailing from Dublin, on 14 October 1967. (Author)

Leinster (1948), pictured before the final passenger sailing from East Princes Dock on 16 November 1968. (K.P. Lewis)

Dublin to Liverpool on 14 October and disembarked her passengers at Princes Landing Stage before sailing immediately for Cork to carry out a short relief on Fishguard–Cork between 16 and 22 October. This, by coincidence, was the route on which she had first served while waiting for her sister to be delivered. She then returned to the Mersey, where she arrived on 23 October to be laid up for sale in Birkenhead. Shortly afterwards she was renamed *Munster I*, releasing her name for use by the new car ferry.

Leinster continued in service, but was only able to provide three nightly sailings per week in each direction. Over Christmas and New Year 1967/68, the service frequency was increased to daily by operating sailings departing at 10.00, from Dublin between 15 and 23 December and from Liverpool between 27 December and 5 January. These were the first occasions on which daylight sailings had ever been scheduled for either vessel. In February 1968, *Innisfallen* again operated the service, while *Leinster* received her overhaul.

The new *Munster* made her maiden voyage on 15 May 1968. The two vessels were able to provide a full nightly service for six nights per week, with additional daytime sailings by *Munster*. Between 21 July and 1 September, *Leinster* sailed additionally on Sundays, giving a daytime sailing from Dublin at 10.30 and returning from Liverpool overnight. *Leinster* remained in service after the summer to cover *Munster's* first annual overhaul; her final sailing was from Liverpool to Dublin on 16 November 1968. On 19 November, she sailed light to Birkenhead to lay up until sold. She also was renamed, becoming *Leinster I*.

Munster I was sold on 24 July 1968 to the Greek Epirotiki Line, and left the Mersey on 8 August, without any change of name for her delivery voyage. After arriving in Greece, she was renamed *Theseus* and refitted extensively for cruising. Both well decks were enclosed, with a swimming pool in the after well, her superstructure was extended fore and aft, all cabins were provided with private facilities, full air conditioning was installed and she received a more streamlined funnel and a new forward mast. In her new guise, she could accommodate 372 passengers in 155 cabins. She was again renamed, this time *Orpheus*, before entering service on cruises to the Greek islands in 1969, where she joined another Epirotiki vessel *Semiramis*. In winter 1969/70 she was chartered by Ensign Cruises of New York to run weekly cruises on a circuit calling at Lisbon, Casablanca, Tangier, Malaga, Cadiz and Portimao, with passengers joining and leaving at Lisbon and Malaga. From May 1970 to October 1971 she was chartered by the American company, Westours, for cruises on the West Coast of North America, from Seattle to Alaska during the summer and from Los Angeles to Mexico during the winter. There was a plaque on board commemorating her visits to Alaska during this period. The charter ended when Holland America Line acquired Westours, and chartered its own ships to them. *Orpheus* then returned to Greece, in November 1971.

For twenty-one years from 1974, *Orpheus* spent spring, summer and autumn on charter to Swan Hellenic, which ran cruises mainly in the Mediterranean to sites of classical and historical interest. Swan Hellenic was acquired by P&O in 1983. While operating for Swan Hellenic, *Orpheus'* passenger numbers were limited to 270. She returned to British waters in various years, usually for cruises around Britain or the British Isles. Each visit to Northern Europe included a positioning cruise before and after the visit. In 1980, she was based at Southampton and made two sailings. The first was a private charter, while the second was around Britain and to the west of Ireland, calling at Dover, Hull, Leith, Kirkwall, Inverewe, Stornoway, Galway, Glengariff, Cork, Waterford, Holyhead, Isles of Scilly and Guernsey. During her call at Holyhead, she went aground in the approaches to the port, blocking the passage of the Dun Laoghaire ferries. In 1981, she returned to Southampton for two similar sailings around Britain and Ireland, again including a call at Cork on each cruise. In 1982, she made two cruises from Southampton around Britain, passing through familiar Irish Sea waters to call at Holyhead. There was then a gap of eight years, during which she continued her Mediterranean cruises for Swan Hellenic, but in July 1990 she sailed on a four-week itinerary from Santander to Irish and Scottish ports, before going on to Scandinavia; she returned to Santander via the Kiel Canal, North Sea and English Channel. In July 1991, she operated a two-week Irish and Scottish cruise, calling at her former home port of Dublin. Her final year with Swan Hellenic was 1995; the Swan Hellenic brochure for that year made a feature of the fact that it was her twenty-first year with Swan Hellenic. By coincidence, her final season began on 5 April 1995, the forty-seventh anniversary of the date on which *Leinster* started her regular Dublin–Liverpool service.

Over the years, *Orpheus* was a most reliable vessel, although she suffered some engine trouble in 1990 and was run aground off Nauplia in 1993. She was occasionally modernised to keep her passenger facilities up to date. The most substantial refurbishment took place before her 1984 season, when she was given a new, more heavily raked bow.

Orpheus (1948), deck view. (S. Turpin)

Leinster (1948), deck view. A bleak deck as befits an overnight ferry, compared with the deck view of *Orpheus*. (Author)

Later, her forward mast was replaced with a lighter version and most of the bulwarks on her Promenade Deck were cut out and replaced with railings.

Orpheus was chartered to Swan Hellenic only during the cruising season, and was generally laid up during the winter. However, in the winters of 1988/89 and 1989/90, she was chartered to an American operator for South American cruises. In winter 1992/92, she operated a few Red Sea cruises for Epirotiki.

After her final season with Swan Hellenic in 1995, *Orpheus* was retained by Epirotiki, and transferred to the management of Royal Olympic Cruises after it had been established by the merger of Epirotiki and Sun Line in 1996. She was refitted in 1997 and continued to operate Aegean cruises. On one occasion, passengers on Swan Hellenic's new ship, *Minerva*, berthed at Kusadasi, watched *Orpheus'* arrival there, and noted the deterioration in her condition. However, she was by this time an old ship. Having passed her fiftieth year, on 28 December 2000 she arrived at an Indian ship-breaker's yard.

Leinster I was sold on 24 December 1968 to Med Sun Ferry Lines, of Cyprus. She was renamed *Aphrodite* and left the Mersey on 31 December 1968. She had a less extensive refit than her sister, with the most obvious change being the enclosure of the after well deck. The alterations included a swimming pool and additional car space. In her new role, she could carry 550 passengers and 100 cars. Her funnel was painted white with a narrow black top and the letters MSL in blue with a mirror image immediately below. Her hull was blue, with red boot topping. She then entered ferry service on Ancona/Brindisi–Piraeus, carrying up to 1,500 passengers. In later years, her sailings were

Aphrodite (1948), formerly *Leinster*. (Author's collection)

extended to include Cyprus and Israel, or the Greek islands and Turkey. Later, her A Deck superstructure was built up aft, giving increased public room space and more open deck space above; an additional lifeboat was fitted on each side. She was damaged by a fire while at Piraeus in March 1972, but survived. On 29 October 1977, she collided with an Italian tanker, *Stamia*. In 1982, she was chartered to a Libyan operator for a service from Piraeus to Libya. She was laid up at Perama, near Piraeus, in December 1983. On 11 October 1987, she arrived in tow at the Turkish port of Aliaga to be broken up.

Munster (1968), Innisfallen/Leinster (1969) and Leinster (1969)

Following its sale to the Irish Government in 1965, B&I had three passenger vessels nearly twenty years old, with cargo holds and space for livestock, but with little vehicle capacity. They were losing money because they were outdated and had high operating costs. With the Irish Government's financial resources, it became possible to spend money on updating B&I's fleet.

The first move was made in early 1967, when B&I signed a contract with the West German shipbuilder Werft Nobiskrug, of Rendsburg, who already had a car ferry on order for the Swedish Lion Ferry. An earlier sister of this ship had been delivered in 1966 as *Kronprins Carl Gustav*. Later, Lion Ferry was also involved in setting up Irish Continental Line between Rosslare and France. By agreement with Lion Ferry, the shipbuilding contract was transferred to B&I. The new ship was to operate on Liverpool–Dublin and replace one old vessel. Her keel was not laid until September

Munster (1968), seen on her first arrival at Liverpool on 12 May 1968. (K.P. Lewis)

1967, but B&I wished to take delivery in May 1968, so could not alter the design of her basic structure, although it was able to influence her interior design.

Towards the end of 1967, B&I announced orders for two further car ferries. The first of these vessels would also be built by Werft Nobiskrug. The second was ordered from the Verolme yard at Cork. As that yard had never previously built such a vessel, plans and technical assistance were to be provided by the West German yard. This contract marked an association with the Verolme yard that would cover six ships over a period of twelve years. The first ship would be particularly fast, with a 24-knot service speed, and was for service from Cork. The second was to replace the remaining conventional vessel on Liverpool–Dublin. The three ships together were expected to cost £7.5 million.

The first new ship was named *Munster* when she was launched on 25 January 1968. She was delivered in May, later than expected. A proposed publicity visit to London was cancelled so that she could be brought into service on the advertised date. She arrived at Dublin on 6 May and crossed over to Liverpool for berthing trials on 12 May, before making her maiden voyage from Liverpool on 15 May. She was a considerable change from her predecessors, doing away with the two-class system. She had capacity for 1,000 passengers, including 238 berths in forty-one two-berth and thirty-nine four-berth cabins and 332 'pullman sleep seats'. There was space for 210 cars on two decks, the higher of which was hinged to make extra room for high vehicles. The public rooms were located on two decks. The Promenade Deck, immediately above the car decks, had a cafeteria at its forward end, and a children's playroom, an entrance area with a shop and a purser's office, a bar and a verandah lounge at its after end. The cafeteria and verandah lounge extended the full width of the ship; the other rooms were to port only, with the galley and catering accommodation to starboard. There was a small open deck space aft of the verandah lounge. The Boat Deck, above the Promenade Deck, had a restaurant and cocktail bar at its forward end, above the cafeteria, and a pullman lounge and open deck space aft, at the sides and ahead of the superstructure. She was fitted with diesel engines, stabilisers and a bow thrust unit.

Munster's funnel colours were the same as those adopted by B&I in 1967, namely white with a black top, with B&I's emblem of an orange arrow within a broken circle superimposed on the white. The hull colours, however, were changed to dark blue, with red boot topping. The timetables for the new service described it as the 'B&I Motorway'.

Munster operated at 22 knots, which enabled her to make a crossing in six-and-a-half hours, including locking into the dock system at Liverpool. She was too large for Princes Dock, so she was allocated a temporary berth and terminal in Carriers Dock, towards the north of the Liverpool dock system, until permanent arrangements could be made. At Dublin, she used the newly built 'Ferryport', situated north-east of the port, away from the centre of Dublin. The old *Leinster*, which operated alongside the new *Munster* until November 1968, continued to use the traditional terminals.

Munster's timetable in her first year was particularly intense, since she was running in conjunction with the old *Leinster*. The two ships were scheduled to provide a nightly service in each direction, with additional daylight sailings by *Munster*. This meant that, during the peak season, *Munster* was making twenty crossings per week, with three sailings every day except Monday, when there were only two. To achieve this schedule meant a sailing every eight hours, so a passage time of six-and-a-half hours was necessary. Her 22-knot speed was the minimum needed to maintain such a schedule. With *Leinster* making eight crossings per week, there were fourteen sailings per week in each direction during the peak summer season. Before and after the peak season, *Munster* operated a single overnight sailing, except on Sundays, until the end of September, when she sailed by day from Liverpool and returned overnight from Dublin. From October, she sailed overnight only, with a standardised departure time of 22.15 from both ports, arriving at 07.00. At first the old *Leinster* continued to operate overnight as well, giving a service every night except Sunday. *Munster* was withdrawn for overhaul between 4 November and 16 November, being covered by *Leinster*. On *Munster*'s return, *Leinster* was withdrawn from service, and *Munster* then operated alone for the remainder of the winter, making just a single crossing on six nights of the week. The service was increased at Christmas and New Year, with a daily round trip in daytime, from Dublin before Christmas and from Liverpool after Christmas. The timings of the crossings during this period were increased to seven hours; it appears that six-and-a-half hours had been too ambitious and such a fast crossing was never scheduled again. The extra half hour was deducted from the turnround time in port.

After the choice of *Munster* for the first ship, the names of the other two new vessels were entirely predictable. They also took the names of their predecessors, with the Irish-built vessel becoming *Leinster* and the German-built vessel *Innisfallen*. *Leinster* was the first to be launched, on 19 November 1968, while *Innisfallen* followed on 7 December.

However, the German yard was much faster at fitting out than the Cork yard, with the result that *Innisfallen* was handed over on 28 March 1969, while *Leinster* did not start her trials until 22 May.

The previous *Innisfallen* had sailed between Fishguard and Cork until she was withdrawn from service on 1 November 1968 and Cork had been without a direct service to Wales since then. British Rail had served notice effective from March 1969 to terminate the 1891 agreement under which the Cork service used Fishguard as its Welsh port. Initially it was not clear which port would be used instead. After investigating various Bristol Channel ports, B&I announced that *Innisfallen* would use Swansea, where a Ferryport was to be built in the tidal area of the port. This gave Cork the direct sailings between two city centres that previous ships had been unable to offer. The decision justified the new vessel's high service speed since, even at that speed, the passage time between the two ports would be nine hours. The main summer schedule required her to make a round sailing every day, including Sundays, departing from Swansea at 22.00 and from Cork at 08.30. This timetable allowed only one-and-a-half hours at Cork, but a more generous four-and-a-half hours at Swansea. Outside the summer season, her pattern followed that of her predecessor, with sailings from Swansea at 22.00 on Tuesdays, Thursdays and Saturdays and from Cork at 21.00 on Mondays, Wednesdays and Fridays. At Cork, *Innisfallen* was to use a new terminal at Tivoli, on the north side of the river Lee about 2 miles downstream from the previous berth at Penrose Quay, in the city centre.

Immediately after her delivery, *Innisfallen* made a series of publicity visits, at London between 5 and 9 April, at Swansea on 10 April, and at Cork between 11 and 13 April. She then sailed to Dublin to make her maiden voyage to Liverpool on 14 April, relieving

Leinster (1969) at Princes Stage on 29 May 1969, before entering service. (K.P. Lewis)

Munster. She made her final sailing on that route on 29 April and then returned to Cork to open the new service on 2 May, carrying around 350 passengers on her first sailing. Her service was interrupted on 7 May, when she suffered a gearbox failure and returned to Cork. She was off service until 10 May.

Leinster was scheduled for immediate entry into service after delivery. On her trials she was the first ship to be tested over Ireland's new 'measured mile'. She left Cobh for Dublin on 28 May, calling at Liverpool on 29 May, and made her maiden voyage to Liverpool on 1 June, when the timetable first required two car ferries on the service. The Liverpool–Dublin schedule in 1969 was more frequent than had ever previously been offered. In the main summer season, there were three sailings per day in each direction on Fridays and Saturdays, departing from both ports at 07.45, 15.45 and 23.45. On the other five days, there were two sailings per day in each direction, with departures from Liverpool at 13.15 and 23.45 and from Dublin at 11.45 and 23.45. On Sunday 3 August, the service was increased to three sailings in each direction. This gave sixteen sailings per week in each direction (seventeen in the busiest week). All sailings were scheduled to take seven hours. Outside the main summer season, there were two sailings every day in each direction.

Apart from their engines and speed, the two new ships were identical. There were a few differences from *Munster*, the most obvious of which was that they had a sky bar on the Compass Deck, above the Bridge Deck. Other differences were sixteen two-berth de-luxe cabins in the after part of the superstructure on the Boat Deck and an open Sun Deck above those cabins. They lacked windows at the sides of the Boat Deck alongside the funnel, as fitted to *Munster*. They were some 20 feet longer than *Munster*, so could carry 1,200 passengers, an increase of 200, and an extra twenty cars. There were more cabins, with seventy-three two-berth and twenty-five four-berth, in addition to the de-luxe cabins. This gave 278 berths and there were also 462 'pullman sleep seats'.

With all three ships in service, both routes settled down to a steady pattern. Initial bookings were considered encouraging, especially on Swansea–Cork. B&I considered ordering a second vessel, similar to *Innisfallen*, for delivery in 1971 and asked a number of shipbuilders to indicate the likely cost and delivery date for such a vessel.

The Liverpool terminal at Carriers Dock, reached through the Langton river entrance, had always been planned as a temporary arrangement. Early in 1969, it was announced that B&I was planning a combined car ferry and container terminal in Liverpool on the site of Trafalgar and Victoria Docks, much closer to the city centre. Access from the river to the new terminal would be through the Waterloo river entrance.

With the end of the autumn season, B&I decided to retain the pattern of two sailings per day in each direction on Liverpool–Dublin, but there were no Sunday sailings, except two over Christmas; these were the only additional Christmas sailings offered. Between January and March 1970, the service was reduced to allow one ship to be overhauled and to cover the other two for their overhauls. The programme became a daytime sailing from Dublin at 11.00 and an overnight sailing from Liverpool at 22.15 on Mondays to Thursdays. There was an overnight sailing from Dublin on Fridays and from Liverpool on Saturdays. *Innisfallen* continued to offer three sailings per week in each direction, although her departure from Swansea was advanced by one hour to 20.00. Over Christmas and New Year, she gave a round sailing daily. During the period between January and April 1970, she was allowed an extra hour for the crossing.

Inevitably, the vessels faced some rough weather during winter. *Leinster* suffered storm damage to her bow on 8 November 1969 and was off service until 25 November. *Munster* continued with her normal schedule in that period. *Innisfallen* took thirty-three hours on passage from Cork on 7 January 1970, with problems caused by gales and steering trouble. A 'Which?' report singled out Swansea–Cork as the 'roughest crossing'. This would have come as no surprise to generations of regular travellers, accustomed to the exposed conditions in the southern Irish Sea. However, it was announced that, for comfort, passengers carried on that route would be restricted in future to 85 per cent of the number on her passenger certificate.

The first vessel to be overhauled early in 1970 was *Munster*, which received attention in Dublin. She was followed by *Leinster* and then by *Innisfallen*, each returning to her respective builder. *Innisfallen* was relieved by *Leinster*, not surprisingly as their accommodation was identical. During these overhauls, additional pullman seats were installed and the children's playrooms were converted into ladies' rest rooms. *Leinster* made a special rugby sailing between Swansea and Dublin over the weekend of 13–15 March. She made a similar sailing later that year for another rugby match on 14 June. The scheduled passage time was around ten hours.

The 1970 summer timetable was similar to that of 1969, but on Liverpool–Dublin the peak season lasted for an extra two weeks and there was a third sailing on three Sundays. The departure times for the twice-daily service were changed to 12.00 and 22.15 from Liverpool and 11.00 and 22.15 from Dublin. On the southern crossing, the daily round trip operated throughout the summer, but in the peak summer the daytime departure from Cork was delayed until 10.00, compared with 08.30 at other times.

During 1970, there were further reports that B&I was likely to order a new vessel, possibly for a new Swansea–Saint Nazaire/Vigo service. Later in the year, it was decided to delay ordering a vessel, but to plan for a new ship in 1976 to operate on Swansea–Cork in summer and to Spain/Portugal in winter. B&I also considered starting an Iberian service earlier than 1976, using a chartered vessel. Finally, it was announced that plans for a new route had been dropped 'for the time being', but that *Innisfallen* would be replaced by a new 7,000 ton vessel in three to four years time.

During summer 1970, *Innisfallen* was off service for three days from 15 July as a result of a dockers' strike at Swansea. She then returned, using an emergency ramp in King's Dock at Swansea. Since this was inside the docks, her schedules were disrupted, as access was only possible for four hours either side of high tide. On the night of 8/9 September, *Innisfallen* went to the aid of a fire-damaged vessel, herself receiving some damage, which resulted in her missing a round trip. On the night of 25 November, force 9 gales caused *Innisfallen* to turn back to Cork after a container had shifted and damaged vehicles.

The 1970/71 winter timetables were similar to the previous winter, except that no additional Sunday sailings were given on Liverpool–Dublin over Christmas; the additional sailings on Swansea–Cork were given over Christmas but not New Year.

Annual overhauls between January and March followed the same sequence as in 1970, but each ship was overhauled at her Irish terminal port. During these overhauls, each vessel was fitted with new lounges and a cafeteria, improvements were made to the catering facilities, and the sky bars on *Leinster* and *Innisfallen* were fitted with 130 extra pullman seats.

The 1971 timetable saw the first sign of retrenchment on Liverpool–Dublin. The twice-daily service did not start until 16 May, compared with 6 April in 1970, and then only operated on Fridays and Saturdays. However, the main summer timetable, from 4 July, was unaltered. The period of the peak summer timetable on Swansea–Cork, with a daily round sailing, was shortened. In retrospect, it can be seen that 1970, which was the second year with all car ferries in operation, had been the high point and a pattern of service reductions now became the norm.

There were no changes in the 1971/72 winter sailing programme, although a scheduled sailing by *Innisfallen* from Swansea to Dublin for a rugby international on 11 March was cancelled. However, changes were to come in the summer timetable. The original timetable showed only a few changes, but there was a slump in advance bookings that was so serious that an emergency timetable was introduced. On Liverpool–Dublin, there was a summer peak service of a single overnight sailing in each direction on Sundays to Thursdays and two sailings in each direction on Fridays and Saturdays. Even Friday's extra sailings operated on fewer weeks than Saturday's. On two Sundays, the service was increased to two sailings in each direction. This reduced the weekly number of sailings in each direction to nine (ten in the two best weeks), compared with sixteen (seventeen) per week in 1970. Indeed, in 1968 *Munster* by herself had operated ten sailings per week in each direction. It was reported that B&I might seek to charter out *Munster* and operate Liverpool–Dublin with *Leinster* alone, but this did not happen and both ships operated on the route throughout the summer. Swansea–Cork also suffered reductions, with a round trip being operated only on Saturdays, Sundays and Wednesdays, giving five round trips per week. The daytime departure from Cork was advanced to 09.30. There was also a round trip on Saturdays for one month after the peak summer season had ended. Demand revived towards the end of the summer and sailings were re-scheduled to cope with heavy traffic from Ireland. Because of the additional traffic, Friday's and Saturday's daylight Liverpool–Dublin sailings were extended to the end of October. Swansea–Cork also had heavier traffic than expected at the beginning of September.

Twice during 1972, *Munster* received damage requiring her to be dry-docked for repairs. On 18 April, she entered Langton dry-dock for repairs to her bow propeller and missed a round trip. On 31 August 1972, she collided with the Bristol coaster *Echo*, when she was arriving at Dublin in dense fog, and damaged her propeller and steering gear. She was drydocked at Dublin, resuming service on 3 September.

The new Liverpool terminal was completed during 1972, but it was not brought into use immediately, as an agreement on charges and manning levels had not been reached. The final sailing from the Carriers Dock terminal was made by *Munster* on 30 September 1972. Next morning, *Leinster* berthed at the new Trafalgar Dock terminal. The first container ship to arrive at the new terminal was *Wicklow*, on 3 October.

The reduced level of traffic to Ireland continued in 1973 and all services were similar to those in 1972, with a few minor changes in the period when additional sailings were operated. However, an additional round trip was operated on Swansea–Cork on Sundays in the autumn. *Munster* suffered some slight damage to her bow at Liverpool on 5 November 1973. She was dry-docked and her sailing that night was cancelled, but she was able to sail light to Dublin next day to take that night's sailing to Liverpool. All sailings between 14 and 18 November were cancelled because of a labour dispute aboard the container ship *Kilkenny*. Several December sailings were cancelled to conserve fuel.

The financial position began to improve in 1974. On Liverpool–Dublin, a marked increase in the number of sailings was planned initially, with three sailings per day in each direction on peak Saturdays, although it was stated that the additional summer sailings would depend on the cost of fuel. In the end, there was only a small expansion in the number of daylight sailings on Fridays and Saturdays, while the Sunday daylight sailings were dropped. There was no change in the number of sailings on Swansea–Cork, but the departure time of the daytime sailing from Cork reverted to 10.00.

Despite the poor traffic figures, B&I was still planning for future growth and, early in 1974, announced that it was considering placing an order for a 7,000-ton ship to operate Swansea–Cork, with delivery in early 1976. This was the first suggestion of new tonnage since the abortive plans in 1970. This announcement was premature, as the order for the new vessel was not placed until 1976.

During *Innisfallen*'s overhaul in April 1975, her engines were converted to burn heavy fuel instead of diesel, giving a saving of £300 per round trip. During the same summer, it was reported that she had been unable to maintain the daily round sailing on Wednesdays to Sundays and had frequently run up to two hours late. Probably the change of fuel and the lack of experience in its use had something to do with her lower operating speed. She had also left passengers at Swansea on some peak nights because of lack of sufficient accommodation. It was clear that a larger ship was needed. The position of Swansea–Cork was not helped by a two-week strike by Cork dockers in the second half of October, resulting in the suspension of the service. In contrast, in 1976 *Innisfallen* ran much better, apart from one notable delay on 5 September, when she arrived at Swansea some four hours late on the daytime sailing from Cork; her return departure was then delayed from 22.00 to 03.20 next morning.

A further change in B&I's funnel colours took place in 1975, when the orange motif showing an arrow inside a broken circle was replaced by the company's name. The new motif was in black and had 'B+I' in large letters, with 'LINE' in smaller letters underneath. The ships' hulls were painted in a darker shade of blue.

By 1977, conditions had improved to the point that a twice-daily Liverpool–Dublin service was started on 3 May and operated through to the end of the year. This gave fourteen sailings per week in each direction. Sailings on Swansea–Cork were increased to six round sailings per week during the peak summer season. Gales on 14 and 15 November disrupted sailings. *Leinster*, which made the 11.00 sailing from Dublin, sailed via the Isle of Man and was stormbound in Laxey Bay for eighteen hours. *Munster*, which was due to sail at 12.00 from Liverpool, was unable to lock out until the morning of 15 November.

Leinster (1969), arriving in the Mersey in July 1976, with new funnel colours. (Author)

At the beginning of 1978, *Innisfallen* left Swansea–Cork for the first time since 1969 to relieve *Munster* and *Leinster* during their overhauls. This allowed Liverpool–Dublin to be operated twice daily throughout the year. During her three-month absence, *Innisfallen* was replaced on Swansea–Cork by a chartered Swedish vessel, *Stena Germanica*. Sailings on Swansea–Cork had a longer peak summer season than in 1977. *Innisfallen* maintained her schedule well, although she suffered from some tidal problems at Swansea.

Major changes were in store with the delivery of the new vessel, *Connacht*, which made her maiden voyage on 7 February 1979. Her entry into service marked the end of *Innisfallen*'s association with Swansea–Cork; she moved north again to relieve *Leinster* and *Munster* on Liverpool–Dublin and for her own overhaul. During these overhauls at Dublin, the accommodation on *Leinster* and *Innisfallen* was improved at a cost of £½ million each, to bring them more into line with *Connacht*. It was planned to run a three-ship service on Liverpool–Dublin during summer 1979, with *Leinster* and *Innisfallen* operating the 1978 timings and *Munster* inaugurating a third sailing with departures from Liverpool at 04.15 and Dublin at 16.15. This would have given the best ever service between the two ports, with twenty-one sailings per week in each direction, but it was not to be. *Innisfallen* re-entered service opposite *Leinster* on 23 June, after completing her overhaul, but bookings did not reach the expected level, so *Munster* was laid up in Liverpool. She was chartered to Brittany Ferries for twenty days from 3 July, to operate Plymouth–Roscoff in place of *Cornuailles*, which had broken down. A second charter, from 4 August, was arranged when another Brittany Ferries' vessel, *Prince of Brittany*, also broke down and *Munster* then operated Portsmouth–St Malo. She returned to Dublin in September and was laid up at the North Wall. *Innisfallen* suffered engine problems at the beginning of August and ran about seven hours late, but there was sufficient room in the timetable for her to catch up within a few days. At the end of September, the service was disrupted by industrial action, which coincided with a Papal visit to Ireland and caused great problems for many Irish people who wished to return home for the visit. Early in October, *Munster* ended her lay-up and replaced *Innisfallen*, which was sent to Germany for major attention to her engines.

Connacht transferred her Welsh terminal from Swansea to Pembroke Dock on 22 May 1979. Towards the end of that year, it was announced that a new Pembroke Dock–Rosslare service, operated by *Munster*, would start in spring 1980, with *Leinster* and *Innisfallen* operating Liverpool–Dublin. When *Innisfallen* returned from Germany, she relieved *Connacht*. From 1979 onwards, the scheduling of B&I's various car ferries became far more complicated.

It came as a great surprise when *Innisfallen*'s sale was announced in February 1980. She was sold to the Italian company Corsica Ferries and handed over to her new owners on 23 February 1980. It was later revealed that B&I had lost £1.1 million in 1979, after five years of uninterrupted growth. The causes of this loss were labour unrest, a dramatic fall in tourist traffic to Ireland, soaring fuel prices and increased interest payments. *Innisfallen*'s sale can be explained by the need to make economies and to cut interest payments by reducing the level of borrowings, especially in view of the capital required for the new ship; it was believed that her sale realised more than £2.5 million.

Innisfallen's departure created a gap in B&I's plans because *Munster* was now needed as the second ship on Liverpool–Dublin and was not available to start the new Pembroke Dock–Rosslare route on 1 May. A more immediate problem was cover for the remaining ships' overhaul programme. This was provided by chartering the Sardinian vessel *Espresso Olbia*, better known as Tor Line's former *Tor Anglia* on Immingham–Gothenburg. She replaced *Connacht* on Pembroke Dock–Cork; *Connacht* in turn sailed north to relieve *Leinster*, making her first appearance on Liverpool–Dublin.

The Liverpool–Dublin service was halted on 21 March 1980 by a Liverpool dockers' strike in support of a national steel strike. *Connacht* was due to return south to resume service on Pembroke Dock–Cork on 23 April, following the completion of *Leinster*'s overhaul, but was trapped in dock in Liverpool by the strike. In her place, *Leinster*, fresh from her overhaul, took over Pembroke Dock–Cork on 24 March. *Espresso Olbia* returned to Gothenburg. The dock strike was over at the beginning of April and *Connacht* was able to return to Pembroke Dock–Cork on 2 April, thus freeing *Leinster*, which returned to Liverpool–Dublin in conjunction with *Munster*. Pembroke Dock–Rosslare was covered by the charter of Townsend Thoresen's *Viking III*, which started the new service belatedly on 23 May.

The 1980 season was better than 1979, but B&I was still below its targets. At the end of September, *Leinster* changed places with *Connacht* and took over Pembroke Dock–Cork. During October, she was renamed *Innisfallen*. This re-naming will be the source of endless confusion, since two ships of identical appearance, built in the same year for the same owner, have each carried the name *Innisfallen*. The only discernable difference was the port of registry. The change was made in order to free the name *Leinster* for a new

Innisfallen (1969), with post-1975 funnel colours. She was registered at Dublin, so is the former *Leinster*. (Author's collection)

car ferry which was launched on 7 November 1980, but the association of the name *Innisfallen* with services from Cork made it clear that, in future, that ship was destined to spend most of her time there.

When *Viking III*'s charter ended, B&I chartered *Stena Nordica* to maintain its latest route. Shortly after *Stena Nordica* had entered service, she suffered a failure of her main engine and limped back to Pembroke Dock on 18 November. *Innisfallen* was called upon to keep Pembroke Dock–Rosslare open, in addition to her normal schedules to and from Cork. She provided a limited daytime Rosslare service on Saturdays, Sundays, Tuesdays and Thursdays in the period normally spent lying over at Pembroke Dock. From 22 December, *Saint Patrick* was chartered from Irish Continental Line to operate the full daily Pembroke Dock–Rosslare service. Her charter ended on 15 January 1981, when *Innisfallen* again took up the same limited Pembroke Dock–Rosslare service. *Stena Nordica* resumed service from Pembroke Dock on 2 February.

1980 saw the end of B&I's plans to start a Cork–Le Havre service. The existing Rosslare–Le Havre/Cherbourg services were operated by Irish Continental Line, which was owned by the Irish Government, as was B&I. The Government had no wish to see competition between two state-owned organisations and told B&I that its new service must be run in co-operation with Irish Continental. Subsequent discussions between the two lines broke down without any agreement.

B&I's 1981 plans were based on the new *Leinster* joining *Connacht* on Liverpool–Dublin. This would at last allow *Munster* to be transferred to Pembroke Dock–Rosslare and end the use of chartered tonnage. *Innisfallen* would continue to operate Pembroke

Dock–Cork. One problem was that *Leinster* was not due in service until early June, but *Stena Nordica*'s charter was due to finish on 5 May. To plug this gap, another Swedish vessel, *Prinsessan Desiree*, was chartered from 6 May until *Munster* became available.

The Liverpool–Dublin service was reduced to single-ship operation in January and February 1981 during the overhauls of *Connacht* and *Munster* at Cork. This was the first time since 1977 that the service had not been operated by two ships. When *Leinster* was delivered, *Munster* was transferred, as planned, to Pembroke Dock. For the first time since 1968 (apart from periods of industrial disputes), none of the first-generation car ferries were sailing between Liverpool and Dublin.

1981 was a year when B&I reached stability in its fleet, without the need for chartered vessels to maintain any of its services. Unfortunately, its financial position was much less satisfactory. It was confirmed that losses in 1980 had been £2.8 million and the loss in 1981 was expected to be much worse, at around £5 million. B&I carried out a major review of its operations. Reports suggested that Pembroke Dock–Cork was a strong candidate for closure. An immediate economy was made on Pembroke Dock–Rosslare, where *Munster*'s schedule was reduced from eleven round trips per week to four, sailing from Rosslare each evening between Wednesday and Saturday, returning from Pembroke Dock early the following morning. She lay idle at Rosslare between Sunday morning and Wednesday evening. The service was withdrawn completely on 22 November because of an industrial dispute with *Munster*'s officers. *Munster* sailed light from Rosslare to Birkenhead, where she arrived on 24 November to lay up. She was put up for sale.

When B&I's results for 1981 were announced, its losses had increased to £7.5 million. It was stated that freight operations, which generated approximately 60 per cent of revenue, were satisfactory, but the passenger and tourism sector remained unprofitable. *Innisfallen*'s Pembroke Dock–Cork service had contributed a loss of £1.2 million to these figures.

Munster was brought out of lay-up in January 1982 to cover *Connacht*'s overhaul. She then covered Pembroke Dock–Cork while *Innisfallen* was overhauled at Avonmouth during February. Her reappearance at Pembroke Dock did not cause any of the problems that had led to her withdrawal. On completion of this relief, she returned to Dublin, where she was available for a bizarre incident. B&I had decided that it wished to reduce its Liverpool–Dublin frequency to a nightly crossing in each direction, using the vessel that had arrived at Dublin in the morning to operate a round sailing to Holyhead during the day. This proposal met with strong resistance from Sealink's employees at Holyhead. *Connacht* was twice refused permission to berth at Holyhead, on 6 and 8 March, and was compelled to return to Dublin. In retaliation, *Munster*, which was 'on trials' in Dublin Bay on 8 March, was 'taken over' by her crew, under a retired captain. She sailed to Dun Laoghaire, where she blocked the port, preventing Sealink's *St David* from berthing. *St David* was forced to return to Holyhead. On her arrival next day, she found that *Munster* was still blocking access. She was finally allowed to berth when *Munster*'s crew were told that there was a sick passenger on board *St David*. Both services were then suspended until the problem had been resolved.

Pembroke Dock–Rosslare was re-started for summer 1982 by *Innisfallen*, which operated four round trips per week from Pembroke Dock, between her overnight Cork sailings. By now her speed had declined to around 19.5 knots, a far cry from the previous *Innisfallen's* original 24 knots. In rough weather, she was not always able to keep to her timetable; some Cork sailings were cancelled to bring her back to schedule. A new Cork terminal at Ringaskiddy, opposite Cobh, cut half an hour off the crossing time, and would have helped with *Leinster's* timing problems. Unfortunately, B&I had failed to agree terms for its use, so *Innisfallen* continued to use the Tivoli terminal.

There was no longer any work for *Munster* in the B&I fleet, but no buyer had been found, so she was chartered for summer 1982 to a new Scandinavian concern, Egersund-Thyboron Linjen A/S, which opened a 130-mile link between Egersund in Norway and Thyboren, north of Esbjerg. *Munster* was scheduled to make a round trip each day, with a crossing time of eight-and-a-half hours. She was collected from the Mersey by a Norwegian crew in mid-April. She returned to the Mersey towards the end of September and, while she was receiving a short overhaul in dry-dock, a writ was attached to her mast alleging non-payment of fuel bills by her charterers. Once again, *Munster* was offered for sale.

During summer 1982, there were rumours that Pembroke Dock–Cork was to close at the beginning of November. This did not happen and it was announced that the service would continue until 7 January 1983. Following pressure from the Irish Government, the service remained open after that date, but finally ended on 2 February. After the closure, *Innisfallen* continued to operate Pembroke Dock–Rosslare, but more frequently.

Munster's final appearance on a B&I service started early in February 1983, when she relieved *Innisfallen* for her overhaul at Liverpool. Later that month, *Innisfallen* relieved *Connacht* and then *Leinster*, while *Munster* continued to cover *Innisfallen's* service. This was the first time *Innisfallen* had ever served on Dublin–Holyhead. Following the completion of her relief work in mid-March, *Munster* was promptly sold to Middle Eastern buyers and, on 22 March, she sailed from Liverpool for the last time, manned by a German crew and bound for Saudi Arabia, via Bremerhaven.

Innisfallen spent summer 1983 on Pembroke Dock–Rosslare. During the four months of the main summer season, she operated a round sailing on four days of the week, in addition to her nightly round sailings. B&I had bowed to considerable pressure from the Irish Government and Cork pressure groups and operated Pembroke Dock–Cork between 16 June and 12 September. Since no B&I vessel was available, a Finnish vessel, *Fennia*, was chartered. This service did use the new terminal at Ringaskiddy. Unfortunately, loadings were very poor, with an average of only 180 passengers and seventy cars per crossing, against a capacity of 1,200 passengers and 230 cars. As a result, *Fennia's* last sailing was the final end of B&I's Cork services, although the Cork–Swansea service would later be revived by Swansea–Cork Ferries.

B&I's financial position worsened further in 1983, with losses of £12 million. The accumulated losses over the previous six years amounted to about £30 million.

After the excitement of the previous few years, 1984 was a quiet year, with *Connacht* and *Leinster* on the Dublin routes and *Innisfallen* on Pembroke Dock–Rosslare. Irish

Continental Line's vessel *Saint Patrick II* relieved all three ships in February and March. *Innisfallen* suffered visor damage during the autumn and was forced to operate as a stern loader, with her bow doors sealed. She was replaced by *Saint Patrick II* on 19 October and proceeded to Liverpool for her visor to be replaced. While there, she was inspected by possible Italian purchasers, but no firm offer resulted, so she returned to Pembroke Dock and resumed her Rosslare sailings on 3 November.

B&I's losses in 1984 amounted to £27.6 million. This figure almost doubled the losses accumulated up to 1983 and made cost reductions even more urgent. They were achieved by entering into a pooling agreement with Sealink, covering both companies' Irish Sea routes to Ireland. For *Innisfallen*, this meant that in 1985 her four daytime round trips each week between Pembroke Dock and Rosslare would not be operated, except between 14 July and 7 September. In return, Sealink agreed to withdraw three Fishguard–Rosslare round sailings each week, except during the same summer period. Following the agreement, *Innisfallen* was withdrawn from Pembroke Dock–Rosslare for most of February and March 1985 without a replacement, for her own overhaul at Liverpool and to cover *Connacht* and *Leinster* for their overhauls.

Despite these changes, B&I was expected to lose a further £6.6 million in 1985 and extraordinary items would increase this to £29.6 million. This led to a plan for further rationalisation with Sealink. *Innisfallen* was to be withdrawn from Pembroke Dock–Rosslare and the service would be closed. A new joint Fishguard–Rosslare service would be started, using a single 'jumbo' ferry, which would replace Sealink's *St Brendan*. These proposals resulted in strikes on all B&I's ships in November 1985 and January 1986. *Innisfallen* closed Pembroke Dock–Rosslare on 5 January 1986 and was laid up at Dublin. However, because *St Brendan* was being overhauled and had been replaced by the smaller *St David*, the Fishguard route was unable to handle all the traffic and *Innisfallen* temporarily reopened Pembroke Dock–Rosslare on 27 January. After the backlog had been cleared, *Innisfallen* was finally withdrawn from that service and then relieved *Leinster* and *Connacht* on the Dublin routes.

Sealink had failed to find a suitable 'jumbo' ferry for Fishguard–Rosslare, so decided to retain *St Brendan*. As her capacity was lower than that of a 'jumbo' ferry, it was agreed that *Innisfallen* would operate alongside *St Brendan* on Fishguard–Rosslare during the summer period, sailing daily at 23.55 from Rosslare and at 06.00 from Fishguard. During the peak summer period, she would also sail at 12.00 from Rosslare and at 17.45 from Fishguard each day between Thursday and Sunday.

Innisfallen spent a lengthy period relieving on the Dublin services, because of extended overhauls of *Connacht* and *Leinster*. She was due to start her Fishguard–Rosslare sailings on 22 May, but *Connacht* was still off service, so B&I chartered the Belgian vessel *Prins Philippe*, which normally operated on Dover–Ostend, to cover *Innisfallen*'s Fishguard sailings. *Connacht* resumed service on 14 June and *Innisfallen* then sailed light to Fishguard to test the ramp there. This was her first visit to Fishguard and the first call there by any B&I vessel since *Innisfallen* (1948) had made her final sailing from Fishguard on 1 November 1968. She then crossed light to Rosslare and took over from *Prins Philippe* on the 23.55 sailing on 15 June.

Innisfallen's last sailing on Fishguard–Rosslare was the 06.00 sailing from Fishguard on 15 September. From Rosslare, she sailed light to Birkenhead, to be laid up and sold. Her buyers, the Greek Strintzis Lines, paid around £1.7 million for her and planned to use her in their Greece–Italy service. She crossed the Mersey to Liverpool for some repairs before her delivery voyage. She was then renamed *Ionian Sun*, with her registry in Greece, and left at the end of October 1986. The final first-generation B&I car ferry had departed.

The first vessel to leave the fleet had been the original *Innisfallen*, sold in February 1980 to Corsica Ferries, which renamed her *Corsica Viva* and placed her in service between the Italian mainland and the Corsican ports of Bastia and Calvi. In 1985, she was chartered for a Caribbean service between Dominica, Martinique and St Lucia as *Dominican Viva*. After the charter, she returned to the Mediterranean in 1988, and was renamed *Corsica Viva I*. She sailed from Savona to Ajaccio in Corsica and Porto Torres in Sardinia. Four years later, she was transferred to a direct ferry service to Sardinia, and renamed *Sardinia Viva*. In 1993, her owners decided to start a Caribbean service on their own account, so she was transferred to the Guadeloupe flag and renamed *Caribia Viva*. Her route was between the French West Indian islands Guadeloupe and Martinique. The new service was not a success and the ship returned to La Spezia early in 1994. In summer that year, she sailed under charter between Bari, Patras and Çesme, and later between Tunis and Genoa.

In autumn 1994, her owners chartered her for one year to a British company, Meridian Ferries, which planned to use her as the second ship in a new Folkestone–Boulogne service. Meridian Ferries also had a purchase option. She arrived at Sunderland for repairs on 26 November 1994. This work concentrated on raising the headroom on her vehicle deck and replacing part of her badly corroded double bottom. It was originally planned that she would be renamed *Spirit of Folkestone* and start a passenger service on 6 December, but Sea Containers, Folkestone's owners, decided that the service should only be for freight. The date proved to be over-optimistic, since there had been a delay in arranging her delivery from Italy and because of the extent of the work required on her. She sailed from the Wear to the Tees on 11 January 1995 for engine repairs. She then returned to Sunderland and remained there until 2 February. Before her departure, she was named *Spirit of Independence*, in preference to *Spirit of Folkestone* and registered in the Bahamas. She entered freight-only service from Boulogne on 5 February, operating three round sailings each day. Her repairs were not completed and she visited shiprepairers on the river Medway on three separate occasions at the end of February.

Spirit of Independence's appearance had altered very little since her days as *Innisfallen*. The only structural changes noticeable were the loss of a few windows on the Promenade Deck, an extra support for her Sun Deck and a small enclosed area at the forward end of the Sun Deck immediately aft of the funnel. She was also fitted with cranes for the liferafts stored on that deck. Her funnel was painted dark blue, with a black top, an orange 'M' and a turquoise wave below. The hull was also blue, similar to her B&I hull colouring, but carried one deck higher. It had the word 'MERIDIAN' in orange, with two turquoise waves below.

Spirit of Independence was manned by a Polish crew, whose wage costs were much lower than those of British or French seamen. The use of Polish seamen caused problems with French seamen, who were already in dispute with their employer, SNAT, over a new manning agreement. It seemed possible that any failure of those negotiations might result in French ferries employing non-French nationals, so the seamen were in no mood to allow another operator to use foreigners. The French seamen started a riot at Boulogne on 23 February. The problem spread to other ports, especially Calais, and caused ships to be diverted. On 8 March, French seamen fired a distress flare at *Spirit of Independence*, smashing a lounge window. The subsequent fire gutted a rest lounge. These riots lost Meridian a great deal of business and so both of the company's ships were laid up in Boulogne on 16 March, owing some £50,000 in unpaid port dues. Legal action was taken against the ships for unpaid bills. A liquidator was appointed on 17 March, with Meridian Ferries owing around £1.5 million. The money due against *Spirit of Independence* was paid by Corsica Ferries, which took possession of its vessel, painted out the Meridian markings and moved her to Dover on 27 March. She sailed from Dover on 4 April, returning to Italy to be laid up at La Spezia.

It appeared that her owners had no further use for her and she was sold in 1996. In 1998, she became *Happy Dolphin* and opened a service between La Spezia and Bastia, Corsica. Her owners became bankrupt in 2001 and she was arrested and sold to pay the creditors. Her Turkish buyers planned to operate her between Turkey and Italy under the name *Sancak II*. The company's previous vessel, *Sancak I*, originally the Swedish vessel *Saga*, had just been burned out. These plans did not materialise and in 2003 she took up service on Brindisi–Çesme/Izmir as *Derin Deniz*. She was listed for sale in August 2004, and arrived at Alang, India, in October 2004, to be broken up.

The second ship to go was *Munster*. She was sold in March 1983 to Jordanian buyers, who renamed her *Farah*. Soon afterwards, she was transferred to a Panamanian company and renamed *Farah I*. She was used to carry pilgrims and on ferry work between Jordan and Egypt. In 1990, she was sold to the Dalian Steam Shipping Co. of China and renamed *Tian Peng*. She has retained that name ever since, but has recently been deleted from Lloyd's Register, implying doubt about her continued existence.

The final vessel to be sold was *Innisfallen* (ex-*Leinster*). She was sold in October 1986 to the Greek Strintzis Lines, who refurbished her at a cost of around £4 million, including fitting a swimming pool, casino, cinema, shops and disco. She was given more cabins above the car deck, increasing the number of her berths to 446. Her passenger capacity was increased to 1,400. She was renamed *Ionian Sun* and placed in service between Italy and Greece. The routes between these two countries were growing rapidly; by 1989, Strintzis had four vessels operating between Ancona and Patras. A long sea journey, each single crossing was scheduled to take around thirty hours, allowing each ship to make two round sailings per week.

B&I had finally abandoned Cork after the summer service in 1983. There was still strong local demand for a service from Cork, but Swansea, with its good transport links to other parts of Britain, was favoured over the more isolated Pembroke Dock. The efforts of three Irish and two Welsh local authorities came to fruition in 1987, when a new company, Swansea–Cork Ferries, was established and chartered the Polish vessel *Rogalin*, renamed *Celtic Pride*, for a summer service between the two ports. The service was repeated successfully with the same ship in 1988. It was not operated in 1989 because delays in obtaining financial backing had prevented an early start to negotiations for a vessel. By the time negotiations were started, charter rates were too high. Negotiations for the 1990 season were started in good time and resulted in the charter of *Ionian Sun* from Strintzis Lines.

Ionian Sun was particularly welcome because of her past associations with Cork. It was planned to rename her *Celtic Pride II*, and that name did appear above her bridge, but officially she remained *Ionian Sun*. She commenced service on 9 May and operated until 30 September. During the main season, she made six round sailings per week, reduced to four in the shoulder seasons. Her off-service day during the peak period was Tuesday. She sailed from Cork by day and from Swansea overnight, with a scheduled ten-hour passage time. The same time had been allowed to her when she first relieved on the route in 1970, but her engines were now twenty years old and not capable of the same performance, especially in bad weather. Her normal passage time was around eleven hours. As a result, there were frequent delays and her one day off service each week was needed to catch up on her timetable.

Ionian Sun's appearance left no doubt of her former identity, but there were more changes than had been the case with *Innisfallen*. The main external alterations were the creation of additional deck space aft, in typical Greek fashion, by the extension of the Boat Deck right to the stern and of the Sun Deck further aft. The area of the Sun Deck was roughly doubled and the new area was supported on an aftwards extension of the cabin area on the Boat Deck. The Sun Deck was also fitted with side screens for part of its length. Her funnel was painted dark blue, with a black top and with two red and one white bands. Her hull was dark blue, with the blue paint one deck higher ahead of the superstructure than on the rest of the hull.

When the season was over, *Ionian Sun* returned immediately to Greece and arrived at Piraeus on 10 October, having suffered some engine problems during the voyage. She never returned, and the service in 1991 and 1992 was again operated by *Celtic Pride* (ex-*Rogalin*). However, the route's potential, demonstrated by *Ionian Sun*, had clearly impressed Strintzis Lines, which bought Swansea–Cork Ferries in 1993. Strintzis then used another of its vessels, *Superferry*, to operate an extended season between Swansea and Cork each year until 1999, when it sold the company to a local consortium.

After her return to Greece, *Ionian Sun* was used on an Aegean route from Rafina, on the Greek mainland on the eastern side of the Attica peninsula, to the Cyclades islands. In 1993, she was chartered, along with another Strintzis vessel, to the Tunisian operator Cotunav. This charter only lasted for a few months, and she then returned to the Italy–Greece ferry. In 1994 she was again in the Adriatic, operating on the shortest crossing, the budget Igoumenitsa–Corfu–Brindisi route. With an average crossing time of around eight hours, which was a little longer than her Liverpool–Dublin time, she was able to make one round sailing every day during her summer season. She remained on that service until 1998, when she returned to Rafina, again serving the Cyclades.

In 1999, she transferred back to the Adriatic, to operate a twice-daily domestic service from Killini, in the north-west of the Peloponnese, to the island of Kefalonia. In 2001, she was sold to an owner in the United Arab Emirates and renamed *Merdif*. She was put up for sale again in October 2003, and was broken up in 2004.

Cú na Mara

Although B&I carried many foot passengers on its car ferries, its management believed that it was losing passengers to the airlines because of the length of the sea crossing between Liverpool and Dublin. Accordingly, when a new type of fast craft, known as a jetfoil, was announced, B&I was keen to acquire one or more as a means of competing with the airlines.

The jetfoil was a new method of fast sea transport developed by Boeing, combining aviation and marine technology. It was an aluminium-hulled craft with steel hydrofoils fore and aft, propelled by gas turbine engines ejecting up to 150 tons of water every minute at high speed. The operations of the craft were controlled by a computer, which set the positions of flaps on the foils, in order to turn and steady the craft. It banked like an aircraft when turning, with a radius of 645 feet at the normal speed of 42 to 45 knots, and it could stop in less than 500 feet by reversing the water stream. The computer took account of sea conditions, allowing the jetfoil to be used in waves up to 12 feet high. The water inlet was situated in the after foil structure. The craft could operate conventionally, floating on its hull, but this was normally done only at the beginning and end of a sailing.

Cú na Mara (1979), pictured at speed. She was B&I's jetfoil, and only served for two seasons. (Irish Ferries)

When the jetfoil was used conventionally, a set of diesel engines was used in preference to the gas turbines, giving greater fuel economy. From stationary, the craft took about two minutes to reach a speed of 25 knots, when it rode up onto its foils.

B&I ordered a jetfoil, costing £6.6 million, in mid-1978. It also took out an option on a second jetfoil, to be exercised by the middle of 1979. The company planned to use the first jetfoil to operate a summer-only Liverpool–Dublin service, offering two round trips per day in the peak season, with a crossing time of three-and-a-half hours, only half the time taken by the car ferries. The service, which was to operate from terminals near the centre of each city, close to Pier Head and O'Connell Bridge, would provide a realistic and lower-price alternative to aircraft, starting in spring 1980. B&I hoped to charter out the craft during the winter. There were plans for the second jetfoil to be used on a new Belfast–Glasgow route. The option for a second craft was extended to autumn 1980 and then to the end of 1980, but nothing further was heard of it.

B&I's jetfoil was named *Cú na Mara* in a ceremony at Seattle in November 1979. Her name was Gaelic for '*Hound of the Sea*'. She arrived at Liverpool on 13 February 1980 on board the Swedish cargo vessel *Antonia Johnson*, and was towed to Trafalgar Dock for equipment checks before the start of trials and crew training during February and March. In the course of her training period she visited Holyhead on 11 April. She made her maiden voyage from Dublin on 25 April.

Cú na Mara had two passenger decks. The upper deck had a lounge and the lower deck had a main lounge and a forward lounge. The lounges had 250 seats in total, arranged in rows similar to an aircraft. A staircase in the centre of the craft gave access between the decks. There were also outside staircases at either side at the after end. There was a small open area with side screens aft on the upper deck, reached from the rear of the upper lounge, or from the lower deck by the outside staircases. The jetfoil was painted white, with three coloured bands below the windows on the upper deck and a single green band below the windows on the lower deck. She was heavily branded with 'B+I', 'Jetfoil' and 'Boeing' markings.

The terminals achieved the objective of proximity to both city centres. The Liverpool terminal was at the Mersey Ferries' landing stage, where special gangways were built to accommodate the jetfoil. A small building on the landing stage was used as a waiting and customs room. The Dublin terminal was at Custom House Quay. In the early season, the jetfoil sailed from Dublin at 09.00 on Mondays to Fridays, returning from Liverpool at 15.15. The Saturday sailing offered the opportunity of a long day in England, with a departure from Dublin at 07.30 and a return from Liverpool at 19.20. The Sunday sailing offered an afternoon round trip, departing from Dublin at 15.15 and from Liverpool at 19.20. The main season ran from 26 May to 8 September inclusive giving two round trips every day, with departures from Dublin at 07.05 and 15.15, and from Liverpool at 11.10 and 19.20. The late season's timetable was a combination of the two earlier periods, with two round trips on Mondays, Fridays and Saturdays, a single round trip at 09.00 from Dublin and 15.15 from Liverpool on Tuesdays, Wednesdays and Thursdays and an afternoon round trip on Sundays. This timetable offered many opportunities for passengers from Dublin to make a day excursion to Liverpool, with reasonable time ashore. The fare structure encouraged this, with day excursion and weekend tickets available at weekends outside the peak season at little more than the single fare. No similar day excursion opportunity was ever advertised to passengers from Liverpool, as the jetfoil was in Dublin for only fifty minutes after making the morning sailing from Liverpool.

There was one early upset to the service on the evening of 2 July, when *Cú na Mara*, while departing from Liverpool, struck the Isle of Man steamer *Manxman*, tied up at the landing stage. The service was suspended at once and *Cú na Mara* was berthed in Trafalgar Dock for repairs. She was due to re-enter service on 11 July, but repairs took longer than expected and required Boeing engineers to be flown from Seattle. She eventually returned to service on 13 July. *Manxman* was virtually undamaged.

The service settled down quickly and became very popular. By the end of August, 50,000 passengers had travelled on the craft. However, as autumn arrived, the weather began to take its toll on sailings. On 22 October, *Cú na Mara* was forced to turn back in force 9 wind conditions when making a third attempt to sail to Dublin from Liverpool. The service continued operating until 3 November, when it was withdrawn for the winter. Although it had originally been planned to charter out the craft for the winter, there had later been suggestions that she would operate throughout the year. It seems probable that the withdrawal was the consequence of poor passenger numbers in October. It was announced that Boeing would be modifying *Cú na Mara* during the winter to improve both her fuel consumption and her bad weather performance.

A short charter was arranged for *Cú na Mara* after her modifications had been completed. The Belgian RTM, which operated the Ostend–Dover ferry service, had ordered two jetfoils for a fast passenger service on the same route, starting at the end of May. *Cú na Mara* was chartered to RTM for two months, operating out of Dublin, to train RTM's seventy crew members. She visited Douglas on 4 May, to assess the possibility of using the harbour as a storm port in the event of severe weather conditions developing while she was at sea.

The 1981 season started on 8 May. It was clear that Boeing's alterations were expected to produce some improvement in performance, as the scheduled crossing time was reduced by fifteen minutes to three-and-a-quarter hours. This faith was justified on the first day of service, when *Cú na Mara* immediately cut the fastest eastbound crossing time to 170 minutes. In addition to the reduced crossing time, the 1971 timetable showed other modifications. As previously, the early season offered a single daily round sailing, but with a weekday departure at 12.00 from Dublin, returning at 16.00 from Liverpool. Saturday still offered a long day trip to Liverpool and on Sunday there was again a round sailing in the afternoon. Between 29 May and 18 July and again from 30 August to 5 October, there were two round trips on Fridays and Saturdays. These sailings departed from Dublin at 07.45 and 15.50, and from Liverpool at 11.45 and 19.50. For the peak summer there were again two crossings in each direction every day except Sunday. There was only one round sailing on Sundays, in the afternoon, except for three peak Sundays, when two round sailings were operated. The service was due to end on 5 October, nearly one month earlier than in the previous year.

Further mechanical problems occurred on 27 May, when a fault in a transmission assembly caused *Cú na Mara*, with 170 passengers on board, to return to Dublin. She was withdrawn from service, returning on 29 May. She was again withdrawn from service for a few days in early July, following further mechanical trouble.

During the period in which the jetfoil had been in service, B&I had been hard hit by increasing fuel prices and by a decline in tourism caused by the Northern Irish troubles. An extensive review of operations was carried out to identify economies, resulting in a decision to withdraw the jetfoil service. The final sailings took place, as scheduled, on 5 October. The jetfoil had carried around 75,000 passengers in her second season, which was similar to the number carried in her longer first season.

Cú na Mara went to Arklow to lay up. She was advertised for sale at a price around £6.6 million, similar to her original cost to B&I. It was reported she was to be chartered for one year from 8 August 1982 to a new British company, Seajet International, which planned to start a Newhaven–Dieppe jetfoil service. However, the charter went to a P&O jetfoil. A further report towards the end of 1983 stated that B&I was negotiating the sale of *Cú na Mara* to Brazilian owners. This sale did not materialise and she remained at Arklow until January 1985, when she was sold to a Japanese company for around £5 million. She was handed over in mid-January and renamed *Ginga*.

Ginga's new owners were Sado Kishen Kaisha, which operates ferry services from the main Japanese island of Honshu to the small island of Sado, off the west coast of Honshu. The island is a little larger than the Isle of Man and has many attractions for visitors, in its coastline, scenery, historic sites and buildings, flora, and traditional local festivals. The company operates services on three routes from mainland ports to the island. The principal route is from Niigata, on Honshu, to Ryotsu, on Sado Island. This is served by three jetfoils, including *Ginga*, which take one hour for the 36-mile crossing. During the peak summer, there are eleven jetfoil crossings in each direction; during most of January and February, this falls to three crossings, which can be maintained by two jetfoils. There is a railway service between Tokyo and Niigata, with the fastest train scheduled to take 100 minutes between the two places; connecting trains are advertised for many of the jetfoil sailings. Two car ferries also serve the route.

Ginga's appearance has changed little since her B&I days, although her twin exhausts have acquired casings, which have been painted in her owner's funnel colours. The jetfoils are distinguished from each other by the paint colour around their windows. *Ginga*'s colour is pink. Her passenger capacity has been increased slightly, to 260. Her normal service speed is still around 43 knots, with a maximum of 47 knots. She has remained in service with the same owners ever since, so it appears that *Ginga*'s owners have found routes where jetfoils can operate successfully.

Jetfoils proved little more successful on other North European routes. Common themes of their failures have been the lack of fuel economy, poor mechanical reliability and an inability to operate in all winter conditions around the British Isles. It seems that B&I's experiment, which could have transformed sea travel between Liverpool and Dublin, was doomed to failure. It is good to see that *Cú na Mara* has found a service on a shorter route, where her future appears more certain.

Cú na Mara became *Ginga* in 1986, and is seen in service in Japanese waters. (Sado Kisen Kaisha)

Connacht and *Leinster/Isle of Inishmore/Isle of Inishturk* (1981)

The start of the new Swansea–Cork service had been very successful and, as early as 1969, B&I considered ordering a second ship for the service and possibly also for a service to Spain/Portugal. The plan for a second vessel was dropped in 1970 but revived in 1974, when B&I expected to have a 7,000-ton ship in service by 1976. However, the order, for a vessel of 6,800 tons costing £15 million, was not placed until then. The ship was ordered from the Verolme yard at Cork, which had built *Leinster* in 1969 and three cargo vessels subsequently. It later emerged that B&I had not wished to place the order with Verolme, as other foreign builders had quoted a lower price, but had been under pressure from the Irish Government to provide work for Irish shipbuilders.

B&I had several changes of mind over its new vessel's deployment. First reports stated that she would be used on Liverpool–Dublin, which would allow either *Leinster* or *Munster* to be transferred to Swansea, to give a nightly Cork service. A later report stated that the new ship would operate to Cork, but from Pembroke Dock rather than from Swansea, as she would have too great a draught for Swansea. That statement was disputed by the Swansea Harbour Authority, which pointed out that *Stena Germanica*, whose dimensions were similar to those of the new vessel, had operated successfully from Swansea for three months. It was indisputable that such a route would reduce the sailing time by around two hours. That report also revived the suggestion that B&I would operate a Continental service, this time from Cork to Le Havre. The next report suggested that the ship would start a new Pembroke Dock–Rosslare service. The final

Connacht (1978). (Author's collection)

version was that she would operate Pembroke Dock–Cork, with *Innisfallen* moving to Liverpool and *Munster* starting Pembroke Dock–Rosslare. This version proved to be closest to reality.

The new vessel's keel was laid on 8 August 1977. Her launch was on 20 June 1978, when she received the name *Connacht*. This was in line with B&I's style, albeit an addition to the B&I repertoire. The City of Dublin Steam Packet Co. had used *Connaught*, the anglicised version of *Connacht*, and B&I had used the name *Lady Connaught*. *Connacht* was handed over on 14 January 1979, more than one week late. She sailed to Dublin before starting a promotional tour, visiting Liverpool on 17 January and London between 19 and 22 January. She then returned to Cork for two weeks for final attention to her passenger accommodation, which delayed her maiden voyage from Cork to Swansea from 24 January to 7 February. Her final cost was £16.5 million.

Connacht had a capacity for 1,500 passengers and around 350 cars or thirty-nine freight units. These figures were a substantial increase on the earlier ships; one improvement permitted by the extra space was the provision of more cabins above the car deck. Passengers were accommodated on five decks, three above and two below the two car decks. The Boat Deck amidships had special and de-luxe two-berth cabins with private facilities, with an observation lounge aft. The Service Deck had a cocktail lounge forward, with a restaurant immediately aft. Both of these rooms extended across the full width of the ship. Amidships, there was one lounge on either side of the vessel, with a full width cafeteria aft and a full width bar at the extreme after end. The Upper Deck was immediately above the car decks, with four-berth cabins in its forward half, convertible to day cabins with seats for six adults, an entrance hall including a shop and a purser's office amidships, and a full width television room aft. The two passenger decks below the car decks contained both two- and four-berth cabins.

Connacht had the dark blue hull introduced by the previous car ferries. Her funnel used the colour scheme introduced in 1975, which was white with a black top and with B&I's emblem 'B+I LINE' in white with a blue shadow. 'B+I' was in large letters and 'LINE' was in smaller letters underneath.

Connacht's use of Swansea was only a temporary measure, pending the start of Cork–Pembroke Dock in May. She carried out a berthing trial at Pembroke Dock on 15 May, before her final departure from Swansea on 20 May. Her first service arrival at Pembroke Dock was on 22 May. Pembroke Dock was a former naval base, which was trying to attract merchant shipping. Apart from its proximity to Ireland, its principal advantages were deep water and a sheltered approach through Milford Haven, which had long been recognised by major oil companies who had oil terminals and refineries there. Cork and Waterford services had operated from Neyland (also known as New Milford), on the northern shore of the Haven, from 1856 until the early 1900s. The City of Cork Steam Packet Co. took over New Milford–Cork from the Great Western Railway in 1876 and operated that service until 1906, when its Welsh terminal was moved to Fishguard, on completion of the harbour there.

During the main summer season, *Connacht* operated a round trip every day, with departures from Cork at 09.30 and from Pembroke Dock at 22.00. Outside the main season, *Connacht* gave a round trip from Cork on the Sunday and a single overnight sailing each night on the remaining six days. The daytime sailing was scheduled to take eight hours, but an extra hour was allowed overnight. *Leinster* had been scheduled to take ten hours for the crossing between Swansea and Cork, so this shorter crossing contributed to greater reliability in bad weather.

B&I appears to have been highly satisfied with *Connacht* and reports that a sister was to be ordered first appeared around the time *Connacht* entered service. Confirmation of the order for the new ship, also to be built by the Verolme yard at Cork, at a cost of around £20 million, followed soon afterwards. Her keel was laid on 26 November 1979. It was stated that the new vessel was to be delivered in 1981 and would be the first of a new generation of ferries planned for Liverpool–Dublin.

Connacht received her first overhaul early in 1980, and was covered by *Innisfallen*. From 13 February, the chartered *Espresso Olbia* replaced *Innisfallen*. On her return from overhaul, *Connacht* relieved *Leinster* on Liverpool–Dublin. *Connacht* was due to resume her normal route on 23 March, but was trapped at Liverpool by a dock strike. *Leinster* filled the gap until the end of the strike, allowing *Connacht* to re-enter service on 2 April.

The summer of 1980 was disappointing for B&I, despite a growth of 10 per cent in passenger numbers. B&I had been hoping for a much greater improvement, with its Cork service well established at Pembroke Dock and its new Rosslare service, operated by the chartered *Viking III*, contributing for the first time. The major shortfall was on the southern services. After the 1980 summer season, on 29 September, *Connacht* was moved to Liverpool–Dublin and replaced by *Leinster*. Not long after she was transferred,

Leinster (1981), the last passenger vessel built for B&I in the colours introduced in 1986. (Irish Ferries)

Leinster was renamed *Innisfallen*, to release her former name for the new car ferry, which was launched on 7 November.

The 1980/81 Liverpool–Dublin winter service was covered by *Connacht* and *Munster*. There was no spare vessel, so the service was maintained by a single ship during overhaul periods. *Connacht* received a very brief overhaul only and operated a Pembroke Dock–Rosslare sailing on 21 January, before returning to Liverpool–Dublin on 22 January.

Leinster's entry to Liverpool–Dublin was scheduled for June 1981, but her delivery was about one month behind schedule. She entered service with an overnight crossing from Liverpool on 3 July. *Leinster* had cost £23.5 million, £3.5 million more than the figure originally expected and £7 million more than *Connacht's* cost only two years previously. She was virtually identical to *Connacht*, but there were a few internal alterations based on experience with *Connacht*. Her passenger and vehicle capacities were identical to her sister's.

The Liverpool–Dublin service was now at a peak in terms of ships, with two large modern sister ships. Unfortunately, the schedule did not make full use of the vessels' potential. There was a sailing every night, but daytime crossings were only made on two days each week, with no increase during the summer. The departure time of the overnight sailings was 22.15 from both ports; the daytime sailings departed from Liverpool at 12.00 and Dublin at 11.00. Overnight crossing times were eight-and-three-quarter hours, while the daytime crossing took seven hours. The ships had been designed with less beam than normal for similar vessels, to allow them to fit the Waterloo entrance lock at Liverpool. They used Liverpool's Trafalgar Dock terminal and B&I's Dublin Ferryport.

Connacht was relieved for her annual overhaul in January 1982 by *Munster*. For the first time, this overhaul was carried out at Liverpool, rather than in Ireland. B&I insisted that the decision had been made on commercial grounds; after this, overhauls of the B&I fleet were often carried out in Britain. *Leinster* received her guarantee overhaul at Cork.

In an effort to improve the utilisation of the two vessels, which spent daytime in port for five days every week, B&I decided that in 1982 the vessel that had arrived at Dublin in the morning would operate a round sailing to Holyhead, before sailing back to Liverpool overnight. The vessel at Liverpool would remain inactive during the day. B&I had never previously operated to Holyhead. The new service was due to start on 1 March 1982, but there was a week's delay to allow discussions between B&I and Sealink to be completed. *Connacht* made a trial run to Holyhead on 6 March, but was denied access by Sealink employees at Holyhead, who bitterly resented any attempt to encroach upon Sealink's exclusive use of the port for Irish services. *Connacht* returned to Dublin without berthing. There were repeat performances when *Connacht* made the first commercial sailing on 8 March and next day when *Leinster* made her first crossing. In the meantime, *Munster* had blocked the entrance to Dun Laoghaire harbour on 8 March, preventing Sealink's *St David* from berthing. Both companies' services were then suspended until a settlement could be agreed. After a satisfactory conclusion to the discussions had been reached, *Connacht* sailed to Holyhead on 5 April to carry out berthing trials and *Leinster* made the first successful commercial crossing on 6 April. The new service had departure times of 11.35 from Dublin, arriving at Holyhead at 15.30, and 16.45 from Holyhead, arriving back at Dublin at 20.15. The berth at Holyhead at first varied between the railway berth in the inner harbour, used by Sealink's vessels, and the Salt Island berth, which had been used by the first Sealink car ferries while the former mail-boats, *Cambria* and *Hibernia*, were still in service. Later, B&I's service settled down at the railway berth.

After all the problems of getting the new service started, traffic was slow to build up. This was worsened by an officers' strike on 1 June, which brought all B&I's services to a standstill for three days. At one time, volumes were so poor that B&I was negotiating the charter of *Connacht* to Sealink to replace *St Edmund*, which was away in the Falklands, on Harwich–Hook of Holland. Fortunately, traffic picked up during the season. A minor interruption occurred in October, when fishermen blockaded Irish ports for twenty-four hours. *Leinster* and *Connacht* were both trapped in Dublin by the blockade.

The Irish Sea can suffer extreme weather conditions, especially in winter. However, a record was set on 1 February 1983, when *Leinster* was prevented from making the evening sailing to Dublin by hurricane-force winds. She was trapped in Trafalgar Dock for over sixteen hours, with 300 passengers on board. The conditions were so severe that it was not even possible to use a gangway for passengers to go ashore.

Both ships received their annual overhauls in February and March 1983. *Innisfallen*, which was available because her Pembroke Dock–Cork service had been closed, maintained the services at their normal frequency. In a reference to the building of *Connacht* and *Leinster*, B&I stated that one reason for the closure had been the company's financial position, brought about by the Irish Government's insistence that those ships must be built in an Irish shipyard, when they could have been built abroad at a lower cost.

The most notable feature of 1983 was the announcement of the closure of the Waterloo river entrance at Liverpool. The decline in the number of coastal vessels had reduced the use of the entrance and the termination of P&O's Belfast service, and the transfer of most Dublin cargo traffic to Pandoro/B&I's joint ro-ro service from Fleetwood, sealed its fate. This left B&I's two car ferries as the only regular users of the entrance. It was extremely disappointing for B&I, as it owned two almost new ships whose narrow beam, which reduced their earning capacity, had been designed specifically to allow them to use that entrance. A new berth was allocated at Brocklebank Branch Dock, close to Belfast Car Ferries' new terminal at Langton Dock; an existing dock shed was converted to provide a new terminal building. Unfortunately, the new terminal was inferior to the Trafalgar Dock terminal, which had won a design award when it was built in 1969, so B&I at first resisted the transfer. After agreement had been reached, *Connacht* made the final sailing from Trafalgar Dock on 18 October; *Leinster* arrived at the new terminal next morning. The new terminal was about 2 miles closer to the sea, but no reduction in journey times was possible, because the ships used the Langton river entrance whose lock operated very slowly.

The 1984 overhauls were covered by Irish Continental Line's *Saint Patrick II*, which was better known at Liverpool as the relief vessel for Belfast Car Ferries' Liverpool–Belfast service. She also covered the Holyhead sailings. During these overhauls, the names of the two routes operated by the car ferries were painted on both ships' hulls. *Leinster's* time away from her normal routes was extended, because she covered *Innisfallen* on Pembroke Dock–Rosslare during March. It was her first time on that service and she made a most favourable impression.

On 2 May 1984, *Connacht* left her berth in Liverpool to take part in a parade of ships to celebrate the opening by the Queen of the International Garden Festival in Liverpool. She was immediately astern of *Saint Colum I*, which headed the procession. Afterwards, *Connacht* returned to dock.

At the end of June, Liverpool–Dublin received a short-term boost when a strike by Sealink employees at Holyhead prevented B&I from landing its passengers. Both vessels made daytime sailings between Liverpool and Dublin for the duration of the strike, in addition to their normal overnight crossings. Despite this, rumours began to grow that B&I wished to abandon Liverpool completely. The rumours were fuelled on 7 November, when *Leinster* carried out berthing trials at Dun Laoghaire. A spokesman for B&I insisted that the object of the exercise was simply to test the suitability of Dun Laoghaire's facilities to handle B&I vessels in an emergency, but the growing scale of B&I's losses made it plain that drastic remedial action was needed. The probable reason for the trial at Dun Laoghaire became apparent later.

Connacht's and *Leinster's* 1985 overhauls were undertaken in Liverpool. Summer 1985 saw further changes, made to improve B&I's finances. A pooling agreement was reached with Sealink, under which Sealink would not operate a second vessel between Holyhead and Dun Laoghaire during the summer, as was its normal practice. Additional sailings from Holyhead would be provided between 14 June and 8 September by switching *Connacht* to a full-time Dublin–Holyhead service, making two round sailings each day. *Leinster* would remain on Liverpool–Dublin, with an overnight sailing from Liverpool at the usual time of 22.15 and a daytime sailing from Dublin at 09.00. It is likely that the unbalanced nature of this service caused a further reduction in the numbers using

Liverpool–Dublin. Economies were also made in crew numbers, resulting in a twenty-four-hour strike by *Connacht's* crew on 12 July. From 9 September, the service reverted to the previous pattern.

The pooling agreement with Sealink was extended further for 1986, with a plan for B&I to withdraw from Dublin and base its Liverpool and Holyhead services at Dun Laoghaire. B&I and Sealink would share revenue from the two services. Both B&I ferries would be refurbished at a total cost of £5 million. There were also to be major changes in the Rosslare services. The reason for *Leinster's* berthing trial at Dun Laoghaire in November 1984 was now clear. The announcement of the changes was met by a strike at the end of November 1985, which resulted in the delay of the transfer to Dun Laoghaire until after summer 1986. This delay was instrumental in allowing sufficient time for other developments, and so the transfer never happened.

A condition of the pooling agreement with Sealink was that a B&I vessel would be used to cover Sealink's Holyhead–Dun Laoghaire service for five weeks during January and February 1986, while the regular vessel, *St Columba*, was being overhauled. *Leinster* was allocated to this duty from 7 January, but her crew refused to work the route unless they had parity of terms with Sealink's employees. *St Columba's* crew came out in sympathy and both companies' Dublin and Dun Laoghaire services were suspended. A return to work was agreed on 10 January, on condition that B&I crews did not have to operate on Sealink services.

The 1986 overhauls of *Leinster* and *Connacht* included the refurbishment previously announced. Each overhaul was carried out in Liverpool, taking six weeks. *Innisfallen*, as usual, covered for the regular vessels. *Leinster* was the first to be refurbished. The main changes were made to the Service Deck and the Upper Deck. The area at the forward end of the Service Deck, which had previously housed the restaurant and cocktail bar, now contained a self-service cafeteria. The former cafeteria area, further aft on the same deck, had been converted to a carvery restaurant and a disco bar. The Upper Deck had undergone the greatest transformation, with its cabins removed and replaced by a rest lounge with Pullman-style seats and a lounge bar on the port side. A cinema was added amidships and a bureau de change in the entrance area. The TV room was converted into a large duty-free shop. To complete the transformation, the deck was renamed Entrance Deck, although it later reverted to Upper Deck. The cabins on the Upper Deck had originally been provided in response to complaints about the old car ferries that all the cabins, except for a few de-luxe cabins, had been below the car deck. This refurbishment recreated the same situation and indicated clearly that B&I could not see a long-term future for its overnight Liverpool–Dublin service. The long overnight Pembroke Dock–Cork service had already been abandoned and it was only on these long crossings that passengers gained much benefit from cabins. *Leinster* still had berths for 256 passengers in the cabins below the car decks, in addition to the berths in the fifteen de-luxe cabins on the Boat Deck and this was felt to be sufficient for a four-hour crossing.

In addition to her internal refurbishment, *Leinster* received B&I's striking new colour scheme. Her funnel colours were white and dark blue, separated by two diagonal blue stripes; the hull and after superstructure were dark blue, while the forward and amidships superstructure was white. The arrangement was finished off with a white fleet title and route information on the hull and two blue horizontal stripes sweeping up aft to separate the dark blue and white.

Leinster returned to service on 14 April 1986 and *Connacht* was then withdrawn for similar alterations. She returned to service on 14 June. The summer service in 1986 was similar to that of the previous year, except that the two ships switched round, with *Leinster* operating to Holyhead and *Connacht* to Liverpool. Bad weather over the August Bank Holiday disrupted sailings, with consequent problems for returning holidaymakers; *Leinster* missed two round trips in three days and *Connacht* was running eight hours late at one time. The service reverted to the winter pattern on 8 September.

By the autumn, it was clear that B&I would not transfer from Dublin to Dun Laoghaire. In addition, Dublin Corporation had put forward a proposal for a unified ferry port in Dublin, to which it was suggested Sealink's Dun Laoghaire services should be transferred. B&I was considering the replacement of either *Connacht* or *Leinster* with a ferry capable of carrying eighty freight units and 400 passengers. However, B&I's problems were far from over. A stoppage, which resulted in the loss of a round sailing between Dublin and Holyhead, took place on 13 October. Later, 370 redundancies were announced. The response from the unions was to threaten further industrial action. To add to B&I's woes at this time, on 21 October *Connacht* collided with the cargo vessel *Saphir* when both vessels were arriving at Dublin. *Connacht* was delayed for twelve hours for repairs to her bow visor.

Connacht (1978), seen in later B&I colours. (Irish Ferries)

B&I had agreed with Sealink that *Leinster* would be made available from 12 January, to cover the overhauls of *St Brendan* and *St Columba*. This was prevented by a strike of B&I's officers, which also affected the company's cargo and ro-ro vessels. The strike lasted for almost two months, with sailings not resuming until 11 March. The Holyhead service was suspended from 19 March to allow each ship in turn to be withdrawn for a quick overhaul at Dublin. *Connacht* was first to be withdrawn, but celebrated her return by taking thirty hours, in very rough weather, to complete her first crossing to Liverpool, which left Dublin on 27 March. She spent much of that time sheltering off Anglesey and the Isle of Man. The full service resumed on 5 April; the summer service was two weeks shorter than in the previous two years. As *Innisfallen* had been sold in autumn 1986, B&I had no vessel available as its contribution to Sealink/B&I's joint Fishguard–Rosslare service in 1987, so *Senlac* was chartered from French Railways to cover the summer service until 12 September and *Saint Colum I* was chartered from Belfast Ferries over Christmas and New Year. The latter vessel ended B&I's participation in Fishguard–Rosslare on 12 January 1988.

Despite all the actions taken to improve B&I's financial position, its losses continued and a drastic new plan was produced to save the company from liquidation. It was proposed that Liverpool–Dublin would be closed, with all crossings from Dublin using Holyhead. This would require only one ship, which would free one of the two ferries, probably *Connacht* as she was the older of the pair, for sale. The funds from this sale would be used to pay redundancy to around 600 employees. The Fleetwood–Dublin ro-ro service, operated jointly by B&I's *Tipperary* and Pandoro's *Ibex*, would transfer its English terminal to Liverpool. Finally, the pooling arrangement with Sealink on Holyhead–Dun Laoghaire and B&I's participation in the Fishguard–Rosslare service would be terminated, being replaced by a reinstated Pembroke Dock–Rosslare service. The closure plans were resisted strongly by B&I's employees, but a threat by the Irish Government to withdraw all state aid to B&I forced them to accept the plan.

Once agreement had been reached, events moved quickly and the final sailings between Liverpool and Dublin were scheduled to take place on 10 January 1988. These sailings were to be given westbound by *Connacht* and eastbound by *Leinster*, but bad weather over New Year disrupted the schedule. This worsened on 5 January when *Connacht* developed engine trouble and her departure from Dublin was delayed from its usual time of 22.00 until 02.15. Her crossing to Liverpool operated on only two of her four engines and took almost twelve hours. *Leinster* had made a normal westbound crossing from Liverpool, arriving in Dublin on the morning of 6 January, and was immediately switched to operate twice daily between Dublin and Holyhead. *Connacht* remained in Liverpool for her engines to be repaired and then moved south to reopen Pembroke Dock–Rosslare, which had been closed two years previously.

These events marked the end of a long chapter in the long history of the Liverpool–Dublin passenger service, which had been operated by B&I since 1919. Both Irish Continental Line and Sealink showed interest in starting a service from Liverpool to Dublin or Dun Laoghaire, respectively, and B&I briefly considered resuming a seasonal Liverpool–Dublin service. However, Sealink acted quickly and employed a spare car ferry, *Earl William*, on a service that started on 25 April. This blocked any prospect of a resumption of a B&I service.

Leinster immediately took up the Holyhead schedule, with sailings from Holyhead at 05.30 and 17.15, and from Dublin at 11.45 and 23.00. B&I was not happy with these times and campaigned for them to be brought forward. *Connacht*'s times on Pembroke Dock–Rosslare were 02.15 and 14.15 from Pembroke Dock and 08.30 and 20.30 from Rosslare. Her round sailing in daytime was advertised only for the summer period, but heavy traffic meant that she frequently operated daytime sailings outside that period.

Connacht did not operate from Pembroke Dock for long, as she was sent to Rendsburg during March for her annual overhaul and extensive engine repairs. Germany was chosen for this overhaul because her engines were German. On her return, she relieved *Leinster* at Holyhead for overhaul at Dublin. *Connacht*'s six-week absence from Pembroke Dock was covered by chartering DFDS's *Prins Hamlet*. Completion of the overhaul programme allowed *Connacht* to return to Pembroke Dock for the summer, during which she was sold to Brittany Ferries, with delivery at the beginning of October. Irish Continental Line's *Saint Patrick II* replaced her at Pembroke Dock.

The changes made in B&I finally produced good financial results in 1988, when it produced a trading profit in the first three months. In the year, it made a trading profit of £1.8 million, although this was swallowed up by interest on money owed to the Irish Government. Its debt was so large that there was no prospect of it being cleared by trading profits, so a financial reconstruction of the company was needed.

For her annual overhaul in 1989, *Leinster* followed in the footsteps of *Connacht*, with a six-week visit to Germany between 14 January and 1 March. This overhaul also included major work on her engines. Her Dublin–Holyhead sailings were covered by chartering *The Viking* from Sally Line. Soon after *Leinster*'s return, she lost a daytime round sailing between Dublin and Holyhead on 15 March, when her crew refused to lash down lorries on her car deck during an industrial dispute.

Leinster enjoyed an uneventful summer on Holyhead–Dublin, with good summer loadings even on the 05.30 departure from Holyhead. B&I continued to press Sealink to improve its slots at Holyhead and the Irish Office of Public Works, which owned Dun Laoghaire harbour, added its weight to the demand.

Pembroke Dock–Rosslare had been operated during summer 1989 by *Earl Harold*, chartered from Sealink. When her charter ended, a Faroese vessel, *Norröna*, was brought in to replace her. During storms on 16 December 1989, B&I's linkspan at Rosslare was torn from its shore mountings and deposited upside down in the harbour. Pembroke Dock–Rosslare was suspended and then, from 20 December, replaced by a special Dublin–Pembroke Dock service, operated by *Norröna*. Since the increased distance involved a sailing time of ten hours, *Norröna* was unable to carry out the daily double round sailing advertised from 21 December. The surplus traffic was diverted from Pembroke Dock to Holyhead where, because *Leinster* was already fully booked for the Christmas rush, *Lady of Mann* was chartered from the Isle of Man Steam Packet Co. to carry the diverted traffic, making two daily round sailings to Dublin.

Munster (1970). She was built for service from Harwich to Germany, and chartered by B&I in 1990-92. (Irish Ferries)

B&I's trading profit in 1989 showed a further increase, to £3 million. The company was so pleased with this improvement that it announced plans to introduce two jumbo ferries, each with capacity for 1,500 passengers and 400 cars, by 1990/91. As with the early announcements over the building of *Connacht* and *Leinster*, this statement would prove to be reasonably accurate over the nature of the vessels, but optimistic over timing.

The pressure on Sealink to improve B&I's slots at Holyhead produced results. New timings, around one-and-a-half hours earlier, were introduced from 15 January 1990, although they were still about two hours later than B&I had originally wanted. The Holyhead timings clashed with those of *St Columba*, so *Leinster* changed from the railway berth in the inner harbour to the Salt Island berth. This new berth, which had sometimes been used in the early days of B&I's Holyhead service, suffered from fewer tidal restrictions than the railway berth. However, it was close to the channel leading to the inner harbour, so any ship berthed there was affected by the wash from Sealink vessels approaching or leaving the inner harbour.

Leinster was accustomed to the rough conditions of the Irish Sea in winter and to the delays and cancellations brought about by those conditions. A more unusual delay occurred on 31 January 1990, when she and the Holyhead lifeboat stood by Sealink's *St Columba*, when she was disabled by a fire in her port engine. At the time, there was a full gale, with a 30-foot swell on the sea.

The Pembroke Dock–Rosslare service had not enjoyed the presence of either a B&I vessel or any regular ship since the departure of *Connacht* in October 1988. Late in 1989, B&I arranged to charter a Singapore-registered vessel, *Cruise Muhibah*, for the route.

Unlike the previous charters, this was a long-term charter for two years, with an option to purchase or to extend the charter for a further three years. The vessel had been built in 1970 for Prins Ferries as *Prins Oberon* and had sailed between Harwich and Bremerhaven before being sold to Singapore. She was refitted at Dublin, where she was re-registered, repainted in B&I colours and renamed *Munster*. She was the last B&I vessel to be given a traditional B&I name. After her refit, she took up Pembroke Dock–Rosslare on 27 April 1990. This allowed *Norröna* to move north to relieve *Leinster* for her annual overhaul at Dublin. Unfortunately, *Norröna* was unsuccessful on the northern route and experienced great difficulty berthing at Salt Island.

The Irish Government had owned B&I since 1965. The first steps towards privatisation took place in 1990, with discussions between Irish Continental Group and B&I over a possible merger. Later in the year, the Irish Government invited three companies, Irish Continental Group, P&O and the Danish DFDS, to tender for the possible purchase of B&I. The trade unions were opposed to any privatisation and the problem of the loans made to B&I by the Irish Government had to be resolved before any sale could take place. It would be well into 1991 before a decision was taken.

During 1990, *Leinster* suffered occasional interruptions to her schedule. She lost two days towards the end of April and another four days in early May, because of yet more industrial action. A potentially more serious event occurred on 22 November, when she suffered an engine failure while departing from Dublin on the morning sailing to Holyhead. She lost power and drifted, touched bottom, was holed and finished with her bows through the catwalk leading from the berth. Tugs assisted *Leinster* back to the berth to discharge her passengers. Later in the day she entered dry-dock, resuming service on 28 November.

Leinster was withdrawn from service for her annual overhaul in Dublin from 12 February 1991 and replaced by *Munster*, transferred from Pembroke Dock. *Norröna* was again chartered, this time to cover for *Munster*, which was no more successful at Holyhead than *Norröna* had been in 1990. She suffered from draught limitations at Salt Island, did not fit the linkspan properly and was unable to use a passenger gangway. She needed a bus to transfer passengers between her vehicle deck and the railway station.

On 28 February 1991, Irish Continental Group signed a memorandum of agreement with the Irish Government to buy B&I for £6.5 million. The agreement was conditional on the Irish Government writing off B&I's debts and on its assets being worth at least £700,000. B&I's employees were opposed to the sale and threatened further strike action, which duly took place on 18 April, when all services were suspended. Negotiations to complete the sale were protracted and it did not become effective until 1 January 1992, by which time the purchase price had become £8.5 million and the amount to be written off had exceeded £36 million. Under the agreement, Irish Continental Group committed itself to spending £30 million over five years on an improved vessel for Pembroke Dock–Rosslare and on increasing *Leinster*'s capacity.

Irish Ferries had started to implement their plans for B&I long before the sale had been completed. They believed that *Munster* had no future with B&I and a group travelled to Germany to inspect Fred Olsen's *Braemar*, but she was sold to other buyers.

Isle of Innisfree (1986) approaching Holyhead in October 1993. She was built as a Danish ferry and chartered by B&I in 1992-95. (Author)

Efforts to find a replacement for *Munster*, whose initial charter was due to finish at the end of March 1992, continued into 1992.

The first sign of the new ownership came in February 1992, when *Saint Patrick II* covered *Leinster*'s overhaul. *Saint Patrick II* relieved *Munster*, which moved north to relieve *Leinster* between 14 February and 2 March, while *Leinster* was overhauled at Birkenhead. *Munster* was no more successful at Holyhead in 1992 than she had been previously.

Munster returned briefly to Pembroke Dock–Rosslare, but a successor had been identified and chartered. The new vessel was *Stena Nautica*, which had been built in 1986 for Danish State Railways as *Niels Klim* and sold in 1991 to Stena Line. She was taken on a two-year charter, with an option to renew. She was refitted in Denmark, where she was named *Isle of Innisfree*. This name was the winner in a competition to choose a new name and marked a break with B&I's traditional style. *Isle of Innisfree* also introduced a further change of hull colour for B&I, with much of the previous dark blue area of the hull being painted white, leaving three lines and a triangular area of dark blue at the after end of the superstructure, matching the colours on the funnel. The name of the owners and the two routes, which had previously been in white on the dark blue background, became dark blue on a white background. The new ship joined Pembroke Dock–Rosslare on 31 March. *Munster* sailed to Dublin for a long lay-up, which ended in a tow to Norway, followed by service in the Mediterranean and finally conversion into a floating casino.

Leinster continued in service at Holyhead, but suffered problems there in 1992 because of changes introduced by Sealink. *Leinster* and *St Columba* had similar schedules and the departing *St Columba*'s wash affected *Leinster* at the Salt Island berth, requiring loading or unloading to be suspended. The problem became more serious when Sealink introduced a second ship, *Stena Cambria*. Sealink's departures bracketed B&I's departures, giving Sealink the first and last sailings from Holyhead in the early hours of the morning and in the afternoon. As a result, B&I's vessel was passed by both Sealink vessels and operations were suspended twice, causing severe disruption to schedules. B&I complained to the European Commission, which ruled that Sealink should alter its timetables. The two companies then reached an agreement to modify Sealink's timetable to give B&I thirty minutes clear time to complete its own operations.

B&I's next plan for *Leinster* involved fitting her with a complete new deck accommodating 120 cars and leaving more space for freight on the existing decks. It appears that this would have involved raising her superstructure to make room for the extra deck. The plan was soon abandoned in favour of introducing a larger ship, using a new berth in Holyhead's outer harbour when it was ready. As an interim measure, it was decided to transfer *Isle of Innisfree* to Holyhead and *Leinster* to Pembroke Dock.

Leinster was withdrawn on 18 March 1993 for her annual overhaul in Dublin and replaced by Irish Ferries' *Saint Killian II*. She was too long for the Salt Island berth, so became the first user of the new outer harbour linkspan. During her overhaul, *Leinster* was given a £2.5 million refit, involving the construction of motorists' and club-class lounges on the Upper Deck. These lounges replaced the former rest lounge, which had itself been created only in 1986. *Leinster's* hull was repainted to match that of *Isle of Innisfree* and her name received the same treatment, becoming *Isle of Inishmore*. So passed into history B&I's final 'Irish Province' name. *Isle of Inishmore* resumed service between Dublin and Holyhead on 4 April, remaining on that route for just one month. She made her final sailing on 3 May and then swapped places with *Isle of Innisfree*, taking over Pembroke Dock–Rosslare on 4 May.

Isle of Inishmore proved herself reliable on her new route, but was unable to cope with all the potential coach and freight business. B&I was looking for a replacement, and *Isle of Inishmore* was inspected by French and Egyptian interests, but no sale resulted. On 8 September, she developed problems with her port propeller. The shaft became twisted, resulting in increased vibration, so both port engines had to be switched off. She returned to Rosslare and then went to Birkenhead for dry-docking. She resumed service on 13 September. On 10 October, a passenger was reported missing overboard from *Isle of Inishmore* on passage to Rosslare. Two lifeboats and a helicopter assisted in the unsuccessful search for the woman, until it was called off at 22.30.

Isle of Inishmore was again in the news on 26 January 1994 when, in severe weather, a lorry overturned on the vehicle deck, causing some damage to the ship. She was immediately withdrawn from service and went to Birkenhead for an early overhaul. On the following day, B&I's Holyhead berth was damaged by *Isle of Innisfree* and became unusable. *Isle of Innisfree* was too large for any other berth at Holyhead. She was immediately sent south, to take over the suspended Pembroke Dock service and Holyhead–Dublin was suspended until *Isle of Inishmore* became available on 7 February, after her overhaul had been completed. She was able to use the Salt Island berth, but she operated a revised timetable to avoid clashes with Sealink's catamaran, *Stena Sea Lynx,*

Isle of Inishmore (1981) approaching Pembroke Dock in August 1995, in Irish Ferries' colours. (Author)

which had become the regular user of that berth. When repairs to the outer harbour berth had been completed, B&I's two vessels switched back to their normal routes on 27 February.

Isle of Innisfree was too slow for Holyhead–Dublin and B&I looked unsuccessfully for a vessel to replace her for 1995. Rather than continue with a search indefinitely, B&I placed an order with a Dutch shipbuilder for a new vessel costing £46 million, with delivery in time for the 1995 season. The new vessel was to have more space for freight, at the expense of some passenger accommodation. There was also an option to order a second ship on similar terms.

The second major change in 1994 was to phase out B&I's name and replace it with Irish Ferries, which was used for the Continental services. The company's brochures and timetables for 1994 referred to B&I as 'an Irish Ferries company'. The change of name became effective on 1 January 1995. *Isle of Inishmore*'s registered ownership did not change, although the two new vessels subsequently built for the former B&I services were owned by Irish Continental Group. Shortly after the name change, *Isle of Inishmore* was re-liveried in Irish Ferries' colours. Her funnel became dark green with a black top and with a large Irish Ferries houseflag outlined in white over the dark green. The flag was a white shamrock on broad diagonal bands of light blue, green and dark blue, with white lines separating the bands. Her hull became white with green boot topping and displayed 'IRISH FERRIES' in dark blue and a wave made up from the same three coloured bands as on the houseflag. *Isle of Innisfree* did not receive the new colours, as she was due to be handed back to her owners in March 1995 but, during December, B&I's name on her hull was painted out, leaving the two routes in place.

The plan for the early months of 1995 was that *Saint Patrick II* would relieve *Isle of Inishmore* on Pembroke Dock–Rosslare at the end of January. When *Isle of Innisfree*'s charter ended in March, she would be replaced by *Saint Patrick II* at Holyhead until the new ship, which was named *Isle of Innisfree* when she was launched on 27 January 1995, entered service in May. These plans were, however, changed significantly. *Isle of Inishmore* started her overhaul at Falmouth on 2 February and was replaced, as planned, by *Saint Patrick II*. On 20 February, *Isle of Inishmore* resumed service on Holyhead–Dublin and *Isle of Innisfree* returned to Pembroke Dock, to complete her service with Irish Ferries on the route for which she had originally been chartered. Some minor damage to Holyhead's outer linkspan was caused by *Isle of Inishmore*, arriving in a gale on the morning of 6 March.

Saint Patrick II, which had in the meantime been overhauled, took over Holyhead–Dublin on 14 March, to allow *Isle of Inishmore* to switch to Pembroke Dock–Rosslare on 15 March, when *Isle of Innisfree*'s charter ended. *Saint Patrick II* experienced major operational problems at Holyhead, culminating in a fire in an engine room exhaust on 19 March. She was repaired at Birkenhead and the two ships were then switched again, with *Isle of Inishmore* taking up service on Holyhead–Dublin on 23 March. She remained on that route until the new *Isle of Innisfree* entered service. For most of her time at Holyhead, she used the outer harbour berth, but she switched to the railway berth in the inner harbour for about a month to facilitate alterations to the other berth necessary to accommodate *Isle of Innisfree*. This was the first time for nearly six years that she had used the railway berth. On 27 April, she developed problems with her bow thrust unit while she was leaving Dublin. She required this unit to assist her in berthing in the inner harbour and so was forced to lie off Holyhead until 18.20, when she berthed with the aid of a local tug. The bow thrust unit continued to give trouble, so she was withdrawn from service on 9 May, when she made Irish Ferries' final ever departure from Holyhead's railway berth, which was due to be blocked off by port developments. She was then dry-docked at Dublin and resumed service on 13 May, using Holyhead's outer harbour berth. The new *Isle of Innisfree* entered service on 23 May and *Isle of Inishmore* was at last able to return south and release *Saint Patrick II* for her summer Continental service.

Although Irish Ferries did not take up its option for a near sister to *Isle of Innisfree*, it did continue its negotiations with her builders for a second vessel. On 26 September, the company announced an order for a second new superferry, costing £60 million. The vessel's capacity was greater than that of *Isle of Innisfree* in all areas and she would carry a higher proportion of passengers, as *Isle of Innisfree*'s passenger accommodation had proved to be insufficient at peak periods. She would enter service during 1997 between Holyhead and Dublin, which would result in *Isle of Innisfree* being transferred to Pembroke Dock–Rosslare and *Isle of Inishmore* being withdrawn.

After an uninterrupted summer at Pembroke Dock, *Isle of Inishmore* was withdrawn for four days in September for rudder repairs at Swansea. She was covered by *Saint Patrick II*, which had finished her summer Continental sailings. *Isle of Inishmore* was damaged when she grounded at Rosslare during gales on 24 October, and was towed free early next morning by a Cork tug. The damage required attention at Falmouth, so *Saint Patrick II* made a further appearance on Pembroke Dock–Rosslare, until *Isle of Inishmore* returned on 15 November. During her time at Falmouth, there were widespread rumours that she had been sold for service in Canada. The sale did not materialise, as her proposed new service had depended on the people of Quebec Province voting for independence from the rest of Canada, but the vote went the other way.

The work carried out on *Isle of Inishmore* at Falmouth did not include her annual overhaul, which was undertaken at Birkenhead in February 1996. *Saint Patrick II* again covered her. This year was free of the route changes characteristic of 1995 and *Isle of Inishmore* operated regularly from Pembroke Dock. She was due to be withdrawn at the end of September, being replaced by *Saint Patrick II* in anticipation of the transfer of *Isle of Innisfree* in 1997, and it seemed likely that she would be sold to other Canadian buyers. However, the sale fell through because a grant towards the cost of a terminal was not approved. Irish Ferries' plans changed with the announcement that its services from Ireland to the Continent would be closed for winter 1996/97; *Saint Patrick II* would be laid up at Le Havre and advertised for sale. As a result, *Isle of Inishmore* remained in service, but her name was changed to *Isle of Inishturk* on 5 November, to free her name for the new vessel. *Isle of Inishmore* was launched on 9 October and delivered in January 1997; she entered service between Dublin and Holyhead on 2 March. *Isle of Innisfree* transferred to the southern route, commencing on 22 March. *Isle of Inishturk* was then withdrawn from service and laid up at Le Havre with *Saint Patrick II*. She was sold to the Canadian Government.

The first of the two ships, *Connacht*, was sold in 1988 to Brittany Ferries. She was handed over in October and sent to Papenburg, Germany, for a refit that included fitting thirty-six cabins above the car deck. This restored some of the cabins that B&I had removed in 1986, gave her 471 berths and made her more suitable for overnight service. The rest of her passenger accommodation was upgraded and her engines were given a major overhaul; the work was completed before Christmas. She was renamed *Duchesse Anne* but, before entering service for Brittany Ferries, she was chartered for two weeks to the Dutch company SMZ for its Hook of Holland–Harwich service. A civic reception was held on board at Portsmouth on 10 February, before she started her Portsmouth–St Malo service on 13 February. Initially, she operated the service alone, but was joined by another Brittany Ferries vessel, *Armorique*, from 25 May, when a twice-daily service was operated in both directions. *Armorique* finished her summer service on 18 September and *Duchesse Anne* soldiered on alone until mid-November, when the service ended for the winter. She had one particularly rough crossing after leaving St Malo on 29 October, when she took twenty-five hours to cross to Portsmouth, having sheltered off the Cherbourg peninsula for some hours. A crew member was seriously injured when he was crushed against the ship's side by a coach, and some cars were damaged.

After her 1989/90 overhaul, *Duchesse Anne* relieved on Plymouth–Roscoff. She resumed her own Portsmouth–St Malo service on 26 February 1990 and was again joined by *Armorique* for the summer. At the end of October, she suffered damage when gales caused her to be diverted to Cherbourg during a crossing from Portsmouth. She was blown against rocks while waiting to pick up a pilot and lost three propeller blades.

She was sent to Brest for emergency dry-docking and replaced by *Armorique*. After her repairs, *Duchesse Anne* operated freight sailings between Poole and Cherbourg, and between Portsmouth and Caen.

For 1992, *Duchesse Anne* again operated on Portsmouth–St Malo but during March her English port was Poole, as alterations were being carried out at Portsmouth. As in previous years, the end of her season on Poole–St Malo was marred by an incident; this year, she collided with a local dredger, *Timac*, in the approaches to St Malo on 9 December. The dredger sank and her master was drowned, but her remaining six crew members were picked up by local rescue services. *Duchesse Anne*'s bow visor was damaged, requiring repairs at Brest. She was again replaced by *Armorique*.

Duchesse Anne's programme was more varied in 1993. At the beginning of February, she relieved *Barfleur* on Truckline's Poole–Cherbourg service. She reopened Portsmouth–St Malo on 18 March and remained there until 13 June. She was then replaced by the larger *Bretagne*. *Duchesse Anne* immediately moved to a new base at Roscoff. She was used over the weekend as an extra vessel on Roscoff–Plymouth, but also operated some France–Cork sailings. Her Irish programme started on a Sunday evening, with a Roscoff–Cork sailing. From Cork, she sailed to St Malo on Monday, returning from there on Tuesday. She sailed on her return crossing to Roscoff on Wednesday and then sailed on Roscoff–Plymouth until the following Sunday. Her first Cork sailing left Roscoff on 20 June, arriving next day. It was her first visit to Cork since September 1980 as *Connacht*. The occasion was marked by a reception on board, to which her first B&I master and her designer were invited. Roscoff–Plymouth was also operated by another Brittany Ferries vessel, *Quiberon*, but Cork–St Malo was a new venture, operated by *Duchesse Anne* alone. Her Irish season lasted until 15 September, when she made her final departure from Cork to Roscoff.

After her main 1993 summer season, *Duchesse Anne* was used in a variety of roles. On 25 September, she was in Southampton Water to view the start of the Whitbread Round-the-World yacht race, when she was struck by P&O's *Pride of Winchester*. Neither vessel was badly damaged. She returned briefly to Portsmouth–St Malo in the middle of October to cover *Bretagne* and was at Portsmouth again in November for freight sailings to Caen.

Brittany Ferries introduced another route in 1994 and *Duchesse Anne* was chosen to operate it. This time it was between St Malo and Poole. *Duchesse Anne* was to make four round sailings each week, departing from St Malo each evening between Thursday and Sunday inclusive, returning from Poole on the following morning. The rest of the week was employed on sailings to Cork, but this year, in a reversal of the previous year's pattern, the first and last sailings were from St Malo and the round sailing from Cork was to Roscoff. The Poole service was the first regular service to be operated to that port by Brittany Ferries. It was a seasonal summer service, commencing on 13 May and finishing at the end of September.

Duchesse Anne's 1995 season was very similar to the previous year, but started earlier, on 5 April. On 1 September, she was damaged while leaving St Malo when one of her stabilisers hit a submerged rock. She returned to St Malo, and her passengers spent the night on board. Brittany Ferries described the incident as 'minor', saying that there was no risk to passengers. She was dry-docked at Brest and quickly returned to service. She closed the route for the winter on 1 October.

Eurotunnel's opening in 1995 had implications for all operators between Britain and northern Europe, including Brittany Ferries. A considerable volume of traffic that had previously used the ferries now transferred to the tunnel. *Duchesse Anne*'s St Malo–Poole service started later, on 16 May, but ended at its usual time, on 30 September. Her Irish sailings followed the previous year's pattern. However, the decline in traffic had caused financial problems for Brittany Ferries, so *Duchesse Anne* was withdrawn from service immediately after completing her summer programme and put up for sale. Her final call at Cork, her birthplace, was on 25 September. She was bought almost immediately by the Croatian company, Jadrolinija, for Adriatic service. She was delivered to her new owners in October and renamed *Dubrovnik*. In the main, she operates coastal sailings between Rijeka, Split and Dubrovnik, but some sailings are extended from Dubrovnik to Bari, Ancona and Igoumenitsa.

Isle of Inishturk was sold in 1997 to the Canadian Government, which placed the ship in service between Prince Edward Island and the Isles de la Madeline, in the Gulf of St Lawrence, to replace an older ferry, *Lucy Maud Montgomery*. She left Le Havre for Halifax, Nova Scotia, on 6 June, then received minor modifications and was renamed *Madeleine* before entering service in July on a 77-mile crossing from Souris, at the eastern end of Prince Edward Island, to Cap aux Meules. Her new name had previously been held by a small coaster, which had served a similar route until 1986. The sale of *Isle of Inishturk* was notable for the disposal from the fleet of Irish Ferries of the last vessel that had any connection with the former British & Irish Steam Packet Co.

B&I Postscript

The withdrawal of B&I's Liverpool–Dublin service in January 1988 marked the end of B&I's association with Liverpool as a ferry port. However, there were to be a few further sailings between the two cities by vessels owned by Irish Ferries, B&I's parent company and successor.

On 13 December 1995, an international football match between Ireland and Holland was held at Liverpool's football ground. *Saint Killian II* made a round trip from Dublin to Liverpool, to carry football supporters to the match. She left Dublin's Ferryport at 07.45, and was due to arrive at Liverpool at 15.00. As she was not carrying cars, she berthed at the landing stage. Her return sailing left Liverpool at 23.59, arriving at Dublin at 07.30 next morning. The fare for the round trip, including a berth on the return sailing, was a massive IR£89. *Saint Killian II* was also scheduled to make a further round sailing, at a slightly lower fare of IR£79, leaving Dublin on 12 December and returning from Liverpool on 14 December. This sailing would have required passengers to spend two nights in Liverpool and involved the ship in light running, but was cancelled because of lack of support.

On 23 February 2003, Irish Ferries flagship *Ulysses* damaged her berth at Holyhead. She arrived at the Twelve Quays river berth at Birkenhead on 25 February to carry out berthing trials and then started a freight service to Dublin early next morning. The service continued until the final departure from Birkenhead on 28 February. *Ulysses* did carry coaches on at least one sailing, but not foot passengers.

FOUR

SEALINK

Earl William

With B&I's withdrawal on 6 January 1988, Liverpool was left without a Dublin passenger service for the first time since 1946. However, early in 1988 Sealink announced plans to operate a year-round Liverpool–Dun Laoghaire service. That port was a few miles south of Dublin and already used by Sealink, so it was Sealink's natural choice. Dun Laoghaire was not a totally new destination for a service from Liverpool, as the City of Dublin Steam Packet Co. had operated its mail service on that route. The new service was planned to start on 28 March 1988, using *Earl William*, which would sail from Liverpool overnight and from Dun Laoghaire during the day.

Earl William had been built in 1964 as *Viking II* for the Norwegian company Thoresen Car Ferries. Together with her sister, *Viking I*, she operated on Southampton–Cherbourg/ Le Havre. They introduced Scandinavian-style drive-through decks for cars and design for passengers. British Rail had recently withdrawn its overnight Southampton– Le Havre service, using the turbine passenger/cargo vessel *Normannia*, on the grounds that the service did not pay.

Viking II was built by the Norwegian shipbuilders Kaldness of Tonsberg. She was launched on 30 April 1964 by three schoolgirls from Southampton, Cherbourg and Le Havre and delivered on 15 July. She entered service on 20 July with a Southampton– Cherbourg crossing. Her appearance was striking, with an orange hull (for visibility at sea) and a white and pale green superstructure. Her twin exhausts, at each side of the ship, were pale green, with her owner's houseflag. The hull bore the name 'THORESEN CAR FERRIES' in white lettering. She could carry 940 passengers and 180 cars.

After a short period in service, the ship's name was altered to *Carferry Viking II*, because there was already another Norwegian ship named *Viking II*. However, the words 'CARFERRY' on her hull were virtually invisible, and she continued to be known by her former name.

Viking II (1964) at Liverpool in October 1964. She later became *Earl William*. (Author's collection)

Following her first summer in service, *Viking II* was sent on a tour around Britain to 'show the flag', with calls at Liverpool, Avonmouth, Southampton, Hull, Newcastle and Leith. In Liverpool, she berthed at Princes Landing Stage on 27 and 28 October 1964 and was visited by more than 10,000 people.

In February 1965, *Viking II* was chartered to the Atlantic Steam Navigation Co. to operate winter reliefs on its Tilbury–Antwerp service. The charter ended in late March.

Despite the losses of the Railway service, the new ships proved a financial success and were joined by a third very similar ship, *Viking III*, in 1965 and a freight-only vessel, *Viking IV*, in 1967. In 1968, Townsend Car Ferries, which operated car ferry services from Dover in competition with the Railway ships there, acquired Thoresen Car Ferries. This did not lead to any immediate changes in the routes or appearance of the 'Vikings', but in due course the words on the hull were changed to 'TOWNSEND THORESEN'.

In November and December 1968, *Viking II* was used for six weeks as a winter relief vessel on Townsend's Dover–Zeebrugge service. This was repeated in January 1970, by which time *Viking II* had been refitted, giving her a new bar and restaurant and rearranging her lounges. *Viking II* was chartered again, in January 1971, when she operated Stena Line's Gothenburg–Kiel/Fredrikshavn services.

A second generation of 'Vikings' was ordered by Townsend Thoresen, with delivery commencing in January 1975. *Viking II* was transferred to Felixstowe in October 1974, to start a new Zeebrugge car ferry service. In May 1975, the second new 'Viking', *Viking Valiant*, joined her on the route. The fourth and final new 'Viking' was

Viking Viscount, which was completed in May 1976 and took over from *Viking II* on Felixstowe–Zeebrugge. *Viking II* had been chartered from April 1976 to Lion Ferry, to sail between Grenaa, Denmark and Varberg, Sweden. After that charter had finished, Townsend Thoresen had no further use for *Viking II*, so she was put up for sale. On 22 December 1976, she was delivered to Holyhead for new owners who had bought her on Sealink's behalf.

It may seem surprising that Sealink had bought a relatively small twelve-year-old ship, but she was needed for the Channel Islands services, where the size of the harbours precluded the use of larger vessels. Her refit for her new service was carried out at Holyhead and lasted more than a year. She was renamed *Earl William*, which was in line with the style then being used by Sealink. Her hull was painted dark blue with 'Sealink' in large white letters and her superstructure was white. Her funnels were red with a black top, with a white 'railway line' emblem on the red. Her passenger accommodation was increased to 1,100. On completion of the work, she entered service from Portsmouth on 16 January 1978. In December 1978, she damaged a propeller shaft after a chain became entangled in her propeller and was withdrawn from service for almost three months until a new shaft could be fitted at Avonmouth.

In March 1981, the larger *Earl Granville* replaced *Earl William* on Portsmouth–Channel Islands. *Earl William* was transferred to Weymouth, where she continued on Channel Island services. In early October, she grounded near St Helier, retired to a dry-dock in Cherbourg for repairs and did not reappear until 18 December. She suffered further damage on 20 November 1982, when she struck the breakwater at Jersey, remaining off service until 18 January 1983. In the latter part of her time at Weymouth, her routing became more complex, as she also operated a Weymouth–Cherbourg schedule, which included Channel Islands–Portsmouth sailings each Saturday.

Under the Government's privatisation programme, Sealink was sold to Sea Containers on 19 July 1984. In preparation for the sale, the emblems on *Earl William*'s funnels had been removed earlier in the year. One of Sea Containers' first decisions was to reorganise and upgrade the Channel Islands services. *Earl William* and *Earl Granville* were sent to Aalborg in Denmark to be refitted for a luxury service from Portsmouth, carrying just 400 passengers. *Earl William* was repainted in the new Sealink colours, a white hull and superstructure, with blue boot topping, a broad blue band and the words 'SEALINK BRITISH FERRIES', also in blue. Her twin exhausts were painted blue, with two gold bands resembling those on an officer's sleeve. The new service started at the end of April 1985.

It came as no surprise to observers that the new service with its high fares was unsuccessful. The majority of the traffic on Portsmouth–Channel Islands was lost to a new company, Channel Islands Ferries, which was associated with Brittany Ferries. After her first season on this new service, *Earl William* was given a motorists' lounge at the after end of her Bridge Deck and the wording on her hull was changed to 'BRITISH FERRIES'. The 1986 season was also unsuccessful and on 30 September it was announced that Sealink and Channel Islands Ferries would operate a joint Channel Islands service. This provoked a sit-in by the crews of Sealink's vessels. *Earl William* was at Guernsey, but subsequently moved to Weymouth to continue the sit-in. It proved impossible to reach agreement with Sealink's crews, but eventually *Earl William* was moved to the river Fal and laid up.

In spring 1987, the Home Office chartered *Earl William* to house asylum seekers in Britain. She returned from Falmouth to Weymouth in May 1987 to pick up supplies, and then sailed to Harwich, where she was moored in the former train ferry dock. On 19 October 1987, during the great hurricane, she broke loose from her berth early in the morning with her 'residents' on board. She drifted into the Channel, causing damage to small craft moored there and then grounded on a sandbank. She had an 18-inch hole in her stern above the waterline. She was refloated and her 'residents' were sent ashore. She never returned to her role as an accommodation ship, and on 4 December 1987 sailed from Harwich for the river Fal, to be laid up again.

Her next use was on Liverpool–Dun Laoghaire and for this her hull again received the words 'SEALINK BRITISH FERRIES'. She had a certificate for 600 passengers and could carry 160 cars and a small number of lorries. She operated overnight from Liverpool, departing at 22.00 and arriving at Dun Laoghaire at 09.45, immediately after the Holyhead vessel's scheduled departure. The return sailing departed from Dun Laoghaire at 11.00, arriving at Liverpool at 18.30. Because of industrial action at Sealink, the service did not start until 25 April 1988 with *Earl William*'s inaugural sailing from Dun Laoghaire. Her Liverpool berth was at the Brocklebank Dock terminal previously used by B&I and now shared with Belfast Ferries. The service was suspended on 11 August, because *Earl William* had developed problems with both her propellers. She was sent to Cardiff for dry-docking and returned to service from Dun Laoghaire on 24 August. *Earl William* was overhauled during November. Her former partner on the Channel Islands route, *Earl Granville*, covered her, but was unable to maintain a reliable crossing time. *Earl William* was able to keep to the timetable, but was sometimes delayed at Dun Laoghaire by the late departure of the Holyhead sailing.

Traffic built up well, especially for the overnight sailing, but the service lost money in 1988. It was decided to make the 1989 service seasonal, between mid-May and the end of September, but this decision was reversed after reduced berthing charges had been negotiated. During the summer, Sealink gave notice to the Mersey Docks & Harbour Company and Belfast Ferries that it was considering ending the service on 30 September. The service's revenue was reduced by a dockers' strike in summer 1989, which prevented *Earl William* from carrying cars. It was not closed at the end of September, but its financial results were poor and, in November, Sealink announced its decision to close the service in January 1990. The final sailing was from Dun Laoghaire on 9 January. She left Liverpool on 11 January to lay up at Milford Haven, but returned to Liverpool on 28 January on charter to Belfast Ferries, following engine problems in *Saint Colum I*. She ended her sailings on 28 February, when her passenger certificate expired, but a new certificate allowed her to resume the same service for a few days until 8 March, when she returned to Milford Haven.

Earl William's next service was early June 1990 when she operated Folkestone–Boulogne, covering a shortage of Sealink vessels caused by repairs and strikes by French seamen.

Unfortunately, there were numerous complaints about her internal condition after her lay-up and she suffered an engine failure. She then sailed to the Fal to lay up again. She next came out of lay-up in February 1991, when she sailed to Holyhead to take over from *Stena Cambria*, which had been damaged in Holyhead harbour on 10 February. *Earl William* took up service from Holyhead on 14 February, but was in even worse condition than when she had been on the Dover Straits. Sealink's markings had been removed from her rust-stained hull, there were problems with her bow thrust unit, the hydraulics of her bow visor were not operating and her once powerful engines had difficulty in completing the crossing in the scheduled three-and-a-half hours. Her certificate only allowed her to carry 300 passengers. *Stena Cambria* re-entered service on 19 February and *Earl William* returned to her lay-up berth in the river Fal. *Stena Cambria* later went round to Dover until a newly purchased ship had been altered. Because the new ship was delayed, *Stena Cambria* was unable to return to Holyhead by the end of June when the service required two passenger ships, so *Earl William* returned to Holyhead–Dun Laoghaire on 27 June. On this occasion, she had been painted externally and the two bands had been removed from her twin exhausts. This time, she had a certificate for 450 passengers, which was raised to 800 during her time at Holyhead. She had no problems during her two-week stint on the service, except for being unable to use her bow door. Following *Stena Cambria*'s return, she went briefly to Dover with the intention of operating Western Docks–Calais, replacing the French *Chartres* whose return from Gulf War service had been delayed. However, concern over the standard of her accommodation prevented her from being used, so she returned to Milford Haven. This marked the end of her service with Sealink.

Before being sold, *Earl William* was chartered to a Tunisian operator for four weeks to operate from Tunis to France. She left Milford Haven on 22 August 1991, but the Tunisian authorities refused to issue a certificate for her to enter service, as they were not satisfied with her machinery and accommodation. After a legal row, *Earl William* returned to Milford Haven via Gibraltar. The final straw in these unsatisfactory events was when she took on some bad fuel at Gibraltar, with the consequence that her engineers had to change her engine filters several times every hour. She arrived back 'home', at Milford Haven, on 11 September.

After a further period of lay-up, *Earl William* was sold to the Greek owners Neptunus Lines. She was registered in Malta, renamed *William* and sailed for Greece on 5 April 1992. Subsequently, she was renamed *Pearl William*, with the change effected by a badly painted 'P' in front of her former Sealink name. An earlier proposal to rename her *European Pearl* did not materialise. She was placed in service on Bari–Igoumenitsa–Patras. In 1993, she was chartered to European Seaways and sailed on Brindisi–Igoumenitsa. She still retained her final Sealink colours, but for this charter the words 'EUROPEAN SEAWAYS' were added in small letters on her hull. In the following year, she operated a longer route between Italy, Greece and Turkey, calling at Bari, Brindisi, Igoumenitsa, Piraeus and Çesme. In 1996, she was sold to P&L Ferries, a Turkish company, which was planning a new weekly service from the northern Greek port of Thessaloniki to Istanbul and Odessa. However, at first she remained in the Adriatic, operating between

Brindisi and Igoumenitsa. For this service, she was renamed *Mar. Julia*. She was sold again in 1997 and then chartered to Stern Lines, who renamed her *Çesme Stern* and operated her on a service from Bari, through the Corinth Canal, to Çesme, in Turkey. After a short period in service, she was arrested in February 1998, and laid up at Bari, reportedly with major engine problems; she remained there until July 2001, when her condition had deteriorated. She was then sold to Windward Lines for Caribbean service, intended to be between St Lucia, Barbados, St Vincent, Trinidad and Venezuela, and refitted in Croatia, when her hull was painted orange, similar to its original colour. This work became the subject of a major disagreement between owner and builder. Under the new name *Windward II*, she sailed for the Caribbean but was detained at Las Palmas. She was due to enter service in October 2003, but on 19 October, when arriving to take up service, she rammed a coastguard vessel, TTS *Nelson*, leaving a hole in the bow. The cost of the repairs was put at US$1,000,000; as *Windward II's* owners failed to pay up, on 30 January the Court ordered her arrest. She was then placed under armed guard at Port of Spain, Trinidad. At forty years of age, her future looks very uncertain.

Sealink's failure is not surprising. Although *Earl William*, with good overnight accommodation, was well suited to passenger service on the route, there was insufficient space for commercial traffic. There had never been great demand from passengers for a daylight Liverpool–Dublin/Dun Laoghaire service, since the length of the route compares badly with the Holyhead route. In contrast, there was demand for a long overnight sailing, so that passengers could enjoy a full night's sleep. A passenger service on this route was unlikely to be successful if it was operated by only one ship, making for an unbalanced service.

FIVE

P&O IRISH SEA

P&O European Ferries (Irish Sea) Ltd, shortened for trading purposes to P&O Irish Sea, operates a Liverpool–Dublin ro-ro passenger and freight service. It also serves Scotland–Northern Ireland and, until recently, Rosslare–Cherbourg, although that route has now been closed. Until April 2004, it operated Fleetwood–Larne, Mostyn–Dublin and Dublin–Cherbourg. Originally, the operating company was Pandoro, but in a 1998 reorganisation it became P&O Irish Sea.

Pandoro was established in 1975. The Belfast Steamship Co. (owned by P&O) ran the overnight Liverpool–Belfast car ferry service, carrying some conventional cargo but with little space for commercial vehicles. Declining passenger numbers and the ships' poor commercial vehicle capacity made the future of the service look increasingly uncertain. The Belfast Steamship Co. had joined with British Rail to start a Heysham–Belfast freight ro-ro service, initially using chartered vessels. Other P&O group companies, Ferrymasters (Ireland), Northern Ireland Trailers, and Ulster Ferry Link Line, had competing freight services to Northern Ireland.

In November 1973, the British Transport Docks Board began to develop a ro-ro terminal at Fleetwood. There was speculation over the user of the terminal until an announcement in July 1974 that the Belfast Steamship Co. would operate a Fleetwood–Larne freight ro-ro service from early 1975. Two vessels built for Stena Line had been purchased and would be named *Bison* and *Buffalo*. The new operator was called Pandoro and took over the operations of the other P&O group companies.

The 'animal' style of nomenclature adopted by Pandoro was first used by J&G Burns (later G&J Burns) in 1833, for the paddle steamer *Antelope*, but it was not until 1853 that the style, including the names *Buffalo*, *Bison* and *Puma*, was adopted regularly for all Burns' new cross-Channel vessels. The style was abandoned in 1929, but revived in 1958 by Coast Lines' subsidiary Link Line. It was used by Burns & Laird Lines for the 1967 car ferry *Lion*, and for some of P&O's south coast and North Sea ferries.

The connection of the Belfast Steamship Co. with the new service was emphasised on 11 February 1975 when the wife of its managing director named the first vessel *Bison*. *Bison* opened Fleetwood–Larne during February.

In a change to the original plan, Pandoro and B&I agreed to operate a Fleetwood–Dublin service jointly, with the ship being supplied and managed by Pandoro. A new company, W&L Shipping, was set up to charter *Buffalo* from Pandoro. W&L stood for Wyre and Liffey, the rivers on which the two terminals were located. *Buffalo* entered service in March.

The services quickly grew to the point where additional tonnage was needed, so two ships were ordered from Japan. The intention was for both new ships to operate Fleetwood–Dublin, allowing *Buffalo* to be transferred to Fleetwood–Larne, alongside *Bison*. Meanwhile, to provide a second ship for Larne, a succession of vessels was chartered from Stena Line: *Stena Trailer* in spring 1977, *Jaguar* (ex-*Stena Timer*) in autumn 1977 and *Union Melbourne*, an enlarged sister of *Bison* and *Buffalo*, in autumn 1978. The first new ship was named *Ibex* and delivered in May 1979. The second was launched as *Puma*, but chartered to B&I on completion and delivered as *Tipperary*.

Bison, *Buffalo* and *Union Melbourne* covered Fleetwood–Larne from November 1979. In September 1980, *Union Melbourne* was purchased from Stena. *Bison* and *Union Melbourne* were then modified, and *Union Melbourne* was renamed *Puma*. The extra capacity freed one ship, so *Ibex* was transferred in December 1980 to North Sea Ferries at Hull, being renamed *Norsea* and later *Norsky*. *Buffalo* took the place of *Ibex* on Fleetwood–Dublin, leaving *Bison* and *Puma* on Fleetwood–Larne.

Following B&I's decision to close its Liverpool–Dublin car ferry service, the English terminal of the joint Pandoro/B&I service was moved to Liverpool on 1 January 1988. *Buffalo* was lengthened at that time, being replaced temporarily by P&O's *Viking Trader*, transferred from Portsmouth. At the end of 1988, *Tipperary* followed her sister to North Sea Ferries and was renamed *Norcape*. As a replacement, *Bison* was chartered to B&I and transferred to Liverpool–Dublin, while *Viking Trader* took up permanent station on Fleetwood–Larne.

The Belfast Steamship Co.'s Liverpool–Belfast car ferry service closed in 1981, and was replaced in 1982 by a new service operated by Belfast Car Ferries. After that service had ended in 1990, Pandoro started a Liverpool–Belfast service on 5 August 1991, using *Merchant Venture*, chartered from Cenargo. It was withdrawn on 21 December 1991, following the advent of Norse Irish Ferries in November.

From the beginning of 1993, Pandoro took over the Ardrossan–Belfast service, but moved its Irish terminal to Larne. The vessel operating the service was *Belard*, which carried no passengers. She was later replaced by *Merchant Valiant*, renamed *Lion* in 1995, which again had no passenger accommodation.

In 1993, Pandoro announced that it wished to order two new vessels to replace *Bison* and *Buffalo*. Yards in Europe and the Far East were asked to tender for the construction of ships substantially faster than their predecessors, reducing the Liverpool–Dublin crossing time to six-and-a-half hours. A new on-river Mersey terminal would allow up to one hour to be taken off crossing times. However, time passed without any orders. Modifications made to various vessels in the fleet suggested that a lower-cost way of increasing capacity had been found.

Pandoro started a Rosslare–Cherbourg service in November 1993, using *European Clearway*. She has also occasionally been used on routes between Britain and Ireland. In 1996, Pandoro started a weekend Dublin–Cherbourg service, supplementing the Rosslare–Cherbourg route. The vessel used initially was *Puma*.

In 1993, to accommodate B&I's new car ferry *Isle of Innisfree*, which was too large for B&I's ferryport, Pandoro's Dublin service was moved from its regular berth in the river Liffey to the ferryport. B&I gave Pandoro twelve months' notice of its intention to withdraw from the joint service. Pandoro then entered into a fifty-one-year lease of a new Dublin terminal at the North Wall extension. Operations were transferred from the ferryport to the new terminal when the joint service ceased. *Bison's* charter ended in June 1994, on the expiry of B&I's notice. She returned to Fleetwood–Larne, swapping routes with *Puma*.

Between 1994 and 1997, to meet growing competition from foreign-flagged ships, Pandoro gradually changed its ships' port of registry from London to Hamilton, Bermuda. This allowed it to replace British seafarers with foreign crews.

Traffic on Liverpool–Dublin continued to grow. The Polish *Arcade Eagle* was chartered as a third vessel for the service; later she was succeeded by the Canadian *Atlantic Freighter*. In mid-1995 *Norsky* (ex-*Ibex*) returned from the North Sea and took over Liverpool–Dublin from *Atlantic Freighter*. Later she reverted to her original name. In May 1996 she was rebuilt; the chartered *Commodore Clipper* covered her schedule. The service was further expanded by the addition of *Leopard* (ex-*Viking Trader*) in summer 1996. Using another chartered vessel, *Tidero Star*, the service then provided four sailings per day in each direction. Its daily frequency was reduced to three sailings at the end of 1996, when *Leopard* was transferred back to Fleetwood. In 1997, *Tidero Star* was replaced by another chartered vessel, *Seahawk*.

Pandoro's operations were combined with P&O's Cairnryan–Larne service in 1998 as P&O Irish Sea. After the Second World War, the Atlantic Steam Navigation Co. had started a Preston–Larne ro-ro service. The company was acquired in 1971 by Townsend Thoresen, which closed the Preston–Larne route in July 1983 and replaced it with a new Cairnryan–Larne route. Townsend Thoresen was acquired by P&O in 1986. The vessels operating on Cairnryan–Larne in 1998 were the summer-only fast ferry *Jetliner* and the ro-ro ferries *Pride of Rathlin* (ex-*Pride of Walmer*, ex-*Free Enterprise VII*), *European Endeavour* (ex-*European Enterprise*) and *European Trader*. The new company was the renamed Atlantic Steam Navigation Co.

Pandoro's services were intended primarily for freight, although a few cars were carried on the Fleetwood services. This arrangement was formalised in 1999, when both Liverpool–Dublin and Fleetwood–Larne were advertised to motorists. The price for a car and two passengers varied between £99 and £140, depending on the season, including meals but excluding a cabin. Foot passengers were not carried, except on Cairnryan–Larne. These arrangements were gradually extended; by 2002 all ships with passenger space were advertised to motorists.

The merger created the opportunity to re-think the Scottish services. The result was the transfer in 2001 of the northern terminal from Ardrossan to Troon. Ardrossan had always been a difficult port in rough weather. The transfer solved that problem and gave a shorter sea crossing. An earlier change, in 2000, had been the replacement of *Jetliner* by another fast ferry, *Superstar Express*. She began operating from Troon, in addition to Cairnryan, in 2003.

The Liverpool–Dublin service had been operated by three ships in 1998 and 1999, but was back up to four ships in 2000, with *European Leader*, *European Envoy*, and the chartered *Celtic Sun* and *Celtic Star*.

After many years of using ships transferred from other P&O companies on Cairnryan–Larne, a new vessel was ordered from Japan. She was delivered in 2000 as *European Causeway*. The order was followed by two more: a sister ship, *European Highlander*, to operate Cairnryan–Larne and a similar but slightly larger vessel, *European Ambassador*, to operate Liverpool–Dublin.

European Ambassador's arrival in 2001 allowed *European Leader* to be switched to Fleetwood–Larne, with Liverpool–Dublin being operated also by *European Envoy* and the two chartered ships. However, all was not well with the service. For many years, there had been plans for a P&O on-river terminal at Liverpool, matching the one being built at Birkenhead for Norse Merchant Ferries, but the plans had experienced a succession of delays. P&O believed that completion of the Birkenhead terminal would put it at a disadvantage compared with Norse Merchant's Dublin service, because of the latter's shorter berth-to-berth time. Early in 2001, P&O announced that it was starting a new Mostyn–Dublin service, using *Celtic Sun* and *Celtic Star*. The route's shorter crossing would counter the advantage about to be gained by Norse Merchant. However, the plan was altered, with *European Ambassador* and *European Envoy* changing places with *Celtic Sun* and *Celtic Star*, which could only carry unaccompanied trailers. Mostyn was a long-established small port on the river Dee, which had hitherto catered only for relatively small vessels. P&O signed a fifteen-year contract and the port raised the money needed for dredging and to develop ro-ro and other port facilities. Originally the transfer date was in July 2001, but there were several postponements, so the service did not begin until 19 November.

When the charter of *Celtic Sun* ended in September, she was replaced on Liverpool–Dublin by *Pride of Suffolk*, transferred from P&O's Felixstowe–Europoort service. She was later renamed *European Diplomat*. It was expected that *Celtic Star* would be replaced by either *Pride of Suffolk*'s sister ship, *Pride of Flanders*, or *European Seafarer*, but instead both ships were replaced in January 2002 by *Norbank* and *Norbay*, formerly on P&O's Hull–Europoort service. *European Diplomat* took over Rosslare–Cherbourg in March 2002.

The new Mostyn service achieved a good volume of business, but there were problems. Initially, the basic weekday timetable was for each ship to make a daily round trip. *European Ambassador* sailed from Mostyn at 23.00 and returned from Dublin at 13.30; *European Envoy* sailed from Dublin at 19.30 and returned from Mostyn at 08.30. However, the actual sailing times sometimes differed from these by several hours and a tide-table was more useful than the printed timetable; passengers were advised to confirm the sailing time by telephone or on the company's website. Considerable dredging had been carried out before the service began, but it still appeared difficult for such large ships to use the Channel around low water. There was also an argument, not involving

P&O but probably reflecting on the same problem, about obtaining permission for additional dredging needed for access to the port by a vessel built to deliver wings for the European Airbus from Mostyn to France. Not surprisingly, it was difficult to maintain a satisfactory level of business when the timetable was so unreliable.

In addition to her Mostyn sailings, *European Ambassador* operated P&O's Dublin–Cherbourg weekend service during the summer, starting in 2002. This service proved very attractive to motorists and the 2003 season was extended.

In view of the problems with Mostyn–Dublin, its future came under review, but the extent of the changes came as a surprise. In May 2003, P&O announced that it had agreed to sell its Liverpool–Dublin and Fleetwood–Larne services and the five ships on those routes to Stena. P&O would close Mostyn–Dublin and charter *European Ambassador* and *European Envoy* to Stena. Stena would take a 50 per cent share in Cairnryan and switch its Stranraer base there. Stena already operated two vessels on Holyhead–Dun Laoghaire, so it was not surprising that the British Competition Commission found that the sale of Liverpool–Dublin to Stena would damage the level of competition on the central corridor services. As a result, a modified contract was completed on 19 April 2004, with Stena buying the Fleetwood–Larne service, together with *European Pioneer*, *European Leader*, *European Seafarer* and the two Mostyn ships. P&O retained the Liverpool–Dublin service, together with *Norbank* and *Norbay*, but closed Mostyn–Dublin.

There was speculation that P&O intended to sell Liverpool–Dublin when it could find a suitable buyer. However, there were no suggestions that the service was unprofitable. The elimination of the capacity of the two ships sailing from Mostyn led to a general improvement in profitability in the central corridor of the Irish Sea, and P&O's route achieved a 10 per cent volume gain in 2004. At the end of September 2004, P&O announced the result of a complete review of its ferry operations. Most of the changes affected English Channel routes, but the closure of Rosslare–Cherbourg on 19 December 2004 was included. The review stated specifically that Liverpool–Dublin would be retained, along with Larne–Cairnryan/Troon. In 2005, *Superstar Express* was replaced on the latter route by the former *Cherbourg Express*, now simply renamed *Express*.

Bison/European Pioneer and *Buffalo/European Leader*

Bison and *Buffalo* were the first pair of a trio ordered by Stena from J.J. Sietas, a Hamburg shipbuilder. Their contracts were sold to P&O, and they were launched as *Bison* and *Buffalo*. They had a speed of 18.5 knots and capacity for ninety trailers. There was a fixed internal ramp to the Upper Deck and a lift between the Main and Lower Decks. Their accommodation was limited to twelve lorry drivers, so they could carry hazardous cargoes on the Upper Deck.

Bison was launched on 31 October 1974 and completed in January 1975. She entered service on 11 February, carrying trade cars from Liverpool to Larne, but soon afterwards opened the new Fleetwood–Larne service. *Buffalo* was launched on 6 January 1975 and completed in March. She entered service in April on the Fleetwood–Dublin joint service.

Bison (1975) in June 1995, showing the accommodation added in 1994/95, but before the addition of an extra deck. (Author)

Bison carried out berthing trials at Warrenpoint on 20 June 1976. There had been a ro-ro berth there for some time, although it had never previously been used.

During their summer overhauls in 1979, *Bison* and *Buffalo* were given blue hulls, in place of their original black ones. With the arrival of *Ibex* and *Tipperary* on Fleetwood–Dublin in 1979, *Buffalo* moved to Fleetwood–Larne. *Bison* opened a new short-lived Liverpool–Larne route, which started on 15 October 1979, and was also served by *Buffalo* and *Union Melbourne*. On 5 January 1980, *Buffalo* arrived at Dover to cover for P&O's *Lion,* which had suffered gale damage. *Buffalo* sailed to Boulogne, loading at Dover's camber as she was too large for the ro-ro berths. She arrived back in Liverpool on 29 January.

In the second half of 1980, *Bison* was sent to the Tyne for lengthening. Afterwards, she was the same length as *Union Melbourne,* which had been built as an identical sister ship but lengthened immediately after completion. The alterations included additional passenger accommodation, with berths for forty drivers, and a bow thrust unit. For the first time, a Pandoro vessel could carry more than twelve passengers and required a passenger certificate. *Union Melbourne* followed her, receiving similar passenger accommodation, and was renamed *Puma.* Both ships resumed regular service on Fleetwood–Larne.

Buffalo was not altered, and returned to Fleetwood–Dublin in January 1981, replacing *Ibex.* She operated in conjunction with *Tipperary.* In November 1981, Pandoro's services were affected by strikes in support of the Belfast Steamship Co.'s seamen; *Buffalo* was occupied by her crew, blocking the Fleetwood berth for more than a week and preventing calls by *Tipperary.*

B&I closed its Liverpool–Dublin car ferry service in January 1988, although it agreed to retain a freight service from Liverpool. To meet this commitment, the British terminal

Buffalo (1975), arriving at Fleetwood. (Author's collection)

of the joint service was moved to Liverpool. The final Dublin–Fleetwood sailing was on 23 December 1987 and the new service started on 4 January 1988. The two ships involved were still *Buffalo* and *Tipperary*. However, because of continued growth on the Dublin route, *Buffalo* was withdrawn around the time of the transfer for lengthening and to be given additional passenger accommodation, making her similar to *Bison* and *Puma* after their 1981 alterations. The contract for the work was awarded to Hall Russell of Aberdeen, but she was lengthened at Leith and then towed to Aberdeen for the work to be finished and the accommodation block fitted.

At the end of 1988, *Tipperary* was sold to North Sea Ferries. To replace her, *Bison* was transferred from Fleetwood–Larne and chartered to B&I, which provided her crew. *Bison* was given a white B&I funnel. Later the words 'B&I Line' were painted on her superstructure. By that time Pandoro's colours, carried by *Buffalo*, were a dark blue funnel with the P&O flag, a dark blue hull with the word 'PANDORO' in white, and a white superstructure.

A national dock strike in the second half of July 1989 closed Liverpool, so *Bison* and *Buffalo* were switched to a Dublin–Pembroke Dock service. There were similar diversions during a Liverpool dock strike in summer 1990, but on that occasion, *Buffalo* also operated a Dublin–Cherbourg sailing. During that year, greater traffic brought about an increase in the Liverpool–Dublin service from six to seven days per week.

On 26 May 1993, *Buffalo* was present at the Royal Fleet Review off Anglesey, commemorating the Battle of the Atlantic. Other ferries present were *Lady of Mann* and *Stena Cambria*. The Review took place in appalling weather.

Bison (1975) at Birkenhead in October 1996, showing the extra vehicle deck added at the stern in July 1995. (G. Ditchfield)

From June 1994, Pandoro became the sole operator of Liverpool–Dublin. *Bison* returned to Pandoro colours and switched to Fleetwood–Larne. She was sent to Cammell Laird's to be fitted with hull sponsons, bringing her into line with new safety standards and increasing her vehicle capacity. She returned there over Christmas/New Year 1994/95 when her upper freight deck was widened and her main and upper vehicle decks were renewed. She was given additional cabins and a large passenger lounge. She returned there again in July 1995, when a third deck for twenty extra trailers was added behind the existing accommodation. This deck had been made possible by the additional buoyancy provided by the hull sponsons. *Bison* returned to Fleetwood on 4 August 1995. She was renamed *European Pioneer* in 1997.

Buffalo remained on Liverpool–Dublin until July 1996, when she was transferred to Fleetwood, in an exchange with *Leopard* (ex-*Viking Trader*). The next year, she reverted to Liverpool–Dublin. In summer 1998, she was sent to Falmouth to be lengthened by 15m and for additional passenger accommodation to be added. While it is fairly common for a ship to be lengthened, this event, involving a second lengthening, was rare. Before returning to service, she was renamed *European Leader*. Two years later, *European Pioneer* attended the same yard for an upgrade to her passenger accommodation.

European Leader ran aground near Crosby Coastguard Station around 06.30 on 17 September 2000, after a complete power failure. A lifeboat was launched, and the Coastguard placed a local dredger and tug on standby. She was undamaged and refloated on the rising tide around 10.25. Not to be outdone, *European Pioneer* ran aground close to the Channel entrance, while leaving Fleetwood on 2 December 2000. She refloated on the next tide and, after an inspection, continued her voyage to Larne.

European Leader (1975) approaching Liverpool in September 1999, showing the accommodation added in 1998. She was formerly *Buffalo*. (Author)

With the delivery of *European Ambassador* in 2001, *European Leader* returned to Fleetwood–Larne, joining *European Pioneer* and *European Seafarer*. These three ships remained on the service until 19 April 2004, when it was taken over by Stena. The first Stena sailings were made at 22.00, by *European Leader* from Larne and *European Pioneer* from Fleetwood. The new owners retained the same ships and schedules for the service. The only obvious changes were the replacement of the ships' '*European*' prefix by '*Stena*', and their funnels being repainted in Stena's colours.

The fact that the two ships have lasted on their original route for nearly thirty years is a tribute to the versatility of their original design, which allowed them to be modified to meet the increasing demands of a modern service. It is an interesting turn of events to see them back with the owner for whom they were originally designed. However, it seems likely that in the near future both ships, along with *Stena Seafarer*, will be replaced by new ships designed specifically with the tidal conditions at Fleetwood in mind.

Puma/European Seafarer

Puma started life as the sister ship of *Bison* and *Buffalo*, from the same builder. She was launched on 3 March 1975 and completed in May for her owners, Northern Coasters Ltd, a Stena subsidiary that owned vessels chartered to other companies. Stena chartered her to the Union Steamship Co. of New Zealand, which chose her first name, *Union Melbourne*. Like her two sisters, she had passenger accommodation for twelve drivers. She was moved almost immediately to another German shipbuilder, Werft Nobiskrug

Union Melbourne (1975) arriving at Fleetwood. (Author's collection)

of Rendsburg, which lengthened her by 17.3m, so increasing her trailer capacity to 110. She then went to New Zealand. After her first charter had ended, she was chartered to Pandoro and arrived in the Irish Sea in autumn 1978. She entered service on Fleetwood–Larne on 13 November, still painted in her New Zealand colours, replacing the chartered *Jaguar*. Later, she was repainted in Pandoro colours. It was planned to rename her *Puma*, but the change was not made at that time; the name was allocated instead to one of the two new vessels built for Fleetwood–Dublin.

Union Melbourne was purchased by P&O in September 1980 and renamed *Union Trader*. She was sent to the Tyne, where accommodation for forty drivers was added and a bow thrust unit was fitted. On completion of the work on 20 November, she received the long-projected name of *Puma*. She returned to Fleetwood and took up Fleetwood–Larne along with *Bison*. *Viking Trader* replaced *Bison* in January 1989. In summer 1990, *Puma* operated some Dublin–Pembroke Dock sailings to help clear freight during a Liverpool dock strike.

In July 1994, *Puma* was sent to Cammell Laird's for a refit, which included replacement of her last four-berth cabins with new two-berth cabins, in addition to a full-width lounge. She did not return to Fleetwood, but swapped routes with *Bison* and transferred to Liverpool–Dublin after relieving for a week on Rosslare–Cherbourg. For three weekends in January 1995, *Puma* operated an extended Liverpool–Dublin–Fleetwood–Larne–Liverpool roster to cover *Bison's* dry-docking and annual overhaul.

In summer 1996, *Puma* started yet another route for Pandoro, this time between Dublin and Cherbourg. The service comprised one round sailing each weekend, supplementing Pandoro's Rosslare–Cherbourg service. During the week, *Puma* continued to operate on Liverpool–Dublin. However, she was later switched to Fleetwood–Larne, changing places with *Buffalo*. In 1998, she was renamed *European Seafarer*.

European Seafarer took over Rosslare–Cherbourg in November 2001. However, her service there finished in mid-January 2002, when *European Diplomat* took over. *European Seafarer* then returned to Fleetwood–Larne, but enjoyed a less settled period. On 30 March, she made a rare round sailing on Larne–Troon. She was laid up at Liverpool in June, but from 3 August relieved *European Envoy* on Mostyn–Dublin. She was briefly on Liverpool–Dublin in January 2003 and then covered Rosslare–Cherbourg during *European Diplomat*'s overhaul. Finally, she returned to Fleetwood–Larne.

This nomadic pattern continued in 2004. For several weekends during the summer, she sailed from Campbeltown to Mostyn carrying windmills for the North Wales offshore wind farm. For most of July, she covered Cairnryan–Larne for *European Causeway* and *European Highlander*, and then returned to Fleetwood–Larne. On 1 September, while en route to Larne from Fleetwood, she spotted two fishermen clinging to the hull of their upturned boat. A nearby Irish Coastguard rescue helicopter winched the two men up and airlifted them to the Isle of Man. *European Seafarer* was out of service between 4 November and 20 December undergoing engine repairs.

Having spent the early months of 2004 on Fleetwood–Larne, *European Seafarer* took over Cairnryan–Larne between 10 and 18 April. Completion of the sale to Stena took place on 19 April. By then *European Seafarer* had returned to Fleetwood–Larne and took P&O's final sailing on the route, departing from Larne at 16.00. As with the other two ships on the route, her funnel was repainted in Stena's colours and she was renamed, becoming *Stena Seafarer*. In addition to serving on Fleetwood–Larne, she was also used to cover other Stena routes. She carried out berthing trials at Stranraer, Belfast, Dublin and Holyhead in the autumn of 2004, and was expected to relieve on Stena's Holyhead–Dublin service in the winter of 2004/05. However, instead she was required to relieve *Stena Caledonia* on the North Channel.

European Seafarer (1975) off Prestatyn in August 2002. She was formerly *Puma*. (Author)

Ibex/European Envoy

Ibex was the first of two ships ordered by Pandoro from the Japanese shipbuilders Mitsui, of Tamano. She was launched on 27 December 1978 and completed in May 1979. She had a capacity for 125 trailers on three decks; loading was by a stern ramp to the main deck, with a fixed internal ramp to the upper deck and a lift to the tank-top deck. All three vehicle decks extended under the forward accommodation block, which had berths for twelve drivers. Her service speed was 19 knots, enabling her to complete the sea crossing in seven hours. She was fitted with stabilisers and twin bow thrusters.

Ibex arrived at Fleetwood on 2 July 1979 to take over Fleetwood–Dublin from *Buffalo*. However, alterations to the ro-ro berth at Dublin had not been completed, so she took up service on Fleetwood–Larne, becoming the largest ferry ever to have berthed at Larne. This released *Bison* to take over Fleetwood–Dublin while *Buffalo* was overhauled. Problems arose while turning *Ibex* in the river Wyre; in strong winds a tug was needed to assist in berthing her. Following *Bison*'s return from overhaul, *Ibex* was withdrawn from service and laid up at Belfast. It was assumed that both ships would behave similarly, so a skeg was fitted to the second vessel's propellers during fitting out. This was successful in trials, so *Ibex* was similarly equipped at Belfast and returned to Fleetwood on 14 September. Further delays were then caused by industrial troubles, but she finally started her regular service on 26 October.

The second ship was launched for Pandoro as *Puma* on 20 April 1979. However, on completion she was chartered to B&I and renamed *Tipperary*, as B&I's contribution to the joint service. The result was that *Puma/Tipperary* never sailed for Pandoro. After her delivery voyage from Japan, she paid a fifteen-hour visit to Pembroke Dock on

Ibex (1979) departing from Fleetwood. (Author's collection)

26 October, apparently to check whether the port could be used in an emergency. She entered service at the end of October, enabling B&I to close its Liverpool–Dublin container service, operated by *Wicklow*.

Ibex and *Tipperary* together operated Fleetwood–Dublin for a little over a year but, at the end of 1980, *Ibex* was chartered to North Sea Ferries, a company in which P&O held a 50 per cent stake, was renamed *Norsea* and was placed in service between Ipswich and Rotterdam. At the end of 1988, North Sea Ferries obtained *Tipperary* for service on Ipswich–Rotterdam, replacing a chartered vessel. She joined *Norsky*, the former *Ibex*, which had been renamed again in 1986 to release the name *Norsea* for a new passenger ferry. *Norsky* had remained a British vessel but, in keeping with the Anglo-Dutch ownership of North Sea Ferries, *Tipperary* was bought by a Dutch company. She was registered under the Dutch flag as *Norcape*.

North Sea Ferries closed its Ipswich–Rotterdam service on 23 April 1995. *Norcape* was transferred to one of the company's main services, Hull–Zeebrugge, but *Norsky* was transferred back to Pandoro. She was repainted in Pandoro's colours and her port of registry was changed to Hamilton, Bermuda, before she entered service on Liverpool–Dublin on 10 May. The service had grown to the point where *Bison* and *Buffalo* could not handle all the traffic available and she took over from a chartered Canadian vessel, *Atlantic Freighter*. During a short overhaul in August her original name, *Ibex*, was restored.

On 11 May 1996, *Ibex* was sent to Cammell Laird's for a new deck to be added. Accommodation for up to seventy passengers was fitted above the accommodation block forward. She returned to service in August. In 1997, she received her fourth name, becoming *European Envoy*.

On 11 August 1999, *European Envoy*, on a sailing from Liverpool, was involved in a search with *Dawn Merchant* for a man who had fallen from Irish Ferries' fast ferry *Jonathan Swift*. The man was found suffering from hypothermia, and taken to hospital.

In 2000, the frequency of the Liverpool–Dublin service was four sailings daily each way by *European Envoy*, *European Leader*, *Celtic Sun* and *Celtic Star*. *European Ambassador* replaced *European Leader* in January 2001. The major change took place in November 2001 when *European Envoy* and *European Ambassador* moved from Liverpool to Mostyn. Although Mostyn's initial vehicle bookings were very encouraging, the problems of the new port soon became apparent. *European Envoy* grounded on a sandbank adjacent to the Channel at about 05.00 on 18 December as she approached Mostyn, and remained there until she refloated on a rising tide about four hours later. Divers inspected her after she docked but found no damage. On 3 January she was diverted to Liverpool as gales prevented her from making an attempt to dock at Mostyn. A third incident on 9 January involving *European Ambassador* required *European Envoy* to be diverted to Liverpool again. She had another diversion to Liverpool on 20 February, because of bad weather.

During the early months of 2004, Mostyn–Dublin was gradually run down. By 21 March, *European Envoy* had ceased to carry passengers. Over the last weekend in March, *European Envoy* covered Liverpool–Dublin sailings, then returned to Mostyn for the final days of the service. On 1 April, a lorry driver failed to collect his vehicle from *European Envoy* when she arrived at Dublin from Mostyn. An unsuccessful air/sea search was mounted, concentrated around her position at midnight. The final sailing left Mostyn on the evening of 4 April. *European Envoy* was sold to Stena and returned to the Mersey until 21 April, when she departed under the name *Envoy*, having been re-sold to KystLink of Norway for the Langesund, Norway–Hirtshals, Denmark, service, on which she makes one round sailing daily. She returned to Liverpool–Dublin on charter to P&O, in July 2005, to cover overhauls of the regular ships.

Viking Trader/Leopard/European Navigator

Viking Trader was ordered by Stena as the lead vessel in a group of three ships that were a slightly smaller version of *Bison*. They were built in Austria by Osterreichische Schiffswerften, of Korneuburg on the river Danube, in the heart of Europe. Her hull, up to bulwark height, was launched on 15 January 1976, when she was named *Stena Tender*. Her superstructure was constructed separately on a barge. The plan was to tow the hull and the barge together down the Danube through Yugoslavia and into Romania to Galati, which is about 100 miles above the point where the Danube emerges into the Black Sea. The two halves of the ship would be joined together there. It was at this stage that theory and practice diverged. A collapsed road bridge in Vienna delayed the tow. When that obstacle had been passed, the level of river water had fallen and the hull grounded. There was a delay until October 1976 before there was sufficient water for the hull to be refloated. The tow then resumed but, by the time it had reached the bridge at Novostad in Yugoslavia, the river level had risen substantially. The hull was able to get under the bridge, but the barge and superstructure were unable to follow. As a result, there was a further delay until spring 1977, when the river fell sufficiently for the barge to pass under the bridge. By this time, Stena had sold the uncompleted ship to the United Baltic Corporation for operation by its subsidiary MacAndrews & Co. After the separate parts had been joined, she was towed to the West German yard, Werft Nobiskrug, at Rendsburg, to be lengthened by 27.1m. She arrived there on 14 October 1977, some twenty-one months after being launched. On completion of her lengthening, which gave her capacity for seventy trailers, she was renamed *Goya* and placed in service between Southampton and Bilbao.

Her two sisters were built at the same yard, but fared much better. The second ship was launched on 22 June 1976 as *Stena Topper*. She was completed in May 1977 and leased to Sealink for fifteen years. She went to Harland & Wolff at Belfast to have accommodation for seventy passengers added, was renamed *Darnia* and entered service at Stranraer in August 1978. The final ship was launched on 28 January 1977 as *Stena Timer*. She was completed in April 1977, apparently earlier than *Stena Topper*, and was chartered to Pandoro, renamed *Jaguar* and used on Fleetwood–Larne. Her charter ended in 1978, when her name reverted to *Stena Timer*.

Goya lasted only until 1980 with MacAndrews. There then followed a quick succession of changes of owner and name, in which she became *Federal Nova* in 1980, *Caribbean Sky* in 1981, *Manaure VII* in 1982 and *Oyster Bay* in 1983. Finally, in early October 1983, she was sold to Cenargo. She was chartered for five years to Townsend Thoresen, who renamed her *Viking Trader* and placed her on their freight service between Southampton and Le Havre. Her name was a reminder of the Thoresen '*Vikings*' which had re-started Southampton–Le Havre in 1964. She was given an orange hull, which had always been a characteristic feature of the '*Vikings*', with the words 'TOWNSEND THORESEN' in white letters. Her funnel was blue/green, with a narrow black top and the white letters 'TT' in outline. The letters also appeared at the forward end of her superstructure.

In 1984, *Viking Trader* was given accommodation for seventy-six passengers, including forty berths. On 3 November 1984, she transferred her British terminal to Portsmouth. The passenger vessels had transferred at the start of 1984, but Portsmouth had no berth suitable for *Viking Trader* at the time. She was laid up at Southampton on 1 October 1986, as part of a deal with French trade unions to secure the sale of a French-flagged ship. In early January 1987, she returned to service, covering overhauls of other Townsend Thoresen ferries at Felixstowe and Cairnryan. She resumed her Le Havre sailings in the spring.

Townsend Thoresen was taken over by P&O on 5 December 1986. The first sign of the change was the repainting of the funnels of all Townsend Thoresen's vessels in P&O's colours. At that time, the colours were pale blue, with the P&O houseflag. *Viking Trader* retained a narrow black top. She also retained her orange hull, marked 'TOWNSEND THORESEN'.

Early in 1988, *Viking Trader* was chartered to Pandoro to operate on Liverpool–Dublin while *Buffalo* was lengthened. When *Buffalo*'s alterations were finished, *Viking Trader* returned to Portsmouth. In autumn of that year, at the end of her charter, *Viking Trader* was bought by P&O. She was then transferred to Pandoro and took over on Fleetwood–Larne, replacing *Bison*, which transferred to Liverpool–Dublin in January 1989. She was overhauled in Liverpool in January 1989, when she was given Pandoro colours, including a dark blue funnel with the P&O flag.

Viking Trader then served on Fleetwood–Larne until mid-1996. She operated some Dublin–Pembroke Dock sailings in summer 1990, to help clear a backlog that had built up during a strike at Liverpool. In June and July 1994, she operated some Fleetwood–Dublin sailings between her Larne sailings, to help cover for *Bison*. In early January 1995, she operated one round Rosslare–Cherbourg sailing.

It was announced during 1995 that Pandoro intended to standardise its nomenclature on its 'animal' theme; *Viking Trader* would be renamed *Jaguar*. However, it was then found that there was already a vessel with the name *Jaguar* on the British Register, with the result that she retained the name *Viking Trader*. After a lengthy delay, the name *Leopard* was chosen instead and the change was made in summer 1996. Following the change, she was transferred to Liverpool–Dublin in July 1996. However, her stay at Liverpool was short-lived; she returned to Fleetwood in December 1996 for reliefs on Fleetwood–Larne and then reopened Fleetwood–Dublin in January 1997. She made one round sailing per day, departing from Fleetwood in the early morning and Dublin in the early evening, with a passage time of eight hours. She also covered weekend Dublin–Liverpool sailings for *Puma*, which had started a new weekend Dublin–Cherbourg service. In June 1997,

Viking Trader (1977) in June 1995. (Author)

she transferred briefly to Cairnryan–Larne to cover for the overhauls of the regular ships. Later, she moved back to Liverpool–Dublin, which she operated as *European Navigator*, having received her ninth name in 1998. She was back on Cairnryan–Larne in summer 1999, again providing overhaul cover, and she also offered an additional daily sailing because of increased demand. While she was away from Liverpool–Dublin, the chartered *Celtic Star* operated her sailings. Afterwards, she again returned to Liverpool–Dublin, covering other overhauls. Towards the end of 1999, she returned to Fleetwood–Larne, introducing a third daily round sailing. On 7 January 2000, a sudden change in the direction of the wind blew her aground at Larne at the end of a crossing from Fleetwood. An inspection found little damage, so she remained in service.

The company's more northerly Scottish terminal was moved from Ardrossan to Troon in July 2001. *European Navigator* became associated with this new route in its early days, replacing *European Mariner* (ex-*European Highlander*, ex-*Lion*). From 1 March 2002, she began carrying cars and motorists on the service and she featured in the route description in the company's 2002 brochure. Despite this, she served elsewhere occasionally during the year. On 22 June, she visited Campbeltown to collect fourteen windmills, bound for a wind farm off Rosslare. She developed a leak in her engine cooling system on 30 August, while sailing between Troon and Larne, and the resulting flood led to engine failure. The emergency services were placed on full alert as the ship lost power and started to drift. The Troon and Girvan lifeboats were launched in case it was necessary to evacuate her. However, she anchored and the problem was corrected, allowing her to complete her voyage. She was withdrawn for overhaul on 22 September, but was recalled hastily when her replacement, *European Mariner*, was chartered for service to Shetland.

When *European Mariner* returned to Troon–Larne, *European Navigator* was withdrawn. She left Larne on 1 February 2003, bound for Birkenhead. Her buyers took delivery on

European Navigator (1977) in the Mersey in September 1999. She was formerly *Viking Trader*. (Author)

17 February, and renamed her *Black Iris*, under the Jordanian flag. She is operated by the Arab Bridge Maritime Co., owned equally by the Governments of Jordan, Egypt and Iraq. Her route is a three-hour crossing of the Gulf of Aquaba, between Aquaba, Jordan, and Nuweibah, Egypt.

European Ambassador

European Ambassador was ordered from the Japanese shipbuilder Mitsubishi, of Shimonoeki. She was a development of *European Causeway*, built for Cairnryan–Larne. P&O had options to build two similar ships, but the final option, for a sister to *European Ambassador*, was not taken up. The result was that *European Ambassador* was a 'one-off' and never formed part of a properly balanced service.

She was launched on 18 August 2000 and left Japan on 13 December, on her 10,800-mile delivery voyage to Liverpool. She made refuelling stops at Singapore (18 December) and Jeddah (26–27 December), then transited the Suez Canal (29 December), and picked up more crew at Gibraltar (2 January). After a publicity call at Dublin (6 January), she docked at Liverpool early on 7 January. A reception was held on board that evening and she entered service next evening. Her regular pattern was overnight from Liverpool at 22.00, returning from Dublin by day. Her timetable made her the first ferry to arrive at Dublin in the morning (05.30).

European Ambassador had three vehicle decks, housing 123 trailers or 375 cars or combinations thereof. For vehicles, there were two main decks and a third small deck. Access to the two main vehicle decks was by bow and stern ramps; internal ramps connected all three decks. Passenger accommodation was located above the vehicle decks and was reached from them by lifts to the reception area and shop. There were two principal public rooms: Fables Restaurant (self-service) and the Poets Bar, located forward with seats for 105 passengers. Other public rooms were a sixty-seat restaurant aft for commercial vehicle drivers, a club-class lounge offering additional facilities for sixty-one passengers, a video lounge, two video games rooms and a children's play area. There were en-suite cabins for 220 passengers, comprising ninety-eight two-berth, twenty-nine four-berth and two four-berth club-class cabins with a TV and fridge. Her total passenger capacity was 405.

After her entry into service, *European Ambassador* had an official naming ceremony in Dublin on 26 January. Afterwards, there was a reception on board for invited guests, followed by a cruise around Dublin Bay and along the Wicklow coast, with music by an Army Band.

After P&O had signed a long-term agreement for the use of Mostyn, it was announced that *European Ambassador* and *European Envoy*, would transfer there. *European Ambassador*'s first sailing on the route was on 20 November. Her service speed of 25 knots allowed her to make the crossing in six hours, but her companion needed seven-and-a-half hours. *European Ambassador*'s propellers became entangled in a mooring rope on 9 January 2002, preventing her from leaving and resulting in the diversion of the incoming *European Envoy* to Liverpool. Regular problems were caused by low tides. By the end of the summer 2002, some of *European Ambassador*'s sailings had been re-timed to take seven-and-a-half hours.

Each summer weekend in 2002, *European Ambassador* made a Dublin–Cherbourg round sailing. She departed from Dublin on Saturday afternoon, after an overnight crossing from Mostyn, and was back at Dublin on Monday morning. She could be spared from Mostyn–Dublin for most of this period, as there was less freight traffic at weekends, but her key Sunday evening crossing from Dublin was taken by *Norbay*. The Dublin–Cherbourg season was due to run from 1 June to 3 September, but was extended for another two months because of its success. The final sailing of the season called at Rosslare on 2 November, but was diverted to Brest because of industrial action at Cherbourg. On 11 January 2003, *European Ambassador* made an out-of-season Dublin–Cherbourg sailing, calling also at Rosslare southbound, to cover for *European Diplomat*. The 2003 Dublin–Cherbourg season ran between April and November and carried foot passengers. It was advertised also as a mini-cruise with five hours ashore in France, costing from £59 including meals and a club-class seat. The 2003 service was extended to 31 March 2004, with all southbound out-of-season sailings calling at Rosslare, avoiding one Rosslare–Cherbourg round trip by *European Diplomat*.

There were only a few small changes to *European Ambassador*'s programme in 2003. In the early months, she operated a Saturday afternoon Dublin–Liverpool sailing, returning overnight. There was no cover for her missed Sunday evening crossing from Dublin, suggesting that P&O's disenchantment with the service had begun.

With the announcement of the sale of P&O's services to Stena came the news that Mostyn–Dublin was to be closed, with both ships being chartered to Stena. The run-down of Mostyn–Dublin began on the weekend of 20–21 March, when *European Ambassador* was withdrawn from the route. She transferred to Liverpool–Dublin, covering *Norbay's* overhaul and maintaining Dublin–Cherbourg until 4 April, when that service ended. *European Ambassador* remained on Liverpool–Dublin until 8 April and then dry-docked at Liverpool. She was handed over to Stena on 19 April and left Liverpool that afternoon with most of her P&O markings removed. After a call at Larne next morning to pick up spares, she sailed to Gothenburg, where she arrived on 20 April. She was renamed *Stena Nordica* and replaced *Stena Traveller* on Stena's Karlskrona–Gdynia route during May. She is expected to have additional cabins fitted later. She was due to return to the Irish Sea in May 2005, to perform reliefs for Stena, but this did not happen.

Norbank and *Norbay*

Norbank and *Norbay* are the two ships regularly employed on P&O's Liverpool–Dublin service at the time of writing. Their names, which do not follow P&O's usual patterns, give a clue to their origins. In December 1965, a new company, North Sea Ferries, began an overnight Hull–Rotterdam service. In 1981, the company came under the joint ownership of P&O and the Royal Nedlloyd Group. A third generation of ferries, *Norsea* and *Norsun*, took over the service in 1987. *Norbank* and *Norbay* were built in 1993 and 1994 to provide extra capacity on the route. Unlike *Norsea* and *Norsun*, which berthed inside Hull's enclosed docks, they used a new river berth which allowed the pair, with their 22-knot speed, to reduce the passage time by three hours, affording a later departure. This was aimed at attracting freight from routes further south. P&O acquired Royal Nedlloyd's 50 per cent share in North Sea Ferries in September 1996 and later the operation became P&O North Sea Ferries. In 2001, two new larger ships, *Pride of Rotterdam* and *Pride of Hull*, took over, replacing the four previous ships. *Norbank* was switched to Felixstowe–Rotterdam in May 2001, but she and *Norbay* were transferred to P&O Irish Sea in January 2002 and took over Liverpool–Dublin.

Both ships were built near Rotterdam by Van der Giessen-de Noord. In keeping with the Anglo-Dutch ownership of the company, *Norbank* was registered at Rotterdam by Nedlloyd, while *Norbay* was registered at Hull by P&O. They were designed to carry 156 trailers on three decks, loaded across a stern ramp to the main deck, with internal ramps to the other vehicle decks. A staircase from the vehicle decks to a catwalk ahead of the funnel leads to the passenger accommodation forward. The accommodation on C Deck comprises a reception area and shop, a self-service dining area and a bar/lounge. There are fifty-seven two-berth cabins on B Deck. The ships were designed for conversion to carry additional passengers, which has not happened.

Norbank was launched on 5 June 1993 and her first arrival at Hull was on 4 November; *Norbay* was launched on 13 November 1993 and entered service at the end of February 1994. Following P&O's acquisition of 100 per cent of North Sea Ferries in 1996, *Norbank* retained her Netherlands registry.

After the completion of the two new ferries for Hull–Rotterdam in 2001, it was planned that *Norbank* and *Norbay* would be transferred to Felixstowe–Rotterdam.

Norbank (1993), sailing out of the Mersey in June 2004. (Author)

Norbank was indeed transferred in May 2001 but, instead of *Norbay* joining her, both ships were transferred to Liverpool–Dublin in January 2002. This followed the transfer of *European Ambassador* and *European Envoy* from Liverpool to Mostyn in November 2001 and ensured that some passenger accommodation continued to be available on Liverpool–Dublin. The ships replaced by the new arrivals were *Celtic Star* and *Pride of Suffolk. Norbay's* registration was transferred to Bermuda before she started on her new route, but *Norbank's* registration was unchanged. This led to the unusual situation of a Dutch ship in service between Britain and Ireland.

Each sister made one round sailing per day, except on Sunday and Monday when no daytime sailing was provided. *Norbank* sailed overnight from Liverpool, returning by day, with *Norbay* sailing in the reverse direction. The overnight sailings were reversed on Sundays. From 2 June to 2 September 2002, *Norbay* made a Sunday night sailing from Dublin to Mostyn during *European Ambassador's* Dublin–Cherbourg weekend sailings. This schedule then required her to sail light to Liverpool for her Monday evening departure to Dublin. A local coach operator arranged to carry two coachloads of passengers on each light sailing. The fare included lunch (or breakfast on early morning departures) and afternoon tea. These excursions proved very popular and were quickly sold out. However, the arrangement was not repeated in 2003.

Norbank suffered a small fire in a furniture van on board on 15 June 2003, while awaiting departure from Liverpool. The fire brigade attended, but there was little delay to the sailing. *Norbay* visited Larne on 26 October 2003 for an underwater survey by divers.

The sale of P&O's central corridor operations to Stena took place on 19 April 2004, but did not include Liverpool–Dublin as originally intended. *Norbank* and *Norbay* have continued to operate the service ever since.

SIX

ISLE OF MAN STEAM PACKET CO./SEA CONTAINERS/IRISH SEA EXPRESS

The closure of Sealink's Dun Laoghaire service in 1990 left Liverpool without any passenger service to the Dublin area. This situation was unprecedented in peacetime, except for the few winter months between the closure of B&I's service and the start of Sealink's service. Some years were to pass before the restoration of a service. When it occurred, it came from an unexpected direction.

The Isle of Man Steam Packet Co. had been formed in 1830. The company appears in the volume of this series dealing with the Liverpool–Cork route, as it roundly defeated the Saint George Steam Packet Co. and drove it off the Liverpool–Douglas route. Its history has probably been recorded more often than that of any other cross-Channel company and does not need repetition here. Suffice to say that from the early 1970s the company suffered a decline in its traditional holiday business. It failed to respond appropriately to the establishment of a competitor in 1978, so its position had become very weak by 1984, when it did belatedly buy a passenger/freight ro-ro vessel. Sealink, by then a subsidiary of Sea Containers, acquired a shareholding in the company in 1985 as the price for a merger of the two companies' services, including the complete abandonment of Liverpool services. The Isle of Man Steam Packet Co. became a full subsidiary of Sea Containers in 1996.

Sea Containers was keen to build a network of Irish Sea services. As an experiment, a Fleetwood–Dublin service was started in the autumn of 1996, using *Lady of Mann*. It was expected that this service would be repeated in 1997, but instead the more realistic Liverpool–Dublin route was chosen. *Lady of Mann* operated the service daily, except on Wednesdays when the sailings were taken by *SeaCat Isle of Man*. The service, which began on 12 June 1997, was described as 'seasonal', but actually ran through to January 1998.

Sea Containers' second generation of fast craft consisted of SuperSeaCats. The new Liverpool–Dublin service by *Lady of Mann* had clearly been successful, as it was announced that the third of these vessels, *SuperSeaCat Three* was destined for Liverpool–Dublin when she was delivered in 1999. In the meantime, *SuperSeaCat Two* operated the 1998 service. *SuperSeaCat Three* completed two seasons on Liverpool–Dublin, but was transferred to the Straits of Dover in 2001 and replaced by another SeaCat, *Rapide*. She lasted only one season on the route and *SuperSeaCat Three* returned in 2002. It was planned that she would remain on the service in 2003, but she suffered engine problems in February 2003, causing *SuperSeaCat Two* to return.

Sea Containers had been suffering financial difficulties and offered various assets for sale. In June 2003 it accepted an offer by Montagu Private Equity for the Isle of Man Steam Packet Co. The pattern of Liverpool–Dublin sailings remained unchanged for the rest of 2003 and was similar for 2004. After rumours of substantial changes in 2005, in November 2004 the Steam Packet announced the complete cessation of Liverpool–Dublin, and a concentration on serving the Isle of Man. *SuperSeaCat Two* would be used exclusively on Manx services in 2005.

However, this announcement did not mark the end of fast-craft services between Liverpool and Dublin. It was announced that *SeaCat Isle of Man* was to be chartered to a new operator, Irish Sea Express. She was renamed *Sea Express I*, and entered service between Liverpool and Dublin on 27 April 2005. Her new operator provided her crew, but management of the craft remained with the Isle of Man Steam Packet Co., thus providing a link with the previous operator.

Lady of Mann

Lady of Mann operated Liverpool–Dublin each day except Wednesday during the first year of the service (1997). Since then, she has made occasional sailings on the route, when weather or technical problems have prevented a fast craft from taking a sailing.

Lady of Mann was the fourth and final ship in the series of 'side loaders' delivered to the Isle of Man Steam Packet Co. between 1962 and 1976 As with her earlier sister, *Mona's Queen*, she was built by the Ailsa Shipbuilding Co., of Troon, Ayrshire. The order was placed in August 1973, at a price of £3.8 million. Her launch took place on 4 December 1975, the sponsor being Mrs Keith Rae, the wife of a director of the company. The company expected to take delivery of her in time for TT, but there were delays and she did not arrive in Douglas until 29 June, long after the motorcyclists had left the Island. This delay resulted in the cancellation of the inaugural car ferry sailing from Fleetwood to Douglas on 13 June.

As built, *Lady of Mann* had accommodation for 1,600 passengers and around 100 cars. The passenger accommodation was typical of Isle of Man ships of the era. There were two main passenger decks: Shelter and Promenade, with a lounge forward on each deck. Further aft, there were two smoke rooms and bars, a dining saloon, two further lounges and fifteen private cabins. There were two lounges below the car deck, one for ladies and a 'sleeping lounge'. The Boat Deck allowed passengers to sit in the open on wooden seats, and deck chairs could be taken onto the various levels of the vehicle ramps, with a favourite spot being immediately aft of the Shelter Deck superstructure. *Lady of Mann's* engines were built by Crossley Brothers, of Manchester, and gave her a maximum speed of 23 knots; her normal service speed was 21 knots. She was painted in traditional Steam Packet colours: a black hull with red boot topping, separated by a white line, white superstructure and red 'funnel' with a black top and black bands. This 'funnel' was in fact a dummy; the real engine exhaust was located about three-quarters aft and painted yellow. In keeping with a Steam Packet tradition for new ships, the name '*LADY OF MANN*' on her bow was painted in yellow, but was repainted black after her first year in service.

Lady of Mann made her maiden voyage from Douglas to Liverpool on 30 June. Her schedule called on her to serve all the company's main ports except Llandudno. Her first sailing to Belfast was on 13 July, to Ardrossan on 16 July, to Fleetwood on 18 July and to Dublin on 28 July. It is customary for each new Isle of Man vessel to make a sailing around the Island; *Lady of Mann* performed hers on 11 July. She also made two evening cruises from Douglas to the Calf of Man. The winter service required two ships operating between Douglas and Liverpool, each vessel normally making a single daily crossing, Sundays excepted. As their diesel engines were more economical than the steam turbines of their predecessors, *Lady of Mann* and *Mona's Queen* were the regular winter vessels. On 5 October, *Lady of Mann* made her first call at Peel on the west coast of the island, as berthing at Douglas had been made impossible by the strength and direction of the wind.

Lady of Mann returned to Troon in April 1977 for her guarantee overhaul. She re-entered service in May and, on 21 June, represented the Steam Packet in a Royal Review of shipping in the Mersey. By that time, the Isle of Man Harbour Board was considering the provision of ro-ro facilities at Douglas and, later in the year, the Manx Government authorised the spending of £650,000 to assist the establishment of a competitive ro-ro service. The competition was duly provided in 1978 by the newly formed Manx Line. One effect of the increased competition was that the Steam Packet cancelled its planned order of another car ferry for delivery in 1981. *Lady of Mann* made her first visit to Manchester on 27 March 1978 for her annual overhaul. During the winter of 1978/79, there was an abnormally large number of diversions to Peel; on 24 December 1978, *Lady of Mann* and *Mona's Queen* were both at Peel, which is believed to be the first occasion when two Steam Packet vessels had been there together.

In May 1979, a programme of charter sailings was operated. Unusual trips by *Lady of Mann* were Dublin to Douglas, Warrenpoint to Douglas (diverted from Peel), Belfast to Peel, Workington to Douglas and Holyhead to Douglas. She also made several charter sailings from Liverpool during this period. On 19 May, her morning departure from Liverpool was delayed for two hours by a bomb scare. In spring 1980, she again operated a charter programme, which included a sailing from Greenore to Douglas on 6 May. This call by *Lady of Mann* is believed to have been the first there by a Steam Packet vessel for forty-five years. In February 1981, *Lady of Mann*'s annual overhaul was carried out at Govan, where she arrived on 22 March. After her return in time for Easter, *Lady of Mann* carried out many of the, by now, annual spring charters, calling at Douglas, Peel, Belfast, Warrenpoint and Dublin. In May 1982, her catering facilities were altered by the installation of a cafeteria in place of the dining saloon. In the following spring, she received a more extensive refit. Her Boat Deck bar was converted to a Grill Room, partly replacing the dining saloon lost in the previous refit, and she was given aircraft-type seats and fixed seating in the cafeteria. During this refit, the words 'ISLE OF MAN STEAM PACKET' were painted on her sides in two wavy rows 8 feet high. It was hoped that this would produce free publicity for the company when she appeared on TV programmes. The letters proved too small to be read at a distance and were replaced by a single straight row of much larger letters in 1984. On 5 July 1983, she operated the annual Tynwald Day excursion, from Douglas to Fleetwood. On 13 July, she made the first call at a new terminal at Dublin. As usual, *Lady of Mann* operated most of the limited programme of spring charters in 1984. However, the sailing from Greenore actually used Warrenpoint because of bad weather on the day. From 7 January 1985, during overhauls, a single vessel operated the Liverpool winter service, rather than by the customary two ships. Despite a Liverpool turnround time of only eighty minutes, *Lady of Mann* was able to keep to the schedule, even in gale conditions. The announcement of the Steam Packet's merger and withdrawal from Liverpool was made on 1 February 1985. In future, the company's main service, Douglas–Heysham, would be operated by the newly acquired and refitted *Mona's Isle* and the former competitor *Manx Viking*, with support sailings and other routes being operated by *Lady of Mann* and *Mona's Queen*.

Lady of Mann had been overhauled at Birkenhead in March 1985. As a precaution against a protest occupation, she left Birkenhead on 27 March and went to Douglas to lay up until Easter. However, *Mona's Isle* was unable to enter service on Douglas–Heysham as planned on 1 April and *Manx Viking*'s passenger certificate expired on 3 April. These events forced the 'new' Steam Packet to bring *Lady of Mann* into service early to operate Douglas–Heysham alongside *Mona's Queen*. *Mona's Isle*, which had been refitted and 'improved' on the Clyde, did manage to operate a programme of Irish sailings over Easter, but berthed at Dun Laoghaire rather than at Dublin. *Lady of Mann* assisted her by making one trip to Dublin on Easter Tuesday, 9 April. The problem preventing *Mona's Isle* from operating on Douglas–Heysham was a lack of deadweight capacity for freight and a failure to fit the Heysham linkspan. She finally entered Douglas–Heysham on 21 April, but only after a return visit to the Clyde for alterations to her stern ramp. *Lady of Mann* was laid up at Douglas from 21 April until 19 May, although she was also called on for a supplementary Heysham sailing on 12 May. Belfast Car Ferries' *Saint Colum I*, operating on Liverpool–Belfast, had suffered engine problems and was off service between 25 and 30 June. *Lady of Mann* was chartered to operate three single sailings between Heysham and Belfast over the weekend of 28 and 29 June. On 14 August, en route from Douglas to Dublin, she stood by a yacht in difficulties in a force 8 gale and took two of the yacht's crew on board. Later, during the same sailing, two passengers became ill and were lifted off by an Air-Sea Rescue helicopter from RAF Valley. Next day, also on a Douglas–Dublin sailing, another passenger became ill and the same procedure was followed. In August, a number of major decisions were taken, involving the replacement of the entire fleet by around 1987. The immediate decision was to withdraw *Mona's Isle* in October and sell her, the replacement being Sealink's *Antrim Princess*. *Lady of Mann* and *Mona's Queen* were both to be replaced by new ro-ro tonnage, probably for the 1987 season. The board also decided to reintroduce a seasonal weekly service to Liverpool in 1986 and close the Fleetwood and Ardrossan routes. *Lady of Mann's* season ended on 19 September and she was laid up at Birkenhead; this was the first year that she had not been scheduled to operate on the main winter service. However, the lay-up provided the opportunity to carry out work converting her ladies' lounge into a duty-free shop for use on her Dublin sailings. During the overhaul, the lettering was removed from her hull.

The Steam Packet must have been thoroughly glad to see the end of 1985. It decided that the seasonal Liverpool service would operate twice weekly, on Tuesdays and Saturdays, rather than once weekly, as originally planned. In a move that would have implications for the future Liverpool–Dublin service, Associated British Ports managed to retain Fleetwood as a port of call for Steam Packet vessels by chartering *Lady of Mann* or *Mona's Queen* for a twice-weekly summer 'Fun Boat' service between Fleetwood and Douglas. *Lady of Mann* re-entered service for Easter, but was then laid up again. She reopened Liverpool–Douglas on 20 May. One week later, she made the same sailing during gales which caused the cancellation of some Heysham sailings. With her new duty-free lounge, she was the vessel of choice for all but one of the Dublin sailings and so left the Fleetwood 'Fun Boat' sailings to *Mona's Queen*. She also served Belfast and gave additional sailings to Heysham during TT and occasionally at other times. The end of *Lady of Mann's* season was on 18 September, but she was back in service between 23 and 28 October for a special programme of autumn excursions, including a day excursion from Douglas to Fleetwood for Blackpool Illuminations.

By 1987, the worst of the Steam Packet's problems were over, although profit levels were still low. *Antrim Princess*, which had been renamed *Tynwald*, was performing well, although problems still arose during periods of bad weather. She operated the main Douglas–Heysham service, with the other routes in the hands of the side-loaders. The seasonal Liverpool service was scheduled for two sailings weekly, increasing to three in the main summer season. There was a sign of the gradual return to Liverpool on 25 May when both *Lady of Mann* and *Mona's Queen* were alongside Liverpool landing stage together. Associated British Ports again, through charter, arranged two sailings per week from Fleetwood. The Douglas–Ardrossan service had ceased after the 1985 season, but was replaced by a Douglas–Stranraer service in 1986. *Lady of Mann* made her first sailing on the route on 11 June 1987. She operated a Round the Island sailing on 21 June, the Tynwald Day excursion to Fleetwood on 6 July and another Round the Island cruise, for charity, on 30 August. She retired to dock early, on 16 September, for repairs to a faulty bow rudder. Once again, she came out of dock for the last weekend of October, operating special excursions to Dublin, Liverpool and Fleetwood.

The Steam Packet's 1988 timetable had one of the two side-loaders based on Liverpool throughout TT and a further improvement in the Liverpool–Douglas schedule, with at least three sailings per week throughout the season. A further change for the new season was a reduction in *Lady of Mann's* passenger certificate from 1,600 to 1,200 as a result of revised regulations following the sinking of *Herald of Free Enterprise* off Zeebrugge. Unusually, *Lady of Mann* was not in service over the winter or at Easter, the additional sailings being provided by *Mona's Queen*; *Lady of Mann* did not enter service until 24 May. She was the vessel chosen to operate the Liverpool 'shuttle' sailings before and after TT. Once again *Lady of Mann* operated the Tynwald Day excursion, to Fleetwood on 5 July, carrying a capacity crowd. On 25 July, in the early hours of the morning, she was struck by *Tynwald*, which was arriving at Douglas from Heysham. Her sailings for that day were cancelled while she was repaired. On 8 August, *Lady of Mann* shared Liverpool landing stage with the Royal Yacht *Britannia*. Her season ended on 25 September, but she was brought back out of dock on the following day after *Tynwald* had suffered technical problems; she returned to dock on 30 September.

A further improvement to Liverpool–Douglas took place in 1989. There were three sailings weekly, rising to four in July and August; there were also excursion sailings at Easter and the Spring Bank Holiday. The winter relief vessel was again *Mona's Queen*; this freed *Lady of Mann* for an extended overhaul and refit, costing £2.5 million, intended to increase her car capacity from 105 to 135 and to provide improved accommodation for 1,000 passengers. The work was undertaken at Birkenhead by Wright & Beyer and included grit blasting, red-leading and repainting the hull, superstructure and funnel. The passenger accommodation was remodelled, with the former Shelter and Promenade Decks gutted and all sliding passenger doors removed. The Boat Deck was given ten new cabins and timber decking (previously painted metal), the Promenade Deck had two lounges, an information bureau, a shop and a cafeteria, and the Shelter Deck was split fore and aft, with a bar and lounge forward and additional car space aft. The area below the main car deck was used for a duty-free shop, video lounge and children's play area. Her bridge front was adorned with a large circular motif showing the name of the company and the Legs of Man. Twin gold bands extended from each side of the motif round the front and sides of the superstructure; the words 'ISLE OF MAN STEAM PACKET COMPANY' appeared between the two gold lines on each side of the ship. The engine exhaust, previously in yellow and black, was painted in the company's full funnel colours; the painting of the dummy funnel amidships was unchanged. After completing her refit, *Lady of Mann* was due to make a Douglas–Peel sailing on 20/21 May, followed by promotional visits to Londonderry, Belfast and Dublin. The Londonderry visit would have been particularly interesting, as there had never been a Steam Packet service to the maiden city, but delays in completing the work forced the cancellation of these special events. *Lady of Mann*'s alterations were not complete when she was due to re-enter service on 26 May, but she was brought to a condition in which she could operate on a temporary certificate for 950 passengers. She was 're-commissioned' two days later at a special ceremony at Douglas, followed by an evening cruise south to the Calf of Mann and north to Laxey, including diversions into the bays at Port St Mary and Port Erin. *Lady of Mann* was needed in service to cover TT, for which she was again based at Liverpool. After TT, she returned to Birkenhead to complete her refit. She returned to service on 7 July, with a certificate for 1,000 passengers. Her reduced capacity caused problems on 26 July, when she took a Fleetwood sailing in place of *Mona's Queen* and was forced to leave 200 passengers behind. On the other hand, her increased car capacity proved a boon on 8 August, when she carried 138 cars from Liverpool, a record for a side-loader. In the autumn, *Mona's Queen* was chartered for service on the south coast, leaving *Lady of Mann* to make additional sailings over the Manx Grand Prix and Car Rally periods. The weather was so bad on 20 September that, most unusually, *Lady of Mann* was forced to turn back to Douglas on a Dublin sailing, after taking three hours to reach the Calf of Man. She operated an 'Illuminations Special' excursion from Douglas to Fleetwood on 24 September and retired to her winter berth in Liverpool on 27 September. She was chartered to B&I in December, after an accident to the linkspan at Rosslare. Surplus car traffic was diverted to Holyhead and *Lady of Mann* was chartered to carry this traffic, making two daily Holyhead–Dublin round sailings between 21 and 23 December.

Lady of Mann had only a short period in dock after her return on 24 December. On 31 January 1990, Sealink's *St Columba*, on her regular Dun Laoghaire–Holyhead service, suffered an engine room fire while she was 12 miles from South Stack, Anglesey. Fire-fighters were transferred to the ship by helicopter and she was later towed to Holyhead. *Lady of Mann* was chartered to take her place, making her first crossing on 9 February. As she could not carry the lorries normally handled by *St Columba*, she was partnered by Sealink's freight ferry *St Cybi* which, as *Dundalk*, had been built in 1974 for B&I. The charter lasted until 7 March, when Sealink's *Horsa* took over. When she returned to service for Easter, *Lady of Mann* started with a single sailing from Holyhead to Dublin on charter to B&I, to provide extra capacity following a fire on the chartered *Norröna*, operating on Pembroke Dock–Rosslare; this was her third period of service from Holyhead during the winter of 1989/90. Following her Easter programme, *Lady of Mann* was overhauled by Harland & Wolff at Belfast. She re-entered service on 17 May and once again provided the Liverpool 'shuttle' sailings during TT. At this time, Sea Containers, who already held 41 per cent of the shares in the Steam Packet, launched a bid to take over the whole company. The defence document produced by the Steam Packet referred to the recent purchase of Sealink's *Channel Entente*, which had replaced *Tynwald* on Douglas–Heysham, and stated that, after her refurbishment, she and *Lady of Mann* would have as much car capacity as the three passenger ships in the fleet before *Lady of Mann's* recent refit. This indicated that there was no future for *Mona's Queen* on Isle of Man routes, but the document stated that the company was examining several possibilities for her redeployment. As a result of blocking action by the Manx Government, Sea Containers' bid was withdrawn, but their ultimate intention was clear. Later, James Sherwood, chairman of Sea Containers, gave their thinking about the future of Manx services in an interview for the *Manx Independent*. Two SeaCats plus a large freight ro-ro ship would operate Douglas–Heysham. *Lady of Mann* would be retained for seasonal routes, supplementary Heysham sailings and SeaCat backup, but *Channel Entente* would be sold. After the main summer season, on 27 September, *Lady of Mann* took over Douglas–Heysham from *Channel Entente*, to allow her to be refitted. Before returning, *Channel Entente* was renamed *King Orry*. At the end of October, *Lady of Mann* made two Irish Bank Holiday weekend round trips to Dublin between her Heysham sailings. *King Orry* entered service on 9 December and *Lady of Mann* was then laid up. However, this proved short-lived and she returned to service on 3 January, providing passenger and car cover while *King Orry* was used for freight sailings during the overhaul of the normal freight vessel, *Peveril*, and then to cover for an unexpected dry-docking of *King Orry*. She remained in service until 26 January.

A further stage in the revival of Liverpool–Douglas occurred in January 1991, when the winter Saturday sailings went to Liverpool rather than Heysham. This was very popular with Manx residents, as it gave them the opportunity to spend Saturday afternoon shopping or watching a major football match, neither of which was possible from Heysham. *Lady of Mann* made the first sailing of the new service on 12 January. She again covered the winter service between 28 February and 6 March after *King Orry* had suffered further problems, but was not required over Easter. Liverpool's summer service was increased to five days per week at peak periods, with a slight reduction in the number of Heysham sailings. The passenger service was operated by just two ships, *Lady of Mann* and *King Orry*. As a result of *Mona's Queen's* withdrawal, most of the Liverpool sailings except on Sundays and virtually all the Fleetwood, Belfast and Dublin sailings were taken by *Lady of Mann*; the number of Irish sailings was reduced significantly. After her overhaul, *Lady of Mann* re-entered service on 19 May with a charity cruise from Douglas to Ramsey, when she called at the south breakwater in Ramsey Harbour. This was the first call at Ramsey since 1970, when Queen's Pier had been closed, and the first passenger call at the south breakwater since before 1939. *Lady of Mann* ended her season on 18 September. Quite unusually, she remained laid up for the rest of the year. At this time, relationships between the Steam Packet's board and Sea Containers were strained. Sea Containers proposed a number of conditions for not proceeding with a full bid for the Steam Packet, two of which were the use by the Steam Packet of a SeaCat and a charter of *Lady of Mann* as winter cover for Sea Containers' proposed Stranraer–Belfast service by a SeaCat.

An innovation in the Steam Packet's 1992 sailing schedules was the introduction of through-bookings from Liverpool or Heysham to Belfast, with the ship calling at Douglas. There was a weekly service to/from each English port; the Liverpool sailings were made by *Lady of Mann*, sailing from Liverpool on Fridays and from Belfast on Mondays. *Lady of Mann* entered service on 10 January, covering *King Orry* for her overhaul, and remained in service until 16 February, after which she called at Belfast to test the side-loading arrangements at a new Donegal Quay berth. After overhaul, she re-entered service on 21 May. Three days later, she offered a special excursion from Fleetwood to Douglas in celebration of the sesquicentenary (150th anniversary) of the first Fleetwood sailing on 31 May 1842. While her Fleetwood passengers were ashore, she made another excursion, round the south of the Island to Peel. *King Orry* was withdrawn on 7 June for emergency propeller repairs and, over the next thirty-six hours, *Lady of Mann* covered all but one of the sailings of the two-ship schedule. After a long period of great reliability, the inevitable occurred on 4 August when *Lady of Mann* developed engine problems during an evening crossing to Fleetwood on a 'Fun Boat' excursion. The ship's departure from Douglas had already been delayed until 20.30 by tidal conditions at Fleetwood. Three hours out of Douglas, with deteriorating weather and one engine out of service, it was decided to divert her to Liverpool. Her arrival there was delayed until 05.30 next morning, when passengers had to be transported back to Fleetwood. *Lady of Mann's* engine problems were soon sorted out and she was back in service later the same day. On 10 September, she was a few miles out from Dublin on passage to Douglas when she spotted a capsized yacht. After a delay of around three hours searching for survivors, it was realised that the yacht had sunk during the previous week. Five days later, *Lady of Mann* added another port to her long list of calls, with a visit to Barrow to operate a charter to Associated British Ports, celebrating the 125th anniversary of the Port of Barrow and the opening of the new dock entrance and deep-water channel to Barrow's Ramsden Dock. Afterwards, she spent 16–17 September relieving *King Orry* on Douglas–Heysham and was then laid up. As usual her services were soon required again. On 14 November, *King Orry* suffered steering problems and then ran aground in the Crosby Channel while leaving Liverpool. She was refloated with the help of two tugs, which towed her back to Liverpool. *Lady of Mann* made her first relief sailing in the early hours of 16 November. Those duties ended on 21 November. At this time, there were conflicting reports about the future of *Lady of Mann*. The Steam Packet was examining the use of fast craft, but they were unlikely to be available for 1993, so *Lady of Mann* featured in the company's plans for that year. In contrast, Sea Containers announced that they wished to use her in British Columbia, from Victoria to Seattle/Port Angeles. The proposal was subject to the agreement of the Government of British Columbia, which in the event asked its own BC Ferry Corporation to operate the service.

Lady of Mann was back in service as a relief for *King Orry* between 22 January and 20 February 1993. After the single-ship service provided over Easter in 1992, the Manx Government offered a subsidy for a two-ship service in 1993, so *Lady of Mann* was also in service. After her overhaul and before the start of the 1993 summer season, she was scheduled to take part in the Royal Review of the Fleet, off Anglesey on 26 May, carrying 492 passengers from Liverpool. The Review was being held to commemorate the Battle of the Atlantic, which had been commanded from Liverpool. Conditions that day were poor, with winds gusting up to 60 knots. *Lady of Mann* was unable to anchor and had to manoeuvre with her engines in order to remain on station for eight hours. Other ships taking part were the Royal Yacht *Britannia*, Pandoro's *Buffalo* and Stena Line's *Stena Cambria*. This sailing was followed by another excursion, landing at Port St Mary in the south of the Island, on 30 May. This was *Lady of Mann's* fourth Manx port of call. She then took up her TT sailings but, on 2 June, she hit the Battery Pier at Douglas, damaged her bow and was withdrawn for temporary repairs involving the construction of a collision bulkhead behind the bow. During *Lady of Mann's* absence, her sailings were covered by chartering *SeaCat Scotland* from Sea Containers and *Pioneer* from Caledonian MacBrayne. Once TT was over, *Lady of Mann* was withdrawn again between 17 and 21 June while permanent repairs were carried out. After the summer, she was docked for the remainder of the year.

The next year, 1994, saw the start of major changes in the pattern of *Lady of Mann's* activities. In December 1993, the company and the Manx Government agreed the terms of a user agreement which designated the Steam Packet as the sole provider of passenger and freight ro-ro services to the island in return for operating at least a guaranteed minimum number of sailings each year. Under this agreement, the Manx Government was to provide a new deep-water ro-ro berth at Douglas.

As usual, *Lady of Mann* took over from *King Orry*, from 6 January 1994, while *King Orry* was overhauled. It was announced that *SeaCat Boulogne* would enter Manx service in June, replacing *Lady of Mann*. The SeaCat, by now renamed *SeaCat Isle of Man*, entered service rather later than planned, on 28 June. *Lady of Mann* remained in service for TT, making her 'final' calls at Fleetwood on 21 June, Dublin and Belfast on 26 June and Liverpool on 27 June. She returned light to Birkenhead on 28 June after a 'sail past' Douglas harbour entrance dressed overall, and was laid up for the remainder of the summer to provide cover if rough weather prevented the SeaCat from sailing. In fact, the Irish Sea had one of its calmest summers for years so *Lady of Mann* was not used.

Lady of Mann was needed again in February 1995, when she relieved *King Orry* for her usual winter overhaul. She was out also for TT and operated what were again widely believed to be her 'final' sailings, to Belfast on 11 June and a single to Liverpool on 12 June. Several Portuguese shipowners were on board during her Belfast sailings and she had also been inspected in service by Greek shipowners, so rumours of her sale were rife. After her final Liverpool sailing, she retired to Birkenhead and soon afterwards moved to Bidston dry-dock, whence she emerged on 17 July flying the Portuguese flag. Her port of registry had been changed to Madeira, but she was still in full Isle of Man Steam Packet colours. She had been chartered to the PS Line, of Funchal, Madeira, to operate a summer service from Funchal to Porto Santo. The work in dry-dock had included fitting a watertight door near her stern to prevent sea water flooding down onto the car deck. After finishing her charter in Madeira, *Lady of Mann* returned to dock in Birkenhead on 16 November.

As usual, in 1996 *Lady of Mann* carried out the normal programme of winter reliefs for *King Orry*. *SeaCat Isle of Man*'s charter was not renewed, so *Lady of Mann* had a full programme of summer Isle of Man sailings, operating to Liverpool, Fleetwood, Belfast and Dublin, as well as to Heysham over TT. The Isle of Man Steam Packet Co. became a full subsidiary of Sea Containers during the summer and then announced ambitious expansion plans. It was to order a new ro-ro freight vessel with some passenger accommodation, and charter a SeaCat and a SuperSeaCat. This announcement appeared to leave no room for *Lady of Mann* in the fleet. However, in October, she was based at Fleetwood for an innovative programme, designed to test out possible new routes. She operated three round trips to Douglas, including day excursions on Saturdays and Sundays and two round trips to Dublin. One of the Dublin sailings was a Monday round trip and the other crossed to Dublin on Thursdays, returning on Fridays. It was stated that, if the sailings were successful, the company would operate a regular Fleetwood–Dublin service in 1997, to cater for 'a huge untapped market from Ireland to Blackpool'. She would also make regular Fleetwood–Douglas sailings.

However, there was still a debate within the company over the service to be operated. The late Captain Vernon Kinley was a strong advocate of using *Lady of Mann* to restore a Liverpool–Dublin service and his view finally prevailed. Her first sailing was on 12 June, having entered service earlier in the season, when she was chartered to take part in the film 'The Boxer', being filmed in Dublin. On 22 May, she restored another lapsed service – the one from Llandudno to Douglas, which had last been operated in 1982 by *Manxman*. This service had traditionally been the province of the Liverpool & North Wales Steamship Co., but the Steam Packet took it over in 1962. It also took over Liverpool–Llandudno in 1963, following the liquidation of the Liverpool & North Wales Steamship Co. Before starting this sailing, *Lady of Mann* had carried passengers from Liverpool to Llandudno, making the first such sailing by a Steam Packet vessel since 1980. It was also the first 'triangular' Liverpool–Llandudno–Douglas sailing. The sailing was advertised as a commemoration of the centenary of the first sailing between the two places by a Steam Packet vessel, on 19 July 1897. On leaving Llandudno pier, Captain Kinley turned *Lady of Mann* off the pier and made a ceremonial 'sail past'. The sailing was notable for being accompanied for part of the crossing by a helicopter from RAF Valley, which landed a man on board and later took him off again. The evening return to Llandudno was the occasion for a fireworks display on shore. *Lady of Mann* then carried out her usual TT programme before starting Liverpool–Dublin on 12 June. She was able to make the Dublin crossing in about six-and-a-half hours; with a departure from Liverpool at 08.30 and a return from Dublin at 16.30. Wednesday's sailing was taken by *SeaCat Isle of Man*, while *Lady of Mann* operated a Fleetwood–Douglas round trip. When the late Captain Kinley, who had a great understanding of the need to make each voyage interesting to passengers, was captain on *Lady of Mann*'s Liverpool–Dublin sailings, he took the ship inside the Skerries when conditions permitted. The service generated a good level of support, frequently with capacity loads of vehicles. Non-landing cruises at £10 per head, marketed as the 'Dublin Flyer', were offered, giving passengers the opportunity to make duty-free purchases on board. On Wednesday 6 August, *Lady of Mann* performed a day trip from Douglas to Fleetwood, also giving a three-hour Morecambe Bay and oil-rig cruise from Fleetwood. She had performed almost impeccably during most of her period of service, but suffered major engine problems on 7 November, when her port engine seized up, causing her to be withdrawn for repairs, which lasted until 6 December. She then remained on Liverpool–Dublin until 5 January 1998, when she was withdrawn to provide cover for *King Orry* during her winter overhaul.

In 1998, Liverpool–Dublin was scheduled for *SuperSeaCat Two*, but *Lady of Mann* was expected to feature in the year's programme. It was planned that she would be based at Dublin in the peak summer season, operating a service to Liverpool. She was also programmed to make a weekly excursion sailing from both Llandudno and Fleetwood to Douglas. Her services were required for Easter and she then returned to dock to complete her overhaul, when her hull was painted in Sea Containers' blue and some of the Isle of Man Steam Packet Co. markings on her superstructure were removed. Services to the Channel Islands operated by Condor Ferries had been put out to tender and *Lady of Mann* was expected to sail to Weymouth for berthing trials early in May. Sea Containers' plan for the Channel Islands was to use a SuperSeaCat with backup from either *Lady of Mann* or *King Orry*, which was about to be replaced by a new *Ben-my-Chree*. In the event, *Lady of Mann* did not go there and Condor's tender was successful.

Lady of Mann was back in service for TT, having first operated two day trips to Douglas, from Fleetwood on 27 May and from Llandudno on 28 May. The plans for her summer programme were abandoned when she was chartered by the Portuguese Açor Line for summer service in the Azores. Following the end of TT, she returned to dock where a dance floor was fitted in her forward lounge and a blue whale was painted on her sides. She left the Mersey on 19 June, manned by a Portuguese crew, but still registered at Douglas. Her programme involved inter-island sailings, but there were none of the whale-watching cruises implied by her repainting. She arrived back at Liverpool on 24 September and her whales were removed. This charter marked the start of an era in which *Lady of Mann* was used for winter and TT service but not in summer – a reversal of the traditional pattern for Manx vessels. The autumn of 1998 was particularly stormy and *Lady of Mann*, which spent her off-service periods in Liverpool's Alexandra Dock, was called upon on several occasions to cover sailings for *SuperSeaCat Two*, *SeaCat Danmark* and *Ben-my-Chree*, including an occasional Liverpool–Dublin crossing. On 29 December, she took one of these Dublin sailings, in lieu of *SuperSeaCat Two*. While departing from Dublin on her return crossing, she suffered propeller damage after hitting a fender, lost all engine power and was towed back to her berth. She was dry-docked at Dublin and left there for Liverpool on 6 January 1999, using one engine only. More repairs were needed at Liverpool before her return to the Manx winter service on 9 January, but her repairs were not finally completed until 21 January.

After her Azores charter in 1998, *Lady of Mann* had a much quieter year in 1999, remaining in the Irish Sea throughout the summer. While on the winter service, she experienced severe weather when approaching the Rock Light at the end of a passage from Douglas on 21 February, and had to call for two local tugs to assist her in berthing. This had happened occasionally, especially with ships departing from the landing stage in strong westerly winds, but it was rare for an Isle of Man ship fitted with bow thrusters to need such help. In early April, she operated additional sailings in connection with the student games being held in the Isle of Man. During her overhaul in May, she was given a circular Legs of Mann marking below her bridge. She operated day excursions to the Isle of Man: from Llandudno on 26 May and from Fleetwood on the following day. *Lady of Mann* then operated a programme of TT sailings between Douglas and Heysham, returning to dock afterwards. She re-emerged from dock for a summer programme between 23 July and 13 September, mainly from Douglas to Heysham or Liverpool. There were several highlights in her summer programme, of which the main ones were a Vernon Kinley memorial cruise from Douglas to Port St Mary on 24 July and further excursions from the mainland to the Isle of Man, from Llandudno on 3 and 23 August and from Fleetwood on 10 August. The return sailing to Fleetwood was particularly fast, taking only two hours fifty minutes. This was, so far, the final year in which *Lady of Mann* operated an Irish Sea summer season. She had barely ended her summer sailings when autumn gales on 18 September saw her back in service, relieving *SuperSeaCat Three* on Liverpool–Dublin. She repeated this support on several occasions over the next month. Her relief activity peaked during December, when she was needed to relieve *SuperSeaCat Three* on twenty-one of the twenty-four days before Christmas. She suffered an engine room fire at Liverpool on 1 December, before her departure for Dublin, but it was dealt with quickly by crew and shore fire-fighters.

The millennium year's summer programme again raised a question mark over *Lady of Mann*'s future. In previous years, the SuperSeaCats had been operating two round trips per day on Liverpool–Dublin, but the 2000 programme had only a single sailing, with *SuperSeaCat Three* making an evening round trip from Liverpool to Douglas. As *SeaCat Isle of Man* was scheduled to make a round trip from Douglas to Liverpool every morning, the Liverpool–Douglas programme was provided entirely by fast craft. This appeared to leave *Lady of Mann* without a summer role. The situation was exacerbated by the fact that, under the new SOLAS ('Safety of Life at Sea') regulations, she would require a substantial sum to be spent on her by May 2001 if she was to be retained in service. Sea Containers had never undertaken to spend that money.

The millennium had barely started when *Lady of Mann* took a sailing from Liverpool to Douglas on the evening of 3 January in place of *SuperSeaCat Three*. Her period of full winter service, relieving *Ben-my-Chree* for overhaul, took place between 19 January and 23 February, and her TT period ran from 26 May to 12 June. This was followed by a more ambitious day excursion programme than had been seen in previous years: from Fleetwood on 13 June, from Llandudno on 14 June, to and from Whitehaven on 15 June, from Warrenpoint on 16 June and around the Isle of Man on 17 June. Before TT, there were rumours in the Isle of Man that *Lady of Mann* had been sold for further service to either Portuguese or Philippine buyers and that her sailing on 17 June would be her 'final' sailing. Instead, she returned to dock where she was prepared for a further charter in the Azores. The changes were fewer than for her previous Azores charter; in particular, there was no dance floor and no 'whale', but a small kiosk was fitted on her car ramp. After completing her charter on 20 September, she arrived back at Liverpool on 1 October. She was first used on 2 October at the start of an Irish Bank Holiday weekend. She was in regular service from 9 November, when she took over the Liverpool–Douglas sailings from *SuperSeaCat Three*.

Lady of Mann remained on winter service to the Isle of Man continuously until 26 February 2001 and was then withdrawn for her own overhaul. Sea Containers had decided to bring her in line with SOLAS requirements so that work, together with a general refurbishment, was carried out at the same time, at a total cost of £1.4 million. The SOLAS work involved fitting three transverse bulkheads on the car deck and inflatable Marine Evacuation Systems on the port and starboard sides under the bridge wings. A new lounge, to be used exclusively by 'first service' passengers and featuring banquette seating as well as airline-style seats, was created to replace the smokers' lounge. The main forward lounge was transformed into the Cafe Express, which had a mixture of banquettes and chairs around small tables with 'at seat' service. The centre lounge, also on the main passenger deck, was refurbished. There was a new lounge on Deck Four with seating for around forty passengers in the 'Blue Riband club'. *Lady of Mann* was scheduled to re-enter service on 19 May with the most ambitious excursion programme yet seen. The highlight of the programme was over the weekend of 19 and 20 May with a trip from Douglas to Troon, revisiting her birthplace for her Silver Jubilee. This was to be followed by excursions from Llandudno on 21 and 24 May, to and from Whitehaven on 22 May, from Fleetwood on 23 May and around the Isle of Man on 27 May to commemorate the 125th anniversary of the Mothers' Union. Immediately afterwards, she was to start her usual programme of TT sailings. However, matters went seriously adrift following an outbreak of foot-and-mouth disease in Great Britain. To prevent the spread of the disease to the Isle of Man, the Manx Government cancelled TT. It would have been uneconomic to crew up *Lady of Mann* just for her excursion programme, so it was cancelled. After completing her overhaul, which also included painting her forward mast white, she left Liverpool light for Douglas on 11 June. She was open to the public at Douglas for two days for inspection of her refurbishment and then left on 15 June, bound for the Azores. As a result, in her Silver Jubilee year, she was totally absent from the Irish Sea during the main season and the first paying beneficiaries of her upgrade were those using her Azores services. During her Irish Sea service, *Lady of Mann* had become well accustomed to rescuing passengers stranded by fast craft. However, on 24 August she was called upon to help with passengers from her fastest 'craft' ever – an Airbus A-330 aircraft which had made an emergency landing in the Azores after running out of fuel! *Lady of Mann* transferred around 300 passengers from the island of Terceira to Ponta Delgada. She suffered engine problems on 1 September, while berthed at Faial, missing one round sailing while the problem was fixed. Her charter ended on 20 September and she returned to Liverpool. She took up her winter Liverpool–Isle of Man schedules on 9 November, replacing *SuperSeaCat Three*, and also took some Christmas Dublin–Douglas sailings.

Lady of Mann came off service on 7 January 2002 and berthed at Douglas until *Ben-my-Chree* was ready to depart for her overhaul, but continued to operate Douglas–Liverpool at weekends. From 19 January, when *Ben-my-Chree* finally started her overhaul, *Lady of Mann* also undertook the weekday Douglas–Heysham service. After *Ben-my-Chree* had returned to service and *SuperSeaCat Three* had started her 2002 season, *Lady of Mann* went on stand-by to cover the SuperSeaCat. After her own overhaul, she emerged to undertake the by now regular programme of day excursions prior to her TT sailings. The excursions were from Llandudno on 19 May, from Warrenpoint on 20 May, to and from Llandudno on 21 May, to and from Fleetwood on 22 May and to and from Whitehaven on 23 May. The end of one Llandudno sailing was marked by a most unpleasant incident, when a man was stabbed on Llandudno pier. After TT, *Lady of Mann* once again departed for the Azores, leaving Liverpool on 27 June and arriving back on 4 October. Her autumn programme comprised the usual pattern of bad weather and breakdown cover for the Manx and Liverpool–Dublin routes, with extra sailings for the Irish Bank Holiday weekend. On 28 October, the exercise undertaken by the RAF in 1997 proved its worth when a passenger suffering severe chest pains and breathing difficulties was lifted off by a helicopter from RAF Valley while *Lady of Mann* was off Port St Mary on a sailing to Dublin. *Lady of Mann* added another film performance to her many versatile roles on the weekend of 18–20 November when she was filmed at Douglas during the shooting of a film entitled 'The Ceilidh War', intended for the American market.

The 2003 programme followed a similar pattern to that established in 2000. After the usual winter reliefs, *Lady of Mann* had her own annual overhaul, which was extended because of unexpected repairs to the starboard propeller and shaft. She took up her TT sailings on 24 May and on that day also operated an evening sailing around the Isle of Man for the benefit of the Manxman Steamship Co. After TT, she made her usual series of excursion sailings, featuring Llandudno (twice), Fleetwood and Whitehaven, and followed this with a charter by the Church Army from Heysham to Douglas on 14 June. Instead of lying at Douglas between the two legs of that charter, she made another Round the Island sailing during the afternoon. She then returned to the Azores for her fifth summer there, beginning on 29 June. She was running in partnership with a Portuguese vessel, *Golfhino Azul*, but that ship proved unreliable and her passenger certificate was withdrawn on 16 July. *Lady of Mann* struggled to cover both ships' schedules until 23 June, when the Portuguese ship was granted a limited passenger certificate, but *Lady of Mann* had to cover sailings to the outer islands for the rest of the summer. She arrived back at Liverpool on 5 October, re-entering service on 24 October with a Douglas–Dublin sailing for the Irish Bank Holiday. From 4 November, she took over from *SuperSeaCat Two* on Liverpool–Douglas, but this year offered a daily sailing, rather than Thursday to Sunday only, which had been the case in previous years.

Early in 2004, *Lady of Mann* again provided relief cover for *Ben-my-Chree*, sailing from Douglas to Heysham between Monday and Wednesday and to Liverpool on the other four days. After her winter reliefs, she was laid up at Liverpool on 23 February, but returned to service again whenever the weather was too windy for the fast craft to operate. She was chartered for a Round the Island sailing on 30 May, and carried out her usual excursion programme, covering Llandudno, Fleetwood and Whitehaven, after TT. However, the second excursion from Llandudno, on Friday 18 June, was cancelled after berthing at Llandudno pier, due to high winds. She was again on charter in the Azores during the main summer, and arrived back at Liverpool on 2 October. As in previous winters, she operated Isle of Man sailings in bad weather, weekend Douglas–Liverpool sailings and overhaul reliefs for *Ben-my-Chree*.

Lady of Mann's 2005 programme was similar to that of 2004, including her special excursions. However, one novelty was a return to Troon, where she had been built, previously planned to take place in 2001. The sailing was intended to commemorate the 175th anniversary of the formation of the Isle of Man Steam Packet Co. The return sailing, on 21 May was a special 175-mile voyage, taking nine hours and passing the coasts of Arran, Kintyre and Northern Ireland. After her TT programme, she was scheduled to be on charter in the Azores between 15 June and 12 September.

Lady of Mann's future is again subject to speculation, as new SOLAS requirements come into force in 2005, and the company appears unwilling to spend the money needed for her to remain in service. Her engines appear to be in excellent condition and very reliable. All those who have enjoyed many years of sailing on *Lady of Mann* hope that the great survivor, the last ship built for the 'old' Steam Packet, will manage it yet again.

SeaCat Isle of Man/Sea Express I

SeaCat Isle of Man operated Liverpool–Dublin each Wednesday during 1997. Since then, she has made occasional Liverpool–Dublin crossings, although her main employment, except in 1998, has been on Isle of Man summer services.

The SeaCat was a new type of ferry, with twin hulls and waterjet propulsion, operating at much higher speeds than conventional ships. There had been two previous attempts to build fast 'vessels': hovercraft, which could carry cars but were reaching the end of their lives, with no replacements being built, and jetfoils, which could only accommodate foot passengers and proved uneconomic in British and European waters.

The inventor of the hovercraft was Sir Christopher Cockerell, and the craft was very much a British development. It worked on the principle that the craft 'floated' on an air cushion produced by the craft's engines, with reduced water resistance enabling it to travel at high speed, and allowing it to come ashore onto a sloping ramp after each voyage. A research hovercraft was built by Saunders Roe at East Cowes in 1959 and crossed the English Channel between Calais and Dover on 25 July of that year, with Sir Christopher on board. The first commercial hovercraft service in the world was started in 1962 by British United Airways with a Vickers VA3 hovercraft, from Moreton, Wirral, to Rhyl, but it lasted only for a single summer. The Dover Straits crossing proved particularly suitable for hovercraft, and two companies established services there – Hoverlloyd on Ramsgate–Calais and Seaspeed on Dover–Calais. The two operations were merged in 1981, taking the name Hoverspeed, and based at Dover. Hoverspeed was bought by its directors in 1984 and sold by them in 1986 to Sea Containers. The five hovercraft in service were not seen by Sea Containers as having a long-term future, so investigations were begun into their replacement by wave-piercing catamarans.

Sea Containers' first orders for catamarans were for its Isle of Wight service from Portsmouth. They were built in Tasmania. Following further development work to ensure that the new craft were suitable for carrying cars and for open-sea operations, Sea Containers ordered five larger craft, with an option for a further five, from Tasmania. The craft ordered were built of aluminium, had capacity for 450 passengers and eighty cars and were driven by four diesel engines, giving a speed of 42 knots. The passenger accommodation featured a central lounge with side lounges, an observation deck giving a view ahead through the bridge area and a lounge bar. There was a small open deck aft for use in fine weather, but in practice it was used mainly by smokers who were prohibited from smoking inside. The engines were connected directly to waterjets that provided the power and steering for the craft. The SeaCats appeared more financially rewarding than hovercraft, despite much higher fuel costs than for conventional ships. It was also hoped that they would allow Sea Containers to compete more effectively with the Channel Tunnel and attract airline passengers.

The first SeaCat to be delivered to Sea Containers was *Hoverspeed Great Britain*. She sailed from Tasmania across the Pacific and along the east coast of America, calling at Punta Arenas, Rio de Janeiro and Nassau. She arrived at New York on 11 June 1990. From there, she attempted a record transatlantic crossing on her delivery voyage, to allow her to claim the 'Blue Riband' from the liner *United States*, which had captured it from Cunard's *Queen Mary* in 1952 and held it unchallenged since then. The crossing was completed in three days, seven hours, fifty-four minutes – nearly three hours less than the previous record. On arrival in Britain, *Hoverspeed Great Britain* took over Portsmouth–Cherbourg. She entered service on 14 August but suffered some technical problems in her first season. The fact that Sea Containers were considering the use of SeaCats for Irish Sea services became clear when the craft carried out berthing trials at Douglas in November 1990 and then made a round trip to Heysham.

SeaCat Isle of Man was the second SeaCat to be delivered to Sea Containers. She first appeared on Manx services in 1994, but she dated from 1990 and had operated under three earlier names on other routes. She was launched on 29 April 1990 by Mrs Rosa Pawsey, the wife of the head of Sea Containers' firm of Naval Architects, as *Hoverspeed France*, but was first used in service to Tasmania during the Australian summer. She left Hobart on 12 April 1991 and travelled to Britain via the Suez Canal. After experiencing engine problems in the Mediterranean, she put into Sicily on 10 May for temporary repairs. She arrived at Southampton on 18 May and further work was carried out before she entered service with Hoverspeed on Dover–Boulogne on 1 July. Later that month, she was joined by *Hoverspeed Great Britain*. The two craft covered services from Dover to both Boulogne and Calais, alongside the two former Seaspeed hovercraft. On 15 October, *Hoverspeed France* claimed the record for the fastest crossing between Dover and Calais, in a time of thirty-four minutes, twenty-three seconds. The previous record had been fifty-two minutes, forty-nine seconds. On the day after her record, *Hoverspeed France* struck a pier at Dover's Eastern Docks and was withdrawn for repairs.

For the 1992 season, the two SeaCats were joined by a third, *Hoverspeed Boulogne*, and they opened a third route, Folkestone–Boulogne, from 11 April. However, within a short space of time, *Hoverspeed France* had been chartered to Italy, for a service between Sardinia and Civitaceccia on the mainland. She was registered in Italy and sailed out under her new name of *Sardegna Express*, ready to begin her service on 1 July. The charter was for five years, but within months it was in difficulties and *Sardegna Express* returned to Portsmouth on 21 November. Initially, it was announced that in 1993 she was to open a new service between Gothenburg in Sweden and Frederikshavn in Denmark as *SeaCat Denmark*, but there was a change of plan, with another SeaCat taking her place. *Sardegna Express* was retained on the Dover Straits and renamed *SeaCat Boulogne*. She operated in conjunction with *SeaCat Calais*, formerly *SeaCat Tasmania*.

The Isle of Man Steam Packet Co. had hoped to charter a SeaCat for its 1993 services, but pulled out of the negotiations. The plan had been to operate a daily Belfast–Liverpool service, calling at Douglas in both directions. *SeaCat Boulogne* remained in service on the Dover Straits throughout the remainder of 1993.

In the early months of 1994, *SeaCat Boulogne* was fitted with a forward ride control system, to improve her sea-keeping qualities. She relieved *SeaCat Scotland* on Stranraer–Belfast from mid-January and then returned to Folkestone. In March, she was chartered to the Isle of Man Steam Packet Co. for the summer. She was originally due to start immediately after TT, but was delayed until the end of June. She was renamed

SeaCat Isle of Man, and left Dover on 20 June, bound for Liverpool. Her arrival at Liverpool on the following day was planned to allow time for berthing trials before her entry into service, but she experienced problems at Liverpool because of the weather and then had difficulties with her ride control system due to shells being sucked into it at Fleetwood. Despite these problems, she entered service on 28 June as planned, operating between Douglas and Fleetwood and making the crossing in just ninety-four minutes. Unfortunately, on her return sailing from Fleetwood, a rope was sucked into her waterjet inlets as she arrived at Douglas. The embarrassment was made worse by the presence on board of both the chairman and the managing director of the company. She lost one round trip while the rope was removed. *SeaCat Isle of Man* then settled down very well, aided by a period of exceptionally good weather. She made her inaugural sailings to Liverpool on 29 June, Dublin on 30 June and Belfast on 1 July. Her speed attracted many passengers, and Manx Airlines blamed the introduction of *SeaCat Isle of Man* for a 7 per cent reduction in passenger numbers on their Liverpool–Douglas route. The only incidents of note occurred on 8 August when she collided with a large sea creature, believed to be a porpoise, and on 23 August when she was damaged in a collision with the berth at Fleetwood. It was not until 28 August that the first gale force winds occurred, causing the suspension and cancellation of sailings by *SeaCat Isle of Man*. Her final speed record of the year was achieved on 19 September, with a crossing between Liverpool and Douglas in two hours ten minutes. Her charter was extended by one week to 26 September. She then took over Stranraer–Belfast from *SeaCat Scotland*, which had been chartered for Middle-East service as *Q-Ship Express*. *SeaCat Isle of Man* served on that route for the rest of the year and until 9 January 1995, despite having collided with *Norse Mersey* in the Belfast channel on 8 November.

During her overhaul early in 1995, *SeaCat Isle of Man* was fitted with 100 additional seats. She was then chartered to Condor Ferries to operate on their Weymouth–Channel Islands service from 16 March to 20 May, replacing the ferry *Havelet*. On 17 April, the local ferry *Saint Malo*, sailing from Jersey to Sark, ran aground on submerged rocks near Jersey's Corbière lighthouse. *SeaCat Isle of Man* was the first vessel to reach the scene and took off 136 passengers. She resumed Manx service on 24 May. This was the first year she had been in service over TT and her vehicle capacity was restricted to 126 motorcycles and about forty cars to ensure that she adhered to the timetable. As in 1994, she served the Manx routes to and from Liverpool, Fleetwood, Dublin and Belfast. Once again, the weather was exceptionally favourable, with no wind or weather delays between 28 May and 25 August. On 27 August, *SeaCat Isle of Man* assisted a yacht in trouble off Spanish Head, while she was on passage between Dublin and Douglas. Her inflatable boat was launched and assistance rendered by her crew, at least one of whom fell into the water. The Port St Mary lifeboat was launched to rescue the yacht's crew, allowing the SeaCat to continue to Douglas. On 12 September, she made her first sailing around the Isle of Man with a full load of passengers, establishing a new record of one hour, fifty-two minutes. From 26 September, *SeaCat Isle of Man* relieved *King Orry* on Douglas–Heysham. Unfortunately, this coincided with the start of Irish Sea winter weather. On 27 September, the weather forced her morning sailing to be diverted to

Liverpool, where there were great difficulties in unloading because of the movement of the pontoon against the landing stage. Her departure for Douglas was delayed until 19.50, but she ran into heavy seas around Formby and was damaged. *SeaCat Isle of Man* returned to Liverpool and her passengers were accommodated overnight in local hotels, awaiting an emergency sailing on the following day by *King Orry*. *SeaCat Isle of Man* was sent to Cammell Laird for repairs. These events emphasised to the Steam Packet the importance of retaining some back-up for fast craft by a conventional ship and helped the case for retaining *Lady of Mann*. Around this time, the Isle of Man Steam Packet Co. decided that it would not operate a SeaCat in 1996, so *SeaCat Isle of Man* was handed back to Sea Containers in December and returned to Dover–Calais.

At the start of 1996, *SeaCat Isle of Man* was still on Dover–Calais, but her next move was not long in coming. Sea Containers and the Norwegian Color Line announced a new joint venture company, Color SeaCat AS, to start a new SeaCat service between Langesund in Norway and Frederikshavn in Denmark. The service was to be operated by *SeaCat Isle of Man*, renamed *SeaCat Norge*, and *SeaCat Danmark*. *SeaCat Norge* was back at Newhaven by early October and resumed on Dover–Calais on 29 November.

Following the acquisition of the Isle of Man Steam Packet Co. by Sea Containers in 1996, it came as no great surprise that a SeaCat was used on Manx services in 1997. At first, it had been planned to use *SeaCat Scotland*, but other route changes forced her retention on Stranraer–Belfast, so the craft chosen was *SeaCat Norge*. She was overhauled at Liverpool in February/March 1997, when her name reverted to *SeaCat Isle of Man*. After completing her overhaul, and having substituted Newhaven for Nassau as her port of registry, she returned to Dover–Calais, which she worked until 15 May. She then moved north, ready for her re-entry into Manx service on 21 May. For this summer, *SeaCat Isle of Man* sailed from Douglas to Liverpool, Dublin and Belfast. She also took Liverpool–Dublin every Wednesday (except during TT, when the service was suspended), in lieu of *Lady of Mann*. With her faster speed, she was able to complete a single Liverpool–Dublin sailing in four-and-a-quarter hours, so allowing her to fit in Isle of Man sailings at either end of the day. Unfortunately, she was not as reliable as she had been during her previous two Manx seasons, suffering problems with one of her waterjets. This forced her withdrawal from service on 1–2 June. She suffered further problems over the remainder of TT, when she was working very hard, and problems with the same waterjet continued for the rest of the summer, resulting in frequent delays. When the weather began to deteriorate, from late August onwards, the extent of the delays increased. The problems were at their worst on Wednesdays. As a result, despite suggestions that her service was to be extended, she was withdrawn as scheduled on 23 September. Earlier in the season, she had featured on successive days in separate incidents involving the Police, while she was operating from Douglas to Liverpool. On 16 August, a jet skier 'drove' his craft between her two hulls when she was nearing New Brighton. He crashed into a buoy and was arrested as he swam ashore. Next day, a passenger was spotted with an imitation firearm and an Armed Response Unit met the craft. After her withdrawal, *SeaCat Isle of Man* remained off service until December, when she relieved *Hoverspeed Great Britain* at Dover.

The 1998 season saw *SeaCat Isle of Man* replaced by *SeaCat Danmark*, which was not scheduled to operate on Liverpool–Dublin. *SeaCat Isle of Man* remained on the Dover Straits throughout the year, sailing on both Dover–Calais and Folkestone–Boulogne. On 4 July, she sighted the Isle of Man Steam Packet Co.'s new ship, *Ben-my-Chree,* on her delivery voyage from the Netherlands to Douglas and sent radio greetings to her. This season was the last when *SeaCat Isle of Man* did not serve on Manx routes.

SeaCat Isle of Man's 1999 season started much earlier than in previous years, on 31 March. *SeaCat Danmark* had been moved to Heysham–Belfast, which was re-started by Sea Containers after a gap of almost twenty-five years, but she was also scheduled to operate Belfast–Douglas sailings twice weekly, in place of *SeaCat Isle of Man*. *SeaCat Danmark* broke down on 15 August, so one of her Belfast–Douglas–Belfast trips was operated (in the reverse direction) by *SeaCat Isle of Man*. The latter had a good reliable season until 18 September, when her sailings were cancelled as a result of gales. On 18 October, she operated a day trip from Douglas to Dublin, but was forced to put back to Dublin by bad weather on her return sailing. Her unfortunate day-trippers were returned via Holyhead and Heysham, arriving back at Douglas some forty-six hours after their departure.

SeaCat Isle of Man's first season of the new millennium was uneventful, apart from the usual weather cancellations, especially towards the end of the season. The season ran from 30 March to 30 October. The 2001 season was due to see *Hoverspeed Great Britain* on Heysham–Belfast from 29 March, but she was late in arriving. As a result, there were some early interruptions to *SeaCat Isle of Man*'s Isle of Man service, as she was required to assist on Heysham–Belfast. On a few occasions during the summer, she made Liverpool–Dublin sailings in place of the regular vessel for that year, *Rapide*. On 6 July, during Tynwald week, she operated an evening Round the Island sailing. After completing her Isle of Man season on 29 October, *SeaCat Isle of Man* took over from *SeaCat Scotland* on Belfast–Stranraer/Troon, on which she served until January 2002. She was then laid up until her spring overhaul.

SeaCat Isle of Man re-entered service on Belfast–Troon for a few days towards the end of March 2002, before taking up her normal Isle of Man service. She undertook another evening Round the Island cruise on 19 June and was due to make an evening 'fireworks cruise' on charter to Laxey Harbour Commissioners on 4 July. However, the cruise was cancelled and *SeaCat Isle of Man* spent the time carrying passengers who had been stranded as a result of technical problems on board *SuperSeaCat Three*. Her season ended on 24 October, but she returned to Isle of Man services on 26 and 27 October to assist with passengers delayed by gales in the intervening period. She then moved to Belfast to take over Belfast–Troon from *SeaCat Scotland*.

The 2003 season marked a major change in the destiny of the Isle of Man Steam Packet Co., with its sale by Sea Containers to Montagu Private Equity. As usual, *SeaCat Isle of Man* was withdrawn from Belfast–Troon early in January for her own overhaul. The service was closed during her absence but re-started on 1 March by *SeaCat Isle of Man* until she resumed her Isle of Man schedules on 28 March. She suffered some damage on 26 May after striking debris, and was withdrawn from service for the damage to her hull and T-foil to be repaired, but was back on service late on 28 May. Her, by now, annual evening trip Round the Island took place on 25 June. On 24 July, *SeaCat Isle of Man*'s sailing from Douglas to Liverpool had to return to Douglas to disembark two passengers who had become ill. After her Isle of Man season, *SeaCat Isle of Man* was overhauled in November and then laid up for the winter.

SeaCat Isle of Man's 2004 season started on 25 March. Her funnel had been repainted with the Steam Packet's traditional black bands. Her programme was very similar to those of previous years. On 3 May, she made an excursion around the Island, during which she passed her sister *SeaCat France*, under tow in Ramsey Bay, but a tenth anniversary cruise on 23 June failed to take place due to bad weather. The next day, the weather forced her to turn back off the Bar lightship and return to Liverpool. On 3 July, she needed the assistance of a tug when leaving Liverpool landing stage. On 23 August, she stood by a yacht in distress for one hour.

SeaCat Isle of Man made her final Isle of Man sailings in 2004 on 20 October. She did not make her final scheduled sailings next day because of bad weather, but sailed light from Douglas to Birkenhead on 23 October, and was laid up in the A&P basin at Birkenhead (formerly Cammell Laird). Following the cessation of the Steam Packet's Liverpool–Dublin Service, she was returned to Sea Containers. After a winter's inactivity, she was chartered to a new operator, Irish Sea Express, and renamed *Sea Express I*. Following a refit, she reopened the Liverpool–Dublin fast-craft service on 27 April. Her schedule calls for her to make up to two round sailings per day between the two cities. The service will operate throughout the year, except in January and February. In addition, after completing her daily Dublin schedule, *Sea Express I* is to operate Liverpool–Douglas evening return sailings over the TT period, on eight days between 1 June and 12 June. Her operators are also planning to start a Liverpool–Belfast service by fast craft in 2006. Carryings have not come up to expectations, and some of the second round trips have been cancelled.

SuperSeaCat Two and *SuperSeaCat Three*

SuperSeaCat Two and *SuperSeaCat Three* have, between them, operated Sea Containers' Liverpool–Dublin service each year between 1998 and 2004, except 2001.

Despite the similarity of the names, SuperSeaCats are an entirely different type of craft from SeaCats. They are monohulled, in contrast to SeaCats' catamaran hulls, and their design originated in Italy, rather than Australia. However, operationally they are a development of SeaCats, but with greater capacity. Unfortunately, their naming by Sea Containers has been highly unoriginal, using only a numerical sequence.

Sea Containers' order was for six SuperSeaCats, with an option for two more. The orders were placed with the Italian shipbuilders Fincantieri. They were built in sections at the builder's yards at Rivo Trivoso, near Genoa, and La Spezia, with a capacity for 774 passengers on two decks. There was a separate business-class lounge, duty-free shop, cafeteria and bars, amusement area and mother and baby room. They carried 175 cars, loaded through stern doors only and had a speed of 38 knots.

The first two were due for delivery in 1997 and the next pair in 1998. The final ones were never built. As with some other cross-Channel ships built in Italy in recent years, the ships were registered at an Italian port, in this case La Spezia, and their owners were an Italian company.

The original plan was for the first of the new craft, *SuperSeaCat One*, to take over Hoverspeed's Folkestone–Boulogne service, with *SuperSeaCat Two* replacing *SeaCat Danmark* on the Color SeaCat Gothenburg–Frederikshavn service. However, instead, *SuperSeaCat One* went to Scandinavia. *SuperSeaCat Two* arrived at Dover from her builders on 14 June 1997 and then sailed to London, berthing alongside HMS *Belfast* for a press and VIP presentation on 17 June. Her departure under Tower Bridge at 18.00 was accompanied by more publicity. She returned to Dover and carried out berthing trials at Calais before entering service on Dover–Calais on 26 June, leaving Folkestone–Boulogne in the hands of a SeaCat.

SuperSeaCat Three was scheduled on completion to take up Liverpool–Dublin. However, her delivery date had slipped to 1999 and *Lady of Mann's* success in 1997 meant that the services of a SuperSeaCat were urgently required on Liverpool–Dublin in 1998, so Sea Containers decided to use *SuperSeaCat Two*. She arrived in the Mersey for the first time on 20 January 1998 for preparatory work in dock. Prior to starting the service, *SuperSeaCat Two* carried out various trial trips, including two to the Isle of Man. Waterjet problems during these trials forced her to spend a further period in dock and it seemed doubtful whether the necessary spares could be obtained from Europe in time. However, she was ready just in time to start the service on 12 March, as scheduled. As she was flying the Italian flag, *SuperSeaCat Two* had an Italian captain on board, but also carried a Manx captain, who held Liverpool and Dublin pilotage certificates. The first day's sailings were delayed by berthing problems at both ports, but they were soon ironed out. With her high speed, which enabled her to cross between the two ports in under four hours, *SuperSeaCat Two* was capable of making two round trips per day and her main season schedule, starting on 3 April, took advantage of this. She departed from Liverpool at 08.15 and 18.00 and from Dublin at 13.00 and 23.00. She suffered an engine failure on her second outward trip from Liverpool on 4 April and had to return to the river before being towed to the landing stage. There followed about a week of disrupted sailings due to engine problems and the weather; unfortunately this period included the Easter holiday. There were two further days of cancellations on 6 and 7 May. During TT, *SuperSeaCat Two* helped out with some Isle of Man sailings, usually in lieu of the day's second round trip to Dublin. Over this period, she continued to suffer problems with one of her four waterjets and finally she was withdrawn from service on 22 and 23 June. Following these repairs, the craft ran much better and completed some of her Liverpool–Dublin crossings in three hours twenty minutes. Unfortunately these improvements were only short-lived and *SuperSeaCat Two* continued to suffer from technical problems and delays for much of the season. It was inevitable that a new type of craft, with much untried technology, would suffer teething problems; this was the view of Sea Containers who announced that the craft would be fitted with an improved ride control system during the forthcoming winter. Further problems arose in September, causing the withdrawal of *SuperSeaCat Two* on 16 September. From 18 September, her schedule was covered by *King Orry*, which had been replaced on the Isle of Man services by *Ben-my-Chree* and was awaiting sale. *SuperSeaCat Two* was back in service on 21 September. Despite the problems, the service proved very popular and the twice-daily round trip sailings were retained after 5 October, when they had been expected to reduce to a single round trip. The only exception was on Tuesdays, when just a single round trip was made to allow time for routine maintenance. Gales in this period forced the complete cancellation of sailings on at least five days. From 5 November, the service was reduced to a single round trip each day, but *SuperSeaCat Two* was then able to make some Isle of Man sailings. There were further disruptions due to the weather over the remainder of the year and Liverpool City Council expressed its displeasure at the loss of tourist traffic earlier in the year as a result of the unreliability of *SuperSeaCat Two*. At some stage during the season, a red Persian cat was painted on each side of her bows. Her first season finally ended on 5 January 1999 with very mixed feelings on the performance of the craft.

The 1999 Liverpool–Dublin season began on 11 March, being operated until 7 April by *SuperSeaCat Two*, which had received the promised upgrade of her stabilisation system. She also gave weekend Isle of Man sailings over this period. *SuperSeaCat Three* took over the service on 8 April. *SuperSeaCat Two* was transferred to Newhaven, where she took over Hoverspeed's seasonal Dieppe service. Her first sailing was on 23 April, the delay having allowed time for crew training. At two hours, this crossing was shorter than either of her Liverpool routes, so she was able to fit in three round trips each day. Initially, the service was due to operate until 31 October, but *SuperSeaCat Two* continued until early January 2000, when she was withdrawn for overhaul.

From 8 April, *SuperSeaCat Three* operated Liverpool–Dublin. She left her builder's yard at La Spezia on 17 March on the three-day voyage to Liverpool. Her layout was similar to that of *SuperSeaCat Two*, but with some improvements based on the operational experience of the older craft. She was fitted with a forward-mounted T-foil to provide a less uncomfortable ride for passengers. The improvements to her accommodation comprised a larger duty-free shop, an improved bar area and a Little Chef Express outlet. There were also changes to her vehicle decks to allow her to carry coaches. *SuperSeaCat Three*'s first season went well, without the problems that had dogged her predecessor. Over TT, her schedule was adjusted to enable her to help out on the Manx services. It was not until mid-September that there was a break in the fine weather; *SuperSeaCat Three* then lost several days' sailings, most of which were picked up by *Lady of Mann*. In mid-October, she made brief overnight visits to Stranraer and Belfast for berthing trials. The weather really caught up with the craft in December and she lost twenty-one out of the twenty-four days' sailings scheduled before Christmas. While berthed in Canada Dock on 20 December, she suffered an outbreak of fire, which was attended by five fire appliances. For Liverpool's millennium celebrations she was berthed at the landing stage and turned into a floating VIP lounge. In addition, there were live broadcasts on Radio One from her open deck and Sky TV cameras were on board to film events in the river. Her season ended on 4 January.

SuperSeaCat Three (1998) in the Mersey in September 1999. (Author)

For the first time ever two SuperSeaCats were based in the Irish Sea in 2000. *SuperSeaCat Two* was replaced on Newhaven–Dieppe by *SuperSeaCat One* and moved to Belfast, where she took over Heysham–Belfast from *SeaCat Danmark*. She opened the service on 18 April and operated two round trips each day during the peak period. *SuperSeaCat Three* remained on Liverpool–Dublin, but the frequency of the service was reduced to one round trip per day. The reason given for the reduction was the abolition of duty-free sales and the consequent reduction in the number of day-excursion passengers. The evening was used to operate a round trip to Douglas. As usual, there were changes to the schedules over TT and both SuperSeaCats helped to carry the TT traffic. *SuperSeaCat Two* again suffered from cancellations due to technical problems and was withdrawn from Heysham–Belfast in mid-October, some three weeks before the scheduled closure date. Unspecified technical reasons and the need to make proper alternative arrangements for passengers were stated to be the reasons for the withdrawal.

A characteristic of Sea Containers' scheduling was the switching of ships between services in different years. This was the case in 2001, when both SuperSeaCats were withdrawn from their Irish Sea services and sent to Dover, where they joined *SuperSeaCat One* to take over Dover–Calais. The replacement craft were SeaCats: *Rapide* at Liverpool and *SeaCat Danmark* at Heysham. Before entering service, *SuperSeaCat Three* visited London between 15 and 17 March, berthing alongside HMS *Belfast*. She was open to the public on the final day. On 15 May, *SuperSeaCat Three* visited Folkestone and carried out berthing trials at the ramp there. In the main summer season, starting on 19 May, the three SuperSeaCats operated an hourly service, giving at least nine return sailings daily. The crossing was scheduled to take forty minutes. They were partnered by *SeaCat Danmark*, which operated Dover–Ostend. All three SuperSeaCats were withdrawn from the short sea crossing after the season; in subsequent years it was operated by SeaCats.

SuperSeaCat Two was laid up at Portsmouth and was expected to serve in 2002 either across the Channel on the longer Newhaven–Dieppe route, or across the Adriatic between Ancona and Split. Instead, she remained at Portsmouth all summer, with reports that she was being cannibalised to provide spares for the other SuperSeaCats. *SuperSeaCat Three* returned to Liverpool–Dublin/Isle of Man in 2002. Her season started on 28 February, with a schedule very similar to 2000's. The season was marked by technical unreliability, culminating with her withdrawal from service on the evening of 16 July. No suitable dry-dock was available at Liverpool so, two days later, she sailed up the Manchester Ship Canal, accompanied by a tug, for dry-docking at Manchester. This was the first ever visit to Manchester by a fast craft of any sort and the first by a Steam Packet vessel since *Peveril* in 1983. She returned from Manchester on 19 July. Despite this work, she continued to suffer problems with her bow thrust unit and experienced a number of delays. She was dry-docked again, this time in Birkenhead, on 3 September, in a further attempt to improve her running. Her schedules were thrown out by bad weather between 25 and 27 October, with *SeaCat Isle of Man* being recalled to service to help clear the backlog. *SuperSeaCat Three*'s season ended on 4 November.

Sea Containers' plans for *SuperSeaCat Three* in 2003 were similar to the previous year's. After completing her overhaul at Birkenhead, she crossed to Liverpool on 19 February in readiness for entering service. However, it was reported that a connecting rod in one of her engines broke under test and she returned to the shipyard for repairs. She was replaced by *SuperSeaCat Two*, which arrived in the Mersey on 16 March and entered service between Liverpool and Dublin on 24 March, one day later than planned. Her port of registry had been changed to Liverpool. She was given a slightly easier schedule, with an evening off duty at Liverpool each Tuesday for routine maintenance. The round trip to the Isle of Man that evening was taken by *SeaCat Isle of Man*. She was withdrawn for two days from 1 July for attention to her waterjets, but suffered more problems later. During the afternoon of 17 July, she joined two lifeboats, the Coastguard and a helicopter from RAF Valley to search for a missing diver off the north coast of Anglesey. The search was eventually called off. After her 2003 season, *SuperSeaCat Two* was laid up for the winter.

SuperSeaCat Three remained under repair until 2 May, when she sailed from the Mersey in the colours of the Finnish Silja Line. She was bound for the Baltic, to take up service between Helsinki and Tallin, joining her younger sister, *SuperSeaCat Four*, which had been operating on that route since 2000.

For 2004, Liverpool–Dublin and some Liverpool–Douglas sailings were being operated by *SuperSeaCat Two*, commencing on 26 February. During the winter, she received some refurbishment, including new leather-style seat coverings, a new shell door was cut in her hull, her funnel was given black bands and the Steam Packet insignia were painted on her sides. She was off service because of high winds on 19 and 20 March, and again on 23 June. One departure from normal took place on 6 July, when she operated an evening charter from Liverpool to the North Hoyle windfarm. Her final Liverpool–Dublin round sailing was on 1 November 2004. She was running on reduced power, so did not arrive back at Liverpool until 21.30. It was not known at the time, but this was the Steam Packet Co.'s final sailing on the route. She was then laid up at A&P, Birkenhead. She continued to sail for the Steam Packet in 2005, partnering *Ben-my-Chree*, but solely on Manx routes, entering service on 18 March. In 2005, her hull carries markings to denote the 175th anniversary of her operators, as do those of their other ships.

Rapide

Rapide was another 'SeaCat'. She operated Liverpool–Dublin in 2001, when the SuperSeaCats were transferred to Dover. The first sailings of the 2003 season were scheduled to be taken by her near sister, *Diamant*, but few of them operated. Since being completed in 1996, *Rapide* had seen service to the Channel Islands, between Ramsgate and Ostend and finally between Dover and Ostend, taking a different name for each route.

Rapide was the thirty-eighth SeaCat to come from Tasmania. She was ordered by Holyman Ferries, which had started operating fast ferries in 1989 with a commuter service in New York harbour, for the services of its subsidiary, Condor Line, from Weymouth to the Channel Islands, at that time being operated by the ferry *Havelet*. There was also an order for a second larger craft. She was christened *Condor 12* in February 1996 and registered at Singapore. On her trials, she achieved a speed of 48.7 knots, with an operating speed of 40 knots. She arrived at Portland on 2 April and was prepared for service, which she entered on 9 April. Her summer season was successful, but the autumn and winter weather produced the usual cancellations. *Havelet* was withdrawn at the end of October, after which the absence of any ferry as backup caused great problems whenever *Condor 12*'s sailings were cancelled. The larger craft ordered along with *Condor 12* was completed as *Condor Express* and entered service on 13th January 1997, replacing *Condor 12*.

The next stage in *Rapide*'s career was a move to Ramsgate, joining the Ostend service. This route had been developed by the Belgian state company RTM, which had transferred its British terminal from Dover to Ramsgate in 1994. When the Belgians withdrew from the service, it was taken over by Sally Line, using conventional vehicle ferries. Holyman Ferries joined forces with Sally as Holyman Sally, introducing *Condor 12* and the new *Holyman Express* to supplement the existing ferries. After a local competition, the ships' names were changed to *Holyman Rapide* and *Holyman Diamant*, respectively, in ceremonies on 1 March 1997. The new service started on the same day. *Holyman Rapide*'s port of registry was changed to Luxembourg. The crossings were advertised to be completed in 100 minutes, but both craft appeared to struggle to keep to the schedules. In July, the timings were increased and the crossing was then advertised to be completed in 'under two hours'. In November, Holyman announced an end to the joint operation with Sally and, a few days later, joined up with Sea Containers, the owners of Hoverspeed, with each company having a 50 per cent stake in the new operation. Both fast craft came to Liverpool for overhaul early in 1998. *Holyman Rapide* was the second craft to be overhauled, and was then chartered to Condor Ferries in mid-February as a relief for *Condor Express* during that craft's winter overhaul. *Holyman Rapide* continued her unreliability and the charter was terminated early, on 5 March. Next day,

Hoverspeed Holyman switched its British terminal from Ramsgate to Dover. The craft then took their third names, dropping the Holyman suffix and becoming *Rapide* and *Diamant*, respectively, and were repainted in SeaCat colours. The new crossings were scheduled to take 125 minutes. *Rapide* carried out berthing trials at Folkestone on 13 April. The 1998 service proved much more reliable than the previous year's.

Sea Containers' involvement in the new service became total early in 1999, when Holyman's 50 per cent interest was purchased. Both craft were overhauled in January/February 1999, *Rapide* at Portsmouth and *Diamant* at Falmouth, when they were painted in Hoverspeed's colours. They were also fitted with a '1st' lounge, available to passengers for a supplement. Both craft again performed well. They were withdrawn in succession during November for their annual overhauls. During the winter, they made some Dover–Calais crossings, in addition to their Ostend runs.

After a stable period, with three seasons operating on Dover–Ostend, the year 2001 marked a further change for both craft. The first three SuperSeaCats were all transferred to Dover. *Rapide* was moved to Liverpool to replace *SuperSeaCat Three*; *Diamant* was to take over Newhaven–Dieppe from *SuperSeaCat Two*. *Rapide* arrived at Liverpool on 16 February and entered service on 1 March. Unfortunately, her passenger and vehicle capacities were each about 15 per cent less than *SuperSeaCat Three*'s. In addition, she was slower than her predecessor, resulting in her morning departure for Dublin being fifteen minutes earlier. While this was not a major problem on the Dublin service, the combined effect of a day's delays led to some very late returns to Liverpool after her evening round trip to Douglas. Although her mechanical reliability was generally good, on 31 March she developed a fuel starvation problem when bound from Douglas to Liverpool and returned to Douglas. On 6 May, *Rapide* stood by a motor yacht that had sent a distress flare after suffering engine trouble 25 miles from Douglas. One of the yacht's crew was taken aboard *Rapide*, but the remaining six stayed on board for the yacht to be towed back to Douglas by a lifeboat. Following the end of *Rapide*'s seasonal programme, she was laid up at Birkenhead.

A further reshuffle within Sea Containers' fleet in 2002 saw the return of *SuperSeaCat Three* to Liverpool, with *Rapide* scheduled to take over Heysham–Belfast. She left Birkenhead on 21 March 2002, bound for Belfast, and on 27 March relieved on Belfast–Troon. She took up her intended route on 28 March, as scheduled. On 21 May, she again made a round trip between Belfast and Troon, covering for *SeaCat Scotland*, at the expense of her usual Heysham sailing. Her reliability was poorer in 2002 than in her previous year. On 26 July, she called at Douglas while on passage from Belfast to Heysham; later that day, she was withdrawn from service for several days. The culmination of her problems occurred on 21 August, when a fire broke out in her engine room when she was one hour into a Belfast–Heysham passage. The voyage was abandoned and the craft returned to Belfast for repairs. It had been intended that Heysham–Belfast would end on 30 September, but the service was abandoned for the remainder of the year because no replacement fast craft could be found. The service was not resumed in 2003. The plan for *Rapide* to take over Belfast–Troon in the autumn also went awry and the service was instead carried on by *SeaCat Isle of Man*.

Rapide remained at Belfast throughout the winter and major work was done there to repair her fire damage. She was due to take over Belfast–Troon on 24 March 2003, but the repairs were not completed in time, so *SeaCat Isle of Man* continued on the route for another two days, leaving a gap of just one day until *Rapide* was able to enter service on 27 March. Her new route had been introduced by Sea Containers in April 1999 as a more convenient alternative to that between Belfast and Stranraer, and had always been operated by fast craft. During TT, *Rapide*'s Troon schedule was altered to allow her to make some sailings between Belfast and Douglas; in previous years, the vessel normally on Heysham–Belfast had undertaken these sailings. On 30 June, the Isle of Man Steam Packet Co. was sold to Montagu Private Equity. The sale did not include Belfast–Troon, which remained with Sea Containers, but the Isle of Man Steam Packet Co. was appointed as manager of the route. This had no practical effect on the activities of *Rapide*. Despite the work carried out on her during the winter, *Rapide* continued to suffer from engine problems and frequently ran late; there were also a number of cancelled sailings.

One highly embarrassing incident affected both *Rapide* and *Diamant* during the year. Sea Containers had planned to transfer their flag from Luxembourg to the Bahamas, and their Luxembourg registrations were cancelled on 25 August 2003. Unfortunately, their new registrations were not opened, and both ships continued in service without a flag until the problem came to light on 8 September and was remedied next day. By then, the ships had made about 130 uncertificated sailings. Despite the fact that no passengers or crew had been put at risk by the omission, Sea Containers was fined £7,000 plus costs by Folkestone Magistrates.

Belfast–Troon had operated year round, but it was announced during the summer of 2003 that, subject to consultation with employees, it would become seasonal, operating only between March and October; the service would be suspended after the sailings on 6 January 2004, to allow *Rapide* to undergo her annual overhaul. She resumed service on the route on 12 March 2004, and operated there until the route's seasonal closure on 1 November. *Rapide*'s final 2004 sailing proved to be the last on the Belfast–Troon service, which was not resumed in 2005. The closure was blamed on rapidly increasing fuel costs and competition from budget airlines. In 2005, *Rapide* joined *Diamant* on Hoverspeed's Dover–Calais service, opening the seasonal route on 17 March 2005. She was renamed *SeaCat Rapide* in June 2005.

SEVEN

NORSE MERCHANT FERRIES

After many years without any Liverpool–Dublin passenger service, it was remarkable that two separate services were started within less than two years. The second of these services, by Merchant Ferries, began early in 1999, using two new ships, *Dawn Merchant* and *Brave Merchant*.

Merchant Ferries was formed in 1986 to operate a Heysham–Warrenpoint freight ro-ro service. It was owned by Cenargo International, which also had other ferry interests. Initially, the service was operated by *Merchant Trader* but, within a few months, she was replaced by the larger *Merchant Venture*. The service prospered and additional ships were added. By 1993, the service also employed *Merchant Victor* and *Merchant Valiant*, but the newly acquired *Merchant Brilliant* and *Merchant Bravery* then replaced them. At the same time, the Mersey Docks & Harbour Co. bought a shareholding in Merchant Ferries, but sold it back in 1997. As early as 1994, Merchant Ferries was expressing interest in a new ro-ro berth at Birkenhead, proposed by the Mersey Docks & Harbour Co. Unfortunately, construction of this terminal, to be named 'Twelve Quays,' was delayed because of disagreements between the dock company and the Merseyside Development Corporation. Even after those differences had been resolved, there were further delays while the necessary consents were obtained, and the terminal did not open until 2002. In 1995, Merchant Ferries' Irish port was switched from Warrenpoint to Dublin; this appears to have been a preliminary step towards the introduction of a Liverpool–Dublin service.

In 1996, Cenargo announced an order for two ro-pax ferries from a Spanish shipbuilder, with delivery in April and June 1998. Cenargo did not specify the route on which the ships would serve, but they were too large for Heysham. Speculation correctly linked them immediately to Liverpool–Dublin. There was also a rumour that they might sail between Spain and the Canaries, a route which would be available to international operators from 1998 (Cenargo was already operating a service between Spain and North Africa). Early in 1998, the order was increased from two to four ships, with an option for a third pair. The second pair was to start a new Liverpool–Belfast service, in competition with Norse Irish Ferries, which had been sailing on the route since 1991.

In 1998 Cenargo launched a bid for Belfast Freight Ferries, which operated a Heysham–Belfast freight ro-ro service. The bid was successful and Merchant Ferries emerged in a strong position, with seven freight ferries in service on the two routes.

Work on the new ships proceeded more slowly than planned. The service had been due to begin in April 1998, but delays caused its start to be put back to 15 February 1999. The full service, also carrying cars and passengers, commenced on 1 March.

Norse Irish Ferries had introduced two new chartered ships, *Mersey Viking* and *Lagan Viking*, to Liverpool–Belfast during the second half of 1997. As a result, one of their existing ships, *Norse Lagan*, became available for service elsewhere. The words 'Liverpool–Belfast' had featured on her superstructure, but 'Belfast' was painted out at that time, leaving 'Liverpool–', causing widespread speculation that she would be used on Liverpool–Dublin, in competition with Merchant Ferries. That may have been a response to Merchant Ferries' plans to operate a Liverpool–Belfast service. Norse Irish Ferries' Dublin service never materialised and *Norse Lagan* was sold to Italian buyers, but the rumours were perhaps a spur to future developments; in September 1999, Norse Irish Ferries was acquired by Cenargo. The combined company served Dublin and Belfast from both Liverpool and Heysham. In October 2000, its name was changed to Norse Merchant Ferries and its ships adopted a common livery.

The two new ships, *Northern Merchant* and *Midnight Merchant*, which were due for delivery in February and April 2000, were expected to take over Liverpool–Belfast from *Mersey Viking* and *Lagan Viking*, whose charters would end in 2001. However, on delivery, *Northern Merchant* was chartered to Norfolk Line for a new Dover–Dunkerque service. Norfolk Line already operated an established Felixstowe–Scheveningen service. It was then suggested that *Midnight Merchant* would become a third ship on Liverpool–Dublin but, on delivery in August 2000, she also was chartered to Norfolk Line, doubling the capacity of its Dunkerque service. In March 2001, Norse Merchant Ferries bought *Mersey Viking* and *Lagan Viking* from their Italian owner and there were reports that, on completion of Twelve Quays, the pair would take over Liverpool–Dublin, with *Dawn Merchant* and *Brave Merchant* joining their younger sisters on charter to Norfolk Line. The Liverpool–Belfast service would then be taken over by two new Italian ships, similar to *Stena Forwarder*, which was operating Holyhead–Dublin. The company also announced that it was planning to operate a seasonal fast ferry between Liverpool and Dublin, starting in summer 2002.

Around that time, it became clear that Cenargo was facing serious financial difficulties. In January 2003 it went into Chapter 11 protection under US insolvency law, and in February this became an Administration procedure under English law. This problem was responsible for many of the subsequent changes. The Dublin service moved to Twelve Quays in September 2002, several months after the Belfast service had moved, but, almost at the same time, *Dawn Merchant* was chartered to Norfolk Line. She was replaced on Birkenhead–Dublin by a chartered freight-only ro-ro, *Lindarosa*. The disappearance of one passenger ship at this time reduced the favourable publicity that the company should have gained from the move to Twelve Quays. Total suspension of the passenger service came in February 2003, when *Brave Merchant* was chartered to the Ministry of Defence for use in the invasion of Iraq. She was replaced by another chartered freight ro-ro, *Norse*

Mersey. After completing her MoD charter in July 2003, *Brave Merchant* resumed service on Liverpool–Dublin in September 2003. The company emerged from Administration in December 2003 and, from that time onwards, its prospects improved steadily. *Brave Merchant*'s sailings are again being advertised to motorists.

In August 2004, the company announced a three-year charter of two 500-passenger ships building at the Italian Visentini yard. They will be delivered in July and December 2005, and replace *Lagan Viking* and *Mersey Viking* on Birkenhead–Belfast. They in turn will replace *Lindarosa* and *Brave Merchant* on Birkenhead–Dublin, restoring a full twice-daily passenger service on the route. The '*Viking*' ships are being renamed *Liverpool Viking* and *Dublin Viking*, respectively, releasing the existing names for the new ships, and making the ships' names more suitable for their new service. An announcement of the resumption of a service for foot passengers from July 2005 was made as a result of the withdrawal of the Isle of Man Steam Packet Co.'s *SuperSeaCat Three* from the route. Growth in freight traffic resulted in the company chartering a third ship, *Leili*, to operate an additional daily freight round trip from October 2004. As planned, *Liverpool Viking* was tranferred to the service in July 2005.

On 29 June 2005, Norfolk Line announced that it had offered to acquire Norse Merchant Ferries, and that the present owners intend to accept the offer. Since three of Norse Merchant's ships are already on charter to Norfolk Line, the proposal makes good operational sense. However, it could lead to future changes in Norse Merchant's activities.

Dawn Merchant and *Brave Merchant*

The order for *Dawn Merchant* and *Brave Merchant* was placed with the Spanish shipbuilder Astilleros Espanoles, for construction at Seville. It was announced that they would carry 2,000 lane metres of cargo, accommodate 260 passengers and have a service speed of 24 knots. The original delivery dates were April and June 1998, with the new service commencing in April. However, a series of building delays resulted in the late delivery of both ships. *Dawn Merchant* was not launched until February 1998; *Brave Merchant*'s launch was expected three months later. These delays caused the start of the service to be put back to July. However, there were further delays in building *Brave Merchant*, whose launch did not take place until the autumn. As a result, the start of the new service was again delayed, to early January 1999, and *Dawn Merchant* was chartered to a Turkish operator, Und RoRo Isletmel, for service between Istanbul and Trieste, covering for the delayed delivery of a new Italian-built ship. Further delays to *Brave Merchant* were caused by damage to the mobile crane hired to lift accommodation modules, in a road accident while on its way to the shipyard.

Dawn Merchant arrived at Dublin on 5 January 1999. After her first crossing of the Irish Sea, she arrived at Liverpool on 7 January for berthing trials at the temporary berth in Canada No.3 Branch Dock. *Brave Merchant* finally arrived at Liverpool on 31 January. On 5 February, in gale conditions, *Brave Merchant* broke loose from her dock mooring, her open stern door mounted the quayside and she was forced to drop anchor. Two tugs were needed to return her to her berth, but she suffered only minor damage to her stern door. The service finally started on 15 February, in a freight-only mode, but two days later *Dawn Merchant* damaged her bulbous bow while manoeuvring in Langton Dock. She was withdrawn for repairs by Cammell Laird, but was back in time for the start of the full passenger service on 1 March.

The passenger accommodation in both ships is housed forward on two decks above the upper vehicle deck. It is reached from the vehicle decks by lift or stairs up to the reception area; there is no access to the passenger accommodation from the quayside. The main passenger deck has a self-service restaurant and separate freight drivers' dining room aft, a shop/reception desk amidships and a bar/lounge forward. The upper deck has fifty-seven two-berth cabins and a forward lounge with ninety-six reclining seats, allowing for 210 overnight passengers. On daytime crossings, the ships' passenger capacity is 250. Both passenger decks have open deck space, mostly facing aft. Unfortunately, for ships spending nearly half their time on daylight sailings, there is a great shortage of seats out on deck; those available might just be capable of seating twelve slim passengers. Vehicles are carried on two decks, with hoistable internal ramps to the upper vehicle deck. Vehicle loading can be carried out through either the stern or the bow ramp.

The ships' names are derived from two famous racehorses – Dawn Run and Dancing Brave. Both ships were registered at Douglas, Isle of Man. As delivered, they had dark grey hulls, with red boot topping and a white superstructure. The twin funnels aft, linked by a lattice structure, were painted white with a narrow dark blue line, the dark blue letters 'MF' and gold emblems. After the merger with Norse Irish Ferries, all the vessels in the fleet were given a common colour scheme. The only change to *Dawn Merchant* and *Brave Merchant* was that the lettering and emblems on the funnels were replaced with three triangular blue, yellow and red pennants. Later, the route was painted on the superstructure.

The new service gave an overnight crossing every night, with additional daytime crossings every day except Sunday and Monday. Initially, *Brave Merchant* gave the overnight crossings from Liverpool, while her sister crossed overnight from Dublin. Both sailings departed at 22.30. Because of the lack of daytime sailings on Sundays and Mondays, this pattern was reversed on Sunday nights. The daytime sailings left Dublin at 09.00 and Liverpool at 10.00. The ships normally used the Langton entrance at Liverpool. This lock is relatively slow and the time spent there could appear excessive, especially around low tide. Further problems arose because Norse Irish Ferries used the same lock. If the Dublin vessel was late arriving, the Belfast vessel, which was operating to a much tighter schedule, could be given priority. The departures of the two sailings were staggered to ensure that the outgoing Belfast ship was well clear of the lock before the Dublin ship was ready to use it. However, the two Dublin ships had sufficient speed and spare time, with a crossing time of seven-and-a-half hours, so normal delays could be absorbed with few effects on the timings of subsequent sailings. Once the two services came under common ownership, the complaints about obstruction by the Belfast ships ceased! Inevitably there were occasional weather delays, especially in winter, but the ships were sufficiently large and well stabilised to be able to cope with all but the worst conditions on the Irish Sea. On rare occasions, the ships used the faster Gladstone entrance, but the time saved there was offset by the additional time needed to transit the dock system. In high winds, tugs were sometimes needed to assist the vessels.

At Liverpool, the temporary dock berth was fitted with portacabin accommodation with basic waiting and refreshment facilities for passengers. At Dublin, the ships used a new berth adjacent to Irish Ferries' berth and the service shared a passenger terminal with Irish Ferries. As there was no direct access for foot passengers, they were taken onto the vehicle deck by a minibus, then made their way up to the passenger accommodation. On disembarkation, they were not allowed down until the vehicles had been unloaded, when their minibus was able to come on board. The overnight sailings arrived very early and all passengers were expected to be ready to disembark on arrival, around 06.00.

Well-run services quickly become uneventful and this one proved no exception. However, *Dawn Merchant* was back in the news on the evening of 11 August 1999 when, along with *European Envoy* and the Dun Laoghaire lifeboat, she assisted with the search for a passenger who had fallen overboard from Irish Ferries' fast craft *Jonathan Swift*.

The new combined company name was launched at Liverpool on 12 February 2001. It had been planned to use *Dawn Merchant* after her arrival from Dublin, but she was delayed by faults at the Langton Lock, which prevented her from entering the dock system. The ceremony was switched to *Brave Merchant*, which fortuitously was available at another berth.

Cenargo took legal action against the Spanish builders of *Dawn Merchant* and *Brave Merchant*, alleging that each ship had six fewer trailer spaces and was slower than specified in the contract. In June 2001, the Court decided that there had been a loss of three trailer spaces (the other three lost spaces had been used to house the internal fire vent system requested by Cenargo), and awarded Cenargo $150,000 for each space lost. The claim for loss of speed gained an award of $180,000. The Court of Appeal overturned the ruling over trailer spaces in April 2002.

Both ships' registry was transferred to Liverpool on 1 March 2002. This was due to Cenargo having signed up for the British Tonnage Tax scheme.

Following *Dawn Merchant*'s charter to Norfolk Line, she was due to leave Liverpool–Dublin early in September 2002. The Mersey terminal moved to Twelve Quays on 9 September and it was planned that the withdrawal of *Dawn Merchant* would coincide with this move. Her replacement was the chartered *Norse Mersey*, which had operated Norse Irish Ferries' service between 1994 and 1997. *Norse Mersey*'s passenger accommodation was limited, so it was restricted to lorry drivers. However, after she had carried out berthing trials at Twelve Quays on 7 September she was detained by the Marine and Coastguard Agency. As a result, *Dawn Merchant* remained on the service and did briefly use the new terminal. Unfortunately, on 9 September, *Lindarosa*, operating on Liverpool–Belfast, collided with Twelve Quays; the resulting damage compelled the Dublin ships to return to Canada Branch Dock. *Norse Mersey* was cleared for service on 12 September and immediately took over from *Dawn Merchant*, which then sailed for Dover, arriving on 14 September. After Twelve Quays had been repaired, the ships returned there on 30 September.

On arrival at Dover, British seamen replaced *Dawn Merchant*'s mixed Polish and Filipino crew. Initially, she operated reliefs for *Midnight Merchant* and *Northern Merchant* while they received belting modifications. She was then used to increase the frequency of the service. Her base was in Dover's eastern docks. Her funnels were repainted in Norfolk Line's colours – black with a large white star on a broad light blue band, the same as for Norfolk Line's

Dawn Merchant (1998) sailing from Dover in August 2003. She is in Norfolk Line's colours. (Author)

parent company, the Danish Maersk shipping line. The name 'NORFOLK LINE' was added to her superstructure, beneath her passenger accommodation. She is unable to carry her full vehicle capacity, as she would need the modifications which have been made to her sisters before she could use the port's double-deck loading berths. Soon after introduction to the service, she hit a breakwater while leaving Dover on 24 October and was forced to return and discharge her vehicles and passengers. Damage above her starboard waterline needed repairing at Dunkerque. This was expected to take about ten days, but she did not return to service until 26 November. In 2003, Norfolk Line ordered two ships from a South Korean shipyard, for delivery in the second half of 2005 and with an option for two further ships. The new ships will replace the three chartered from Norse Merchant Ferries.

Brave Merchant continued to operate Liverpool–Dublin from Twelve Quays, sailing from Liverpool by day and from Dublin overnight. There were no Sunday sailings. Rumours abounded that she was to join her three sister ships on charter to Norfolk Line, but they were denied by the company. During Christmas and New Year 2002/03, she replaced *Mersey Viking* and *Lagan Viking* on Liverpool–Belfast. This was her first period of duty on that service. During her absence, her sailings were covered by another chartered vessel similar to *Norse Mersey*, *Lindarosa*, which had previously been the third ship on Liverpool–Belfast.

Early in 2003, it was announced that *Brave Merchant* had been chartered to the Ministry of Defence to carry military vehicles and supplies to the Middle East for the invasion of Iraq. The charter was for a minimum period of five months, with the option of three-monthly renewals. She left the Mersey on 4 February, bound for Antwerp and then for the military port of Marchwood, near Southampton. *Lindarosa* again provided her cover. It was reported that she was not expected to return to service with Norse Merchant Ferries. After completing her military duties, *Brave Merchant* arrived back at Marchwood from the Gulf on 12 July. She went to Dunkerque for dry-docking, before taking up a charter to Norfolk

Line, covering *Dawn Merchant*'s refit for a short period in late July. She was then chartered to P&O, and operated on Middlesbrough (Teesport)–Rotterdam, replacing *Norking*, which moved to Hull to cover the overhauls of P&O ships based there.

Brave Merchant returned to Irish Sea service on 1 September. Her first duty was on Liverpool–Belfast, relieving *Lagan Viking* until 6 September. She returned to Liverpool–Dublin on 8 September, but in a freight-only mode, carrying a maximum of twelve drivers. This time, she sailed overnight from Liverpool and by day from Dublin. Shortly after the return of *Brave Merchant*, *Norse Mersey*'s charter was terminated; *Brave Merchant*'s partner was *Lindarosa*. On 27 October, while *Brave Merchant* was leaving Birkenhead in strong tidal conditions, a rope broke and became entangled in her propeller, causing underwater damage. The problem only became apparent during the crossing to Dublin and she returned light to Liverpool for dry-docking. She was out of service until 10 November. Over Christmas and New Year 2003/04, she again served on Liverpool–Belfast, while *Mersey Viking* was overhauled.

The carriage of cars and motorists, but not foot passengers, on *Brave Merchant*'s Dublin sailings was resumed on 29 March 2004. The resumption of a motorists' service was partly in response to P&O's closure of its unprofitable Mostyn–Dublin service, which had taken traffic from Norse Merchant. When the first new ship for Liverpool–Belfast was delivered in July 2005, one of the Belfast ships replaced *Lindarosa* on Liverpool–Dublin. This will allow Norse Merchant to resume the carriage of foot passengers on the service. The transfer will be completed in December 2005, after the delivery of the second new ship for Liverpool–Belfast. Both *Brave Merchant* and *Dawn Merchant* have been sold to a Hong Kong organisation, with delivery by the end of 2005.

Iveagh (1892). Her owners were bought by B&I in 1926, but she was not renamed. (R. Brandreth collection)

APPENDIX – FLEET LISTS

Line 1
Name
Names in brackets were projected but never used. Some chartered vessels are included. In the early years, it was not possible to rename a British ship. To get around this, a ship would be 'sold' to a foreign citizen resident in Britain, renamed and then 're-sold' to the existing or a new British owner.

Years in service with owner, or on route (chartered vessels)
Date of entry (or re-entry) into service with that particular owner under that name, and date of disposal are given. Where a ship has had more than one name, the later name is shown under the year in which it was first used, with a reference to the original name.

Dimensions
Dimensions as shown in the official register, or Lloyd's Register, with major changes are given. Information shown in Lloyds's Register altered in 1955 and 1966. The dimensions normally shown are :

	Until 1954	1955–1965	From 1966
Length	Official Register	Overall	Overall
Breadth	Official Register	Extreme	Extreme
Depth	Official Register	Not shown	Moulded

Lloyd's Register started recording metric dimensions in 1975 and most ships built after that date show metric dimensions, but Irish-registered ships list the imperial measures shown in their official registers.

Tonnage
Gross tonnage on first registration. For a few early ships, the figure shown is net tonnage – marked N. Only major tonnage changes are shown. The current method of measuring gross tonnage differs from the earlier method and results in a large increase when a ship is re-measured.

Construction materials
Steel, unless shown otherwise.

Type of ship
Where no type of ship is specified, it is a major passenger ship.

Line 2
Official number

British official numbers were introduced in 1855. The number shown is normally British, unless stated otherwise. Irish ships used the same number sequence as British ships until 1952, when an Irish series, in the 400000s was started. Ships registered under the Irish flag from that date were allocated numbers in the 'Irish' sequence, even if they already had a 'British' number. The earliest ship in this book so renumbered is *Inniscarra*, which was given the number 400016 when she was transferred from the British to the Irish flag in November 1952. Ships already registered in Ireland in 1952 retained their 'British' numbers. Official numbers are not applicable to all ship entries.

Line 3
Builder and yard number

The name of the ship's builder, followed by the yard number (where known), are given. They have been taken from official registers until 1854. From 1855, the builder was not shown in the official register for some years and sources used include Lloyds and other registers and yard lists. In a very few cases, it has not been possible to establish the identity of the builder.

Line 4
Engine builder

The identity and location of the manufacturer of the engines has been taken from the official register, or from Lloyds Register. For the period before those sources showed that information, the sources used were engine builders' records, newspaper reports and secondary sources. This information is not always available for early ships.

Type of engines

Normally steam or motor (shown as oil).

Horse power

Until around 1895, the calculation of hp was standard, but Lloyds Register then introduced a calculation that gave a different result from that shown in the ship's (British) official register. As a result, from that time, the figures shown in Lloyds Register differ from those in the Mercantile Navy List, which continued to show the 'official' hp. Further complications arose with the advent of turbine engines, where neither formula could be applied and with diesel engines, leading to further calculations of hp. The types of hp quoted in this list are as follows:

hp: The figure used before 1895. This is usually the figure quoted in ships' official registers, or in other shipping registers. For early ships, it has sometimes been obtained from the engine builder's records, or from newspapers.

rhp: Registered hp, for ships registered from 1895. This was the same figure as the pre-1895 hp and is found in British ships' official registers and in the Mercantile Navy List.

nhp: Nominal hp, brought in by Lloyds Register around 1895, including early diesel ships. From around 1945, it was replaced by a machinery number (MN), which used the same formula.

bhp: Brake hp, quoted for modern diesel ships.

shp: Shaft hp, used for the Jetfoil.

Paddle or propeller

The number of propellers is shown. CP = controllable pitch.

Speed

Not always shown.

Remaining lines
Ownership and management
The name of the owner of a ship is followed by the name of the manager, if any, in rectangular brackets, e.g. Belfast Steamship Co. Ltd [Coast Lines Ltd]. A change of manager without any change of owner is shown by rectangular brackets alone, e.g. 1978: [James Fisher & Sons Ltd]. The ownership of modern vessels is often complicated. Varying ownerships have no effect on the operators of a ship, which are defined by the trading style adopted and by the route(s) covered. Outright sales are denoted by 'Sold to', transfers to associates by 'To'.

Port of registry and flag
For British and Irish ships, the names of the owner (and manager) are followed by the port of registry in brackets, e.g. {Liverpool}. If there was a major difference between the owner's principal place of business or head office and the port of registry, the business location is shown immediately after the name of the owner, e.g. Oldham Bros, Liverpool {Dublin}. Irish ships were included on the British register until 1939, but have been registered separately since then; their flag is not shown. All other foreign ships show the port of registy and the flag in brackets, e.g. {and/Piraues; Greece}. If the port of registry is unknown, the flag alone is shown, e.g. {Greece}. A port of registry without any other details, e.g. 1952: {Dublin}, indicates a change in the port of registry.

Name *Official number* *Builder. Yard no.* *Engine builder and details*	*In fleet*	*Dimensions* *(length x breadth x depth)*	*Gross* *tons*	*Notes*

Charles Wye Williams & Company 1824–1825
City of Dublin Steam Packet Company (joint stock company) 1825–1833
City of Dublin Steam Packet Company (statutory company) 1833–1924

City of Dublin	1823–1841	132'10" x 22'4½" x 13'0"	207 N	Wood.

Dawson and Pearson, Liverpool.
Fawcett & Co., Liverpool. Steam. 126hp. Paddle wheels.
1823: Launched 4 October as *City of Dublin*.
1823: Completed for Charles Wye Williams & Co. {Liverpool}.
1831: To City of Dublin Steam Packet Co. {Dublin}.
1841: Sold to Joseph Coyne, Runcorn {Liverpool}.
1841: Sold to Government of Mexico. Renamed *Regenerador*.
1845: Lost at Rio de Alvarado, Mexico.

Town of Liverpool	1824–1828	132'5" x 22'2" x 13'3"	204 N	Wood.

John Wilson, Liverpool.
Fawcett & Co., Liverpool. Steam. 126hp. Paddle wheels.
1824: Completed for Charles Wye Williams & Co. {Liverpool} as *Town of Liverpool*.
1828: Grounded 18 March on rocks near Hook Tower Light, Waterford, on voyage from Waterford to Liverpool.

Hibernia	1825–1849	133'0" x 22'7" x 14'0"	210 N	Wood.

Dawson and Pearson, Liverpool.
Fawcett & Co., Liverpool. Steam. 130hp. Paddle wheels.
Laid down as *Free Trader*.
1825: Launched 5 February as *Hibernia*.
1825: Completed for City of Dublin Steam Packet Co. {Liverpool}.
1843: {Dublin}.
1849: Broken up at Liverpool.

Name Official number Builder. Yard no. Engine builder and details	In fleet	Dimensions (length x breadth x depth)	Gross tons	Notes

Britannia   1825–1859   136'0" x 24'3" x 14'0"   219 N   Wood.
8782
Dawson and Pearson, Liverpool.
Gladstone & Foster, Liverpool. Steam. 160hp. Paddle wheels.
Laid down as *Union*.
1825: Launched 19 July as *Britannia*.
1825: Completed for City of Dublin Steam Packet Co. {Liverpool}.
1843: {Dublin}.
1859: Broken up.
1863: Register closed.

Liffey   1826–1846   136'7" x 22'1" x 12'3"   202 N   Wood.
John Wilson, Liverpool.
Clegg & Co. Steam. 110hp. Paddle wheels.
1824: Completed for Dublin and Liverpool Steam Navigation Co. {Liverpool} as *Liffey*.
1826: Dublin and Liverpool Steam Navigation Co. acquired by City of Dublin Steam Packet Co.
1843: To City of Dublin Steam Packet Co. {Dublin}.
1846: Register closed: broken up.

Mersey   1826–1859   129'3" x 22'1" x 12'4"   202 N   Wood.
8780   143'9" x 21'2" x 12'4"   196 N   from 1835.
John Wilson, Liverpool.
Fawcett & Co., Liverpool. Steam. 86hp. Paddle wheels.
1825: Completed for Dublin and Liverpool Steam Navigation Co. {Liverpool} as *Mersey*.
1826: Dublin and Liverpool Steam Navigation Co. acquired by City of Dublin Steam Packet Co.
1831: To City of Dublin Steam Packet Co. {Dublin}.
1833: Lengthened. New steam engines. 120hp. Registered 1835. Old engines transferred to *Lady Lansdowne* (1833
   – river Shannon).
1859: Broken up.
1863: Register closed.

Commerce   1826–1845   144'0" x 22'0" x 16'0"   203 N   Wood.
Grayson and Leadley, Liverpool.
Maudslay, Son & Field, London. Steam. 140hp. Paddle wheels.
1825: Launched 18 July as *Commerce*.
1825: Completed for Dublin and Liverpool Steam Navigation Co. Not registered.
1826: Dublin and Liverpool Steam Navigation Co. acquired by City of Dublin Steam Packet Co.
1826: To City of Dublin Steam Packet Co. {Dublin}.
1845: Sold to John Wilson, Liverpool {Dublin}. Converted to sailing ship.
1845: Sold to Reuben Hemingway {Liverpool}.
1847: Sold to George Hargreaves {Liverpool}.
1847: Sold to Charles S. Middleton {Liverpool}.
1848: Sold to Peter Stuart and Peter Douglas {Liverpool}.
1850: Sprang leak at sea and abandoned 2 April, on voyage from Bonny, West Africa, to Liverpool. Wrecked 3 April
   on Blasket Islands, Co. Kerry, Ireland.

Mona   1826–1847   126'0" x 20'7" x 14'1"   201 N   Wood.
Mottershead and Hayes, Liverpool.
Fawcett & Co., Liverpool. Steam. 100hp. Paddle wheels.
1825: Launched 18 June as *Mona*.
1825: Completed for Mona and Liverpool Steam Packet Co. {Liverpool}. Operated by Dublin and Liverpool Steam
   Navigation Co.

Name Official number Builder. Yard no. Engine builder and details	In fleet	Dimensions (length x breadth x depth)	Gross tons	Notes

1826: Dublin and Liverpool Steam Navigation Co. acquired by City of Dublin Steam Packet Co.
1831: To City of Dublin Steam Packet Co. {Dublin}.
1838: Not in company's fleet list.
1847: Register closed: broken up.

Manchester	1826–1829	142'0" x 24'8" x 14'3"	224 N	Wood.

Dawson and Pearson, Liverpool.
Gladstone & Foster, Liverpool. Steam. 140hp. Paddle wheels.
1826: Launched 25 June as *Manchester*.
1826: Completed for City of Dublin Steam Packet Co. {Dublin}.
1829: Sank 3 December, off the Skerries, Anglesey, on voyage from Dublin to Liverpool.

Shamrock	1826–1843	121'4" x 24'2" x 12'7½"	203 N	Wood.

Bland and Chaloner, Liverpool.
Fawcett & Co., Liverpool. Steam. 80hp. Paddle wheels.
1824: Launched 30 June as *Shamrock*.
1824: Completed for Liverpool and Belfast Steam Packet Co. {Liverpool}.
1826: Liverpool and Belfast Steam Packet Co. acquired by City of Dublin Steam Packet Co.
1831: To City of Dublin Steam Packet Co. {Dublin}.
1843: Sold to David Bannon, Newry, and Malcolm McEachen, Liverpool {Newry}.
1844: Sold to David Bannon {Newry}.
1844: Registered to Malcolm McEachen on trust {Newry}.
1845: Sold to Norman McLeod, James Ingram and Hugh Mackay {Liverpool}.
1845: Sold to John S. de Wolf {Liverpool}.
1845: Sold to Hugh Mackay {Liverpool}.
1848: Abandoned in sinking condition 15 September, in Atlantic about 10°W, on voyage from Liverpool and Cork
   to St John's, Newfoundland.

Leeds	1826–1852	141'3" x 25'0" x 14'8"	243 N	Wood.

John Wilson, Liverpool.
Fawcett & Co., Liverpool. Steam. 130hp. Paddle wheels.
1826: Completed for City of Dublin Steam Packet Co. {Dublin} as *Leeds*.
1834: Grounded 6 November on Furlong Rock. Refloated, but sank at Holyhead. Later raised.
1852: Abandoned in a sinking state 24 January, off Point Lynas, Anglesey, on voyage from Dublin to Liverpool.
Drifted north and later sank. Some remains washed up near Maryport.

Birmingham 8806	1826–1864	140'8" x 25'0" x 14'8"	233 N	Wood.

John Wilson, Liverpool.
Fawcett & Co., Liverpool. Steam. 130hp. Paddle wheels.
1826: Completed for City of Dublin Steam Packet Co. {Dublin} as *Birmingham*.
1864: Register closed: broken up.

Sheffield	1826–1828	145'6" x 24'8" x 14'6"	226 N	Wood.

Dawson and Pearson, Liverpool.
Gladstone & Foster, Liverpool. Steam. Paddle wheels.
1826: Launched 21 June as *Sheffield*.
1826: Completed for City of Dublin Steam Packet Co. {Dublin}.
1828: Wrecked 30 December at Ballywalter, Co. Down, on voyage from Liverpool to Belfast.

Name Official number Builder. Yard no. Engine builder and details	In fleet	Dimensions (length x breadth x depth)	Gross tons	Notes

Mars 1826–? Wood. Tug,
Steam. Paddle wheels. later cattle tender.
1826: Completed as *Mars*. Not registered.
1829: New steam engines by Fawcett & Co., Liverpool. 18hp.
1838: Still in company's fleet list.

Venus 1827–? Wood. Tug.
Fawcett & Co., Liverpool. Steam. 36hp. Paddle wheels.
1827: Completed as *Venus*. Not registered.
1833: Still in company's fleet list.

Nottingham 1827–1846 142'8" x 24'8" x 14'1" 228 N Wood.
Dawson and Pearson, Liverpool.
Fawcett & Co., Liverpool. Steam. 130hp. Paddle wheels.
1827: Launched 29 January as *Nottingham*.
1827: Completed for City of Dublin Steam Packet Co. {Dublin}.
1833: Grounded at Larne in September, but refloated.
1846: Sold to Nicholas Treweek, Amlwch {Beaumaris}. Converted to sailing ship. Engines transferred to *Roscommon*
  (1845).
1846: Abandoned at sea 18 November, waterlogged and dismasted, on voyage from Quebec to Liverpool.

Tyne 1827–1827 68'0" x 19'10" x 11'7" 112 Wood.
William Wallace, Workington.
Sailing brig.
1826: Launched 28 January as *Tyne*.
1826: Completed for Captain Ralph Thompson, Workington, and others {Whitehaven}.
1827: Chartered to City of Dublin Steam Packet Co. for Dublin–Liverpool cargo service.
1828: Sold to Grayson & others {Whitehaven}.
1829: Lost 13 July on island of Inagua, West Indies, on voyage from Port-au-Prince to Trieste.

(Town of Liverpool) Wood.
Seddon and Leadley, Liverpool.
Steam. Paddle wheels.
Ordered by City of Dublin Steam Packet Co.
1829: Launched 7 March as *Town of Liverpool*.
Not registered in name of company. Probably completed as *Ballinasloe*.

Ballinasloe 1829–1864 138'1" x 24'2" x 7'2" 191 N Wood.
8779
Seddon and Leadley, Liverpool.
Steam. 130hp. Paddle wheels.
1829: Completed for City of Dublin Steam Packet Co. {Dublin} as *Ballinasloe*.
1864: Register closed: broken up.

Kingstown 1829–1845 91'2" x 17'0" x 10'4" 71 N Wood.
John Wilson, Chester.
Steam. 60hp. Paddle wheels.
1826: Launched 11 February as *Kingstown*.
1826: Completed for Saint George Steam Packet Co. {Dublin}.
1829: Sold (possibly only chartered) to City of Dublin Steam Packet Co. Sale not registered.
1845: Register closed: broken up.

Name Official number Builder. Yard no. Engine builder and details	In fleet	Dimensions (length x breadth x depth)	Gross tons	Notes

William Huskisson   1832–1840   137'10" x 23'9" x 14'6"   213 N   Wood.
John Scott and Sons, Greenock.
Builder. Steam. 120hp. Paddle wheels.
1826: Launched 10 July as *William Huskisson*.
1826: Completed for Mersey and Clyde Steam Navigation Co. {Liverpool}.
1831: Mersey and Clyde Steam Navigation Co. taken over by Glasgow and Liverpool Steam Shipping Co.
1832: Sold to John Watson {Liverpool}. Operated by Saint George Steam Packet Co.
1832: Sold to City of Dublin Steam Packet Co. {Dublin}.
1840: Abandoned 12 January off Holyhead, on voyage from Dublin to Liverpool, after springing leak. Later sank
   in approaches to river Mersey.

Clarence   1832–1839   96'10" x 15'2" x 8'0"   70   Wood.
James Lang, Dumbarton.
Robert Napier, Glasgow. Condensing steam. 45hp. Paddle wheels.
1827: Completed for Robert Napier, Glasgow, as *Clarence*. Not registered.
1832–39: Chartered to City of Dublin Steam Packet Co.
1839: Sold to Carlisle Canal Co. {Carlisle}.
1847: Sold to James Jack (engineer), Liverpool {Carlisle}.
1847: Sold to Thomas & Henry Hillard, Birkenhead, and Henry Nicholls, Eastham {Liverpool}.
1848: Sold to Robert Singlehurst {Liverpool}.
1848: Sold to Edward Clark {Liverpool}.
1849: Sold to George S. Sanderson {Liverpool}.
1853: Register closed: broken up.

Garryowen   1834–1866   130'0" x 21'6" x 9'3"   263   Iron.
54967
William Laird, North Birkenhead. 3.
Fawcett, Preston & Co., Liverpool. Steam. 80hp. Paddle wheels.
1834: Launched 6 September as *Garryowen*.
1834: Completed for City of Dublin Steam Packet Co. Not registered.
1866: Sold to Peter Stuart and Peter Douglas {Liverpool}. Converted to sailing vessel.
1866: Sailed 3 June from Liverpool to West Africa and converted to a hulk at New Calabar River.
1871: Register closed.

City of Limerick   1836–1859   143.6 x 22.5 x 15.9   459   Wood.
5675
Thomas Wilson, Liverpool.
Steam. 190hp. Paddle wheels.
1835: Launched 26 August as *City of Limerick*.
1836: Completed for City of Dublin Steam Packet Co. {Dublin}.
1838: Sold to British & Irish Steam Packet Co. {Dublin}.
1859: Register closed: broken up.

Athlone   1836–1852   145.5m x 22.7m x 14.6m   434   Wood.
2320
W & T Wilson, Liverpool.
Fawcett, Preston & Co., Liverpool. Steam. 190hp. Paddle wheels.
1835: Launched 11 November as *Athlone*.
1836: Completed for City of Dublin Steam Packet Co. {Dublin}.
1847: Grounded 6 July on Mew Island, Belfast Lough, but refloated and returned to service.
1852: Sold to Samuel Ball, William Williams & Peter P. Brownrigg {Liverpool}. Converted to sailing vessel.
1857: Sold to Thomas Buxton and Joseph Yeoward {Liverpool}.

Name Official number Builder. Yard no. Engine builder and details	In fleet	Dimensions (length x breadth x depth)	Gross tons	Notes

---

1857: Sold to Joseph Yeoward {Liverpool}.

1859: Sprang leak and abandoned with six feet of water in the hold, 8 November, in position 45°N 11°W, on voyage from Liverpool to Galveston.

Royal William   1837–1885   172.5m x 24.6m x 16.6m   645   Wood.
8781
W&T Wilson, Liverpool.
Fawcett, Preston & Co., Liverpool. Side-lever steam. 270hp. Paddle wheels.
1836: Launched 31 May as *Royal William*.
1837: Completed for City of Dublin Steam Packet Co. {Dublin}.
1838: Chartered to Transatlantic Steamship Co. for two round voyages Liverpool–New York.
1885: Converted to coal hulk.
1888: Broken up.

(Roscommon)   490   Wood.
John Wilson, Liverpool.
Steam. Paddle wheels.
Ordered by City of Dublin Steam Packet Co.
1836: Launched 14 September as *Roscommon*.
Not registered in name of company.

(Roscrea)   Wood.
John Wilson, Liverpool.
Steam. Paddle wheels.
Ordered by City of Dublin Steam Packet Co.
Not registered in name of company.

Queen Victoria   1837–1853   154.5m x 22.8m x 15.1m   483   Wood.
                                               169.5m x 22.8m x 15.5m   537   from 1845.
W&T Wilson, Liverpool.
Mather, Dixon & Co., Liverpool. Steam. 250hp. Paddle wheels.
1837: Launched 19 August as *Queen Victoria*.
1837: Completed for City of Dublin Steam Packet Co. {Dublin}.
1845: Lengthened.
1853: Wrecked 15 February, off Bailey Light, Dublin, on voyage from Liverpool to Dublin.

Duchess of Kent   1838–1866   155.m x 23.0m x 15.0m   482   Wood.
8786
W&T Wilson, Liverpool.
Fawcett, Preston & Co., Liverpool. Steam. 250hp. Paddle wheels.
1838: Completed for City of Dublin Steam Packet Co. {Dublin} as *Duchess of Kent*.
1866: Register closed: broken up.

Royal Adelaide   1838–1850   175.7m x 24.4m x 16.5m   642   Wood.
W&T Wilson, Liverpool.
Mather, Dixon & Co., Liverpool. Steam. 270hp. Paddle wheels.
1838: Completed for City of Dublin Steam Packet Co. {Dublin} as *Royal Adelaide*.
1850: Wrecked 30 March on Tongue Sand, off Margate, on voyage from Cork to London.

Name Official number Builder. Yard no. Engine builder and details	In fleet	Dimensions (length x breadth x depth)	Gross tons	Notes

Devonshire   1838–1840   157.0m x 23.5m x 16.7m   598   Wood.
731
Hunter and Dow, Kelvinhaugh, Glasgow.
Claude Girdwood & Co., Glasgow. Steam. 230hp. Paddle wheels.
1837: Completed for Goole Steam Navigation Co. as *Vanguard*. Not registered.
1838: Renamed *Devonshire*. Registered by Goole Steam Navigation Co. {Goole}.
1838: Sold to City of Dublin Steam Packet Co. {Dublin}.
1840: Sold to British & Irish Steam Packet Co. {Dublin}.
1859: Register closed: broken up.

Duke of Cambridge   1838–1866   158.1m x 23.5m x 16.5m   602   Wood.
8794
Hunter and Dow, Kelvinhaugh, Glasgow.
Claude Girdwood & Co., Glasgow. Steam. 220hp. Paddle wheels.
1838: Completed for Goole Steam Navigation Co. as *Jason*. Not registered.
1838: Renamed *Duke of Cambridge*. Registered by Goole Steam Navigation Co. {Goole}.
1838: Sold to City of Dublin Steam Packet Co. {Dublin}.
1866: Sold to unnamed buyer. Broken up by 1870.
1870: Register closed.

Thames   1838–1841   153'0" x 27'0" x 15'0"   331 N   Wood.
Henry Fletcher, Son, and Fearnall, Poplar, London.
Boulton & Watt, Birmingham. Steam. 160hp. Paddle wheels.
1826: Completed for Dublin & London Steam Packet Co. {Dublin} as *Thames*.
1838: Sold to City of Dublin Steam Packet Co. {Dublin}.
1841: Wrecked 4 January on Rosevear Carn, Isles of Scilly, on voyage from Dublin to London.

Prince   1839–1867   164.9m x 23.6m x 16.2m   626   Wood.
8788
W&T Wilson, Liverpool.
Fawcett, Preston & Co., Liverpool. Steam. 250hp. Paddle wheels.
1839: Completed for Dublin and Liverpool Steam-Ship Building Co. Registered in name of City of Dublin Steam
Packet Co. {Dublin} as *Prince*.
1851: Registered in names of trustees of Dublin and Liverpool Steam-Ship Building Co. {Dublin}.
1867: Register closed: broken up.

Princess   1839–1866   165.9m x 23.7m x 16.0m   637   Wood.
8789
Thomas Wilson, Liverpool.
Fawcett, Preston & Co., Liverpool. Steam. 250hp. Paddle wheels.
1839: Completed for Dublin and Liverpool Steam-Ship Building Co. Registered in name of City of Dublin Steam
Packet Co. {Dublin} as *Princess*.
1851: Registered in names of trustees of Dublin and Liverpool Steam-Ship Building Co. {Dublin}.
1866: Register closed: broken up.

Erin go Bragh   1840–1867   126.4m x 22.4m x 10.9m   324   Iron.
12225
Grantham, Page & Co., Liverpool.
Mather, Dixon & Co., Liverpool. Steam. 100hp. Paddle wheels.
1840: Completed for Dublin and Liverpool Steam-Ship Building Co. Registered in name of City of Dublin Steam
Packet Co. {Dublin} as *Erin go Bragh*.
1851: Registered in names of trustees of Dublin and Liverpool Steam-Ship Building Co. {Dublin}.

Name Official number Builder. Yard no. Engine builder and details	*In fleet*	*Dimensions* *(length x breadth x depth)*	*Gross* *tons*	*Notes*

1867: Sold to Peter Stuart and Peter Douglas {Liverpool}. Converted to sailing vessel.

1867: Sailed 29 August from Liverpool to West Africa and converted to hulk on Opobo River.

1871: Register closed.

Dover Castle	1841–1863	111.6m x 15.9m x 11.1m	177	Wood.
12236				

J.P. Batley, Shoreham.

Maudslay & Co., London. Steam. 70hp. Paddle wheels.

1833: Completed for John Hayward & others {Dover} as *Dover Castle*.

1838: Sold to John Westrup & Richard Russell (Limerick Shipping Co.), Limerick {Dover}.

1841: Sold to City of Dublin Steam Packet Co. Sale not registered.

1843: Registered to City of Dublin Steam Packet Co. {Dublin}.

1863: Register closed: broken up.

Iron Duke	1844–1893	177.5 mx 26.9m x 17.2m	629	Iron.
8809		222.0m x 28.2m x 17.2m	733	from 1857.

Thomas Wilson, Liverpool.

Fawcett, Preston & Co., Liverpool. Side-lever steam. 320hp. Paddle wheels.

1843: Launched 28 December as *Iron Duke*.

1844: Completed for Dublin and Liverpool Steam-Ship Building Co. Registered in name of City of Dublin Steam Packet Co. {Dublin}.

1851: Registered in names of trustees of Dublin and Liverpool Steam-Ship Building Co. {Dublin}.

1857: Lengthened.

1893: Broken up.

Albert	1845–1886	146.5m x 23.0m x 13.6m	493	Iron.
8783				

Thomas Wilson, Liverpool.

Maudslay, Sons & Field, London. Side-lever steam. 160hp. Paddle wheels.

1845: Completed for City of Dublin Steam Packet Co. {Dublin} as *Albert*.

1886: Broken up.

William Stanley	1845–1852	90.1m x 14.1m x 7.5m	86	Wood.
24186				

Thomas Wilson, Liverpool.

Fawcett, Preston & Co., Liverpool. Steam. 40hp. Paddle wheels.

1837: Completed for Mrs Peggy Smith as *William Stanley*. Not registered.

1845: Sold to City of Dublin Steam Packet Co. {Dublin}.

1852: Sold to William Walters {Chester}.

1854: Converted to sailing ship.

1854: Sold to Gibbs & Bright, but sale not completed.

1854: Sold to Arthur Hunt {Liverpool}.

1855: Sold to Thomas F. Carter, William Roberts and Joseph Jones {Liverpool}.

1859: Damaged 7 April at 44°N 38°W, in a squall, on voyage from Matanzas to the United Kingdom. Abandoned 11 April.

Pearl	1845–1852	160.0m x 20.6m x 13.0m	252	Iron.

Ditchburn & Mare, Blackwall, London.

Auxiliary steam. Single Archimedean screw.

1845: Launched 18 October as *Pearl*.

1845: Completed for City of Dublin Steam Packet Co. {Dublin}.

Name	In fleet	Dimensions	Gross	Notes
Official number		(length x breadth x depth)	tons	
Builder. Yard no.				
Engine builder and details				

1852: On fire at sea 19 June, on voyage from Hartlepool to Rotterdam. Abandoned 45 miles off Yarmouth. Sank 21 June in position 53°N 3°E.

Roscommon   1845–1865   165.5m x 22.4m x 13.6m   448   Iron.
8784
Peter Cato, Liverpool.
Steam from *Nottingham* (1827). 130hp. Paddle wheels.
1845: Launched 15 November as *Roscommon*.
1845: Completed for City of Dublin Steam Packet Co. {Dublin}.
1853: Rescued survivors from wrecked City of Dublin vessel *Queen Victoria* 15 February.
1865: Sold to Joseph Thompson {Liverpool}. Converted to sailing vessel by Bowdler, Chaffer & Co., Seacombe.
1865: Sold to foreigner. Renamed *Amacree*. Re-sold to Joseph Thompson {Liverpool}.
1866: Sold to Joseph Thompson, Liverpool, Thomas L. Birley, Charles Birley and Arthur L. Birley, Kirkham, Lancashire {Liverpool}.
1869: Sold to Thomas L. Birley, Charles Birley and Arthur L. Birley, Kirkham, Lancashire {Liverpool}.
1872: Sold to Joseph Thompson {Liverpool}.
1873: Wrecked 27 January on St Anne's Head, Pembrokeshire, on voyage from Cardiff to Pernambuco, Brazil.

Prince of Wales   1846–1881   174.1m x 21.6m x 11.4m   347   Iron.
8790
Tod and MacGregor, Glasgow. 41.
Builder. Side-lever steam. 80/200hp. Paddle wheels.
1846: Completed for Dublin and Liverpool Steam-Ship Building Co. Registered in name of City of Dublin Steam Packet Co. {Dublin} as *Prince of Wales*.
1851: Registered in names of trustees of Dublin and Liverpool Steam-Ship Building Co. {Dublin}.
1881: Registered in name of City of Dublin Steam Packet Co. {Dublin}.
1881: Sold to Liverpool, Llandudno and Welsh Coast Steam Boat Co. Ltd {Liverpool}.
1883: Broken up.

Windsor   1846–1887   204.7m x 26.9m x 16.0m   727   Iron.
8800   246.5m x 28.4m x 16.4m   816   from 1868.
Thomas Vernon & Co., Liverpool.
Bury Curtis & Kennedy, Liverpool. Side-lever steam. 325hp. Paddle wheels.
1846: Launched 28 January as *Windsor*.
1846: Completed for Dublin and Liverpool Steam-Ship Building Co. Registered in name of City of Dublin Steam Packet Co. {Dublin}.
1851: Registered in names of trustees of Dublin and Liverpool Steam-Ship Building Co. {Dublin}.
1868: Lengthened.
1887: Broken up.

Emerald   1846–1870   130.0m x 20.0m x 12.3m   249   Iron.
8807
Peter Cato, Liverpool.
Fawcett, Preston & Co., Liverpool. Auxiliary steam. 60hp. Single Archimedean screw.
1846: Launched 15 January as *Emerald*.
1846: Completed for City of Dublin Steam Packet Co. {Dublin}.
1870: Sold to John F. Bewley {Dublin}. Converted to sailing ship.
1871: Sold to Robert Tedcastle {Dublin}.
1877: Sold to Robert Tedcastle and Joseph Studholme {Dublin}.
1887: Sold to William McMaster {Liverpool}.
1892: Sold to Elizabeth A. McMaster {Liverpool}.
1894: Sold to Elizabeth A. McMaster, Liverpool, and William Owen, Amlwch {Liverpool}.

Name	*In fleet*	*Dimensions*	*Gross*	*Notes*
Official number		*(length x breadth x depth)*	*tons*	
Builder. Yard no.				
Engine builder and details				

1896: Sold to William Jones and William Owen, Amlwch {Liverpool}.

1908: To Hannah Jones, as executrix, and William Owen, Amlwch {Liverpool}.

1909: Sold to William Thomas and John Thomas, Amlwch {Liverpool}.

1911: Sold to Dartmouth Coaling Co. Ltd, London {Liverpool}. Converted to coal hulk.

1924: Broken up.

Diamond	1846–1872	130.0m x 20.0m x 12.5m	256	Iron.
8785				

Peter Cato, Liverpool.

Fawcett, Preston & Co., Liverpool. Auxiliary steam. 60hp. Single Archimedean screw.

1846: Launched 28 March as *Black Diamond*.

1846: Completed for City of Dublin Steam Packet Co. {Dublin} as *Diamond*.

1872: Sold to John F. Bewley {Dublin}. Converted to sailing ship.

1872: Sold to Robert Tedcastle {Dublin}.

1877: Sold to Robert Tedcastle & Co. {Dublin}.

1887: Sold to James Tyrrell & Co., Arklow {Dublin}.

1897: Sold to Robert Killen & Co. {Dublin}.

1902: Sold to Samuel Jack {Dublin}.

1902: Sold to Robert Boustead, Saltcoats, Ayrshire {Dublin}.

1902: Sold to Wals & Boustead {Nantes; France}. Renamed *Robert Boustead*.

1907: Converted into pontoon.

(*Trafalgar*)		224.2m x 29.1m x 17.7m	1,091	Iron.
13990		229.4m x 32.0m x 17.8m	1,125	from 1855.

Tod and MacGregor, Glasgow. 43.

Builder. Oscillating steam. Paddle wheels.

Ordered by and laid down for City of Dublin Steam Packet Co. as *Trafalgar*. Order transferred to Peninsular and Oriental Steam Navigation Co.

1847: Launched 1 June as *Sultan*.

1847: Completed for Peninsular and Oriental Steam Navigation Co. {London}.

1855: Lengthened, new engine and converted to screw by Caird & Co., Greenock. 200hp.

1870: Sold to Aspinall, Corner & Co., Japan {London}.

1870: Sold to Frederick Cornes {London}.

1871: Sold to Union Steam Navigation Co., Shanghai [Olyphant & Co.] {London}.

1873: Sold to China Navigation Co. Ltd {London}.

1889: Hulked; registry closed.

1899: Registry reopened to provide proof of nationality {London}.

1920: Sold to Chinese buyers.

No further information.

Trafalgar	1848–1881	189.0m x 28.5m x 17.8m	793	Iron.
8810				

Tod and MacGregor, Glasgow. 47.

Builder. Oscillating steam. 350hp. Paddle wheels.

1848: Completed for Dublin and Liverpool Steam-Ship Building Co. Registered in name of City of Dublin Steam Packet Co. {Dublin} as *Trafalgar*.

1851: Registered in names of trustees of Dublin and Liverpool Steam-Ship Building Co. {Dublin}.

1881: Broken up.

Name Official number Builder. Yard no. Engine builder and details	In fleet	Dimensions (length x breadth x depth)	Gross tons	Notes

Fairy   1849–1881   129.0m x 16.3m x 8.3m   153   Iron.
8808
Tod and MacGregor, Glasgow. 55.
Builder. Steeple steam. 65hp. Paddle wheels.
1849: Launched 3 May as *Fairy*.
1849: Completed for City of Dublin Steam Packet Co. {Dublin}.
1881: Sold to Liverpool, Llandudno and Welsh Coast Steam Boat Co. Ltd {Liverpool}.
1881: Broken up.

Eblana   1849–1883   205.5m x 25.2m x 15.7m   653   Iron.
8787
Tod and MacGregor, Glasgow. 53.
Builder. Steeple steam. 350hp. Paddle wheels.
1849: Completed for City of Dublin Steam Packet Co. {Dublin} as *Eblana*.
1883: Broken up.

Prince Arthur   1851–1881   195.0m x 23.2m x 12.3m   427   Iron.
                                                                    Two funnels.
8811
Miller, Ravenhill and Salkeld, London.
Ravenhill & Miller, London. Diagonal oscillating steam. 220hp. Paddle wheels.
1851: Completed for City of Dublin Steam Packet Co. {Dublin} as *Prince Arthur*.
1881: Sold to Liverpool, Llandudno and Welsh Coast Steam Boat Co. Ltd {Liverpool}.
1891: Sold to Richard Barnwell, Govan (representing Fairfield Shipbuilding & Engineering Co. Ltd) {Liverpool}.
1891: Sold to John Williams {Liverpool}.
1891: Sold to Rasmussen and Racine {Stavanger; Norway}.
1893: Broken up.

St Columba   1854–1873   205.3m x 26.4m x 15.1m   589   Iron.
8778   250.1m x 27.2m x 14.1m   654   from 1869.
John Laird, Birkenhead. 65.
Forrester & Co., Manchester. Side-lever steam. 375hp. Paddle wheels.
Ordered as *Kathleen*.
1847: Completed for Admiralty as HMS *St Columba*.
1850: Chartered to City of Dublin Steam Packet Co.
1854: Sold to City of Dublin Steam Packet Co. {Dublin}.
1869: Lengthened. Engines 350hp.
1873: Wrecked 21 June in dense fog, on the Skerries, on voyage from Dublin to Liverpool.

Leinster   1860–1897   343.0m x 35.0m x 19.0m   1,383   Iron.   Two
pairs of funnels.
28718
J.D.A. Samuda, Poplar, London.
Ravenhill, Salkeld & Co., London. Oscillating steam. 700hp, 1,305nhp. Paddle wheels.
1860: Completed for City of Dublin Steam Packet Co. {Dublin} as *Leinster*.
1884: New boilers. Two funnels.
1897: Sold to Isle of Man Steam Packet Co. Ltd, Douglas {Dublin}.
1897: Broken up at Belfast.

Name Official number Builder. Yard no. Engine builder and details	In fleet	Dimensions (length x breadth x depth)	Gross tons	Notes

Ulster | 1860–1897 | 336.7m x 35.2m x 18.8m | 1,421 | Iron.
Two funnels.

28720
John Laird, Birkenhead. 228.
James Watt & Co., Birmingham. Oscillating steam. 750hp, 1,299nhp. Paddle wheels.
1860: Launched 25 February as *Ulster.*
1860: Completed for City of Dublin Steam Packet Co. {Dublin}.
1897: Sold to Isle of Man Steam Packet Co. Ltd, Douglas {Dublin}.
1897: Broken up.

Connaught | 1860–1897 | 338.0m x 35.2m x 18.8m | 1,412 | Iron.
Two pairs of funnels.

28722
John Laird, Birkenhead. 230.
Ravenhill, Salkeld & Co., London. Oscillating steam. 700hp, 1,304nhp. Paddle wheels.
1860: Launched 21 April as *Connaught.*
1860: Completed for City of Dublin Steam Packet Co. {Dublin}.
1887: New boilers. Two funnels.
1897: Sold to H.E. Moss & Co. {Dublin}.
1898: Broken up at Brest, France.

Munster | 1860–1897 | 336.6m x 35.2m x 18.8m | 1,432 | Iron.
Two funnels.

28724
John Laird, Birkenhead. 229.
James Watt & Co., Birmingham. Oscillating steam. 750hp, 1,345nhp. Paddle wheels.
1860: Launched 21 April as *Munster.*
1860: Completed for City of Dublin Steam Packet Co. {Dublin}.
1897: Sold to S.W. Higginbottom and others {Dublin}.
1898: Broken up at London.

St Patrick | 1865–1894 | 239.6m x 27.2m x 15.7m | 737 | Iron.
51467
Miller & Ravenhill, Blackwall.
Builder. Oscillating steam. 400hp. Paddle wheels.
1848: Completed for Admiralty as HMS *Llewellyn.*
1850: Chartered to City of Dublin Steam Packet Co. Retained name *Llewellyn.*
1865: Sold to City of Dublin Steam Packet Co. {Liverpool}. Renamed *St Patrick.*
1865: {Dublin}.
1879: To Dublin and Liverpool Steam-Ship Building Co. {Dublin}. Registered in names of trustees.
1894: Broken up.

Kildare | 1867–1896 | 240.5m x 27.0m x 14.7m | 748 | Iron.
58392 | | 262.5m x 27.0m x 14.7m | 842 | from 1873.
Laird Brothers, Birkenhead. 345.
Builder. Diagonal oscillating steam. 300hp, 534nhp. Paddle wheels.
1867: Launched 18 May as *Kildare.*
1867: Completed for City of Dublin Steam Packet Co. {Dublin}.
1873: Lengthened.
1896: Broken up.

Name Official number Builder. Yard no. Engine builder and details	In fleet	Dimensions (length x breadth x depth)	Gross tons	Notes

---

Mullingar 1868–1896 2390m x 27.0m x 14.5m 784 Iron.
58401 261.0m x 27.4m x 14.5m 761 from 1871.
Walpole, Webb & Bewley, Dublin. 25.
Fawcett, Preston & Co., Liverpool. Oscillating steam. 300hp. Paddle wheels.
1868: Launched 4 December as *Mullingar*.
1868: Completed for City of Dublin Steam Packet Co. {Dublin}.
1871: Lengthened.
1877: New steam engines by Laird Brothers, Birkenhead. 300hp, 476nhp.
1896: Broken up.

Longford 1870–1896 249.5 x 27.1 x 14.7 817 Iron.
58423
Laird Brothers, Birkenhead. 374.
Builder. Diagonal oscillating steam. 300hp, 535nhp. Paddle wheels.
1870: Launched 18 June as *Longford*.
1870: Completed for City of Dublin Steam Packet Co. {Dublin}.
1879: Registered in names of trustees of Dublin and Liverpool Steam-Ship Building Co. {Dublin}.
1888: Sank Tedcastle McCormick steamer *Dublin* in collision 26 October, in Liverpool Bay.
1896: Broken up.

Leitrim 1874–1899 249.4m x 27.2m x 14.7m 796 Iron.
67779
Laird Brothers, Birkenhead. 417.
Builder. Compound oscillating steam. 300hp, 477nhp. Paddle wheels.
1874: Launched 1 September as *Leitrim*.
1874: Completed for City of Dublin Steam Packet Co. {Dublin}.
1896: Sank 20 December after collision with steamship *Nicosian* at Liverpool. Raised and laid up.
1899: Sold for breaking up at Preston. Register closed. Partly dismantled. Sold to Severn Port Warehousing Co. Ltd, Gloucester, and converted to twin-screw self-propelled grain elevator for use at Sharpness. Compound steam engines by Fawcett, Preston & Co., Liverpool. 71rhp. 7 knots.
1901: {Gloucester}.
1959: Sold to British Transport Commission {Hull}.
1963: To British Transport Docks Board {Hull}.
1963: Broken up at Dunston-on-Tyne.

Cavan 1876–1897 250.2m x 27.2m x 14.8m 803 Iron.
67794
Laird Brothers, Birkenhead. 433.
Builder. Compound oscillating steam. 300hp, 476nhp. Paddle wheels.
1876: Launched 27 May as *Cavan*.
1876: Completed for City of Dublin Steam Packet Co. {Dublin}.
1897: Register closed: vessel sold for breaking up.
1899: Register reopened on restoration to seaworthiness, following conversion to sailing ship. Owned by Paul Rogers (shipbuilder), Carrickfergus {Belfast}.
1899: Sold to Christian Christians {Swansea}.
1903: Sold to R. Razetto {Genoa; Italy}. Renamed *Ero*.
1904: Sold to William Brown {London}. Renamed *Cavan*.
1905: Sold to William Brown, London, & Stephen Brown, Newcastle, NSW {Newcastle, NSW}.
1932: To Stephen Brown {Newcastle, NSW}, as executor following death of William Brown in 1927.
1932: Sold to William Jones {Newcastle, NSW}.
1932: Register closed: vessel to be broken up.

Name Official number Builder. Yard no. Engine builder and details	In fleet	Dimensions (length x breadth x depth)	Gross tons	Notes

---

Mayo   1880–1903   262.6m x 27.2m x 14.7m   760   Iron.
81435
Laird Brothers, Birkenhead. 479.
Builder. Compound oscillating steam. 300hp, 477nhp. Paddle wheels.
1880: Launched 24 July as *Mayo*.
1880: Completed for City of Dublin Steam Packet Co. {Dublin}.
1903: Broken up.

Standard   1882–1887   174.5m x 24.9m x 13.7m   422   Iron.
8691
C.J. Mare & Co., Blackwall, London.
J&G Rennie, London. Diagonal steam. 100hp. Single screw.
1854: Completed for Dublin and Liverpool Screw Steam Packet Co. {Dublin} as *Standard*.
1856: Sold to Malcomson & Co. {Dublin}.
1863: Sold to Dublin and Liverpool Screw Steam Packet Co. {Dublin}. Registered in names of James Stirling &
    Henry A. Cowper.
1867: Registered in name of James Stirling {Dublin}.
1882: Dublin and Liverpool Screw Steam Packet Co. acquired by City of Dublin Steam Packet Co., following death
    of James Stirling in 1882.
1882: To City of Dublin Steam Packet Co. {Dublin}.
1887: Broken up.

Star   1882–1886   160.2m x 21.2m x 12.9m   281   Iron.
28723
Laurence Hill & Co. Port Glasgow. 30.
A&J Inglis, Glasgow. Vertical steam. 85hp. Single screw.
1860: Completed for Dublin and Liverpool Screw Steam Packet Co. {Dublin} as *Star*. Registered in names of James
    Stirling & Henry A. Cowper.
1867: Registered in name of James Stirling {Dublin}.
1882: Dublin and Liverpool Screw Steam Packet Co. acquired by City of Dublin Steam Packet Co., following death
    of James Stirling in 1882.
1882: To City of Dublin Steam Packet Co. {Dublin}.
1886: Broken up.

Express   1882–1910   191.4m x 23.8m x 13.2m   398   Iron.
67772
R. Irvine & Co., West Hartlepool. 15.
Blair & Co. Ltd, Stockton on Tees. Compound steam. 110hp, 140nhp. Single screw.
1874: Launched 17 February as *Express*.
1874: Completed for Dublin and Liverpool Screw Steam Packet Co. {Dublin}. Registered in name of James Stirling.
1882: Dublin and Liverpool Screw Steam Packet Co. acquired by City of Dublin Steam Packet Co., following death
    of James Stirling in 1882.
1882: To City of Dublin Steam Packet Co. {Dublin}.
1910: Broken up.

Meath   1884–1906   262.6m x 27.1m x 14.8m   843   Iron.
88992
Laird Brothers, Birkenhead. 524.
Builder. Compound oscillating steam. 279hp, 468nhp. Paddle wheels.
1884: Launched 28 June as *Meath*.
1884: Completed for City of Dublin Steam Packet Co. {Dublin}.
1906: Broken up at Preston.

Name *Official number* *Builder. Yard no.* *Engine builder and details*	*In fleet*	*Dimensions* *(length x breadth x depth)*	*Gross* *tons*	*Notes*

Belfast   1884–1919   192.3m x 24.2m x 13.5m   425   Iron.
88994
Irvine & Co., West Hartlepool. 52.
Blair & Co. Ltd, Stockton-on-Tees. Compound steam. 110hp, 134nhp. Single screw.
Ordered by Dublin and Liverpool Screw Steam Packet Co. Ltd.
1884: Launched 4 October as *Belfast*.
1884: Completed for City of Dublin Steam Packet Co. {Dublin}.
1919: Sold to London Maritime Investment Co. Ltd {Dublin}.
1919: To British & Irish Steam Packet Co. Ltd {Dublin}.
1922: Sold to Latvijas Kugneezibas Sabeedriba Austra {Riga; Latvia}. Renamed *Austra*.
1924: To Schiffahrts Ges. 'Austra' {Riga; Latvia}.
1927: Broken up.

Ireland   1885–1899   366.3m x 38.3m x 19.2m   1,952   Two
                                                                                            funnels.
88998
Laird Brothers, Birkenhead. 531.
Builder. Oscillating steam. 846hp, 1616nhp. Paddle wheels.
1885: Launched 29 April as *Ireland*.
1885: Completed for City of Dublin Steam Packet Co. {Dublin}.
1899: Sold to Samuel W. Higginbottom, Liverpool {Dublin}.
1899: Sold to Liverpool and Douglas Steamers Ltd {Liverpool}.
1900: Sold to Thomas W. Ward, Sheffield {Liverpool}.
1900: Sold to Percy Millward, London {Liverpool}.
1900: Broken up at Brest, France.

Galway   1891–1907   262.5m x 27.2m x 14.7m   881
95333
Blackwood & Gordon, Port Glasgow. 224.
Builder. Compound diagonal steam. 225hp, 398nhp. Paddle wheels. 15 knots.
1891: Launched 11 June as *Galway*.
1891: Completed for City of Dublin Steam Packet Co. {Dublin}.
1907: Sold to Mayor, Commonalty and Citizens of the City of London {London}.
1915: Broken up.

Louth   1894–1919   260.6m x 34.1m x 15.8m   1,249
99760
Blackwood & Gordon, Port Glasgow. 229.
Builder. Triple expansion steam. 400rhp, 330nhp. Single screw. 14 knots.
1894: Launched 24 May as *Louth*.
1894: Completed for City of Dublin Steam Packet Co. {Dublin}.
1919: Sold to London Maritime Investment Co. Ltd {Dublin}.
1919: To British & Irish Steam Packet Co. Ltd {Dublin}.
1920: Renamed *Lady Louth*.
1920: To City of Cork Steam Packet Co. Ltd {Liverpool}. Renamed *Bandon*.
1921: {Cork}.
1931: To British & Irish Steam Packet Co. Ltd {Dublin}. Renamed *Lady Galway*.
1936: To British & Irish Steam Packet Co. (1936) Ltd {Dublin}.
1938: Renamed *Galway*.
1938: Broken up at Port Glasgow.

Name Official number Builder. Yard no. Engine builder and details	In fleet	Dimensions (length x breadth x depth)	Gross tons	Notes

Wicklow 1895–1919 260.2m x 34.1m x 15.8m 1,248
104963
Blackwood & Gordon, Port Glasgow. 230.
Builder. Triple expansion steam. 258rhp, 330nhp. Single screw. 14 knots.
1895: Launched 28 March as *Wicklow*.
1895: Completed for City of Dublin Steam Packet Co. {Dublin}.
1918: Taken over by Shipping Controller [British & Irish Steam Packet Co. Ltd].
1919: Returned to City of Dublin Steam Packet Co.
1919: Sold to London Maritime Investment Co. Ltd {Dublin}.
1919: To British & Irish Steam Packet Co. Ltd {Dublin}.
1920: Renamed *Lady Wicklow*.
1936: To British & Irish Steam Packet Co. (1936) Ltd {Dublin}.
1938: Renamed *Wicklow*.
1938: Owner renamed British & Irish Steam Packet Co. Ltd.
1947: To Belfast, Mersey and Manchester Steamship Co. Ltd {Belfast}.
1948: Broken up at Llanelli.

Carlow 1896–1919 260.0m x 34.1m x 15.8m 1,274
104968
Blackwood & Gordon, Port Glasgow. 232.
Builder. Triple expansion steam. 398.7rhp, 330nhp. Single screw. 15 knots.
1896: Launched 3 March as *Carlow*.
1896: Completed for City of Dublin Steam Packet Co. {Dublin}.
1919: Sold to London Maritime Investment Co. Ltd {Dublin}.
1919: To British & Irish Steam Packet Co. Ltd {Dublin}.
1920: Renamed *Lady Carlow*.
1925: Broken up at Troon.

Ulster 1896–1924 360.0m x 41.5m x 27.3m 2,632 Two funnels.

104972
Laird Brothers, Birkenhead. 611.
Builder. Triple expansion steam. 1,000rhp, 529nhp. Twin screws. 23 knots.
1896: Launched 27 June as *Ulster*.
1896: Completed for City of Dublin Steam Packet Co. {Dublin}.
1920: Laid up at Holyhead.
1924: Broken up in Germany.

Leinster 1896–1918 360.0m x 41.5m x 27.3m 2,632 Two funnels.

104974
Laird Brothers, Birkenhead. 612.
Builder. Triple expansion steam. 1,000rhp, 529nhp. Twin screws. 23 knots.
1896: Launched 12 September as *Leinster*.
1896: Completed for City of Dublin Steam Packet Co. {Dublin}.
1918: Torpedoed and sunk 10 October by German submarine *UB-123*, 7 miles from Kish Light Vessel, on voyage
   from Kingstown to Holyhead.

Munster 1897–1924 360.0m x 41.5m x 27.3m 2,632 Two funnels.

104975
Laird Brothers, Birkenhead. 613.

Name	In fleet	Dimensions	Gross	Notes
Official number		(length x breadth x depth)	tons	
Builder. Yard no.				
Engine builder and details				

Builder. Triple expansion steam. 1,000rhp, 529nhp. Twin screws. 23 knots.

1896: Launched 21 October as *Munster*.

1897: Completed for City of Dublin Steam Packet Co. {Dublin}.

1920: Laid up at Holyhead.

1924: Broken up in Germany.

Connaught	1897–1917	360.0m x 41.5m x 27.3m	2,632	Two funnels.

104980

Laird Brothers, Birkenhead. 614.

Builder. Triple expansion steam. 1,000rhp, 529nhp. Twin screws. 23 knots.

1897: Launched 21 September as *Connaught*.

1897: Completed for City of Dublin Steam Packet Co. {Dublin}.

1917: Torpedoed and sunk 3 March by German submarine *U-48*, 29 miles SW of Owers Light Vessel, English Channel, on voyage from Le Havre to Southampton.

Kerry	1897–1919	260.0m x 34.1m x 15.8m	1,277	

104976

Blackwood & Gordon, Port Glasgow. 237.

Builder. Triple expansion steam. 398.7rhp, 330nhp. Single screw. 15 knots.

1897: Launched 6 February as *Kerry*.

1897: Completed for City of Dublin Steam Packet Co. {Dublin}.

1919: Sold to London Maritime Investment Co. Ltd {Dublin}.

1919: To British & Irish Steam Packet Co. Ltd {Dublin}.

1920: Renamed *Lady Kerry*.

1924: Broken up at Birkenhead.

Cork	1899–1918	260.3m x 34.1m x 15.7m	1,280	

111023

Blackwood & Gordon, Port Glasgow. 242.

Builder. Triple expansion steam. 399rhp, 330nhp. Single screw. 15 knots.

1899: Launched 12 April as *Cork*.

1899: Completed for City of Dublin Steam Packet Co. {Dublin}.

1918: Torpedoed and sunk 26 January by German submarine *U-103* 9 miles NE from Point Lynas, Anglesey, on voyage from Dublin to Liverpool.

Kilkenny	1903–1917	269.7m x 36.2m x 15.7m	1,419	

117513

Clyde Shipbuilding & Engineering Co. Ltd, Port Glasgow. 234.

Builder. Triple expansion steam. 536rhp, 309nhp. Single screw. 15 knots.

1902: Launched 30 December as *Kilkenny*.

1903: Completed for City of Dublin Steam Packet Co. {Dublin}.

1917: Sold to Great Eastern Railway Co. {Harwich}.

1919: Renamed *Frinton*.

1923: To London & North Eastern Railway Co. {Harwich}, following railway amalgamation.

1926: Sold to William H. Burgess, Palmer's Green, Middlesex {Harwich} (a public officer of Samos Steam Navigation Co. Ltd).

1926: To Samos Steam Navigation Co. Ltd, London {Harwich}.

1927: To Steam Navigation of Samos (D. Inglessi Fils) {Samos; Greece}.

1941: Destroyed by aircraft 22 April, at Megalo Lefko, Greece.

Name Official number Builder. Yard no. Engine builder and details	*In fleet*	*Dimensions* *(length x breadth x depth)*	*Gross* *tons*	*Notes*

Carrickfergus   1910–1917   220.8m x 29.1m x 14.6m   726
99959
Harland & Wolff Ltd, Belfast. 266.
Builder. Triple expansion steam. 219hp, 225nhp. Twin screws. 13.25 knots.
1893: Launched 4 February as *Mystic*.
1893: Completed for Belfast Steamship Co. Ltd {Belfast}.
1910: Sold to City of Dublin Steam Packet Co. {Dublin}. Renamed *Carrickfergus*.
1917: Sold to Sligo Steam Navigation Co. Ltd {Sligo}.
1919: Sligo Steam Navigation Co. Ltd acquired by Coast Lines Ltd.
1931: To Burns & Laird Lines Ltd {Glasgow}. Renamed *Lairdsben*.
1936: Sold to Smith & Co. for breaking up.
1937: Broken up at Port Glasgow.

Dublin and London Steam Packet Company 1826–1836
These ships were owned by Richard Bourne and his associates and operated on Dublin–London, which was run
   jointly with the City of Dublin Steam Packet Co. The list excludes ships so owned, but used exclusively by the
   Peninsular Steam Navigation Co.

Thames   1826–1838
See *Thames* (1838) in City of Dublin Steam Packet Co. fleet list.

Shannon   1826–1837   153'0" x 27'0" x 15'0"   325 N   Wood.
Henry Fletcher, Son, and Fearnall, Poplar, London.
Boulton & Watt, Birmingham. Steam. 160hp. Paddle wheels.
1826: Completed for Dublin and London Steam Marine Co. {Dublin} as *Shannon*.
1837: To Richard Bourne, Frederick Bourne, James Hartley, William H. Fortescue & Simon Boileau {Dublin}.
1837: Sold to British & Irish Steam Packet Co. {Dublin}.
1845: New engines. 230hp.
1846: Damaged by fire 5 December at Plymouth. Scuttled. Raised later in December and repaired at Dublin.
1855: Broken up.

City of Londonderry   1830–1838   139'6" x 24'8½" x 14'6"   231 N   Wood.
                                                    152.8m x 22.5m x 14.5m   319 N   from 1837.
N. and R. Haselden, Whitby Locks, Cheshire.
Side-lever steam. 200hp. Paddle wheels.
1826: Launched 1 November as *City of Londonderry*.
1827: Completed for Liverpool and Londonderry Steam Navigation Co. {Liverpool}.
1830: Sold to Richard Bourne {Dublin}.
1837: Lengthened. Sold to Richard Bourne and others {Dublin}. Chartered to Peninsular Steam Navigation Co.
1838: {London}.
1840: Chartered to Peninsular and Oriental Steam Navigation Co.
1845: Register closed: broken up.

Royal Tar   1832–1838   144'0" x 27'9" x 6'7"   308 N   Wood.
John Duffus & Co., Aberdeen.
Builder. Steam. Paddle wheels.
1832: Completed for Richard Bourne and others {Dublin} as *Royal Tar*.
1834: Chartered to Brodie M'Ghie Willcox and Arthur Anderson for two round voyages from London to Lisbon.
1834: Chartered to Government of Spain. Renamed *Reyna Governandola*.
1836: Charter ended. Renamed *Royal Tar*.
1838: New engines. 265hp. Chartered to Peninsular Steam Navigation Co.

Name	In fleet	Dimensions	Gross	Notes
Official number		(length x breadth x depth)	tons	
Builder. Yard no.				
Engine builder and details				

1838: {London}.
1841: Sold to Peninsular and Oriental Steam Navigation Co. {London}.
1847: Sold to Government of Portugal (Portuguese Navy). Renamed *Infante D Luis*.
1863: Decommissioned.

| **William Fawcett** | 1832–1838 | 130'8" x 22'2" x 14'9" | 185 N | Wood. |
| | | 145'8" x 22'2" x 14'9" | 209 N | from 1832. |

Caleb and James Smith, Liverpool.
Fawcett, Preston & Co., Liverpool. Steam. 120hp. Paddle wheels.
1828: Launched 5 March as *William Fawcett*.
1828: Completed for Joseph Robinson Pim and William Fawcett {Liverpool}.
1832: Lengthened.
1832: Sold to Richard Bourne and others {Dublin}.
1835: Chartered to Peninsular Steam Navigation Co.
1836: Charter ended.
1837: Chartered to Peninsular Steam Navigation Co.
1838: {London}.
1840: Chartered to Peninsular and Oriental Steam Navigation Co.
1845. Register closed: broken up.

Transatlantic Steamship Company 1838–1840 (subsidiary of City of Dublin Steam Packet Company)

| **Royal William** | 1838–1838 (chartered). | | | |

See *Royal William* (1837) in City of Dublin Steam Packet Co. list.

| **Liverpool** | 1838–1840 | 212.9m x 28.5m x 19.3m | 1,150 | Wood. |
| | | | | Two funnels. |

Humble and Milcrest, Liverpool.
George Forrester & Co., Liverpool. Side-lever steam. 450hp. Paddle wheels. 9 knots.
1837: Launched 14 October as *Liverpool*.
1837: Completed for Sir John Tobin {Liverpool}.
1838: Sold to James Hartley and others {Liverpool}. Chartered to Transatlantic Steamship Co.
1840: Sold to Peninsular and Oriental Steam Navigation Co. {London}. Renamed *Great Liverpool*. Sale and change
   of name not registered.
1841: Registered in ownership of Peninsular and Oriental Steam Navigation Co. {London}, but still officially
   named *Liverpool*.
1846: Struck reef off Cape Finisterre 24 February, on voyage from Alexandria to Southampton. Beached near
   Corcubion, Spain, but broke up 27 February in storm.

| **United States** | | 202.0m x 33.5m x 28.5m | 1,673 | Wood. |
| 30714 | | 215.0m x 33.5m x 28.5m | 1,752 | from 1848. |

Thomas Wilson & Co., Liverpool.
Fawcett, Preston & Co., Liverpool. Side-lever steam. 420hp. Paddle wheels.
Original planned name *Atlantic*, then *New York*.
1840: Launched 7 March as *United States* for Transatlantic Steam Ship Co.
1840: Completed for Charles Wye Williams, Joseph C. Ewart and Francis Carleton {Liverpool} as *Oriental*.
1840: Sold to Peninsular and Oriental Steam Navigation Co., but change of ownership not registered.
1843: Registered in ownership of Peninsular and Oriental Steam Navigation Co. {London}.
1848: Lengthened.
1860: Store ship at Bombay.
1861: Machinery removed. Sold to Jairaz Faizul & Co., Bombay {London}.

Name	In fleet	Dimensions	Gross	Notes
Official number		(length x breadth x depth)	tons	
Builder. Yard no.				
Engine builder and details				

1862: Registry closed.

Later broken up at Hong Kong.

Robert Tedcastle & Company 1869–1897

| *Dublin* | 1869–1888 | 174.3m x 27.0m x 13.6m | 494 | Iron. Machinery aft. |

55239

Walpole, Webb & Bewley, Dublin.

Courtney, Stephens & Co., Dublin. Inverted steam. 70hp. Single screw.

1866: Completed for United Kingdom Screw Collier Co. Ltd {Dublin} as *Dublin*.

1869: Owner in liquidation.

1869: Sold to Robert Tedcastle and Joseph Studholme {Dublin}.

1882: Compound steam engines by V. Coates & Co. Ltd, Belfast. 90hp.

1888: Sank 26 October in collision with City of Dublin vessel *Longford*, in Liverpool Bay, about 4 miles west of North West lightship, on voyage from Liverpool to Dublin.

| *Magnet* | 1873–1896 | 195.4m x 32.0m x 13.7m | 609 | Iron. Machinery aft. |

63215

J. Horn, Waterford.

London & Glasgow Engineering & Iron Shipbuilding Co. Ltd, Glasgow. Compound steam. 150hp, 140nhp. Single screw.

1869: Completed for William Malcomson, Portlaw {Liverpool} as *Magnet*.

1870: Sold to Charles Palgrave and Michael Murphy (WB&C Palgrave & Co.) {Dublin}.

1873: Sold to Robert Tedcastle {Dublin}.

1877: Sold to Robert Tedcastle and Joseph Studholme {Dublin}.

1893: Sold to Robert Tedcastle {Dublin}.

1896: Sold to Alexander McCredie, Troon {Dublin}.

1896: Sold to John M. Campbell {Glasgow}.

1896: Sold to Magri, Rinni & Co., Suez {Glasgow}.

1899: Sold to Khedivial Mail Steamship and Graving Dock Co. Ltd, Alexandria {London}. Renamed *Gharbieh*.

1910: Sold to M. Rovetta {Genoa; Italy}.

1910: Broken up at Genoa.

| *Toiler* | 1876–1882 | 101.4m x 19.3m x 10.0m | 118 | Wood. Tug. |

70403

Lancelot Liddle, Willington Gut, Newcastle.

T.R. Scott & Co., North Shields. Lever steam. 50hp. Paddle wheels.

1875: Completed for Edward Marshall {North Shields} as *Toiler*.

1876: To Edward Marshall and others {North Shields}.

1876: Sold to Robert Tedcastle {North Shields}.

1877: {Dublin}.

1877: Sold to Robert Tedcastle and George Fenn {Dublin}.

1880: To Robert Tedcastle and Margaret Fenn {Dublin}, following death of George Fenn in 1879.

1882: Sold to Robert Brown and John Matthews {Aberdeen}. Converted to trawler.

1882: Sold to Robert Brown, John Matthews, William Morrison and others {Aberdeen}.

1883: Sold to William Pyper, John Matthews, William Morrison and others {Aberdeen}.

1885: Sold to Robert Brown, William Morrison, John Matthews and Francis Henderson {Aberdeen}.

1887: Abandoned 31 March, off coast of Caithness, in gale, following bursting of a discharge pipe, which caused ship to become waterlogged.

Name Official number Builder. Yard no. Engine builder and details	In fleet	Dimensions (length x breadth x depth)	Gross tons	Notes

Tolka   1875–1878   144.0m x 21.0m x 10.9m   257   Iron. Machinery aft.
58400
Walpole, Webb & Bewley, Dublin. 23.
Courtney, Stephens & Co., Dublin. Inverted steam. 50hp. Single screw.
1867: Completed for Walpole, Webb & Bewley {Dublin} as *Boulogne*.
1868: Sold to Constant A. Lanceau, Woodchester, near Stroud {Gloucester}.
1868: Sold under a Decree of the High Court of Admiralty to Walpole, Webb & Bewley, Dublin {Gloucester}, as
     mortgagees.
1869: Sold to foreigner. Renamed *Tolka*. Re-sold to John F. Bewley {Dublin}.
1869: Sold to Palgrave, Murphy & Co. {Dublin}.
1872: Sold to Tomlinson, Hodgetts & Co., Liverpool {Dublin}.
1872: Sold to Tomlinson, Hodgetts & Co. and John Miller Jr, Liverpool {Dublin}.
1872: Sold to John Miller Jr {Dublin}.
1872: Sold to John Miller Jr and others {Dublin}.
1875: Sold to Robert Tedcastle {Dublin}.
1877: Sold to Robert Tedcastle and Joseph Studholme {Dublin}.
1878: Sold to William A. Grainger and others {Belfast}.
1879: Compound steam engines by MacIlwaine & Lewis, Belfast. 50hp, 44nhp.
1883: Sold to David McMillan {Belfast}.
1889: Sold to H. Sundför & Co. {Haugesund; Norway}. Renamed *Thor*.
1906: Sank 28 February at Lyngholmen, between Bergen and Haugesund, Norway, after losing anchor chain
     in gale.

Adela   1878–1917   199.8m x 32.2m x 14.5m   675   Iron. Machinery aft.
77398
Henry Murray & Co., Port Glasgow. 91.
Kincaid, Donald & Co., Greenock. Compound inverted steam. 150hp, 181nhp. Single screw.
1878: Launched 27 November as *Adela*.
1878: Completed for Robert Tedcastle & Co. {Dublin}.
1897: To Tedcastle, McCormick & Co. Ltd {Dublin}.
1917: Torpedoed and sunk 27 December by German submarine *U-100*, 12 miles NW from the Skerries on voyage
     from Dublin to Liverpool.

Thistle   1885–1897   198.5m x 25.2m x 13.1m   444   Iron.
52604
A&J Inglis, Glasgow. 24.
Builder. Steam. 140hp. Single screw.
1865: Launched 13 April as *Thistle*.
1865: Completed for John Cameron and Lewis MacLellan {Glasgow}. Traded as Glasgow and Londonderry Steam
     Packet Co.
1867: To Lewis MacLellan, following death of John Cameron.
1867: To Walter MacLellan, Lewis MacLellan, John Reid and Alexander A. Laird [A.A. Laird] {Glasgow}.
1877: Compound inverted steam engines by Hutson & Corbett, Glasgow. 105hp, 213nhp.
1883: Sold to Whitehaven Steam Navigation Co. {Whitehaven}. Registered in names of trustees.
1885: Sold to Robert Tedcastle & Co. {Dublin}.
1897: Sold to D&C MacIver, Liverpool {Dublin}.
1897: Sold to Union Transport Co. Ltd, Manchester {Dublin}.
1900: Sold to Islander Steamship Co. [M. Whitwill & Son] {Bristol}.
1908: Broken up at Hendrik-Ido-Ambacht, Netherlands.

Name Official number Builder. Yard no. Engine builder and details	In fleet	Dimensions (length x breadth x depth)	Gross tons	Notes

Marlay 1890–1902 200.2m x 29.2m x 14.0m 798 Machinery aft.
95329
Workman, Clark & Co. Ltd, Belfast. 70.
Victor Coates & Co., Belfast. Compound steam. 150hp, 170nhp. Single screw. 11 knots.
1890: Launched 20 May as *Marlay*.
1890: Completed for Robert Tedcastle {Dublin}.
1897: To Tedcastle, McCormick & Co. Ltd {Dublin}.
1902: Sank 17 December, off Baily Light, Dublin, in gale, on voyage from Liverpool to Dublin.

Eblana 1892–1919 213.0m x 32.1m x 15.0m 824 Cargo.
Machinery aft.
99746
Ardrossan Shipbuilding Co. Ltd, Ardrossan. 175.
Hutson & Corbett, Glasgow. Compound steam. 185hp, 204nhp. Single screw. 13 knots.
1892: Launched 22 October as *Eblana*.
1892: Completed for Robert Tedcastle & Co. {Dublin}.
1897: To Tedcastle, McCormick & Co. Ltd {Dublin}.
1919: Tedcastle, McCormick & Co. Ltd acquired by British & Irish Steam Packet Co. Ltd.
1919: To British & Irish Steam Packet Co. Ltd {Dublin}.
1924: Broken up.

Cumbria 1896–1919 198.0m x 30.0m x 14.1m 694 Cargo.
104971
Ailsa Shipbuilding Co., Troon. 58.
Dunsmuir & Jackson Ltd, Glasgow. Triple expansion steam. 175rhp, 174nhp. Single screw. 12 knots.
1896: Launched 12 August as *Cumbria*.
1896: Completed for Robert Tedcastle & Co. {Dublin}.
1897: To Tedcastle, McCormick & Co. Ltd {Dublin}.
1919: Tedcastle, McCormick & Co. Ltd acquired by British & Irish Steam Packet Co. Ltd.
1919: To British & Irish Steam Packet Co. Ltd {Dublin}.
1920: To City of Cork Steam Packet Co. Ltd {Liverpool}.
1921: {Cork}.
1925: Broken up at Granton, Firth of Forth.

S.S. McCormick 1883–1895
F. McCormick & Company 1892–1895
J. McCormick & Company Limited 1895–1897

Blackwater 1883–1905 176.0m x 24.6m x 12.9m 538 Iron.
81448
Workman, Clark & Co., Belfast. 21.
W. King & Co., Glasgow. Compound inverted steam. 80hp. Single screw.
1883: Completed for John McCormick {Dublin} as *Blackwater*.
1884: Sold to Samuel S. McCormick & Thomas C. McCormick {Dublin}.
1895: To J. McCormick & Co. Ltd {Dublin}.
1897: To Tedcastle, McCormick & Co. Ltd {Dublin}.
1905: Sank 10 July off the Skerries after collision with steamer *Wexford*, on voyage from Liverpool to Dublin.

Name Official number Builder. Yard no. Engine builder and details	In fleet	Dimensions (length x breadth x depth)	Gross tons	Notes

---

Blackrock — 1892–1919 — 240.0m x 32.1m x 15.2m — 866 — Cargo. Machinery aft

99743
Naval Construction & Armaments Co. Ltd, Barrow. 216.
Builder. Triple expansion steam. 360hp, 297nhp. Single screw. 14 knots.
1892: Launched 10 October as *Blackrock*.
1892: Completed for F. McCormick & Co. {Dublin}.
1895: To J. McCormick & Co. Ltd {Dublin}.
1897: To Tedcastle, McCormick & Co. Ltd {Dublin}.
1919: Tedcastle, McCormick & Co. Ltd acquired by British & Irish Steam Packet Co. Ltd.
1919: To British & Irish Steam Packet Co. Ltd {Dublin}.
1923: Broken up at Ardrossan.

Tedcastle, McCormick & Company Limited 1897–1919

Dublin — 1904–1919 — 200.0m x 29.0m x 11.3m — 727 — Cargo. Machinery aft.

117516
John Fullerton & Co., Paisley. 175.
Ross & Duncan, Govan, Glasgow. Triple expansion steam. 155rhp, 156nhp. Single screw. 11 knots.
1904: Launched 17 February as *Dublin*.
1904: Completed for Tedcastle, McCormick & Co. Ltd {Dublin}.
1919: Tedcastle, McCormick & Co. Ltd acquired by British & Irish Steam Packet Co. Ltd.
1919: To Coast Lines Ltd {Dublin}.
1920: To British & Irish Steam Packet Co. Ltd {Dublin}.
1922: To Coast Lines Ltd {Liverpool}. Renamed *Cardigan Coast*.
1928: Sold to R&DA Duncan Ltd {Belfast}. Renamed *Dublin*.
1940: Sold to S. Instone & Co. Ltd {London}. Renamed *Themston*.
1950: Sold to Tyson, Edgar Shipping Ltd {London}.
1952: Broken up at Rosyth.

Blackwater — 1907–1919 — 185.1m x 27.6m x 11.0m — 678 — Cargo. Machinery aft.

123129
Ailsa Shipbuilding Co. Ltd, Troon. 181.
Builder. Compound steam. 86.6rhp. Single screw. 10.5 knots.
1907: Launched 12 October as *Blackwater*.
1907: Completed for Tedcastle, McCormick & Co. Ltd {Dublin}.
1919: Tedcastle, McCormick & Co. Ltd acquired by British & Irish Steam Packet Co. Ltd.
1919: To Coast Lines Ltd {Dublin}.
1920: Sold to Samuel Kelly {Dublin}.
1923: [William Clint].
1937: To Lady Mary Kelly, as executrix of S. Kelly [William Clint] {Belfast}.
1938: To John Kelly Ltd [William Clint] {Belfast}.
1952: Renamed *Ballygowan*.
1954: Broken up at Rainham, Kent.

Killiney — 1918–1919 — 254.5m x 36.1m x 16.0m — 1,145
140454
Caledon Shipbuilding & Engineering Co. Ltd, Dundee. 245.
Builder. Triple expansion steam. 206.4rhp, 347nhp. Single screw. 14 knots.

Name	In fleet	Dimensions	Gross	Notes
Official number		(length x breadth x depth)	tons	
Builder. Yard no.				
Engine builder and details				

1917: Launched 2 October as *Killiney*.

1918: Completed for Tedcastle, McCormick & Co. Ltd {Dublin}.

1919: Tedcastle, McCormick & Co. Ltd acquired by British & Irish Steam Packet Co. Ltd.

1919: To British & Irish Steam Packet Co. Ltd {Dublin}.

1920: Renamed *Lady Killiney*.

1923: To City of Cork Steam Packet Co. Ltd {Cork}.

1924: Renamed *Ardmore*.

1936: To British & Irish Steam Packet Co. (1936) Ltd {Cork}.

1938: Owner renamed British & Irish Steam Packet Co. Ltd.

1940: Mined and sunk 11/12 November off Great Saltee Islands and Coningbeg Rock, on voyage from Cork to Fishguard.

British & Irish Steam Packet Company 1837–1879
British & Irish Steam Packet Company Limited 1879–1936
British & Irish Steam Packet Company (1936) Limited 1937–1938
British & Irish Steam Packet Company Limited 1938–1986
B&I Line Public Limited Company 1986–1992
B&I Line Limited 1992–1995

Shannon   1837–1855

See *Shannon* (1826) in Dublin & London Steam Packet Co. fleet list.

City of Limerick   1838–1859

See *City of Limerick* (1836) in City of Dublin Steam Packet Co. fleet list.

Devonshire   1840–1859

See *Devonshire* (1838) in City of Dublin Steam Packet Co. fleet list.

| *Prince Albert* | | | | Wood. |

Thomas Wilson, Liverpool.

Steam. Paddle wheels.

Ordered by British & Irish Steam Packet Co.

1841: Launched 16 September as *Prince Albert*.

Not owned by company. Possibly completed as *Duke of Cornwall*.

| *Duke of Cornwall* | 1842–1869 | 170.8 mx 26.4 m x 17.0m | 706 | Wood. |
| 523 | | 176.0m x 29.0 m x 16.0m | 610 | from 1869. |

Thomas Wilson, Liverpool.

Fawcett, Preston & Co., Liverpool. Steam. 280hp. Paddle wheels.

1842: Completed for British & Irish Steam Packet Co. {Dublin} as *Duke of Cornwall*.

1869: Sold to J.F. Bewley & Co. {Dublin}. Converted to sailing ship.

1870: Sold to Thomas Bewley {Dublin}.

1871: Sold to Henry Brown, Passage West {Dublin}.

1871: Sold to Eugene J. McSwiney, Cork {Dublin}.

1873: Sold to James Martin & Son {Dublin}.

1874: Foundered 8 September about 9 miles from island of St Pierre, Canada, on voyage from Dublin to Quebec.

| *Rose* | 1845–1853 | 119.0m x 20.4m x 12.9m | 249 | Iron. |
| 227 | | | | |

Ditchburn & Mare, Blackwall, London.

Auxiliary steam. 60hp. Single screw.

Name Official number Builder. Yard no. Engine builder and details	In fleet	Dimensions (length x breadth x depth)	Gross tons	Notes

1845: Completed for British & Irish Steam Packet Co. {Dublin} as *Rose*.

1853: Sold to J.N. Russell & Co. {Limerick}.

1854: To London and Limerick Steam Ship Co. {Limerick}.

1864: To London and Limerick Steam Ship Co. Ltd {Limerick}.

1865: To Limerick Steam Ship Co. Ltd {Limerick}.

1868: Wrecked 10 July on Mears Rocks, near Coverack, Cornwall, in fog, on voyage from Limerick to London.

| *Shamrock*
592 | 1846–1859 | 129.2m x 19.9m x 12.8m | 282 | Iron. |

Frederick Burrington, Ringsend, Dublin.

Auxiliary steam. 68hp. Single Archimedean screw.

1846: Completed for British & Irish Steam Packet Co. {Dublin} as *Shamrock*.

1859: Stranded 1 November on Holm Sand, off Lowestoft, on voyage from Tyne to Dublin. Split in two next day.

| *Foyle*
13694 | 1850–1866 | 196.5m x 25.8m x 16.8m | 795 | Iron. |

Caird & Co., Greenock. 17.

Builder. Side-lever steam. 400hp. Paddle wheels.

1848: Completed for Ninian B. McIntyre, Londonderry {Greenock} as *Foyle*.

1849: Sold under mortgage to James Mackay, Londonderry & John Thompson, Belfast {Greenock}.

1850: Sold to George Reade & Herbert A. Fletcher, Kilkenny {Greenock}.

1850: Sold to George Reade, Kilkenny {Greenock}.

1850: Sold to British & Irish Steam Packet Co. {Dublin}.

1855–56: Chartered to British Government as Crimean War transport.

1866: Sank 12 September, in Barking Reach, River Thames, in collision with steamer *Collingwood*, on voyage from
  Dublin to London.

1870: Register closed.

| *Lady Eglinton*
25151 | 1853–1889 | 192.8m x 26.9m x 16.4m
228.5m x 279m x 16.5m | 579
768 | Iron.
from 1865. |

Robert Napier & Sons, Govan. 51.

Builder. Beam geared steam. 150hp. Single screw.

1853: Launched 24 January as *Lady Eglinton*.

1853: Completed for Henry A. Cowper {Dublin}. Chartered to British & Irish Steam Packet Co.

1853: Chartered to Canadian Steam Navigation Co. for two round voyages Liverpool–Canada.

1853: Chartered to South American & General Steam Navigation Co. for round voyage Liverpool–South
  America.

1855–56: Chartered to British Government as Crimean War transport.

1857: Sold to British & Irish Steam Packet Co. {Dublin}. Registered in names of trustees.

1858: Chartered to British & Irish Transatlantic Steam Packet Co. for two round voyages Galway–Canada.

1865: Lengthened by Walpole, Webb & Bewley, Dublin.

1879: To British & Irish Steam Packet Co. Ltd {Dublin}.

1889: Sold to Jaques V. Valette and John T. Duncan {Cardiff}.

1891: Broken up at Grays, Essex.

| *Nile*
 | 1853–1854 | 164.2m x 25.3m x 15.4m | 525 | Iron. |

Alexander Denny & Brother, Dumbarton. 15.

Steam. 150hp. Single screw.

1850: Completed for William Miles Moss {Liverpool} as *Nile*.

1853: Sold to James Stirling {Dublin}. Chartered to British & Irish Steam Packet Co.

1854: Wrecked 30 November on Godrevey Rocks, North Cornwall, on voyage from Liverpool to London.

Name Official number Builder. Yard no. Engine builder and details	In fleet	Dimensions (length x breadth x depth)	Gross tons	Notes

Mars 1858–1863 179.8m x 19.0m x 8.4m 229 Iron.
9062
Money, Wigram & Son, Blackwall, London.
Miller & Ravenhill, London. Steam. 90hp. Paddle wheels.
1853: Completed for Gravesend New Steam Packet Co. {London} as *Mars*.
1856: Sold to William S. Andrews {London}.
1858: Sold to British & Irish Steam Packet Co. {Dublin}. Registered in names of trustees.
1863: Sold to James Brown {Dublin} as blockade-runner.
1864: Sold to Samuel O. Johnson {Nassau, NP}.
1865: Sold to James G. Baillie {Nassau, NP}.
1868: Broken up.

Lady Wodehouse 1866–1895 225.0m x 28.5m x 15.8m 736 Iron.
49527
Walpole, Webb & Bewley, Dublin. 11.
MacNab & Co., Greenock. Inverted steam. 180hp, 195nhp. Single screw.
1865: Launched 5 December as *Lady Wodehouse*.
1866: Completed for British & Irish Steam Packet Co. {Dublin}. Registered in names of trustees.
1879: To British & Irish Steam Packet Co. Ltd {Dublin}.
1895: Sold to J. Hurley, Bristol {Dublin}.
1897: Broken up.

Countess of Dublin 1869–1894 220.4m x 28.2m x 15.0m 760 Iron.
58415
Walpole, Webb & Bewley, Dublin. 40.
Thompson, Boyd & Co., Newcastle. Steam. 150hp. Single screw.
1869: Launched 24 June as *Countess of Dublin*.
1869: Completed for John F. Bewley {Dublin}.
1869: Sold to British & Irish Steam Packet Co. {Dublin}. Registered in names of trustees.
1879: To British & Irish Steam Packet Co. Ltd {Dublin}.
1894: Sank 21 February, in Long Reach, River Thames, on voyage from London to Dublin, after colliding with
   LCC sludge steamer *Binnie*. Refloated 26 February.
1894: Broken up.

Cymba 1870–1880 197.3m x 29.8m x 15.8m 673 Iron.
23043   224.3m x 29.8m x 15.6m 790 from 1871.
Smith & Rodger, Glasgow. 17.
Builder. Steeple steam. 90hp. Single screw.
1850: Launched 8 August as *Albatross*.
1850: Completed for Cork Steam Ship Co. {Cork}.
1854–56: Chartered to British Government as Crimean War transport.
1860: Registered in names of trustees. Engines 140hp.
1866: Sold to Malcomson Brothers {Waterford}.
1867: Sold to foreigner. Renamed *Cymba*. Re-sold to William Malcomson {Waterford}.
1869: Sold to Valentine O'Brien O'Connor {Dublin}.
1870: Sold to British & Irish Steam Packet Co. {Dublin}. Registered in names of trustees.
1870: Compound steam engines by T. Richardson & Sons, Hartlepool. 140hp.
1871: Lengthened.
1879: To British & Irish Steam Packet Co. Ltd {Dublin}.
1880: Sold to Robert Fell {Newcastle}.
1885: To Jane E.I. Fell and Isabella S. Fell {Newcastle}, as executrixes, following death of Robert Fell in 1884.

Name Official number Builder. Yard no. Engine builder and details	In fleet	Dimensions (length x breadth x depth)	Gross tons	Notes

1888: Sold to A. Halvorsen {Bergen; Norway}. Renamed *Wessell*. Engines 90hp.

1894: Stranded 21 August on Jemima Rocks, off island of Canna, on voyage from Dram to Barrow in Furness. Condemned, but refloated and completed voyage.

1894: Broken up.

Avoca	1870–1890	228.0m x 31.0m x 16.0m	797	Iron.

49734

George Robinson & Co., Cork.

Scott & Linton, Dumbarton. Inverted steam. 150hp. Single screw.

1865: Launched 28 January as *Avoca*.

1865: Completed for Malcomson Brothers {Waterford}.

1868: Sold to James Payne {London}.

1869: Sold to William Malcomson {Waterford}.

1870: Sold to British & Irish Steam Packet Co. {Dublin}. Registered in names of trustees.

1879: To British & Irish Steam Packet Co. Ltd {Dublin}.

1890: Sank 10 April, 4 miles NE by E from Dungeness, Kent, in collision with steamer *North Cambria*, on voyage from London to Dublin.

Lady Olive	1878–1911	249.8m x 30.3m x 15.9m	1,058	Iron.

77399

A&J Inglis, Glasgow. 150.

Builder. Compound inverted steam. 200hp, 242nhp. Single screw.

1878: Launched 10 December as *Lady Olive*.

1878: Completed for British & Irish Steam Packet Co. {Dublin}. Registered in names of trustees.

1879: To British & Irish Steam Packet Co. Ltd {Dublin}.

1911: Sold to Navigation à Vapeur 'Ionienne' G. Yannoulatou Frères {Andros; Greece}. Renamed *Epiros*.

1918: Sold to N.G. Lyras {Piraeus; Greece}.

1919: Sold to P.M. Lemos {Piraeus; Greece}. Renamed *Melpomeni*.

1921: Sank 10 March between Lodos Point and Cape Baba, Turkey, after striking mine, on voyage from Piraeus to Constantinople.

Lady Martin	1888–1914	269.6m x 34.2m x 16.4m	1,356	

95315

Workman, Clarke & Co. Ltd, Belfast. 60.

Dunsmuir & Jackson, Glasgow. Triple expansion steam. 220hp, 275nhp. Single screw. 13 knots.

1888: Launched 8 October as *Lady Martin*.

1888: Completed for British & Irish Steam Packet Co. Ltd {Dublin}.

1914: Sold to Administration de Nav. à Vapeur Ottomane, Istanbul. Renamed *Bimbashi Riza Bey*.

1915: Detained by British Government as war prize. Sold to British & Irish Steam Packet Co. Ltd {Dublin}. Renamed *Lady Martin*.

1917: Sold to Cunningham, Shaw & Co. [V.S. Lovell] {London}. Renamed *Purfleet Belle*.

1920: Sold to National Steam Navigation Co. of Greece [Embiricos Bros] {Piraeus; Greece}. Renamed *Naxos*.

1924: To Byron Steamship Co. Ltd [M. Embiricos] {London}.

1925: Sold to J. Vlahakis {Greece}.

1926: Sold to Thessaliki Steam Navigation Co. {Piraeus; Greece}.

1928: Sold to A.G. Yannoulatos {Piraeus; Greece}. Renamed *Miaoulis*.

1929: Sold to Hellenic Coast Lines Co. Ltd {Piraeus; Greece}.

1932: Renamed *Naxos*.

1934: Broken up at Savona, Italy.

Name Official number Builder. Yard no. Engine builder and details	In fleet	Dimensions (length x breadth x depth)	Gross tons	Notes

---

Lady Hudson-Kinahan   1891–1914   273.5m x 34.1m x 16.6m   1,368
95336
Ailsa Shipbuilding Co. Ltd, Troon. 29.
Dunsmuir & Jackson, Glasgow. Triple expansion steam. 283hp, 284nhp. Single screw. 12½ knots.
1891: Launched 5 September as *Lady Hudson-Kinahan*.
1891: Completed for British & Irish Steam Packet Co. Ltd {Dublin}.
1914: Sold to Navigation Hellénique John MacDowall {Piraeus; Greece}. Renamed *Elsie*.
1917: Sold to Hellenic Co. of Maritime Enterprises {Piraeus; Greece}.
1919: Renamed *Elsi*.
1927: Sold to Mandafouni Steamship Co. {Piraeus; Greece}.
1931: Sold to M. Kehayoglou {Piraeus; Greece}.
1934: Sold to John Toyias Steamship Co. {Piraeus; Greece}.
1941: Sunk 29 April at Suda Bay, Crete, in air attack. Refloated.
1943: Sunk by mine September.
1945: Wreck broken up.

Lady Wolseley   1894–1915   275.0m x 35.1m x 16.5m   1,450
99752
Naval Construction & Armaments Co. Ltd, Barrow in Furness. 226.
Builder. Triple expansion steam. 285rhp, 283nhp. Single screw. 12.5 knots.
1894: Launched 22 March as *Lady Wolseley*.
1894: Completed for British & Irish Steam Packet Co. Ltd {Dublin}.
1915: Sold to Limerick Steamship Co. Ltd {Limerick}. Renamed *Kinvarra*.
1916: Sold to Frutera Line Ltd [Armstrong, Lloyd & Co.] {Newcastle}. Renamed *River Tyne*.
1916: Foundered 25 October, 30 miles off Oporto, Portugal, on voyage from Lisbon to Hull.

Lady Roberts   1897–1914   275.0m x 36.1m x 16.5m   1,462
104977
Ailsa Shipbuilding Co. Ltd, Troon. 60.
Dunsmuir & Jackson, Glasgow. Triple expansion steam. 280rhp and nhp. Single screw. 13 knots.
1896: Launched 22 December as *Lady Roberts*.
1897: Completed for British & Irish Steam Packet Co. Ltd {Dublin}.
1914: Sold to Societa Maritima Italiana {Genoa; Italy}. Renamed *Sassari*.
1923: Sold to Societa di Nav. Italia {Genoa; Italy}.
1926: Sold to Cia. Italiana Transatlantica S.A. di Nav. {Genoa; Italy}.
1932: Sold to 'Tirrenia' Flotte Reunite Florio-Citra {Genoa; Italy}.
1933: Broken up at Naples.

Calshot   1905–1914   178.5m x 27.1m x 12.4m   549
117527
Ailsa Shipbuilding Co. Ltd, Troon. 137.
Muir & Houston Ltd, Glasgow. Triple expansion steam. 93rhp, 110nhp. Single screw.
1905: Launched 8 May as *Calshot*.
1905: Completed for British & Irish Steam Packet Co. Ltd {Dublin}.
1914: Sold to La Morue Française et Pecheries de Fécamp {St Pierre; France}. Renamed *Pro Patria*.
1928: To La Morue Française {St Pierre; France}.
1933: Sold to Eugenio Passalacqua {Genoa; Italy}.
1933: Oil engines (built 1919–20) by Sulzer Bros Ltd, Winterthur, Switzerland, installed by Franco Tosi S.A., Legnano, Italy. 87nhp.
1942: Sunk by bombing 29 December at Sfax, Tunisia. Salvaged and repaired after war.
1948: Sold to John C. Hamlin, Nicosia {Famagusta}. Renamed *Dora P*.
1950: Sold to Cia. Nav. de Commercio Dora [N. Papalios and S. Petrovits] {Puerto Limon; Costa Rica}.

Name	In fleet	Dimensions	Gross	Notes
Official number		(length x breadth x depth)	tons	
Builder. Yard no.				
Engine builder and details				

1950: Damaged by fire 17 April, off Durban, on voyage from Mauritius to Durban. Towed in. Sunk 9 July off Durban by Naval gunfire.

Camber   1907–1919   67.4m x 18.4m x 8.9m   99   Barge.
123132
P. MacGregor & Sons, Kirkintilloch.
Fishers Ltd, Paisley. Compound steam. 16.5rhp. Single screw. 8 knots.
1907: Completed as *Camber*.
1908: Registered to British & Irish Steam Packet Co. Ltd {Dublin}.
1919: Sold to James Dredging, Towage and Transport Ltd, Southampton {Dublin}.
1919: Sold to Daniel Gower, Cardiff {Dublin}.
1920: Renamed *D. C. G.*
1937: To Daniel Gower (jr), Glamorgan {Dublin}, following death of Daniel Gower.
1939: Sold to Risdon Beasley Ltd {Southampton}. Renamed *Topmast No. 4.*
1941: Sold to British Iron & Steel Corporation (Salvage) Ltd, Glasgow {Southampton}.
1947: Sold to John Lee {Belfast}.
1948: Sold to W.H. Arnott, Young & Co. Ltd, Glasgow {Belfast}.
1951: Broken up.

Lady Gwendolen   1911–1918   300.2m x 39.7m x 17.5m   2,163
132505
Clyde Shipbuilding & Engineering Co. Ltd, Port Glasgow. 294.
Builder. Triple expansion steam. 362rhp and nhp. Single screw.
1911: Launched 13 May as *Lady Gwendolen*.
1911: Completed for British & Irish Steam Packet Co. Ltd {Dublin}. Renamed *Lady Gwendolen*.
1916: Requisitioned by Russian Government. Renamed *Lyudmila*.
1918: Returned to British & Irish Steam Packet Co. Ltd.
1918: Sold to Dundee, Perth & London Shipping Co. Ltd {Dundee}.
1919: Sold to New York, Newfoundland & Halifax Steam Ship Co. Ltd [C.T. Bowring & Co. Ltd] {Liverpool}.
    Renamed *Rosalind*.
1921: {St John's, Newfoundland}.
1923: {Liverpool}.
1929: Sold to Bermuda and West Indies Steamship Co. Ltd {Hamilton, Bermuda}.
1936: Sold to 'Zetska Plovidba' A.D. {Kotor; Yugoslavia}. Renamed *Lovcen*.
1940: Sold to Cia. Centro Americana de Navegacion Ltda ['Zetska Plovidba' A.D.] {Panama; Panama}.
1941: Sold to United States Government {USA}. Renamed *Columbia*.
1942: Renamed *Brigadier General Harry E. Rethers*.
1946: Sold to Chan Kin Cheong {Canton; China}. Renamed *Wah Chung*.
1950: Sold to Grande Shipping Corporation S.A. {Panama; Panama}. Renamed *Teresa*.
1952: Reported broken up in China.

Lady Olive   1914–1917   200.3m x 31.5m x 12.2m   701
132838
Dundee Shipbuilding Co. Ltd, Dundee. 247.
Richardsons, Westgarth & Co. Ltd, Middlesbrough. Triple expansion steam. 107rhp, 171nhp. Single screw.
1913: Launched 6 February as *Tees Trader*.
1913: Completed for Furness, Withy & Co. Ltd {West Hartlepool}.
1914: Sold to British & Irish Steam Packet Co. Ltd {London}. Renamed *Lady Olive*.
1917: Sold to London Welsh Steamship Co. Ltd {London}.
1917: Requisitioned by Admiralty as 'Q' ship (*Q 18*).
1917: Sunk 19 February by gunfire from German submarine *UC-18*, in English Channel, NW of St Malo, France.

Name Official number Builder. Yard no. Engine builder and details	In fleet	Dimensions (length x breadth x depth)	Gross tons	Notes

Danehurst 1915–1915 95.0m x 21.8m x 10.2m 162 Steel/wood.
127945 168 from 1914.
W.J. Yarwood & Sons Ltd, Northwich, as dumb barge.
No engines.
1904: Completed. Not registered.
1907: Registered by Henry Seddon & Sons Ltd, Middlewich {Liverpool} as *Danehurst*.
1914: Compound steam engine by W.J. Yarwood & Sons Ltd, Northwich. 29.9rhp. Single screw. 8.5 knots.
1915: Sold to W.J. Yarwood & Sons Ltd, Northwich.
1915: Sold to Danehurst Shipping Co. Ltd, Widnes {Liverpool}.
1915: Sold to British & Irish Steam Packet Co. Ltd {Liverpool} (owned 22 May–30 July).
1915: Sold to Henry M. Grayson {Liverpool} (a B&I director; owned 30 July–27 October).
1915: Sold to Kymo Shipping Co. Ltd [W.B. Kyffin] {Liverpool}.
1930: Owner in liquidation. Sold to Andrew Smith, Birkenhead {Liverpool}.
1940: Sold to Norwest Construction Co. Ltd {Liverpool}.
1941: Sold to Berrys (Stranraer) Ltd {Stranraer}.
1941: Sold to British Iron & Steel Corporation (Salvage) Ltd {Stranraer}.
1944: Sold to John Cameron, Peterhead {Stranraer}.
1947: Broken up.

Lady Wimborne 1915–1939 260.0m x 38.2m x 14.6m 1,532
139074
Clyde Shipbuilding & Engineering Co. Ltd, Port Glasgow. 314.
Builder. Triple expansion steam. 134.2rhp, 216nhp. Single screw. 11 knots.
1915: Launched 27 May as *Lady Wimborne*.
1915: Completed for British & Irish Steam Packet Co. Ltd {London}.
1921: {Dublin}.
1936: To British & Irish Steam Packet Co. (1936) Ltd {Dublin}.
1938: Renamed *Galway*.
1938: Owner renamed British & Irish Steam Packet Co. Ltd.
1939: To Coast Lines Ltd {Liverpool}. Renamed *Galway Coast*.
1945: Sold to Virtu Steamship Co. Ltd [Anthony & Bainbridge Ltd] {Liverpool}.
1946: Renamed *Virtu*.
1947: {Malta}.
1948: Grounded off Raz Azzaz lighthouse, between Bardia and Tobruk, Libya, 27 February. Refloated 19 May. Towed to Tobruk and laid up.
1950: Broken up at Tobruk.

Lady Martin 1915–1917
See *Lady Martin* (1888).

Lady Cloé 1916–1938 260.0m x 38.0m x 15.0m 1,581
139129
Sir Raylton Dixon & Co. Ltd, Middlesbrough. 592.
Richardsons, Westgarth & Co. Ltd, Middlesbrough. Triple expansion steam. 220rhp, 162nhp. Single screw. 11 knots.
1916: Launched 17 April as *Lady Cloé*.
1916: Completed for British & Irish Steam Packet Co. Ltd {London}.
1921: {Dublin}.
1936: To British & Irish Steam Packet Co. (1936) Ltd {Dublin}.
1938: To Coast Lines Ltd {Liverpool}. Renamed *Normandy Coast*.
1945: Torpedoed and sunk 11 January by German submarine *U-1055* off Point Lynas, Anglesey, on voyage from London to Liverpool.

Name Official number Builder. Yard no. Engine builder and details	In fleet	Dimensions (length x breadth x depth)	Gross tons	Notes

Lady Patricia   1916–1917   249.0 mx 38.2m x 15.9m   1,372
139183
Ardrossan Drydock & Shipbuilding Co. Ltd, Ardrossan. 268.
John G. Kincaid Ltd, Glasgow. Triple expansion steam. 220rhp, 162nhp. Single screw.
1916: Completed for British & Irish Steam Packet Co. Ltd {London} as *Lady Patricia*.
1916: Requisitioned by Admiralty as 'Q' Ship (Q 25).
1917: Torpedoed and sunk 20 May by German submarine *U-46*, in Atlantic, NW of Tory Island.

Lady Patricia   1919–1939   270.6m x 38.1m x 16.2m   1,391
143158
Caledon Shipbuilding & Engineering Co. Ltd, Dundee. 266.
Builder. Triple expansion steam. 280rhp, 196nhp. Single screw. 12 knots.
Ordered by British Government as war standard ship.
1919: Launched 18 February as *War Spey*.
1919: Completed for British & Irish Steam Packet Co. Ltd {London} as *Lady Patricia*.
1921: {Dublin}.
1936: To British & Irish Steam Packet Co. (1936) Ltd {Dublin}.
1938: Renamed *Kerry*.
1938: Owner renamed British & Irish Steam Packet Co. Ltd.
1939: To Coast Lines Ltd {Liverpool}. Renamed *Kerry Coast*.
1941: To Burns & Laird Lines Ltd {Liverpool}.
1944: Sunk 11 March in collision with Norwegian vessel *Mosdale* in Mersey. Registry closed.
1945: Raised 20 May.
1945: Sold to Henry P. Lenaghan & Sons, Belfast {Liverpool}. Renamed *Bangor Bay*.
1946: Sold to Burns & Laird Lines Ltd {Liverpool}. Renamed *Kerry*.
1947: To British & Irish Steam Packet Co. Ltd {Dublin}.
1959: Broken up at Passage West, Co. Cork.

Lady Emerald   1919–1939   270.6m x 38.1m x 16.2m   1,389
143218
Caledon Shipbuilding & Engineering Co. Ltd, Dundee. 267.
Builder. Triple expansion steam. 277.5rhp, 196nhp. Single screw. 12 knots.
Ordered by British Government as war standard ship.
1919: Launched 18 March as *War Garry*.
1919: Completed for British & Irish Steam Packet Co. Ltd {London} as *Lady Emerald*.
1921: {Dublin}.
1936: To British & Irish Steam Packet Co. (1936) Ltd {Dublin}.
1938: Renamed *Carlow*.
1938: Owner renamed British & Irish Steam Packet Co. Ltd.
1939: To Coast Lines Ltd {Liverpool}. Renamed *Brittany Coast*.
1946: To Burns & Laird Lines Ltd {Liverpool} Renamed *Kildare*.
1948: To British & Irish Steam Packet Co. Ltd {Liverpool}.
1952: To Burns & Laird Lines Ltd {Glasgow}. Renamed *Lairdsford*.
1960: Broken up at Troon.

Blackrock   1919–1923
See *Blackrock* (1892) in Tedcastle, McCormick list.

Eblana   1919–1924
See *Eblana* (1892) in Tedcastle, McCormick list.

Cumbria   1919–1920
See *Cumbria* (1896) in Tedcastle, McCormick list.

Name Official number Builder. Yard no. Engine builder and details	In fleet	Dimensions (length x breadth x depth)	Gross tons	Notes

Lady Killiney 1919–1923
See *Killiney* (1918) in Tedcastle, McCormick list.

Belfast 1919–1922
See *Belfast* (1884) in City of Dublin Steam Packet Co. list.

Lady Louth 1919–1920
See *Louth* (1894) in City of Dublin Steam Packet Co. list.

Lady Wicklow 1919–1947
See *Wicklow* (1895) in City of Dublin Steam Packet Co. list.

Lady Carlow 1919–1925
See *Carlow* (1896) in City of Dublin Steam Packet Co. list.

Lady Kerry 1919–1924
See *Kerry* (1897) in City of Dublin Steam Packet Co. list.

Lady Tennant 1920–1923 165.0m x 26.1m x 10.1m 452 Cargo.
Machinery aft.

119083
Napier & Miller Ltd, Yoker, near Glasgow. 132.
D. Rowan & Co., Glasgow. Triple expansion steam. 93rhp. Single screw. 10.75 knots.
1903: Launched 7 December as *Lady Tennant*.
1904: Completed for Nobel's Explosives Co. Ltd {Glasgow}.
1914: Sold to Stornoway Shipping Co. Ltd {Stornoway}.
1916: Sold to M. Langlands & Sons {Stornoway}.
1918: M. Langlands & Sons acquired by Coast Lines Ltd.
1919: To Coast Lines Ltd [M. Langlands & Sons Ltd] {Stornoway}.
1920: To British & Irish Steam Packet Co. Ltd {Liverpool}.
1921: {Dublin}.
1923: Registered at Cork, but cancelled.
1923: To Coast Lines Ltd [M. Langlands & Sons Ltd] {Liverpool}. Renamed *Elgin Coast*.
1930: Renamed *Kilkenny*.
1936: Sold to Captain H.W.B. Ohlmeyer {Hamburg; Germany}. Renamed *Lisa*.
1950: Oil engine by Klöckner-Humboldt-Deutz AG, Köln, Germany. 500bhp.
1962: Sold to Theodoros O. Vavatsioulas and Helene T. Vavatsioulas {Salonica; Greece}. Renamed *Orestis*.
1969: Sold to A. Pastrikos and G. and D. Papageorgiou {Thessaloniki; Greece}. Renamed *Mario*.
1974: Broken up in Greece.

Lady Martin 1920–1938 250.5m x 36.0m x 15.0m 1,189 Cargo.
133548
Sir Raylton Dixon & Co. Ltd, Middlesbrough. 585.
Richardsons, Westgarth & Co. Ltd, Middlesbrough. Triple expansion steam. 178rhp, 138nhp. Single screw. 10.5 knots.
1913: Launched 13 December as *Northern Coast*.
1914: Completed for Powell, Bacon & Hough Lines Ltd {Liverpool}.
1917: Owner renamed Coast Lines Ltd.
1920: To British & Irish Steam Packet Co. Ltd {London}. Renamed *Lady Martin*.
1921: {Dublin}.
1936: To British & Irish Steam Packet Co. (1936) Ltd {Dublin}.
1938: Sold to A/S Eestis Laevandus {Tallinn; Estonia}. Renamed *Pearu*.
1940: Seized by USSR in Baltic during June. Renamed *Vodnik*.
1941: Lost 14 August, east of Prangli Island, probably in German air attack, on voyage from Kronstadt to Tallin.

Name Official number Builder. Yard no. Engine builder and details	In fleet	Dimensions (length x breadth x depth)	Gross tons	Notes

Dublin   1920–1922
See *Dublin* (1904) in Tedcastle, McCormick list.

Lady Kildare   1920–1931   245.0m x 34.1m x 15.6m   1,217   Cargo.
144200
William Beardmore & Co. Ltd, Dalmuir. 613.
Builder. Triple expansion steam. 265nhp. Single screw.
Original planned name *Whippet*.
1920: Launched 26 January as *Setter*.
1920: Completed for G&J Burns Ltd {Glasgow}.
1920: G&J Burns Ltd acquired by Coast Lines Ltd.
1920: To British & Irish Steam Packet Co. Ltd {Dublin}. Renamed *Lady Kildare*.
1931: To Belfast Steamship Co. Ltd {Belfast}.
1932: Renamed *Ulster Castle*.
1950: Broken up at Preston.

Lady Meath   1920–1925   225.0m x 33.1m x 15.5m   862   Cargo and
                                                                                              steerage passengers.
124134
Scott's Shipbuilding & Engineering Co. Ltd, Greenock. 409.
Builder. Triple expansion steam. 247rhp and nhp. Single screw. 13 knots.
1906: Launched 19 July as *Lurcher*.
1906: Completed for G&J Burns Ltd {Glasgow}.
1920: G&J Burns Ltd acquired by Coast Lines Ltd.
1920: To British & Irish Steam Packet Co. Ltd {Dublin}. Renamed *Lady Meath*.
1925: To City of Cork Steam Packet Co. Ltd {Cork}. Renamed *Inniscarra*.
1935: Sold to Wexford Steamships Co. Ltd {Wexford}. Renamed *Menapia*.
1939: Broken up at Port Glasgow.

Lady Valentia   1921–1922   240.1m x 36.1m x 14.6m   1,211   Cargo.
                                                                                              Machinery aft.
144976
A&J Inglis Ltd, Pointhouse, Glasgow. 600.
Builder. Triple expansion steam. 203rhp, 204nhp. Single screw. 11.25 knots.
Original intended name *Ayrshire Coast*.
1920: Launched 29 November as *Northern Coast*.
1921: Completed for British & Irish Steam Packet Co. Ltd {Dublin} as *Lady Valentia*.
1922: To Coast Lines Ltd {Liverpool}. Renamed *Northern Coast*.
1954: Broken up at Passage West.

Brussels   1922–1929   285'3" x 34'0" x 15'6"   1,090   Cargo.
                                                                                              Two funnels.
109884   (1,380   as built).
Gourlay Brothers & Co., Dundee. 202.
Builder. Triple expansion steam. 350rhp and nhp. Twin screws. 15 knots.
1902: Launched 26 March as *Brussels*.
1902: Completed for Great Eastern Railway Co. {Harwich} as passenger ship.
1915: Attempted to ram German submarine 28 March.
1916: Captured by German Navy 22 June. Captain Fryatt executed.
1916: Renamed *Brugge*. Used as submarine depot ship at Zeebrugge.
1918: Scuttled 5 October as blockship at entrance to Zeebrugge harbour.
1918: Taken over by Belgian Government.
1919: Raised 4–6 August.

Name	In fleet	Dimensions	Gross	Notes
Official number		*(length x breadth x depth)*	tons	
Builder. Yard no.				
Engine builder and details				

1920: Transferred to British Government. Renamed *Brussels*.

1921: Sold to Dublin & Lancashire Shipping Co. Ltd, Dublin [Joseph Gale, Preston] {Dublin}. Converted to livestock carrier.

1922: Dublin & Lancashire Shipping Co. Ltd acquired by British & Irish Steam Packet Co. Ltd.

1922: To British & Irish Steam Packet Co. Ltd {Dublin}.

1923: Renamed *Lady Brussels*.

1929: Broken up at Port Glasgow.

(Lydia)	1922–1922	253.0m x 35.1 x 14.8m	1,059	Cargo and livestock.
97217				

J&G Thomson Ltd., Clydebank. 251.

Builder. Triple expansion steam. 494hp, 360nhp. Twin screws.

1890: Launched 16 July as *Lydia*.

1890: Completed for London & South Western Railway Co. {Southampton} (passenger vessel).

1919: Sold to Thomas Sales, through agency of James Dredging, Towing & Transport Co. Ltd. Not registered.

1920: To James Dredging, Towing & Transport Co. Ltd {Southampton}.

1921: Sold to Captain Montagu Yates {Southampton}.

1921: Repossessed by James Dredging, Towing & Transport Co. Ltd. {Southampton}.

1922: Sold to Dublin & Lancashire Shipping Co. Ltd, Dublin. Not registered.

1922: Dublin & Lancashire Shipping Co. Ltd acquired by British & Irish Steam Packet Co. Ltd.

1922: Sold to British & Irish Steam Packet Co. Ltd. Not registered.

1922: To Coast Lines Ltd {Southampton}.

1923: Sold to Nav. à Vaplonienne G. Yannoulato Frères {Greece}. Renamed *Ierac*.

1924/25: Owner renamed S.A. Ionienne de Nav. à Vap. 'Yannoulatos'.

1926/27: Name restyled *Ierax*.

1929: To Hellenic Coast Lines Co. Ltd. {Greece}.

1933: Broken up at Savona, Italy.

Lady Brussels	1923–1929			

See *Brussels* (1922), above.

(Lady Limerick)

Vessel originally ordered from A&J Inglis Ltd, Pointhouse, Glasgow (yard no. 606), by G&J Burns Ltd. Order taken over by British & Irish Steam Packet Co. Ltd. Name of *Lady Limerick* allocated. Order subsequently cancelled.

(Lady Olive)

Vessel originally ordered from A&J Inglis Ltd, Pointhouse, Glasgow (yard no. 607), by G&J Burns Ltd. Order taken over by British & Irish Steam Packet Co. Ltd. Name of *Lady Olive* allocated. Order transferred to Coast Lines Ltd before launch. Vessel launched 22 August 1922 for Coast Lines Ltd as *Ayrshire Coast*.

Lady Louth	1923–1930	276.6m x 37.6m x 15.3m	1,881	
144983				

Ardrossan Drydock & Shipbuilding Co. Ltd, Ardrossan. 330.

John G. Kincaid & Co. Ltd, Greenock. Triple expansion steam. 336nhp. Single screw. 14 knots.

1923: Launched 7 March unnamed.

1923: Completed for British & Irish Steam Packet Co. Ltd {Dublin} as *Lady Louth*.

1930: To Burns & Laird Lines Ltd {Glasgow}. Renamed *Lairdsburn*.

1953: Broken up at Port Glasgow.

Name	In fleet	Dimensions	Gross	Notes
Official number		(length x breadth x depth)	tons	
Builder. Yard no.				
Engine builder and details				

Lady Longford   1923–1930   274.4m x 37.9m x 17.2m   1,679
143723
Ardrossan Drydock & Shipbuilding Co. Ltd, Ardrossan. 308.
John G. Kincaid & Co. Ltd, Greenock. Triple expansion steam. 360rhp, 553nhp. Single screw. 14 knots.
1920: Launched 11 August as *Ardmore*.
1921: Completed for City of Cork Steam Packet Co. Ltd {Liverpool}.
1921: {Cork}.
1923: To British & Irish Steam Packet Co. Ltd {Dublin}. Renamed *Lady Longford*.
1930: To Burns & Laird Lines Ltd {Glasgow}. Renamed *Lairdshill*.
1936: To British & Irish Steam Packet Co. Ltd {Dublin}. Renamed *Lady Longford*.
1936: To British & Irish Steam Packet Co. (1936) Ltd {Dublin}.
1937: To Burns & Laird Lines Ltd {Glasgow}. Renamed *Lairdshill*.
1957: Broken up at Dublin.

Lady Limerick   1924–1930   276.6m x 37.6m x 15.3m   1,945
146419
Ardrossan Drydock & Shipbuilding Co. Ltd, Ardrossan. 329.
John G. Kincaid & Co. Ltd, Greenock. Triple expansion steam. 178rhp, 336nhp. Single screw. 14 knots.
1924: Launched 25 March as *Lady Limerick*.
1924: Completed for British & Irish Steam Packet Co. Ltd {Dublin}.
1930: To Burns & Laird Lines Ltd {Glasgow}. Renamed *Lairdscastle*.
1940: Sank 4 September in collision with steamship *Vernon City*, on voyage between Glasgow and Belfast.

Iveagh   1926–1930   190.0m x 29.0m x 14.0m   550   Passenger/
                                                                                              cargo.
98274
A&J Inglis Ltd, Pointhouse, Glasgow. 224.
Builder. Triple expansion steam. 180hp, 148nhp. Single screw.
1892: Launched 7 July as *Iveagh*.
1892: Completed for Dundalk & Newry Steam Packet Co. Ltd {Newry}.
1911: Engines 114rhp, 148nhp.
1926: Dundalk & Newry Steam Packet Co. Ltd acquired by British & Irish Steam Packet Co. Ltd. Operated as
    part of B&I fleet.
1930: Broken up at Port Glasgow.

Lady Meath   1929–1940   321.2m x 40.1m x 16.4m   1,598   Cargo.
146429
Ardrossan Dockyard Ltd, Ardrossan. 341.
John G. Kincaid & Co. Ltd, Greenock. Triple expansion steam. 195rhp, 222nhp. Twin screws. 13.75 knots.
1929: Launched 28 February as *Lady Meath*.
1929: Completed for British & Irish Steam Packet Co. Ltd {Dublin}.
1936: To British & Irish Steam Packet Co. (1936) Ltd {Dublin}.
1938: Renamed *Meath*.
1938: Owner renamed British & Irish Steam Packet Co. Ltd.
1940: Mined and sunk 16 August, off Holyhead breakwater, on voyage from Dublin to Birkenhead.

Lady Munster   1929–1948   320.3m x 41.3m x 16.8m   1,915   Two funnels.
120714
Harland & Wolff Ltd, Belfast. 379.
Builder. Quadruple expansion steam. 824rhp, 404/788nhp. Twin screws. 18 knots.
1906: Launched 27 February as *Graphic*.
1906: Completed for Belfast Steamship Co. Ltd {Belfast}.

Name Official number Builder. Yard no. Engine builder and details	In fleet	Dimensions (length x breadth x depth)	Gross tons	Notes

---

1923: Sank in collision with American steamer *Balsam* in Victoria Channel, Belfast, 3 June. Raised and returned
   to service.

1923: Engines 660nhp.

1929: To British & Irish Steam Packet Co. Ltd {Dublin}. Renamed *Lady Munster.*

1936: To British & Irish Steam Packet Co. (1936) Ltd {Dublin}.

1938: Renamed *Louth.*

1938: Owner renamed British & Irish Steam Packet Co. Ltd.

1939: {Liverpool}.

1948: To Belfast Steamship Co. Ltd {Belfast}. Renamed *Ulster Duke.*

1951: Sold to Italian shipbreakers.

1951: Sank 15 May, while under tow to La Spezia, Italy.

Lady Kerry	1929–1934	236.3m x 31.2m x 15.3m	877	

104466

Harland & Wolff Ltd, Belfast. 306.

Builder. Triple expansion steam. 263rhp and nhp. Twin screws. 13 knots.

1896: Launched 9 June as *Comic.*

1896: Completed for Belfast Steamship Co. Ltd {Belfast}.

1921: To Laird Line Ltd {Glasgow}. Renamed *Cairnsmore.*

1922: To Burns & Laird Lines Ltd {Glasgow}.

1929: To British & Irish Steam Packet Co. Ltd {Dublin}. Renamed *Lady Kerry.*

1934: Broken up at Preston.

Lady Carlow	1929–1936	236.0m x 31.2m x 15.6m	883	

108619

Barclay, Curle & Co. Ltd, Whiteinch, Glasgow. 410.

Builder. Triple expansion steam. 263rhp and nhp. Twin screws. 14 knots.

1897: Launched 26 October as *Logic.*

1898: Completed for Thomas Gallaher {Belfast}. Chartered to Belfast Steamship Co. Ltd.

1904: Sold to Belfast Steamship Co. Ltd {Belfast}.

1921: To Laird Line Ltd {Glasgow}. Renamed *Culzean.*

1922: To Burns & Laird Lines Ltd {Glasgow}.

1929: To British & Irish Steam Packet Co. Ltd {Dublin}. Renamed *Lady Carlow.*

1936: Sold to Smith & Co. for breaking up.

1937: Re-sold to West of Scotland Shipbreaking Co. Ltd. Broken up at Troon.

Lady Connaught	1930–1953	320.3m x 41.3m x 16.8m	1,913	Two funnels.

120712

Harland & Wolff Ltd, Belfast. 378.

Builder. Quadruple expansion steam. 824rhp, 404/804nhp. Twin screws. 18 knots.

1906: Launched 13 January as *Heroic.*

1906: Completed for Belfast Steamship Co. Ltd {Belfast}.

1914: Requisitioned by Royal Navy as HMS *Heroic.*

1920: Returned to owner.

1924: Engines 651rhp, 649nhp.

1930: To British & Irish Steam Packet Co. Ltd {Dublin}. Renamed *Lady Connaught.*

1936: To British & Irish Steam Packet Co. (1936) Ltd {Dublin}.

1938: Renamed *Longford.*

1938: Owner renamed British & Irish Steam Packet Co. Ltd.

1940: {Liverpool}.

1953: Broken up at Barrow.

Name	In fleet	Dimensions	Gross	Notes
Official number		(length x breadth x depth)	tons	
Builder. Yard no.				
Engine builder and details				

Lady Leinster 132019
Harland & Wolff Ltd, Belfast. 424.
Builder. Triple expansion steam. 840rhp and nhp. Twin screws. 18 knots.

	1930–1947	325.4m x 41.7m x 16.2m	2,284	Two funnels.

1911: Launched 7 September as *Patriotic*.
1912: Completed for Belfast Steamship Co. Ltd {Belfast}.
1930: To British & Irish Steam Packet Co. Ltd {Dublin}. Renamed *Lady Leinster*.
1936: To British & Irish Steam Packet Co. (1936) Ltd {Dublin}.
1938: Renamed *Lady Connaught*.
1938: Owner renamed British & Irish Steam Packet Co. Ltd.
1940: {Liverpool}.
1940: Damaged by mines 26 December. Laid up.
1941: Abandoned to underwriters.
1942: Bought back from underwriters. Converted to livestock carrier by Dublin Dockyard Co.
1944: Converted to hospital ship. Engines 792nhp.
1946: Converted to cruise ship by Harland & Wolff Ltd, Belfast.
1947: To Coast Lines Ltd {Liverpool}. Renamed *Lady Killarney*.
1956: Broken up at Port Glasgow.

Lady Louth 123124
Caledon Shipbuilding & Engineering Co. Ltd, Dundee. 187.
Builder. Quadruple expansion steam. 282rhp, 310nhp. Single screw. 16.5 knots.

	1930–1934	275.0m x 36.7m x 15.5m	1,053	Cattle carrier.

1906: Launched 10 April as *Duke of Montrose*.
1906: Completed for Dublin & Glasgow Sailing and Steam Packet Co. {Dublin}.
1908: Dublin & Glasgow Sailing and Steam Packet Co. acquired by Burns Steamship Co. Ltd.
1908: To Burns Steamship Co. Ltd {Glasgow}. Renamed *Tiger*.
1922: To Burns & Laird Lines Ltd {Glasgow}.
1929: Renamed *Lairdsforest*.
1930: To British & Irish Steam Packet Co. Ltd {Dublin}. Converted to cattle carrier. Renamed *Lady Louth*.
1934: Broken up at Port Glasgow.

Lady Galway
See *Lady Louth* (1919).

	1931–1938			

Lutterworth 99169
Earle's Shipbuilding & Engineering Co. Ltd, Hull. 343.
Builder. Triple expansion steam. 165hp, 249nhp. Single screw. 15 knots.

	1932–1933	240.3m x 32.3m x 15.5m	1,007	Iron. Cargo.

1891: Launched 8 April as *Lutterworth*.
1891: Completed for Manchester, Sheffield & Lincolnshire Railway Co. {Grimsby}.
1897: Owner renamed Great Central Railway Co.
1912: Engines 249rhp, 250nhp.
1923: To London & North Eastern Railway Co. {Grimsby}.
1932: Sold to British & Irish Steam Packet Co. Ltd {Grimsby}.
1933: Broken up at Preston.

Staveley 99173
C.S. Swan & Hunter, Newcastle. 165.
Westgarth, English & Co., Middlesbrough. Triple expansion steam. 250hp, 244nhp. Single screw. 15 knots.

	1932–1933	240.2m x 32.0m x 15.8m	1,047	Iron. Cargo.

1891: Launched 1 May as *Staveley*.

Name	In fleet	Dimensions	Gross	Notes
Official number		(length x breadth x depth)	tons	
Builder. Yard no.				
Engine builder and details				

1891: Completed for Manchester, Sheffield & Lincolnshire Railway Co. {Grimsby}.
1897: Owner renamed Great Central Railway Co.
1923: To London & North Eastern Railway Co. {Grimsby}.
1932: Sold to Manuel Swift, Liverpool {Grimsby}.
1932: Sold to British & Irish Steam Packet Co. Ltd {Grimsby}.
1933: Renamed *Lady Glen*.
1933: Broken up at Preston.

Lady Glen   1933−1933
See *Staveley* (1932).

Lady Cavan   1933−1939   178.0m x 29.6m x 14.1m   602   Cargo.
123248
Earle's Shipbuilding & Engineering Co. Ltd, Hull. 517.
Builder. Triple expansion steam. 79.5rhp, 79nhp. Single screw. 9 knots.
1906: Launched 5 March as *Fido*.
1906: Completed for Thomas Wilson, Sons & Co. Ltd {Hull}.
1917: Owner renamed Ellerman's Wilson Line Ltd.
1922: Sold to H.H. Poole & Co. Ltd {London}. Renamed *Poolmina*.
1930: Sold to Wexford Steamships Co. Ltd [J.J. Stafford] {Wexford}. Renamed *Wexfordian*.
1933: Sold to British & Irish Steam Packet Co. Ltd {Dublin}. Renamed *Lady Cavan*.
1936: To British & Irish Steam Packet Co. (1936) Ltd {Dublin}.
1937: Sank collier *Alder* in collision 4 April in fog at entrance to Strangford Lough.
1938: Renamed *Cavan*.
1938: Owner renamed British & Irish Steam Packet Co. Ltd.
1939: Sold to Michael A. Karageorgis {Piraeus; Greece}. Renamed *Marios*.
1941: Sunk 25 April in air attack at Vostitsa (now Aiyion), Gulf of Corinth, Greece.

Ardmore   1936−1940
See *Lady Killiney* (1919).

Kenmare   1936−1956   274.5m x 37.9m x 17.2m   1,675
143487
Ardrossan Drydock & Shipbuilding Co. Ltd, Ardrossan. 278.
John G. Kincaid & Co. Ltd, Greenock. Triple expansion steam. 360rhp, 553nhp. Single screw.
1921: Launched 24 February as *Kenmare*.
1921: Completed for City of Cork Steam Packet Co. Ltd {Cork}.
1936: To British & Irish Steam Packet Co. (1936) Ltd {Cork}.
1938: Owner renamed British & Irish Steam Packet Co. Ltd.
1956: Broken up at Passage West, Cork.

Innisfallen   1936−1940   321.0m x 45.7m x 15.2m   3,071   Two funnels.
152222
Harland & Wolff Ltd, Belfast. 870.
Builder. Oil. 1,192rhp, 1,193nhp. Twin screws. 18 knots.
1930: Launched 4 March as *Innisfallen*.
1930: Completed for City of Cork Steam Packet Co. Ltd {Cork}.
1936: To British & Irish Steam Packet Co. (1936) Ltd {Cork}.
1938: Owner renamed British & Irish Steam Packet Co. Ltd.
1940: Mined and sunk 21 December in River Mersey. Wreck later demolished by explosives.

Name Official number Builder. Yard no. Engine builder and details	In fleet	Dimensions (length x breadth x depth)	Gross tons	Notes

Finola   1937–1939   200.0m x 30.8m x 13.2m   879   Cargo.
                                                                                               Machinery aft.

143533
Dublin Dockyard Co. Ltd, Dublin. 105.
Ross & Duncan, Govan, Glasgow. Triple expansion steam. 120rhp, 155nhp. Single screw. 10.75 knots.
1920: Launched 27 November as *Finola*.
1920: Completed for Michael Murphy Ltd, Dublin.
1921: {Cardiff}.
1926: Michael Murphy Ltd acquired by British & Irish Steam Packet Co. Ltd.
1937: To British & Irish Steam Packet Co. (1936) Ltd {Dublin}.
1938: Owner renamed British & Irish Steam Packet Co. Ltd.
1939: To Coast Lines Ltd {Liverpool}. Renamed *Glamorgan Coast.*
1947: To British Channel Traders Ltd {London}. Renamed *Stuart Queen.*
1947: To Queenship Navigation Ltd {London}.
1952: To Zillah Shipping Co. Ltd [W.A. Savage Ltd] {Liverpool}. Renamed *Caldyfield.*
1955: Broken up at Preston.

Kilkenny   1937–1971   263.7m x 40.1m x 14.2m   1,320   Cargo.
159788
Dublin Dockyard Co. (Vickers <Ireland> Ltd), Dublin. 169.
Harland & Wolff Ltd, Belfast. Oil. 404rhp and nhp. Single screw. 14 knots.
1937: Launched 14 April as *Kilkenny.*
1937: Towed to Belfast for engine to be fitted.
1937: Completed for British & Irish Steam Packet Co. (1936) Ltd {Dublin}.
1938: Owner renamed British & Irish Steam Packet Co. Ltd.
1971: Sold to Patrick J. O'Connor, Co. Dublin {Dublin}. Renamed *Cork.*
1974: Broken up at Dalmuir.

Leinster   1938–1940   353.0 mx 50.2m x 14.6m   4,302
164343
Harland & Wolff Ltd, Belfast. 995.
Builder. Oil. 1,348rhp, 1,347nhp, 5,100bhp. Twin screws. 17 knots.
1937: Launched 24 June as *Leinster* for British & Irish Steam Packet Co. (1936) Ltd.
1937: Completed for Coast Lines Ltd {Liverpool}.
1938: {Dublin}. Chartered to British & Irish Steam Packet Co. (1936) Ltd.
1938: Charterer renamed British & Irish Steam Packet Co. Ltd.
1940: Charter terminated. {Liverpool}.
1946: To Belfast Steamship Co. Ltd {Belfast}. Renamed *Ulster Prince.*
1966: Renamed *Ulster Prince I.*
1967: Sold to Van Heyghen Frères, Belgium, for breaking up.
1967: Sold to Epirotiki Lines (George Potamianos) Ltd {Greece}. Renamed *Ulster Prince.*
1968: To Epirotiki Steamship Co. Ltd {Famagusta; Cyprus}. Renamed *Adria.*
1969: Renamed *Odysseus.*
1975/76: {Greece}.
1976/77: {Limassol; Cyprus}.
1979: Broken up at Faslane. Demolition completed 1980.

Munster   1938–1939   353.0m x 50.2m x 14.6m   4,302
166226
Harland & Wolff Ltd, Belfast. 996.
Builder. Oil. 1,348rhp, 1,347nhp, 5,100bhp. Twin screws. 17 knots.
1937: Launched 3 November as *Munster.*

Name	In fleet	Dimensions	Gross	Notes
Official number		*(length x breadth x depth)*	tons	
Builder. Yard no.				
Engine builder and details				

1938: Completed for Coast Lines Ltd {Liverpool}.

1938: {Dublin}. Chartered to British & Irish Steam Packet Co. (1936) Ltd.

1938: Charterer renamed British & Irish Steam Packet Co. Ltd.

1939: Chartered to Belfast Steamship Co. Ltd.

1940: Mined and sunk 7 February, off Mersey Bar Lightship, on voyage from Belfast to Liverpool.

Meath   1938–1940
See *Lady Meath* (1929).

Louth   1938–1948
See *Lady Munster* (1929).

Longford   1938–1953
See *Lady Connaught* (1930).

Lady Connaught   1938–1947
See *Lady Leinster* (1930).

Galway   April–June 1938
See *Lady Galway* (1931).

Wicklow   1938–1947
See *Lady Wicklow* (1919).

Cavan   1938–1939
See *Lady Cavan* (1933).

Galway   August 1938–1939
See *Lady Wimborne* (1915).

Kerry   1938–1939
See *Lady Patricia* (1919).

Carlow   1938–1939
See *Lady Emerald* (1919).

Dundalk   1939–1966   186.2m x 35.2m x 12.6m   699   Cargo.
159826
Ardrossan Dockyard Ltd, Ardrossan. 372.
British Auxiliaries Ltd, Glasgow. Oil. 113rhp, 218nhp. Single screw. 12.5 knots.
1938: Launched 10 November as *Dundalk*.
1939: Completed for British & Irish Steam Packet Co. Ltd {Dublin}.
1966: Sold to Varverakis & Co. {Greece}. Renamed *Alexis*.
1966: Sank 5 September 35 miles west of Paphos, Cyprus, on voyage from Constantza, Rumania, to Beirut, Lebanon.

Kerry   1947–1959
See *Kerry* (1938).

Meath   1948–1952   271.0m x 38.1m x 16.2m   1,434   Cargo.
143050
Caledon Shipbuilding & Engineering Co. Ltd, Dundee. 265.

Name	In fleet	Dimensions	Gross	Notes
Official number		*(length x breadth x depth)*	*tons*	
Builder. Yard no.				
Engine builder and details				

Builder. Triple expansion steam. Single screw. 278rhp, 196nhp. 12 knots.
Ordered by British Government as war standard ship.
1919: Launched 17 January as *War Leven*.
1919: Completed for Shipping Controller [J. Moss & Co. Ltd] {London} as *Limoges*.
1919: Sold to Moss Steamship Co. Ltd {Liverpool}.
1922: Sold to Coast Lines Ltd {Liverpool}. Renamed *Western Coast*.
1941: To Burns & Laird Lines Ltd {Liverpool}. Name of *Lairdsvale* allocated, but never formally changed.
1946: Renamed *Meath*.
1948: To British & Irish Steam Packet Co. Ltd {Liverpool}.
1952: To Burns & Laird Lines Ltd {Glasgow}. Renamed *Lairdscastle*.
1958: Broken up at Hendrik-Ido-Ambacht, Netherlands.

Munster	1948–1968	353.2m x 50.2m x 14.5m	4,088	

159871
Harland & Wolff Ltd, Belfast. 1349.
Builder. Oil. 698rhp, 1,590nhp, 5,600bhp. Twin screws. 17.5 knots.
1947: Launched 25 March as *Munster*.
1948: Completed for British & Irish Steam Packet Co. Ltd {Dublin}.
1968: Renamed *Munster I*.
1968: Sold to Epirotiki Steamship Navigation Co. 'George Potamianos' S.A. {Piraeus; Greece}. Renamed *Theseus*.
1969: Renamed *Orpheus*.
1972: To Epirotiki Lines SA {Piraeus; Greece}.
1987/88: To Epirotiki Steamship Co. George Potamianos SA [Epirotiki Lines SA] {Piraeus; Greece}.
1996: [Royal Olympic Cruises Ltd].
2000: Arrived Alang, India, 28 December, for breaking up.

Leinster	1948–1968	353.2m x 50.2m x 14.5m	4,115	

159877
Harland & Wolff Ltd, Belfast. 1352.
Builder. Oil. 698rhp, 1,590nhp, 5,600bhp. Twin screws. 17.5 knots.
1947: Launched 20 May as *Leinster*.
1948: Completed for British & Irish Steam Packet Co. Ltd {Dublin}.
1968: Renamed *Leinster I*.
1968: Sold to Med Sun Ferry Lines Ltd {Famagusta; Cyprus}. Renamed *Aphrodite*.
1975/76: {Limassol; Cyprus}.
1987: Broken up at Aliaga, Turkey.

Innisfallen	1948–1969	327.2m x 50.2m x 14.7m	3,705	

159848
William Denny & Brothers Ltd, Dumbarton. 1405.
Builder. Sulzer oil. 1,589nhp, 6,400bhp. Twin screws. 17 knots.
1947: Launched 12 December as *Innisfallen*.
1948: Completed for British & Irish Steam Packet Co. Ltd {Cork}.
1969: Renamed *Innisfallen I*.
1969: Sold to Isthmian Navigation Co. Ltd [The Hellenic Mediterranean Lines Co. Ltd] {Famagusta; Cyprus}.
  Renamed *Poseidonia*.
1975/76: {Limassol; Cyprus}.
1985: Broken up at Brindisi.

Kildare	1948–1952			

See *Carlow* (1938).

Name Official number Builder. Yard no. Engine builder and details	In fleet	Dimensions (length x breadth x depth)	Gross tons	Notes

Inniscarra 1950–1969 169.5m x 28.1m x 9.8m 584 Cargo.
Machinery aft.

182867 (British)/400016 (Irish)
Burntisland Shipbuilding Co. Ltd, Burntisland. 310.
British Polar Engines Ltd, Glasgow. Oil. 80.6rhp, 184nhp, 800bhp. Single screw. 11.25 knots.
1948: Launched 20 May as *Brittany Coast*.
1948: Completed for British Channel Islands Shipping Co. Ltd {London}.
1950: To British & Irish Steam Packet Co. Ltd {Liverpool}. Renamed *Inniscarra*.
1952: {Dublin}.
1969: Sold to Oldham Bros, Liverpool {Dublin} for breaking up.
1970: Sold to Kassos Maritime Enterprises Ltd {Greece}. Renamed *Elni*.
1971: Sold to Vassilios and Gerassimos Zavitsanos {Piraeus; Greece}.
1971: Sold to Theodoros and Vassilios Zavitsanos, and Theodoros Argiris {Piraeus; Greece}.
1972: Sold to Mrs Kyriaki D. Kallimassia and Mrs Evangelia B. Dimopoulou {Piraeus; Greece}. Renamed *Ria*.
1981: Broken up in Italy.

Glengariff 1956–1963 272.5m x 38.4m x 17.2m 1,599
164098 (British)/400092 (Irish)
Alexander Stephen & Sons Ltd, Linthouse, Glasgow. 550.
Builder. Triple expansion steam. 210rhp, 196nhp. Single screw. 13 knots.
1936: Launched 3 September as *Rathlin*.
1936: Completed for Clyde Shipping Co. Ltd {Glasgow}.
1941: Requisitioned as Convoy Rescue Ship.
1945: Returned to owners.
1953: Sold to Burns & Laird Lines Ltd {Glasgow}. Renamed *Lairdscraig*.
1956: To British & Irish Steam Packet Co. Ltd {Cork}. Renamed *Glengariff*.
1963: Arrived at Passage West, Cork, for breaking up, 30 December.
1964: Broken up.

Wicklow 1960–1970 189.6m x 31.6m x 10.9m 586 Cargo.
Machinery aft.

165759 (British)/400277 (Irish)
J. Koster Hzn. Scheepswerf 'Gideon', Groningen, Netherlands. 158.
Humboldt-Deutzmotoren AG, Köln, Germany. Oil. 144nhp, 825bhp. Single screw. 10 knots.
1937: Launched 18 November as *Sandhill*.
1938: Completed for Tyne-Tees Steam Shipping Co. Ltd {Newcastle}.
1943: Tyne-Tees Steam Shipping Co. Ltd acquired by Coast Lines.
1946: Renamed *Valerian Coast*.
1948: To Aberdeen Steam Navigation Co. Ltd {Aberdeen}. Renamed *Hebridean Coast*.
1951: To Tyne-Tees Steam Shipping Co. Ltd {Newcastle}.
1953: To Belfast Steamship Co. Ltd {Belfast}. Renamed *Ulster Chieftain*.
1956: To Tyne-Tees Steam Shipping Co. Ltd {Newcastle}. Renamed *Durham Coast*.
1960: To British & Irish Steam Packet Co. Ltd {Dublin}. Renamed *Wicklow*.
1960: Oil engine by Humboldt-Deutzmotoren AG, Köln-Deutz, Germany. 63.5rhp, 870bhp. 10 knots.
1970: Sold to Sistallic Shipping Co. Ltd {Famagusta; Cyprus}. Renamed *Sinergasia*.
1973: Sold to Aghios Sostis Maritime Co. Ltd {Famagusta; Cyprus}. Renamed *Sonia*.
1974: Sold to Fortitude Maritime Co. {Greece}. Renamed *Margarita P.*
1976: Sold to Cia. de Nav. Scotia SA {Panama; Panama}.
1979: Arrived at Baia, Italy, to be broken up.
1980: Broken up.

Name Official number Builder. Yard no. Engine builder and details	In fleet	Dimensions (length x breadth x depth)	Gross tons	Notes

Meath   1960–1973   276.0m x 42.1m x 15.4m   1,558   Cargo.
400281 (Irish)/359117 (British)   280.8m x 42.1m x 15.6m   2,478   from 1975.
Liffey Dockyard Ltd, Dublin. 180.
George Clark & North East Marine (Sunderland) Ltd, Sunderland. Oil. 446rhp, 2,500bhp. Single screw. 13 knots.
1959: Launched 4 November as *Meath*.
1960: Completed for British & Irish Steam Packet Co. Ltd {Dublin}.
1974: Sold to Vickers Ltd, London {Barrow}.
1975: Converted into submarine support and oceanographic research vessel by Manchester Dry Dock Co. Ltd.,
Manchester. Renamed *Vickers Viscount*.
1978: [James Fisher & Sons Ltd].
1979: Sold to British Oceonics Ltd, Leith [Premier Shipping & Engineering Ltd] {Barrow}. Renamed *British
Viscount*.
1980: Sold to J.H. Food Machinery Ltd, Hull [Jiltro Ltd] {Barrow}.
1981: Sold to Fairfield Industries (Bermuda) Ltd, Hamilton, Bermuda [J. Marr & Son Ltd] {Hull}. Reported
renamed *Fairfield Viscount*, but no change registered.
1983: Reported renamed *British Viscount*.
1984: To Fairfield Industries Panama SA [Johnasia (S) Pte. Ltd] {Panama; Panama}.
1990: Sold to unspecified owners {St Vincent and the Grenadines}. Renamed *British*.
1990: Broken up in India.

Glanmire   1963–1969   229.0m x 37.2m x 11.5m   814   Cargo.
164095 (British)/400346 (Irish)
Harland & Wolff Ltd, Belfast. 978.
Builder. Oil. 330rhp, 332nhp. Twin screws. 13.5 knots.
1936: Launched 3 September as *Lairdsbank*.
1936: Completed for Burns & Laird Lines Ltd {Glasgow}.
1963: To British & Irish Steam Packet Co. Ltd {Cork}. Renamed *Glanmire*.
1969: Broken up at Dalmuir.

Munster I   1968–1968
See *Munster* (1948).

Munster   1968–1983   342.2m x 57.8m x 18.8m   4,067   Vehicle ferry.
400690
Werft Nobiskrug GmbH, Rendsburg, West Germany. 657.
Maschinenbau Augsburg-Nuernberg, Augsburg, Germany. Oil. 684rhp, 11,400bhp. Two CP propellers. 21.8 knots.
Ordered by Lion Ferry A/B, Sweden.
1968: Launched 25 January as *Munster*.
1968: Completed for British & Irish Steam Packet Co. Ltd {Dublin}.
1983: Sold to Petra Navigation Agencies {Aquaba; Jordan}. Renamed *Farah*.
1983: To Silver Dolphin SA {Panama; Panama}. Renamed *Farah I*.
1987: To Ahmad Armoush {Aquaba; Jordan}.
1987: To Arab Orient Trading Services Ltd. [Petra Navigation & International Trading Co. Ltd] {Aquaba; Jordan}.
1990: To Tourist International Investments Co. Ltd [Petra Navigation & International Trading Co. Ltd] {Valletta;
Malta}.
1990: Sold to Dalian Steam Shipping Co. {Dalian/Dairen; China}. Renamed *Tian Peng*.
1999/2000: To China Passenger Ship Co. Ltd {Dalian, Liaoning Province; China}.
2003: Deleted from Lloyd's Register.

Leinster I   1968–1968
See *Leinster* (1948).

Name Official number Builder. Yard no. Engine builder and details	In fleet	Dimensions (length x breadth x depth)	Gross tons	Notes

Innisfallen I 1969–1969
See *Innisfallen* (1948).

Kildare	1968–1974	247.0m x 43.4m x 7.7m	622	Container ship. Machinery aft.
400751		247.0m x 43.4m x 17.3m	1,632	from 1971.

Schlichting Werft GmbH, Travemünde, Germany. 1361.
Atlas-MaK Maschinenbau, Kiel, Germany. Oil. 277rhp, 1,550bhp. Single screw. 13.1 knots.
1968: Launched 12 October as *Kildare*.
1968: Completed for Shelbourne Shipowning Co. {Dublin}. Leased to British & Irish Steam Packet Co. Ltd.
1974: Sold to Universal Maritime Corporation {Monrovia; Liberia}. Renamed *Pacific Despatcher*.
1976: To Orient Overseas Container Services Inc. {Monrovia; Liberia}.
1982: Sold to Cheng Lie Navigation Co. Ltd {Keelung; Taiwan}. Renamed *Min Lie*.
1985: Sold to E-Hsiang Steamship Co. Ltd {Keelung; Taiwan}. Renamed *Hsiang Lie*.
1990: Sold to Chom Kunpalin {Bangkok; Thailand}. Renamed *Ta Tung No. 1*.
1991: Sold to Pacific Shipping Lines Co. Ltd {Bangkok; Thailand}. Renamed *C. Express*.
1994: Suffered hull damage while moored at Ban Pak Nam, Thailand, in collision with bulk carrier *Timpe* on 30 August.
1996: Reported lost May.

Tipperary	1969–1974	247.0m x 43.4m x 7.7m	622	Container ship. Machinery aft.
400756			1,048	from 1974.
			1,765	from 1995.

Schlichting Werft GmbH, Travemünde, Germany. 1362.
Atlas-MaK Maschinenbau, Kiel, Germany. Oil. 277rhp, 1,550bhp. Single screw. 13.1 knots.
1969: Launched 25 January as *Tipperary*.
1969: Completed for Shelbourne Shipowning Co. {Dublin}. Leased to British & Irish Steam Packet Co. Ltd.
1974: Sold to Moosmie Ltd {Dublin}.
1974: Sold to Scan Heavy Shipping Co. [Blaesbjerg (Holland) BV] {Willemstad; Netherlands Antilles}. Renamed *Thor Scan*.
1980: Sold to Atlantska Plovidba {Dubrovnik; Yugoslavia}. Renamed *Jahorina*.
1987: Sold to Gallego Shipping Corp. {Kingstown; St Vincent and the Grenadines}. Renamed *Hori*.
1988: Sold to Lin Lin Shipping Sendirian Berhad {Kuching; Malaysia}. Renamed *Lin Petaling*.
1989: Sold to Thong Soon Nav. (Pte.) Ltd [Thong Soon Lines Pte. Ltd] {Singapore; Singapore}. Renamed *Equator Jade*.
2003: No owners or flag.
2005: Still in service.

Innisfallen	1969–1980	387.8m x 58.5 mx 37.4m	4,849	Vehicle ferry.
400663			7,187	from 1998.

Werft Nobiskrug GmbH, Rendsburg, West Germany. 660.
Maschinenbau Augsburg-Nuernberg, Augsburg, Germany. Oil. Two CP propellers. 16,000bhp. 24 knots.
1968: Launched 7 December as *Innisfallen*.
1969: Completed for British & Irish Steam Packet Co. Ltd {Cork}.
1980: Sold to Tourship Co. SA (Corsica Ferries) {Panama, Panama}. Renamed *Corsica Viva*.
1985: To Mainvest Funds SA {Panama; Panama}. Renamed *Dominican Viva*.
1988: To Tourism & Shipping SA {Panama; Panama}. Renamed *Corsica Viva I*.
1992: To Nuovo Trans Tirreno Express Srl (Sardinia Ferries) {Italy}. Renamed *Sardinia Viva*.
1993: To Caribia Ferries SA {Guadeloupe}. Renamed *Caribia Viva*.
1994: {Nassau; Bahamas}. Renamed *Spirit of Independence*.
1996: Sold to Jerika Corporation Ltd [Agenzia Marittima Saidelli Srl] {Nassau; Bahamas}.

Name Official number Builder. Yard no. Engine builder and details	In fleet	Dimensions (length x breadth x depth)	Gross tons	Notes

---

1998: Sold to Millennium Shipping Co. Ltd, Gibraltar [Happy Lines] {Madeira; Portugal (MAR)}. Renamed
  Happy Dolphin.
2003: Sold to Derin Denizcilik Nakliyat ve Tikaret Ltd Sirketi {Istanbul; Turkey}. Renamed *Derin Deniz.*
2004: Broken up at Alang, India.

Leinster	1969–1986	367.8 x 57.8 x 18.8	4,849	Vehicle ferry.
400767			7,311	from 1995.

Verolme Cork Dockyards Ltd, Cobh. 800.
Maschinenbau Augsburg-Nuernberg, Augsburg, Germany. Oil. 2,036rhp, 11,400bhp. Two CP propellers.
  21.8 knots.
1968: Launched 19 November as *Leinster.*
1969: Completed for British & Irish Steam Packet Co. Ltd {Dublin}.
1980: Renamed *Innisfallen.*
1986: Owner renamed B&I Line PLC.
1986: Sold to Strintzis Lines Co. Ltd {Limassol; Cyprus}. Renamed *Ionian Sun.*
1988/89: To Strintzis Lines Mediterranean Shipping Co. [Strintzis Lines SA] {Piraeus; Greece}.
1990: Chartered to Swansea–Cork Ferries Ltd.
1993: Chartered to Cotunav (Tunisia). Renamed *Chams.*
1993: Renamed *Ionian Sun.*
1995: [Joint Service Minoan Lines–Strintzis Lines].
1998: To Strintzis Lines Shipping SA (Blue Star Ferries) {Piraeus; Greece}.
2001: Sold to Marco Shipping Agency LLC {Dubai; UAE}. Renamed *Merdif.*
2004: Broken up.

Wicklow	1971–1994	311.3 x 53.3 x 21.8	3,442	Container ship. Machinery aft.
401046				

Verolme Cork Dockyards Ltd, Cobh. 821.
Maschinenbau Augsburg-Nuernberg, Augsburg, Germany. Oil. 687rhp, 3,900bhp. Single CP propeller. 15 knots.
1971: Launched 21 June as *Wicklow.*
1971: Completed for British & Irish Steam Packet Co. Ltd {Dublin}.
1986: Owner renamed B&I Line PLC.
1992: Owner renamed B&I Line Ltd.
1994: Sold to Wilke Shipping Ltd {St John's; Antigua and Barbuda}. Renamed *Wilke.*
1995: Sold to Billion Gold Shipping (Belize) SA [Yantai Hengtong Shipping Co.] {Belize, Belize}. Renamed
  Vince.
2001: To Yantai Hengtong Shipping Co. {San Lorenzo; Honduras}. Renamed *Prince No.5.*
2002: To Tian Mu Shipping Co. Ltd [Yantai Hengtong Shipping Co.] {Phnon-Penh; Cambodia}. Renamed *Tian
  Mu.*
2004: Sold to PT Tata Shipping Co. Ltd {Phnon-Penh; Cambodia}. Renamed *Tian Feng.*
2005: Still in service.

Mayo	1971–1974	249.4 x 38.1 x 10.3	757	Container ship. Machinery aft.
400916				

F Smit v/h Smit & Zoon, Foxhol, Netherlands 204.
Atlas-Mak Maschinenbau GmbH, Kiel, Germany. Oil. 268rhp, 1,500bhp. Single screw. 12.5 knots.
Ordered by Limerick Steamship Co. Ltd.
1970: Completed for Hibernian Transport Companies Ltd, Ireland as *Hibernian Enterprise.* Not registered.
1970: Owner in liquidation.
1970. Sold by liquidator to Palgrave Murphy Ltd {Dublin}.
1971: Sold to Irish Sea Operators Ltd {Dublin}. Chartered to British & Irish Steam Packet Co. Ltd. Renamed *Mayo.*

Name	In fleet	Dimensions	Gross	Notes
Official number		*(length x breadth x depth)*	*tons*	
Builder. Yard no.				
Engine builder and details				

1972: To Grafton Shipping Co. Ltd {Dublin}.

1972: Owner renamed Irish Sea Operators Ltd.

1974: Sold to Commodore Shipping Co. Ltd {Guernsey}. Renamed *Commodore Clipper.*

1988: Sold to Jean P. Metz {Beirut; Lebanon}. Renamed *Celine M.*

1990: Sold to Meromar Chartering Co. Ltd {San Lorenzo; Honduras}. Renamed *Sea Lion I.*

1991: Renamed *Celine M.*

1993: Sold to unspecified owners. Renamed *Larnaca Town.*

1993: Sold to Mediterranean Container Line {San Lorenzo; Honduras}. Renamed *Sea Star III.*

1993: Sold to Celine M Ltd {San Lorenzo; Honduras}. Renamed *Celine M.*

1996/97: {Kingstown; St Vincent and the Grenadines}.

2003: Sold to Mrs Veinn Kaidaban {Union of Comoros}. Renamed *Abdallah.*

2004: {Wonsan; North Korea}.

2005: Still in service.

Sligo	1971–1978	234.9 x 42.7 x 10.0	787	Container ship.
				Machinery aft.

401053

Astilleros Luzuriaga SA, Pasages, Spain. 200.

Naval-Stork-Werkspoor SA, Cadiz. Oil. 277rhp 1,550bhp. Single screw. 12.5 knots.

Ordered by F. Laeisz, Germany.

1971: Launched 11 February unnamed.

1971: Completed as *Astiluzu 200.* Not registered.

1971: Registered to Irish Sea Operators Ltd {Dublin} as *Sligo.* Chartered to British & Irish Steam Packet Co. Ltd.

1972: To Grafton Shipping Co. Ltd {Dublin}.

1972: Owner renamed Irish Sea Operators Ltd.

1978: Sold to Scan Unit Shipping Co., Curacao {Willemstad; Netherlands Antilles}. Renamed *Biscayne Sky.*

1982: Renamed *Scan Glen.*

1985: Sold to Atlanska Plovidba {Dubrovnik; Yugoslavia}. Renamed *Slano.*

1987: Sold to Ariane Shipping Corp. {Panama; Panama}. Renamed *Ariane I.*

1990: To Ariane Shipping Co. Ltd [Morton & Co.] {St. John's; Antigua and Barbuda}. Renamed *Ariane.*

1997: Renamed *Crioula.*

2000: Renamed *Transport.*

2005: Still in service.

Kerry	1972–1978	234.9 x 42.7 x 10.0	787	Container ship.
				Machinery aft.

401146

Astilleros Luzuriaga SA, Pasages, Spain. 201.

Naval-Stork-Werkspoor SA, Cadiz. Oil. 277rhp 1,550bhp. Single screw. 12.5 knots.

Ordered by F. Laeisz, Germany.

1971: Completed as *Astiluzu 201.* Not registered.

1972: Registered to Irish Sea Operators Ltd {Dublin} as *Kerry.* Chartered to British & Irish Steam Packet Co. Ltd.

1978: Sold to Scan Unit Shipping Co., Curacao {Willemstad; Netherlands Antilles}. Renamed *Biscayne Sea.*

1982: Renamed *Scan Venture.*

1983: Sold to Power Navigation SA {Panama; Panama}. Renamed *Fast Trader.*

1987: Sold to Rasco Trading Co., Malvern, PA, USA {Panama; Panama}. Renamed *Rasco Trader.*

1988: Renamed *Pheonix Caribe.*

1989: Sold to Emu Shipping Co. Ltd {Limassol; Cyprus}. Renamed *Samantha.*

1997: Sold to Southwest Transfer Ltd [Morton & Co.] {George Town; Cayman Islands}. Renamed *Transfer.*

2004: To Ariane Shipping Co. Ltd [Morton & Co.] {St. John's; Antigua and Barbuda}.

2005: Grounded 7 January on Lighthouse Reef, Belize, on a voyage from Belize to Mobile. Not expected to be salvageable.

Name Official number Builder. Yard no. Engine builder and details	In fleet	Dimensions (length x breadth x depth)	Gross tons	Notes

---

Kilkenny

1973–1991   311.3 x 53.3 x 9.5   1,514   Container ship. Machinery aft.

401239
Verolme Cork Dockyards Ltd, Cobh. 844.
Maschinenbau Augsburg-Nuernberg, Augsburg, Germany. Oil. 687rhp, 3,900bhp. Single CP propeller. 15 knots.
1973: Launched 4 July as *Kilkenny*.
1973: Completed for Allied Irish Banks Ltd {Dublin}. Leased to British & Irish Steam Packet Co. Ltd.
1986: Name of owner changed to Allied Irish Banks PLC.
1986: Sold to British & Irish Steam Packet Co. Ltd {Dublin}.
1986: Owner renamed B&I Line PLC.
1991: Sank 21 November in Dublin Bay, after collision with *Hasselwerder*, on voyage from Antwerp to Dublin.
1992: Wreck dismantled *in situ*; recovered sections broken up at Dublin.

Dundalk

1975–1980   370.4 x 53.4 x 15.1   2,353   Ro-ro.

401411   6,653   from 1997.
Verolme Cork Dockyards Ltd, Cobh. 874.
British Polar Engines Ltd, Glasgow. Oil. 1,500rhp, 8,400bhp. Two CP propellers. 18 knots.
1974: Launched 12 September as *Dundalk*.
1975: Completed for Allied Irish Banks Ltd {Dublin}. Leased to British & Irish Steam Packet Co. Ltd.
1980: Sold to Stena Caribbean Line Ltd, Cayman Islands [Rederi A/B Concordia] {Dublin}. Renamed *Stena Sailer*.
1984: {Georgetown; Cayman Islands}.
1987: Renamed *Lion Sailer*.
1988: Renamed *Stena Sailer*.
1988: To Hoginaut International Ltd [Swecal Ltd] {Georgetown; Cayman Islands}.
1988: Sold to Ro-Ro 3 Ltd. [Sealink UK Ltd] {Nassau; Bahamas}.
1989: To Sealink (UK) Ltd {Nassau; Bahamas}. Renamed *St Cybi*.
1991: Sold to Wind Ltd. {Gibraltar}. Renamed *Wind Cybi*.
1992: Sold to Olympia II Shipping Co. [Costas and Christos Miras] {Piraeus; Greece}. Renamed *Theseus*. Rebuilt as passenger and vehicle ferry.
1995: To Dimitrios Miras & Co. ENE {Piraeus; Greece}.
1997/98: To Olympia II Shipping Co. [Dimitrios Miras & Co. ENE] {Piraeus; Greece}.
2005: Still in service.

Connacht

1978–1988   380.0 x 60.8 x 20.1   6,812   Vehicle ferry.

401869   9,795   from 1996.
Verolme Cork Dockyards Ltd, Cobh. 955.
Krupp MaK Maschinenbau GmbH, Kiel, Germany. Oil. 3,215rhp, 18,000bhp. Two CP propellers. 21 knots.
1978: Launched 20 June as *Connacht*.
1978: Completed for British & Irish Steam Packet Co. Ltd.
1979: {Dublin}.
1986: Owner renamed B&I Line PLC.
1988: Sold to SA de Economie Mixte d'Equipment Navale [BAISA Brittany Ferries Bretagne–Angleterre–Irelande] {St Malo; France}. Renamed *Duchesse Anne*.
1996: Sold to Morrison Ship Trading Co. [Jadrolinija] {Rijeka; Croatia}. Renamed *Dubrovnik*.
2005: Still in service.

Tipperary

1979–1988   475.3 x 68.0 x 17.2   6,310   Ro-ro.

401950   14,087   from 1995.
Mitsui Engineering & Shipbuilding Co. Ltd, Tamano, Japan. 1164.
Builder. Oil. 3,214rhp, 18,000bhp. Two CP propellers. 18.75 knots.
1979: Launched 20 April as *Puma*, for leasing to P&O Ferries Ltd.

Name	In fleet	Dimensions	Gross	Notes
Official number		*(length x breadth x depth)*	tons	
Builder. Yard no.				
Engine builder and details				

1979: Completed for Ensign Tankers (Leasing) Ltd, London {Dublin} as *Tipperary*. Chartered to British & Irish Steam Packet Co. Ltd.

1986: Charterers renamed B&I Line PLC.

1988: Sold to Norcape Shipping BV [North Sea Ferries Noordzee Veerdiensten BV] {Rotterdam; Netherlands}.

1989: Renamed *Norcape*.

1996: Norcape Shipping BV acquired by P&O group.

1997: To P&O North Sea Ferries BV {Rotterdam; Netherlands}.

1999/2000: To Norcape CV [P&O North Sea Ferries BV] {Rotterdam; Netherlands}.

2005: Still in service.

Cú na Mara	1979−1985	89.2 x 28.0 x 8.0	311	Jetfoil. Aluminium. Machinery aft.

401963

Boeing Marine Systems, Seattle, Washington, USA. 0015.

General Motors − Detroit Diesel Allison Division, Indianapolis, Indiana, USA. Gas turbines. 1,357rhp, 7,600shp. Two water jet propulsion units. 43 knots.

1979: Completed for British & Irish Steam Packet Co. Ltd as *Cú na Mara*.

1980: {Dublin}.

1980: Sold to Midland Montagu Leasing (UK) Ltd, London {Dublin}. Leased to British & Irish Steam Packet Co. Ltd.

1985: Sold to Irelandia Investments Ltd, Co. Tipperary {Dublin}.

1986: Sold to Sado Kisen KK {Ryotsu, Niigata Prefecture; Japan}. Renamed *Ginga*.

2005: Still in service.

Innisfallen	1980−1986	

See *Leinster* (1969).

Leinster	1981−1997	380.8 x 60.8 x 20.1	6,807	Vehicle ferry.
402151			9,700	from 1994.

Verolme Cork Dockyards Ltd, Cobh. 979.

Krupp MaK Maschinenbau GmbH, Kiel, Germany. Oil. Two CP propellers. 18,000bhp. 21 knots.

1980: Launched 7 November as *Leinster*.

1981: Completed for British & Irish Steam Packet Co. Ltd {Dublin}.

1986: Owner renamed B&I Line PLC.

1992: Owner renamed B&I Line Ltd. Registered 1993.

1993: Renamed *Isle of Inishmore*.

1995: Owner renamed Irish Ferries Ltd.

1996: Renamed *Isle of Inishturk*.

1997: Sold to Government of Canada (Transport Canada) [Cooperative de Transport Maritime et Aerien (CTMA)] {Ottawa, ON; Canada}. Renamed *Madeleine*.

2005: Still in service.

Munster	1990−1992	409.9 x 68.3 x 37.3	8,093	Vehicle ferry.
402732			11,403	from 1995.

Werft Nobiskrug GmbH, Rendsburg, West Germany. 663.

Blohm + Voss AG, Hamburg, West Germany. Pielstick oil. Two CP propellers. 16,000bhp. 20 knots.

Original planned name *Prins Charles*.

1970: Launched 21 February as *Prins Oberon*.

1970: Completed for A/B Bonnierföretagen [H. Meyer, Lion Ferry A/B] {Halmstad; Sweden}.

1978: Sold to Deutsche Leasing AG [Prinzelinien Schiffahrts GmbH & Co.] {Bremen; Germany}. Renamed *Prinz Oberon*.

1981: Prinzelinien Schiffahrts GmbH & Co. acquired by DFDS A/S, Denmark.

Name	In fleet	Dimensions	Gross	Notes
Official number		(length x breadth x depth)	tons	
Builder. Yard no.				
Engine builder and details				

1983: To DFDS (Deutschland) GmbH [DFDS A/S] {Hamburg; Germany}.

1984: Sold to Trans-Nordic Line A/B, Rederi A/B Gotland and Gotlandstrafiken A/B [Rederi A/B Gotland] {Visby; Sweden}. Renamed *Nordic Sun*.

1986: Sold to Perbadanan Nasional Shipping Line Berhad (Feri Malaysia) {Port Kelang; Malaysia}. Renamed *Cruise Muhibah*.

1989: Sold to Zatlen Ltd, Dublin {Port Kelang; Malaysia}. Renamed *Munster*.

1990: {Dublin}. Chartered to B&I Line PLC.

1990: Owner renamed EPA (Ireland) Ltd.

1992: Charter terminated.

1993: To EPA Investor No.11 [Blaesbjerg Ferries ApS] {Limassol; Cyprus}. Renamed *Ambassador*.

1994: Renamed *Ambassador II* [EPA Invest A/S].

1996: Sold to Sterling Shipping One LLC, Miami, USA [International Shipping Partners Inc.] {Monrovia; Liberia}.

1998: {Nassau; Bahamas}.

2005: Still in service.

Isle of Innisfree	1992–1995	134.02m x 24.62m x 8.00m	11,602	Vehicle ferry.
716308			19,761	from 1995.

A/S Nakskov Shipsvaerf, Nakskov, Denmark. 234.

B&W Maskinfabrik Division of B&W Diesel A/S, Copenhagen. Oil. 14,420bhp. Two CP propellers. 16.4 knots.

1985: Launched 29 May as *Niels Klim*.

1986: Completed for Government of the Kingdom of Denmark (Danske Statsbaner) (Danish State Railways) {Aarhus; Denmark}.

1991: Sold to Stena Nautica Line Ltd [Sealink UK Ltd] {Hamilton, Bermuda}. Renamed *Stena Nautica*.

1991: Engines 16,950bhp.

1992: Chartered to Irish Continental Group PLC. Renamed *Isle of Innisfree*.

1995: Chartered to Lion Ferry A/B. Renamed *Lion King* {Halmstad; Sweden}.

1996: Renamed *Stena Nautica*.

1998/99: {Hamilton, Bermuda}.

2000/01: To Stena Sphere A/B [Stena Line A/B] {Hamilton, Bermuda}.

2001: To Stena Nautica Line Ltd [Stena Line Scandinavia A/B] {Goteborg; Sweden}.

2005: Still in service.

Isle of Inishmore	1993–1997	
See *Leinster* (1981).		

Isle of Inishturk	1996–1997	
See *Isle of Inishmore* (1993).		

Sealink UK Limited 1988–1990

Earl William	1988–1990	99.50m x 17.73m x 5.67m	3,984	Vehicle ferry.
377458			5,739	from 1997.

K/M Kaldness MV A/S, Tonsberg, Norway. 160.

Lindholmens Varv A/B, Gothenburg, Sweden. Pielstick oil. 10,200bhp. Two CP propellers. 18.5 knots.

1964: Launched 30 April as *Viking II*.

1964: Completed for Otto Thoresen Shipping Co. A/S {Oslo; Norway}.

1964: Renamed *Carferry Viking II*.

1968: Sold to Thoresen Car Ferries A/S {Oslo; Norway} (owned by European Ferries Ltd).

1977: Sold to Lloyds Leasing Ltd [British Railways Board] {London}. Renamed *Earl William*.

1979: [Sealink UK Ltd].

Name	In fleet	Dimensions	Gross	Notes
Official number		(length x breadth x depth)	tons	
Builder. Yard no.				
Engine builder and details				

1992: Sold to Adonis Shipping Co. Ltd {Valletta; Malta}. Renamed *William*.

1992: Renamed *Pearl William*.

1996: Sold to P&L Ferries Shipping Co. SA {Valletta; Malta}. Renamed *Mar. Julia*.

1997: Sold to Lucky Shipping SA {Kingstown; St Vincent and the Grenadines}. Renamed *Çesme Stern*.

2001: Sold to Windward Lines Ltd {Kingstown; St Vincent and the Grenadines}. Renamed *Windward II*.

2003: To Winward II Ltd [Winward Agencies Ltd] {Kingstown; St Vincent and the Grenadines}.

2005: Still in service.

Pandoro Limited 1975–1997

P&O European Ferries (Irish Sea) Limited/P&O Irish Sea 1998–

Bison	1975–2004	125.00m x 19.05m x 11.99m	3,453	Ro-ro.
				Machinery aft.
363569		141.81m x 19.05m x 11.99m	4,259	from 1981.
			11,723	from 1994.
		140.10m x 23.40m x 6.00m	14,387	from 1995.

J.J. Sietas KG Schiffswerft GmbH & Co., Hamburg. 755.

Klöckner-Humboldt-Deutz AG, Köln, West Germany. Oil. 12,000bhp. Two CP propellers. 18.5 knots.

Ordered by Stena A/B, Sweden.

1974: Launched 31 October as *Bison*.

1975: Completed for Peninsular and Oriental Steam Navigation Co. {London}.

1975: To Hain-Nourse Ltd [Belfast Steamship Co. Ltd] {London}.

1977: [P&O Short-Sea Shipping Ltd].

1978: Owner renamed P&O Ferries Ltd.

1981: Lengthened by Middle Dock & Engineering Co. Ltd, South Shields. Passenger accommodation added.

1984: To POETS Fleet Management Ltd, Altrincham {London}.

1991: To Pandoro Ltd {London}.

1995: Widened.

1997: [P&O European Transport Services Ltd] {Hamilton, Bermuda}. Renamed *European Pioneer*.

1998: [P&O Ship Management (Irish Sea) Ltd].

2001: [P&O European Ferries (Irish Sea) Ltd].

2002: To P&O European Ferries (Irish Sea) Ltd [P&O Irish Sea] {Hamilton, Bermuda}.

2004: Sold to Stena Ropax Ltd [Stena Line Ltd] {Hamilton, Bermuda}. Renamed *Stena Pioneer*.

2005: Still in service.

Buffalo	1975–2004	125.00m x 19.05m x 11.99m	3,453	Ro-ro.
				Machinery aft.
363630		141.81m x 19.44m x 11.99m	10,987	from 1988.
		156.50m x 19.42m x 11.99m	12,879	from 1998.

J.J. Sietas KG Schiffswerft GmbH & Co., Hamburg. 756.

Klöckner-Humboldt-Deutz AG, Köln, West Germany. Oil. 12,000bhp. Two CP propellers. 18.5 knots.

Ordered by Stena A/B, Sweden.

1975: Launched 6 January as *Buffalo*.

1975: Completed for Peninsular and Oriental Steam Navigation Co. {London}.

1975: To Hain-Nourse Ltd [Belfast Steamship Co. Ltd] {London}.

1977: [P&O Short-Sea Shipping Ltd].

1978: Owner renamed P&O Ferries Ltd.

1984: To POETS Fleet Management Ltd, Altrincham {London}.

1988: Lengthened. Passenger accommodation added.

1991: To Pandoro Ltd {London}.

1996: {Hamilton, Bermuda}.

Name	In fleet	Dimensions	Gross	Notes
Official number		*(length x breadth x depth)*	*tons*	
Builder. Yard no.				
Engine builder and details				

1997: [P&O European Transport Services Ltd].

1998: [P&O Ship Management (Irish Sea) Ltd]. Lengthened. Renamed *European Leader.*

2001: [P&O European Ferries (Irish Sea) Ltd].

2002: To P&O European Ferries (Irish Sea) Ltd [P&O Irish Sea] {Hamilton, Bermuda}.

2004: Sold to Stena Ropax Ltd [Stena Line Ltd] {Hamilton, Bermuda}. Renamed *Stena Leader.*

2005: Still in service.

Name	In fleet	Dimensions	Gross	Notes
Union Melbourne	1978–2004	124.49m x 19.41m x 11.99m	3,453	Ro-ro.
				Machinery aft.
365913		141.81m x 19.41m x 11.97m	4,043	from 1975.
			4,377	from 1980.
			10,957	from 1994.

J.J. Sietas KG Schiffswerft GmbH & Co., Hamburg. 757.

Klöckner-Humboldt-Deutz AG, Köln, West Germany. Oil. 12,000bhp. Two CP propellers. 18 knots.

Ordered by Stena A/B, Sweden.

1975: Launched 3 March for Stena Line Ltd as *Union Melbourne.*

1975: Lengthened by Werft Nobiskrug GmbH, Rendsburg, West Germany.

1975: Completed for Northern Coasters Ltd {London}. Chartered to Union Steamship Co. of New Zealand Ltd.

1978: Chartered to Pandoro Ltd.

1980: Sold to Stena Shipping Line Ltd, Hamilton, Bermuda {London}. Renamed *Union Trader.*

1980: Sold to Bovis Properties (Southern) Ltd (P&O Group) [POETS Fleet Management Ltd] {London}. Renamed *Puma.*

1984: To POETS Fleet Management Ltd, Altrincham {London}.

1990: To Pandoro Ltd {London}.

1994: {Hamilton, Bermuda}.

1998: [P&O Ship Management (Irish Sea) Ltd]. Renamed *European Seafarer.*

2001: [P&O European Ferries (Irish Sea) Ltd].

2002: To P&O European Ferries (Irish Sea) Ltd [P&O Irish Sea] {Hamilton, Bermuda}.

2004: Sold to Stena Ropax Ltd [Stena Line Ltd] {Hamilton, Bermuda}. Renamed *Stena Seafarer.*

2005: Still in service.

Name	In fleet	Dimensions	Gross	Notes
Ibex	1979–1980	150.02m x 21.77m x 13.01m	6,310	Ro-ro.
379892			14,077	from 1994.
		150.02m x 24.43m x 13.01m	18,653	from 1996.

Mitsui Engineering & Shipbuilding Co. Ltd, Tamano, Japan. 1163.

Builder. Oil. 18,000bhp. Two CP propellers. 18.75 knots.

1978: Launched 27 December as *Ibex.*

1979: Completed for P&O Ferries Ltd {London}.

1980: Chartered to North Sea Ferries Ltd. Renamed *Norsea.*

1986: Renamed *Norsky.*

1986: To POETS Fleet Management Ltd, Altrincham {London}.

1990: To P&O Ferrymasters Ltd, Altrincham {London}.

1995: To Pandoro Ltd {Hamilton, Bermuda}.

1995: Renamed *Ibex.*

1996: Re-built with passenger accommodation and widened.

1997: [P&O Ship Management (Irish Sea) Ltd]. Renamed *European Envoy.*

2001: [P&O European Ferries (Irish Sea) Ltd].

2002: To P&O European Ferries (Irish Sea) Ltd {Hamilton, Bermuda}.

2004: Sold to Stena A/B. Re-sold to KystLink A/S, Norway {Hamilton, Bermuda}. Renamed *Envoy.*

2004: {Langesund; Norway}.

2005: Still in service.

Name Official number Builder. Yard no. Engine builder and details	In fleet	Dimensions (length x breadth x depth)	Gross tons	Notes

Puma 1979–1979
See *Tipperary* (1979) in B&I fleet list.

Puma 1980–2004
See *Union Melbourne* (1978).

Viking Trader	1988–2003	116.95m x 18.14m x 11.70m	2,905	Ro-ro.
377421		137.30m x 18.14m x 11.70m	3,985	in 1984.
			9,085	from 1995.

Osterreichische Schiffswerften AG Linz-Korneuburg, Korneuburg, Austria. 709.
Klöckner-Humboldt-Deutz AG, Köln, West Germany. Oil. 10,200bhp. Two CP propellers. 18 knots.
Ordered by Stena A/B, Sweden.
1976: Launched 15 January as *Stena Tender*.
1977: Towed to Rendsburg, Germany, for lengthening by Werft Nobiskrug GmbH.
1977: Completed for United Baltic Corporation Ltd {London} as *Goya*.
1980: Sold to Federal Commerce & Navigation Ltd, Montreal, Canada [Federal Offshore Services Ltd] {Halifax, Nova Scotia}. Renamed *Federal Nova*.
1980: {Georgetown, Cayman Islands}.
1981: Sold to Seaforth Fednav Inc., Canada {Georgetown; Cayman Islands}. Renamed *Caribbean Sky*.
1981: Renamed *Manaure VII*.
1982: Sold to Philippine Navigation Inc. {Panama; Panama}.
1983: Sold to Timber Shipping Inc. {Panama; Panama}. Renamed *Oyster Bay*.
1983: Sold to Cenargo Ltd [Denholm Ship Management Ltd] {Southampton}. Renamed *Viking Trader*.
1984: Passenger accommodation added.
1988: Sold to P&O European Ferries (Portsmouth) Ltd, Portsmouth {Southampton}.
1988: Sold to POETS Fleet Management Ltd, Altrincham {Southampton}.
1990: To Pandoro Ltd {Southampton}.
1996: {Hamilton, Bermuda}. Renamed *Leopard*.
1998: [P&O Ship Management (Irish Sea) Ltd]. Renamed *European Navigator*.
2001: [P&O European Ferries (Irish Sea) Ltd].
2003: Sold to Arab Bridge Maritime Co. and Salam International Transport & Trading Co. Ltd [International Ship Management Co. Ltd] {Aquaba; Jordan}. Renamed *Black Iris*.
2004: [Arab Ship Management Co.].
2005: Still in service.

Norsky 1995–2004
See *Ibex* (1979).

Ibex 1995–2004
See *Norsky* (1995).

Leopard 1996–2003
See *Viking Trader* (1988)

European Pioneer 1997–2004
See *Bison* (1975).

European Envoy 1997–2004
See *Ibex* (1995).

European Leader 1998–2004
See *Buffalo* (1975).

Name Official number Builder. Yard no. Engine builder and details	In fleet	Dimensions (length x breadth x depth)	Gross tons	Notes

European Seafarer   1998–2004
See *Union Melbourne* (1978).

European Navigator   1998–2003
See *Leopard* (1996)

European Ambassador   2000–2004   170.51m x 25.82m x 9.50m   24,206   Ro-pax.
8000165
Mitsubishi Heavy Industries Ltd, Shimonoseki, Japan. 1068.
Wartsilla Nederland BV, Zwolle, Netherlands. Oil. 53,836bhp. Two CP propellers. 25.7 knots.
2000: Launched 18 August as *European Ambassador*.
2000: Completed for Lombard Facilities Ltd [P&O Ship Management (Irish Sea) Ltd] {Nassau; Bahamas}.
2001: [P&O European Ferries (Irish Sea) Ltd].
2004: Sold to Stena Line Scandinavia A/B {Gothenburg; Sweden}. Renamed *Stena Nordica*.
2005: Still in service.

Norbank   2002–   166.77m x 23.90m x 14.40m   17,464   Ro-pax.
Van der Giessen–de Noord BV, Krimpen am de Ijssel, Netherlands. 961.
Zaklady Urzadzen Tecnicznych 'Zgoda' SA, Swietochlowice, Poland. Sulzer oil. 33,282bhp. Two CP propellers.
23 knots.
1993: Launched 5 June as *Norbank*.
1994: Completed for Norbank CV [North Sea Ferries Noordzee Veerdiensten BV] {Rotterdam; Netherlands}.
1997: Sold to Norships CV [P&O North Sea Ferries BV] {Rotterdam; Netherlands}.
2005: Still in service.

Norbay   2002–   166.77m x 23.90m x 14.40m   17,464   Ro-pax.
723652
Van der Giessen–de Noord BV, Krimpen am de IJssel, Netherlands. 962.
Zaklady Urzadzen Tecnicznych 'Zgoda' SA, Swietochlowice, Poland. Sulzer oil. 33,282bhp. Two CP propellers.
 23 knots.
1993: Launched 13 November as *Norbay*.
1994: Completed for Equipment Leasing (Properties) Ltd [North Sea Ferries Noordzee Veerdiensten BV] {Hull}.
1997: [P&O North Sea Ferries Ltd].
2000: Sold to Equipment Leasing Co. Ltd [P&O North Sea Ferries Ltd] {Hull}.
2000: Owner renamed SGVF (6) Ltd.
2002: {Hamilton, Bermuda}.
2002: [P&O European Ferries (Irish Sea) Ltd].
2003: Owner renamed Norbay (UK) Ltd.
2005: Still in service.

Isle of Man Steam Packet Co. Limited 1997–1998
Sea Containers 1998–2003
Isle of Man Steam Packet Co. Limited 2003–2004
Irish Sea Express Limited 2004–

Lady of Mann   1976–   104.55m x 16.77m x 8.21m   2,990
359761   104.43m x 16.74m x 8.16m   3,176   from 1989.
                                                                           4,482   from 1995.
Ailsa Shipbuilding Co. Ltd, Troon. 547.
Crossley Premier Engines Ltd, Manchester. Pielstick oil. 11,000bhp. Two CP propellers. 21 knots.
1975: Launched 4 December as *Lady of Mann*.

Name Official number Builder. Yard no. Engine builder and details	In fleet	Dimensions (length x breadth x depth)	Gross tons	Notes

1976: Completed for Isle of Man Steam Packet Co. Ltd {Douglas}.

1995: {Madeira; Portugal}.

1995: {Douglas; Isle of Man}.

2005: Still in service.

SeaCat Isle of Man	1994–1995 1997–2004	74.00 x 26.00 x 4.09	3,003	Aluminium alloy. Twin hulls.

730251

International Catamarans Tasmania Pty. Ltd, Hobart, Tasmania. 026.

Ruston Diesels Ltd, Newton-le-Willows, Lancashire. Oil. 19,836bhp. Four water jet propulsion units. 35 knots.

1990: Launched 29 April.

1990: Completed for SeaCat 2 Ltd {Nassau; Bahamas} as *Hoverspeed France*.

1992: Chartered to Sardinia Express SpA. Renamed *Sardegna Express* {Italy}.

1992: Charter ended. Renamed *Hoverspeed France*. {Nassau; Bahamas}.

1994: Renamed *SeaCat Boulogne*.

1994: To Sea Containers Ltd {Nassau; Bahamas}. Chartered to Isle of Man Steam Packet Co. Ltd. Renamed *SeaCat Isle of Man*.

1995: Charter ended.

1996: To SeaCat 2 Ltd {Nassau; Bahamas}. Chartered to Color SeaCat KS, Norway. Renamed *SeaCat Norge*.

1997: {Newhaven}. Chartered to Isle of Man Steam Packet Co. Ltd. Renamed *SeaCat Isle of Man*.

2001/02: To Sea Containers Ltd. {Newhaven}.

2004: Charter ended.

2005: Chartered to Irish Sea Express Ltd. Renamed *Sea Express I*.

2005: Still in service.

SuperSeaCat Two	1998–1999	100.00m x 17.10m x 10.70m	4,662	Aluminium alloy.
906912	2003–			

Fincantieri-Cant. Nav. Italiani SpA, Riva Trigoso, Genoa, Italy. 6000.

Ruston Paxton Diesels Ltd, UK. Oil. 37,388bhp. Four water jet propulsion units. 38 knots.

1997: Completed for Sea Containers Italia SpA {La Spezia; Italy} as *SuperSeaCat Two*.

2003: Sold to K/S UL SuperSeaCat [Isle of Man Steam Packet Co. Ltd] {Liverpool}.

2005: Still in service.

SuperSeaCat Three	1999–2000 2002–2002	100.00m x 17.10m x 10.70m	4,697	Aluminium alloy.

Fincantieri-Cant. Nav. Italiani SpA, La Spezia, Italy. 6003.

Ruston Paxton Diesels Ltd, UK. Oil. 33,644bhp. Four water jet propulsion units. 38 knots.

1999: Completed for Sea Containers Italia SpA {La Spezia; Italy} as *SuperSeaCat Three*.

2005: Still in service.

Rapide	2001–2001	81.24m x 26.00m x 6.52m	4,112	Aluminium alloy. Twin hulls.

386976 (Singapore)

Incat Australia Pty Ltd, Hobart, Tasmania. 038.

Ruston Diesels Ltd, Newton-le-Willows, Lancs. Oil. 29,909bhp. Four water jet propulsion units. 43 knots.

1996: Completed for Holyman Ferries Pte Ltd [Condor Marine Services Ltd, Poole] {Singapore; Singapore} as *Condor 12*.

1997: Sold to Holyman Sally (Luxembourg) SA {Luxembourg; Luxembourg}. Renamed *Holyman Rapide*.

1998: Sold to Hoverspeed Holyman Ltd [Hoverspeed Ltd] {Luxembourg; Luxembourg}. Renamed *Rapide*.

2003: {Nassau; Bahamas}.

2005: Renamed *Seacat Rapide* {Italy}. Still in service.

Name Official number Builder. Yard no. Engine builder and details	In fleet	Dimensions (length x breadth x depth)	Gross tons	Notes

---

Merchant Ferries Limited 1998–2000
Norse Merchant Ferries Limited 2000–

| **Dawn Merchant** | 1998–2002 | 179.93m x 25.24m x 8.70m | 22,152 | Ro-pax. Machinery aft. |

731839
Astilleros Espanoles SA, Sevilla, Spain. 287.
Wartsilla NSD Nederland BV, Zwolle, Netherlands. Oil. 32,300bhp. Two CP propellers. 22.5 knots.
1998: Completed for Cenargo Ltd [V. Ships (UK) Ltd] {Douglas} as *Dawn Merchant*.
2002: {Liverpool}. Manager Bluewater Marine Management Ltd.
2002: Chartered to Norfolk Line.
2004: Owner renamed Norse Merchant (DM) Ltd.
2004: [Meridian Marine Management Ltd].
2005: Still in service.

| **Brave Merchant** | 1998– | 179.95m x 25.24m x 8.70m | 22,152 | Ro-pax. Machinery aft. |

731850
Astilleros Espanoles SA, Sevilla, Spain. 288.
Wartsilla NSD Nederland BV, Zwolle, Netherlands. Oil. 32,300bhp. Two CP propellers. 22.5 knots.
1998: Completed for Cenargo Ltd [V. Ships (UK) Ltd] {Douglas} as *Brave Merchant*.
2002: {Liverpool}. Manager Bluewater Marine Management Ltd.
2003: Chartered for service as military transport to Iraq.
2003: Charter ended.
2004: To Norse Merchant Shipping Ltd [Bluewater Marine Management Ltd] {Liverpool}.
2004: [Meridian Marine Management Ltd.]
2005: Still in service.

| **Liverpool Viking** | 2005– | 186.00m x 26.00m x 9.15m | 21,856 | Ro-ro. |

C.N. 'Visentini' di Visentini Francesco and C. Donada, Italy. 182.
Wartsilla Diesel AB, Trolhattan, Finland. Oil. 21,208bhp. Two CP propellers. 24 knots.
1997: Completed for Levantina Trasporti Srl {Bari; Italy} as *Lagan Viking*.
1997: Chartered to Norse Irish Ferries Ltd.
2001: Sold to Belfast Freight Ferries Ltd [V. Ships (U.K.) Ltd] {Bari; Italy}.
2002: [Bluewater Marine Management Ltd].
2004: [Meridian Marine Management Ltd.]
2004: {Belfast}.
2005: Renamed *Liverpool Viking*.
2005: Still in service.

| **Dublin Viking** | 2005– | 186.00m x 26.00m x 9.15m | 21,856 | Ro-ro. |

C.N. 'Visentini' di Visentini Francesco and C. Donada, Italy. 180.
Wartsilla Diesel AB, Trolhattan, Finland. Oil. 21,208bhp. Two CP propellers. 24 knots.
1996: Launched 7 December unnamed.
1997: Completed for Francesco Visentini Trasporti Fluvio Marittimi {Chioggia; Italy} as *Mersey Viking*.
1997: Chartered to Norse Irish Ferries Ltd.
1998: {Bari; Italy}.
2001: Sold to Belfast Freight Ferries Ltd [V. Ships (U.K.) Ltd] {Bari; Italy}.
2002: [Bluewater Marine Management Ltd].
2004: [Meridian Marine Management Ltd.]
2004: {Belfast}.
2005: To be renamed *Dublin Viking*.
2005: Still in service.

BIBLIOGRAPHY

Periodicals

Marine News
Sea Breezes
British & European Ferry Scene
Ships Monthly
Shipping Today and Yesterday
Ship Ahoy
Cruising Monthly
The Motor Ship
The Marine Engineer
The Shipbuilder
Shipping World
Mitchell's Maritime Register

Reference books

Lloyd's Register
Stock Exchange Register of Defunct Companies
Stock Exchange Official Handbook
Mercantile Navy List
Mercantile Navy List 1857 (Reprinted by Elibron Books, USA, 2003)

Books covering Irish Sea services

Clyde & Other Coastal Steamers (1st edition). C.L.D. Duckworth and G.E. Langmuir. Brown, Son & Ferguson Ltd. 1939.
Clyde & Other Coastal Steamers (2nd edition). C.L.D. Duckworth and G.E. Langmuir. T. Stephenson & Sons Ltd. 1977.
West Coast Steamers (3rd edition). C.L.D. Duckworth and G.E. Langmuir. T. Stephenson & Sons Ltd. 1966.
Across the Irish Sea. Belfast–Liverpool Shipping Since 1819. Robert C. Sinclair. Conway Maritime Press. 1990.
The B&I Line. Hazel Smyth. Gill and MacMillan Ltd. Dublin. 1984.
Irish Passenger Steamship Services – volumes 1 & 2. D.B. McNeill. David & Charles. 1969, 1971.

Coast Lines. Norman L. Middlemiss. Shield Publications Ltd. 1998.

Irish Shipping Limited 1941–1982. H.C. Spong. World Ship Society. 1982.

Ships in Focus – Burns & Laird. Colin Campbell and Roy Fenton. Ships in Focus Publications. 1999.

Irish Sea Shipping Publicised. Robert Forsyth. Tempus Publishing Ltd. 2002.

General maritime books

The History of Steam Navigation. John Kennedy. Charles Birchall Ltd. 1903.

Car Ferries of the British Isles (various editions). Nick Widdows. Ferry Publications.

West Country Passenger Steamers (1st edition). Grahame Farr. T. Stephenson & Sons Ltd. 1956.

West Country Passenger Steamers (2nd edition). Grahame Farr. T. Stephenson & Sons Ltd. 1967.

Railway and other Steamers (2nd edition). C.L.D. Duckworth and G.E. Langmuir. T. Stephenson & Sons Ltd. 1968.

Merchant Fleets – volumes 24, 25, 26 (Britain's Railway Steamers). Duncan Haws. TCL Publications. 1993, 1993, 1994.

The Life and Times of the Steam Packet. John Shepherd. Ferry Publications. 1994.

Stena Line's Ships 1962–1992. Sahlsten, Söderburg and Bång. Stena Line. 1992.

Stena 1939–1989. W.J. Harvey. Stena Line. 1989.

Viking Line 25. Viking Line. 1983.

A Century of North Sea Passenger Ships. Ambrose Greenway. Ian Allan. 1986.

100 Years of Parkeston Quay and its Ships. Philip J. Cone. 1983.

Maritime Harwich as a Ferry Port. Harry G. Hitchman and Philip Driver. 1986.

British Standard Ships of World War 1. W.H. Mitchell and L.A. Sawyer. Sea Breezes. 1968.

The Wilson Line of Hull 1831–1981. Arthur G. Credland and Michael Thompson. Hutton Press Ltd. 1994.

The Pirrie-Kylsant Motorships 1915–1932. Alan S. Mallett and Andrew M.B. Bell. Mallett & Bell Publications. 1984.

North Atlantic Seaway. N.R.P. Bonsor. David & Charles. 1975.

South Atlantic Seaway. N.R.P. Bonsor. Brookside Publications. 1983.

DP&L (Dundee Perth & London Shipping Co. Ltd). Graeme Somner. World Ship Society. 1995.

Liners & Cruise Ships; Some Notable Smaller Vessels. Anthony Cooke. Carmania Press. 1996.

Monks' Navy. R.S. Fenton. World Ship Society. 1981.

A Business of National Importance; the Royal Mail Shipping Group 1902–1937. Edwin Green and Michael Moss. Methuen & Co. Ltd, 1982.

Transactions 1955–1961 (Vol. IX). The Irish Sea Services of British Railways and their Predecessors. E.P. McManus. Liverpool Nautical Research Society. 1963.

Liverpool Shipping: a Short History. George Chandler. Phoenix House. 1960.

Steamers of North Wales (2nd edition). F.C. Thornley. T. Stephenson & Sons Ltd, 1962.

Cross Channel and Coastal Paddle Steamers. Frank Burtt. Richard Tilling. 1934.

Starke/Schell Registers of Vessels Completed. World Ship Society. (Various years).

DFDS 1866–1891. Søren Thorsøe and Others. World Ship Society. 1991.

The Canals of the South of Ireland. V.T.H. Delaney and D.R. Delaney. David & Charles. 1966.

The Hoverspeed Story. Miles Cowsill and John Hendy. Ferry Publications. 1991.

Books on P&O

A Hundred Year History of the P&O. Boyd Cable. Ivor Nicholson and Watson. 1937.

The Story of P&O. David Howarth and Stephen Howarth. Weidenfeld & Nicholson. 1986.

P&O – A Fleet History. Stephen Rabson and Kevin O'Donoghue. World Ship Society. 1988.

Books on wartime

The Fourth Service; Merchantmen at War 1939–45. John Slader. New Era Writer's Guild. 1995.
British War Losses. HMSO. 1947.
British Vessels Lost at Sea 1914–18. HMSO 1919. Reprint by Patrick Stephens Ltd. 1977.
British Merchant Ships Sunk by U-Boats in the 1914–1918 War. A.J. Tennent. The Starling Press Ltd. 1990.
The D-Day Ships. John de S. Winser. World Ship Society. 1994.
Short-sea: Long War. John de S. Winser. World Ship Society. 1997.
B.E.F. Ships before, at and after Dunkirk. John de S. Winser. World Ship Society. 1999.
The Long Watch. The History of the Irish Mercantile Marine in World War Two. Frank Forde. Gill & Macmillan. 1981.

Books on shipbuilding and shipbreaking

British Shipbuilding Yards – volumes 1, 2 & 3. Norman M. Middlemiss. Shield Publications Ltd. 1993, 1994, 1995.
The Denny List. National Maritime Museum. 1974.
Shipbuilders to the World: 125 Years of Harland & Wolff, Belfast. Michael Moss and John R. Hume. Blackstaff Press. 1986.
Beardmore Built; the Rise and Fall of a Clydeside Shipyard. Ian Johnston. Clydebank District Libraries & Museums Department. 1993.
Portrait of a Shipbuilder; Barrow-built Vessels from 1873. Nigel Harris (Ed.). Silver Link Publishing. 1989.
Song of the Clyde; a History of Clyde Shipbuilding. Fred M. Walker. Patrick Stephens. 1984.
Ardrossan Shipyards: Struggle for Survival 1825–1983. Dr Catriona Levy and the Ardrossan Local History Workshop. WEA. 1983.
Ardrossan Harbour 1805–1970. Dr Catriona Levy and the Ardrossan Local History Workshop. WEA. 1988.
Metal Industries; Shipbreaking at Rosyth and Charlestown. Ian Buxton. World Ship Society. 1992.
The Last Tide; A History of the Port of Preston 1806–1981. Jack Dakres. Carnegie Press. 1986.
Shipbuilders' Yard Lists. World Ship Society.
The Shipbuilding Industry. A Guide to Historical Records. L.A. Ritchie (Ed.). Manchester University Press. 1992.
Shipbuilders of the Hartlepools. B. Spaldin. Hartlepool Borough Council. 1986.

Newspapers

Lloyd's List
Liverpool Daily Post
Glasgow Herald
Clare Journal

INDEX

SHIPOWNERS, PORT OPERATORS,
SHIPBUILDERS, ENGINEBUILDERS AND
SHIPBREAKERS

If you are interested in purchasing other books published by Tempus,
or in case you have difficulty finding any Tempus books in your local bookshop,
you can also place orders directly through our website

www.tempus-publishing.com